CRAFT BEVERAGE
BUSINESS MANAGEMENT

MADELEINE PULLMAN // JOHN HARRIS

Kendall Hunt
publishing company

Cover images © 2016 Shutterstock, Inc.

www.kendallhunt.com
Send all inquiries to:
4050 Westmark Drive
Dubuque, IA 52004-1840

Copyright © 2016 by Kendall Hunt Publishing Company

ISBN 978-1-4652-9816-4

Printed in the United States of America

DEDICATION

This book is primarily dedicated to our families who tolerate our many hours of working on our passions and projects. Mellie thanks her husband Tim Brill and faithful companions, Tristan, and Islay, who must wait patiently for a walk during the writing process. Additionally, the book is dedicated to her students who have passed through the Business of Craft Brewing program and provided the motivation for this book. John would like to thank his wife Jane for her support and advice for all these years and his daughters Fiona and Maeve for being awesome.

BRIEF CONTENTS

CONTENTS

ABOUT THE AUTHORS

Madeleine (Mellie) Pullman is the Director of the Business of Craft Brewing On-line Education Program and Willamette Industries Professor of Supply Chain Management at Portland State University. She developed the craft business program, the first of its kind, in 2012 and since then hundreds of students have taken the courses, developed or joined craft businesses, and advanced their careers in the craft industry. She grew up in a beer family; her grandmother's family owned the Schlitz Brewery, now part of the Pabst Brewing Company. In 1986, she became a Brewmaster/Owner of Wasatch Brewery in Park City, Utah and later, Hops Brewery in Scottsdale, Arizona. She earned her Ph.D. in Business Administration, MBA and MS in Mechanical Engineering from the University of Utah. In addition to this book, she has multiple books and articles on the food and beverage industry, sustainability, supply chain management, and experiential service design.

John Harris has been involved in the craft brewing industry for 30 years. In 2013, John opened Ecliptic Brewing in Portland, Oregon where he is the Brewmaster/Owner. He started his career as a brewer at McMenamins Hillsdale Brewpub in 1986. He left to become the founding Brewmaster at Deschutes Brewery in 1988 and then went on to serve as a Brewmaster at Full Sail Brewing in 1992. John was the first Craft Brewer Member of the MBAA National Technical Committee and a past President of the MBAA district NW. He served on the Oregon Brewers Guild Board. John's awards are numerous, gold medals at the World Beer Cup and the Great American Beer Festival. He also received the Brewers Association Russell Schehrer Award for Innovation in Brewing in 2001. When not running his business you might find him playing washboard or staring at the stars with his telescope.

ACKNOWLEDGMENTS

So many people and craft industry folks have contributed to this book that it's hard to know where to start. First, we want to thank Scott Dawson for motivating and supporting the development of the Business of Craft Brewing Program while Dean at Portland State University (PSU). We thank Lynne Curry for corralling our team and patiently editing this manuscript as well as Whitney Dawson for her extensive case research and Jessica Ferrell for graphic elements for this book and videos for the program. Benjamin Curry, Aaron Filipowsky, Joe Jackson, and Patrick Walsh were instrumental to content development while Kristen Peterson and Meghan Oswalt have provided feedback on improving the content over the years at the Center for Executive and Professional Education at PSU. The instructors in the program have been instrumental in finding appropriate material and interacting with our students: Nate Young, Marcus Reed, Maria Pearman Young, Charlie Devereux, and Geoff Westapher.

John Harris would like to thank the following people who allowed him to make beer at their breweries—Mike and Brian McMenamin, Gary Fish, James Emmerson, and Irene Firmat. Thanks to Conrad Santos who gave him his first brewing job and thanks to his mentor, the late Jim Kennedy III for all of his advice and friendship.

Finally, there are so many craft businesses that have contributed to this book through interviews, case examples, field trips, videos, and overall pestering on our part. While it is impossible to make this list comprehensive, some of our best friends include: BTU Brasserie & Brewery, Base Camp Brewery, Boneyard Brewery, Blue Mountain Cidery, Bullrun Distillery, Cider Riot!, The Commons, Craft Brewers Alliance, Craft Brewers Association, Dingle Brewing Company, Dingle Distillery, Dragons Gate Brewery, Ecliptic, The Edge Brewery Barcelona, Finn River Cidery, Gigantic, Hopworks Urban Brewery, Magnolia Brewery, Metalcraft /MCF, Migration, Northwest Cider Association, New Deal Distillery, Oregon Hophouse, Pfriem, Point Blank Distribution, Portland Kettleworks, Rev Nat's Cider, Stein Distillery, Terminal Gravity, Teri Fahrendorf, Worthy Brewing, Rose City Label and many more . . . A super thanks to all our fellow co-workers at all the breweries where we have worked for their help and support.

FEATURES OF THE BOOK

While there are many books out there that cover the personal story of successful craft beverage business operators, this book serves a different purpose. While both of us have started and run successful craft breweries, this book is a practical guide to starting and managing a craft business today. The book not only helps create an initial and on-going business plan but will help with managing, decision-making, and budgeting for the life of the business.

What makes it different from existing books? Well here are a few of the key features:

- ▶ **Broad Audience Appeal:** The book is for anyone interested in the business side of the craft beverage world. While many people may know how to make a craft beverage, less know how to make money in the process. People who will benefit from this book include those who want to join the industry as an employee or startup owner, those in the industry with limited to no business background, those in other industries that interact with craft beverage businesses, and any craft beverage enthusiasts that dreams of opening a business in any part of the world.
- ▶ **Concept Explanation:** Concepts are clearly explained and then current examples are provided of businesses executing that concept in a unique or successful way. The latest and greatest concepts are covered at the time of the publication of this book.
- ▶ **Analysis:** When appropriate, cost and revenue calculations are provided. Chapters show step-by-step methods for calculating costs and financial elements needed for the day-to-day operations as well as strategic decision-making for a craft beverage business. Both startups and on-going businesses will have the ability to calculate the cost of goods sold for their products from grain to glass as well as the other employee and capitol costs driving overhead. Many of the analytical techniques can be done on the back of an envelope but others will benefit from the use of an excel spreadsheet. Suggested Excel Template designs are provided.
- ▶ **Cases:** Each chapter contains several cases covering examples of breweries, cideries, distilleries, meaderies, etc. Some of the cases are long while others are short to show how a business has executed on a concept and how the business owner dealt with the challenges.
- ▶ **Graphical elements:** Each chapter contains photos, charts, tables, and other graphical information that help illustrate the points and clarify the concepts.
- ▶ **Learning activities:** Each chapter concludes with learning activities so that the reader can go out into his or her community and apply the concepts learned in that chapter to that particular environment. For those using the book in a classroom environment, PowerPoint slides and quiz questions are available.
- ▶ **International appeal:** Most of the content and analytical approaches are relevant to craft businesses in any part of the world where alcohol is produced and sold. Some legal and distribution content is specific to the US but has a similar structure in other countries. The formulas are created for Metric or English systems of measurement as well as any currency. Equipment pricing is provided in US dollars only but can readily be converted to other currencies.

CHAPTER ONE

Introduction

Key Terms

business plan	craft cider	mead
certified craft distilled spirit	distilled spirits plant (DSP)	reinheitsgebot beer purity law
craft beer	gluten-free	sessionable
craft beverage	independent	traditional
craft brewery	kombucha	

Overview

This introductory chapter presents the main purpose and content of the book as well as the primary tools you need to function as a craft business professional. Following a brief history of craft beverages is a discussion of trends happening in this exciting industry. The chapter also addresses one of the major challenges of starting a business or introducing a new craft product—naming the business and products and researching trademarks for potential names.

Learning Objectives

▶ Understand the need for business skills as craft beverage professionals and how various will benefit from this book.

▶ Understand the key elements and purpose of a business plan.

▶ Learn the history of the different craft beverage types.

▶ Identify the trends affecting the craft beverage industry.

▶ Understand the importance of uniqueness in a crowded market.

Introduction

The craft alcoholic beverage industry is one of the most dynamic and exciting places to work today. Since the resurgence of small breweries in the 1980s, the **craft beer** industry has been taking the world by storm. Beer continues to dominate this sales category, with emergent craft cider, distilled spirits, and mead industries following a similarly rapid trajectory. Home brewers and cider makers as well as craft beverage enthusiasts are creating and consuming new products either produced in dedicated production facilities or popular brewpubs. There is at least one producer of a craft beverage in any major city following on the successes in places like Portland, Oregon, Seattle, Washington, San Francisco, California, and Denver, Colorado. Other US states and world cities are quickly catching up with new businesses opening with surprising frequency. Rural locations, too, are emerging with exceptional craft beverages set in small towns, orchards, or farms that draw destination craft enthusiasts.

Source: Madeleine Pullman.

FIGURE 1.1   Farmstead brewer

Because of this rapid growth, there is a shortage of talented beer or cider makers as well as skilled business people to run these production facilities or pubs/restaurants. While it is one thing to produce a high quality cider or beer at home and give it to friends, it is a completely different ball game to ask friends to pay and establish a profitable business with these products in the commercial arena. Today, consumers will only pay for high-quality products.

The purpose of this book is to provide an overview of the essential business topics and tools required for you to operate competitively in the craft beverage world. It is set up to facilitate the development of your business plan and includes complete coverage of the potential costs and revenues during startup and in the first few years of operations. A business plan is not just a road map for creating your business but, ideally, is a guiding document you continuously update throughout the life of your business.

Who Will Benefit from this Book?

People who will benefit from content in this book include: a home craft beverage producer who wants to go into commercial business; a brewing enthusiast who would like to work for a craft beverage company; a person who currently works or wants to work in supporting industries like ingredient sales or equipment manufacturing; someone already working in the craft industry who wants to move into more of a business function rather than technical or production; or anyone interested in the ins and outs of the craft beverage business.

Business Plan

The **business plan** provides the structure for this book's content, which covers the significant areas that everyone in the craft beverage business should understand. The key parts of the business plan are illustrated in Figure 1.2.

FIGURE 1.2   Full business plan model

The first step—concept description, and vision—covers your craft beverage business model as well as the story defining your business and vision for the future. The next step is an industry overview that shows the status of the overall industry where your craft business is situated as well as your local conditions. In the third step, the plan defines the competitive context where your business is operating, key competitors, competitive opportunities, and ways to differentiate your concept in the marketplace. In the fourth step, you define the potential customers in your chosen location and develop the approach for marketing and distributing a product to them. The fifth step is your operational plan: the production process, the required equipment, site and facility needed initially and in future years as well as a timeline. The sixth step defines the team, legal organization and human resource requirements as well as the skills of the ownership group. How you will train, retain, incentivize, and develop your team is a fundamental part of the plan. Finally, the financial section details fund raising approach, the projected profit and loss for all the months of the first year and subsequent yearly projections as well as other required financial statements.

In this book, the chapters will highlight critical decisions you need to make in the startup phase as well as ongoing operational phase. Many of these decisions will become part of your business plan and others are on-going decisions with tools to support their analysis. Different parts of the financial statements are developed incrementally so that you understand every part of the financial statements by the end of the book.

What is a Craft Beverage?

There is no concise definition of **craft beverage** since different people define it in different ways, such as: small, local, not industrial or mass-produced, all local ingredients, made by hand, artisanal, and so on. Most of the clarity on the subject comes from industry associations that set a standard for their members. For example, the longest operating craft beverage association, the Brewers Association (an American brewer trade group concerned with the promotion of craft beer and home brewing) defines a craft brewery as the following:

▸ **Small:** Annual production of six million barrels of beer or less (approximately three percent of US annual sales)

▸ **Independent**: Less than 25 percent of the craft brewery is owned or controlled (or equivalent economic interest) by a beverage alcohol industry member who is not themselves a craft brewer.

▸ **Traditional**: A brewer who has a majority of its total beverage alcohol volume in beers whose flavor derives from traditional or innovative brewing ingredients and their fermentation. Flavored malt beverages (FMBs) are not considered beers.

Therefore, a **craft beverage** comes from a **craft brewery** defined above as small, independent, and traditional.

Craft spirits have a similar set of criteria. According to the American Distilling Institute to be a **certified craft distilled spirit,** the spirit must meet the following standards[1]:

- ▶ **Distilled by the Distilled Spirits Plant (DSP):** The spirit must have been run through a still by a certified craft producer, and the Alcohol and Tobacco Tax and Trade Bureau (TTB) approved label must state "distilled by" followed by the name of the DSP.

- ▶ **Independently owned:** Less than 25 percent of the craft distillery (distilled spirits plant or DSP) is owned or controlled (or equivalent economic interest) by alcoholic beverage industry members who are not themselves craft distillers.

- ▶ **Small-scale:** Maximum annual sales are less than 100,000 proof gallons.

- ▶ **Hands-on production:** Craft distillers produce spirits that reflect the vision of their principal distillers using any combination of traditional or innovative techniques including fermenting, distilling, re-distilling, blending, infusing, or warehousing.

The associations for other craft beverages do not have agreed upon definitions, but the general intentions are the same: small (not industrial scale production), independently owned, and the use of traditional ingredients such as orchard-based real fruit or fruit juice, honey, or other innovative ingredients that are neither highly processed nor flavored with artificial ingredients. Legal definitions of various categories (cider, beer, mead, and spirits) can be found in European countries and the United States but are often very confusing and out of line with consumer perceptions of "craft."

A Short History of Brewing

Archeologists who recently found potential beer-brewing tools in the Eastern Mediterranean concluded, "Brewing of beer was an important aspect of feasting and society in the Late Epipaleolithic era."[2] By the 1500s, Germany was the hotbed of everything beer. The **Reinheitsgebot beer purity law** permitted beer to be made only with barley, hops, and water later acknowledging the existence of yeast and permitting wheat. Eventually, other European countries followed suit with commercial beer production and immigrants carried recipes and production techniques to other continents, most notably the United States during Colonial times. Historically, the big beer brewing countries have been Germany, the United Kingdom, France, and Belgium.

In 1873, the United States reached a pinnacle of 4,131 breweries producing 9 million barrels of beer. American production was beginning to overtake Germany's lead right before Prohibition when it dropped close to zero for that period (with the exception of "near beer"). Improved production and distribution techniques such as refrigeration technology, and the forces of Prohibition, led to massive consolidation and closures. After Prohibition was repealed in 1933, the number of breweries began to climb again and the United States took the lead in beer production for the world.

By 1983, consolidation forces had once again driven the industry to a low of 51 brewing concerns operating a total of 80 breweries. As a rebellion against this massive consolidation and industrial brews, small microbreweries begun to spring up during the 1980s and the industry has been off to the races ever since. Today, more than 3,400 craft brewers operate in the United States with 11 percent volume (more than 19 percent in dollar share) of the total US beer market.[3]

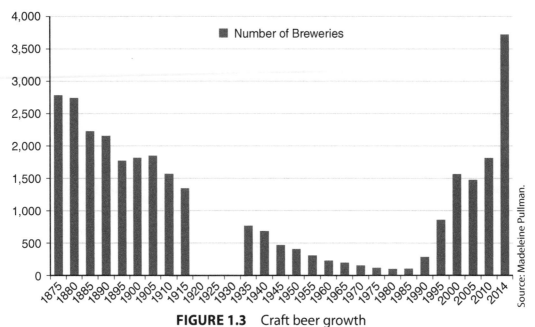

Source: Madeleine Pullman.

FIGURE 1.3   Craft beer growth

Data from Martin H. Stack, "A Concise History of America's Brewing Industry," Economic History Association.

Craft cider ("hard cider") also has a long history dating back thousands of years. The first documented evidence of cider and perry (pear cider) is described by Pliny (AD 23–AD 79). Around 55 BC, Roman invaders found English villagers drinking fermented apple juice. England is still the top producer of apple juice in the world and the largest market for cider and perry today. Early colonists brought cider making to the United States during the 17th Century. The famous apple tree planter, Johnny Appleseed, introduced cider apple trees to many parts of the US in the late 1700s. At that time, cider was the most popular alcoholic beverage in the United States. In the 1900s it lost ground to beer and later to the pressures of Prohibition. Truth be told, the demise of hard cider actually occurred *after* the repeal of Prohibition when it was discovered that it was faster to grow barley and make beer than grow apple trees for cider. While cider has always been popular in England, Ireland, France, and Spain, only a few US-based cider makers, such as Idaho's Seven Sisters Cider (founded 1986) and Vermont's Woodchuck Cider (founded 1991), emerged during the early craft beer movement in the United States. Cider sales did not take off until 2009 but since that point, they have been growing faster than craft beer with 60 to 70 percent sales growth on average each year. It shares a wider demographic appeal with women making up 50 percent of cider drinkers relative to craft beer's roughly 25 percent. Today, cider is emerging as one of the hottest craft beverages. If cider were a beer style, it would come in second place to IPA in terms of popularity and sales.

Similar to the cider story, **mead** is also making a comeback. Mead is considered the oldest alcoholic beverage. Consisting of fermented honey and water, it could be found naturally fermenting in the wilds when a beehive became saturated with rainwater. Popular in Africa, Ancient Greece, Norse and Celtic mythology, and the Middle Ages (implied drink in the popular show, *Game of Thrones*), mead has a rich and long history. The commercial market for mead, on the other hand, has never retained consistent demand.[4] Today, there are several hundred mead producers in the United States. And like cider, starting from a small sales base, mead has seen sales growth close to 100 percent in the last few years as consumers continue to explore all the craft beverages.

Other beverages are also creeping into the craft market space, and this book deals with alcoholic beverages since they have relatively similar concerns in the realm of production, marketing, legal, and financial issues. An example of another beverage is **kombucha**, fermented sweetened tea. Much of the commercially available product falls under 0.5 percent alcohol (the dividing line between alcohol and non-alcohol according to the US Food and Drug Administration). The alcoholic aspects of kombucha drew US national attention when in 2010, the actress Lindsay Lohan, set off a nationwide recall of the drink when tabloids speculated that kombucha activated an alcohol monitoring bracelet that Ms. Lohan wore while out on bail for charges of driving while intoxicated. Today, some companies are intentionally making the product over 0.5 percent alcohol, selling it in pubs and taprooms. While kombucha is more than 2000 years old (from China), it has only emerged as a hot-selling beverage category over the last 10 years. Today kombucha is up to almost $500 million in US sales and international sales are picking up. Of course, the higher alcohol version is only a fraction of those sales, but given the limited tap and shelf space available, craft business people should pay attention to the growth of all craft products in the refrigerated alcoholic beverage space.

©Unity Vibration Kombucha. Reprinted with permission.

FIGURE 1.4   Kombucha

Finally, **craft spirits**, round out the portfolio of the beverages covered in this book. Distilled spirits require more complicated technology than the aforementioned beverages. Distillation is a process of separating the alcohol from a liquid mixture (fermented liquids of any kind: juice, grain liquor, mead, or anything with sugar) by selective evaporation and condensation. A fermentation step is required to make alcohol and the distilling process concentrates that alcohol. Although spirits don't appear in history until about the 12th century, the process of distilling was understood long before that time. The Scottish farmers were making whiskey in the mid-1500s and early US settlers made spirits from fermented fruit or honey. By the late 1700s, both whiskey and rum were produced and consumed by all urban and rural dwellers alike.

In the United States, distilled spirits became the backbone of the underground alcohol market during Prohibition. Because more alcohol is packed into a small quantity of liquid than other beverages; it was easier to transport and hide from the authorities.[5] Like the other alcoholic beverages, the legitimate spirits industry was hit hard by Prohibition and most firms went out of business. However, after the repeal of Prohibition, mass-production-oriented large players re-emerged and dominated the industry.

The US *craft* distillery movement materialized around 1982. Arcane liquor laws, including those that vary from state to state have hampered growth of the movement. Nationwide US federal government's TTB regulations stipulate that you cannot produce alcohol in a still unless the site qualifies as a "distilled spirits plant." In other words, home spirits production is illegal. As a result, craft spirits have not benefited from a foundation of knowledgeable and legal producers and associations like other home craft beverage producers. Despite these obstacles, the craft spirits market today is growing exponentially. The number of craft producers has expanded ten times in the last 10 years, and it is estimated that the number could soon exceed 1,000 producers by 2017. These producers are working to change state and national laws so that it is easier to own and operate a micro-distillery. Craft distilleries are now operating in every US state as well as in most Canadian providences and many European countries.

FIGURE 1.5 Craft distillery

Trends in the Craft Beverage World

With the growth happening in all segments of the craft beverage world, there are several emerging trends:

Lots of Volume and Choices with Limited Shelf Space

New craft businesses are cropping up everywhere and existing players are expanding product lines. Some locations have very high concentrations of breweries, cideries, and distilleries, such as the Pacific Northwest and West Coast of the United States. Other places are less crowded but have many entrepreneurs looking for opportunities within the same markets. Store shelves have limited space for all the packaged beverages available, and many types of craft beverages are all competing for the same shelf space. This level of competition means that expectations of quality are high. Getting on the shelf with a new product not only requires a great product but a solid marketing and distribution strategy.

FIGURE 1.6 Crowded shelves

Rotating Tap Handles

Similar to the retail shelves, bars and pubs have really taken to the rotating tap handle approach. In these cases, as soon as a keg is finished, a different producer's brand replaces the spent keg and very few producers are guaranteed a secure spot in the line-up. It provides their customers with lots of choices and variety since there is always something new to try. For producers, frequent rotation means that accounts are not stable and keeping the attention of the distributor, pub staff, and consumer is an on-going activity. Similar to the retail shelves, pubs are adding cider and other craft products to the mix to expand their scope. The result is that more craft beverage categories are competing against one another for limited taps.

FIGURE 1.7   Multiple taps

Health Attributes

Concerns about gluten—a protein found in wheat, barley, and other grains—have driven demand for cider and mead as well as gluten-free beer. In order to be labeled **gluten-free** beer in the United States, products cannot be made from any type of gluten-containing grain (barley, wheat, rye, or crossbreeds of those grains). Today, gluten-free beers are made from pseudo-cereals, such as sorghum and millet. Those made from de-glutenized barley cannot carry the gluten-free label but can use names that imply gluten-free like the Omission brand—unless the producer can prove that the beverage has less than 20 parts per million (ppm) of gluten. Unfortunately, in the United States, the Food and Drug Administration (FDA) and TTB do not agree on an authorized test for measuring gluten levels in beer made with de-glutenizing processes.[6] In the general public, gluten avoidance shows no sign of waning as a trend, so you can expect more growth in gluten-free craft beverages of all kinds. Similarly, kombucha, as a probiotic beverage, appeals to consumers for the live bacteria health benefits as well as numerous other claims including anti-oxidant content related to the properties of tea in the base.

Styles

Among beers, the darling of the style category has long been the highly hopped and alcoholic IPA. It makes up more than 50 percent of craft beer sales and shows no sign of slowing down. Second to that, consumers have looked to seasonal offerings and variety packs to expand their horizons. Lagers like Pilsner and other lower alcohol **sessionable** beers are gaining in popularity. Sessionable beverages are those suitable to a lengthy drinking session, hence lower in alcohol. More breweries are creating packaged radlers or shandies—lagers mixed with citrus soda or lemonade—to appeal to the lighter alcohol drinkers and expand their brand's demographic reach.

Ingredients

Most experts in the industry expect the cost and scarcity of ingredients to increase. The amount of planted acreage in malting barley, private and public hops, and other ingredients like heirloom or cider apples are not keeping up with demand. Hops and apples have long lead times from planting until the plant reaches adequate yield levels. Certain hop varieties are now extremely difficult to acquire and many have long lead times and a three-year wait. This scarcity makes designing a product around a specific variety a risky proposition. Barley is highly dependent on weather conditions and is not subsidized at the levels of wheat or corn in many countries; so, many farmers have opted out of barley into more lucrative crops. One bright star, craft malting is gaining in popularity and many of the maltsters are starting to grow their own or contract for barley in their local areas.

Craft Brewery Acquisitions

As craft beverages continue to grow in popularity around the world, the large industrial players are taking notice and buying up well-established brands of both craft beer and cider. The craft brewery acquisitions by Anheuser-Busch Inbev (AB-Inbev) have garnered lots of public attention. These powerful major players have the ability to place their products and dominate on-premise, restaurants and bars, and off-premise, convenience stores, grocery and package stores. The pace of acquisition promises to accelerate as more craft breweries look to cash out, those who started breweries in the 1980s retire, and other successful newer brands seek cash to grow into more US regions or even other parts of the world.

SUMMARY

This chapter presented an overview of the book's purpose and audience as well as the history and current trends in craft beverages worldwide. Business management skills and a sound understanding of the elements of business planning are essential to succeed in the rapidly growing yet highly competitive craft beverage industry. As more and more players enter the exciting craft beverage landscape, those with a solid understanding of the tools for business decision-making will have a decisive head start on the others.

ENDNOTES

1. "Craft Certification," American Distilling Institute, http://distilling.com/resources/craft-certification.

2. Brian Hayden, Neil Canuel, and Jennifer Shanse, "What Was Brewing in the Natufian? An Archaeological Assessment of Brewing Technology in the Epipaleolithic," *Journal of Archaeological Method and Theory,* 20, no. 1 (2013): 102–150.

3. National Beer Sales and Production Data," Craft Brewers Association, https://www.brewersassociation.org/statistics/national-beer-sales-production-data/.

4. Harry Wallop, "How Game of Thrones Put Mead Back on the Menu," *The Telegraph* (2015) http://www.telegraph.co.uk/foodanddrink/foodanddrinknews/11584509/How-mead-made-a-comeback.html.

5. Gary Regan and Mardee Haidin Regan, *The Book of Bourbon and other Fine American Whiskeys* (n.p.: Jaren Brown, 2009).

6. Marc Sorini, "Labeling and Advertising Gluten-Free Beer," *New Brewer,* 32, no. 4 (2015): 27–29.

CHAPTER TWO

Concept Development

Key Terms

alternating proprietorship

barrels

bottles and cans

brewpub

cidery

concept

contract arrangement

copyright

craft blender

craft spirits

distilled spirits plant (DSP)

distillery

farmhouse brewery

kegs

large brewery

meadery

microbrewery

naming

off-premises

on-premises

packaging brewery

pub/restaurant

regional craft brewery

taproom

tasting room

three-tier system

trademark

two-tier system

vision

Overview

This chapter explores the different concepts that revolve around the creation of a craft beverage. From a standard production facility to pub or tasting room, there are cost and revenue implications for each business model. Additionally, while a business may start by making beer in a contract facility or in its own production facility, other concepts may be added on as cash becomes available, laws change, or other products, like cider or spirits, are added to the portfolio to expand into other market segments. Additionally, naming and trademarking the business are essential initial steps addressed in this chapter.

Learning Objectives

► Understand why a concept choice with a compelling description is the key part of a business plan.

► Identify the key concepts that are the foundation of all the craft beverage business models.

► Comprehend the pros and cons of various concepts.

► Explore the issues related to naming a business or new product.

► Perform a trademark search for a name and identify potential conflicts.

Introduction

The **concept** describes what your business determines to do, the overall idea that shapes your business identity, and the model for making money. It is the first part of the business plan (see Figure 2.1). While the concept can change over time, every business starts with a concept. In the craft beverage world, the concept outlines who the business is, what the business is going to make, and why the business is producing this beverage or beverage-based concept. It should also describe how the product will reach the consumer's hands (for example via a pub, packaged for retail, or tasting room), and include the business name, story, personality, image, and vision that will tie it all together.

The audience for the business plan is typically a potential investor for either a startup or an expansion of an existing business. After reviewing this description, this reader should have a basic understanding about the product(s) and the concept around the products. A well-developed concept is a bit like writing a story (fiction at this stage); it should convey what makes your idea unique and how it will connect with your target audience. While it may never actually become a reality, it is a chance to dream of what could be, a starting point. It should get the audience so interested that they want to continue through the remaining pages of the document, or your pitch, and then want to

Source: Madeleine Pullman.

FIGURE 2.1 Concept as part of business plan

Source: Madeleine Pullman.

Photo courtesy of Whitney Dawson. Reprinted with permission.

FIGURE 2.2   Concept Photos

invest their hard-earned money. Compelling concept descriptions provide photos or illustrations so the audience can visualize the space and products. Crowdfunding videos that depict a cohesive concept are also an important way to attract investors. Examples of well-done concept descriptions can be found on any of the successful craft beverage pitches on websites like Crowdbrewed, Kickstarter, and others. Here is an example of a short pub concept description with accompanying photos in Figure 2.2.

> *Neighbor is an artisan distilled spirits and craft beer tasting room with a rustic food café located in XYZ neighborhood. Neighbor will serve glasses of our house-made aperitifs, craft cocktails, beers, and ciders, a house-cured salmon platter and sandwich, daily soups and salads, and home-baked desserts. Neighbor brings the neighborhood together in a no-frills, simple, and affordable classic café with a beautiful mix of modern and traditional café styles.*

[handwritten margin note: Nieghborhood, Family + Friendly, gathering Place, high quality, fresh + drinkable]

Vision

Every business plan needs a **vision**. It states the ideal of what your business will become in the long-term (10 to 20 years). And it answers the question, "How is this concept going to be better in some way than those existing craft businesses in your area?" The vision should also be inspiring enough to resonate with the people who will be working in your business. Sierra Nevada Brewery's vision statement is a great example:

> *Inspired by the nearby Sierra Nevada Mountains, our beers are designed to be as bold, wild, and unwavering as those storied granite peaks. With respect to tradition and an unbridled passion for innovation, Sierra Nevada beers are inspired by the philosophy that anything is possible. We are committed to pushing the boundaries of craft beer and we look forward to the day that flavorful beers are the standard throughout the world.*[1]

Beverage Choice and Facility Type

The first decision is to determine what you plan to make: beer, cider, mead, or distilled spirits. Typically, one or more of the owners has a passion or sees a market opportunity for a particular type of beverage. This section details each beverage type definition as well as the facility categories that determine how the product is sold.

Brewery

According to the Brewers Association, breweries are generally classified by size and by focus (on-site consumption versus off-site consumption). Brewing facilities are categorized by barrels produced (one barrel = 31 gallons or 1.17 hectoliters) as:

Microbrewery: A brewery that produces less than 15,000 **barrels** (17,600 hectoliters) of beer per year with 75 percent or more of its beer sold off-site. Microbreweries sell to the public by one or more of the following methods: the traditional **three-tier system** (brewer to wholesaler to retailer to consumer); the **two-tier system** (brewer acting as wholesaler to retailer to consumer); and directly to the consumer through carry outs and/or on-site **taproom** or restaurant sales. Examples of the biggest microbreweries today are Ale Smith (California), Mad River Brewing (Vermont), and Hopworks (Oregon). Some of the other big players are in Texas and California, but they are growing so fast they jump from the microbrewery into the regional category as soon as they reach the top of the list.

Brewpub: A restaurant-brewery that sells 25 percent or more of its beer on-site. The beer is brewed primarily for sale in the restaurant and bar, often dispensed directly from the brewery's storage tanks. Where allowed by law, brewpubs often sell beer to go and/or distribute to off-site accounts. The Brewers Association re-categorizes a company as a microbrewery if its off-site (distributed) beer sales exceed 75 percent. Many of the biggest brewpubs have multiple pubs, such as BJ's Restaurant & Brewhouse (171 pubs), use contract brewing, such as New York's Southampton Publick House, or

FIGURE 2.3 Brewery

Source: Madeleine Pullman.

©Syda Productions/Shutterstock.com

FIGURE 2.4   Brewpub

have alternating proprietorships, such as California's Buffalo Bills Brewery. The range of food offered by brewpubs can be anything from a full-service restaurant to the bare minimum of snack offerings.

Regional craft brewery: A brewery making between 15,000 to 6 million barrels per year. An independent regional brewery has either an all-malt flagship or at least 50 percent of its volume in all-malt beers or in beers that use adjuncts to enhance rather than lighten flavor. Well-known examples are Boston Beer, Sierra Nevada, and New Belgium.

Large brewery: A brewery with annual beer production over 6 million barrels. Currently, no craft breweries produce more than 3 million barrels per year. The large brewery category now includes the four major brewery corporations: Anheuser-Busch InBev, MillerCoors, Constellation, and Heineken USA.

Brewery concepts overall: Since the 1980s, brewpubs were the most popular craft concept. For example, in 1994, there were about one-and-a-half times as many brewpubs as microbreweries and almost three times as many in 2004. Around 2010 the number of microbreweries started to catch up to the number of brewpubs and then surpassed it in 2011. Now, there are more microbreweries than brewpubs. This trend is also occurring in other countries. One reason is that the tasting room has become a great alternative to having a brewpub. Beer can be sold directly to customers with a simple

TABLE 1.1   Brewery concept trends[2]

Year	Brewpub	Microbrewery	Regional	Total
1994	329	192	16	537
2004	1005	362	46	1413
2010	1053	620	81	1754
2012	1155	1149	97	2401
2013	1280	1464	119	2863
2014	1412	1871	135	3418
Source: Madeleine Pullman. Adapted from Brewers Association.				

set up of taps and picnic tables. Another reason is that many nanos make up the microbrewery category. For food, most microbreweries bring in food carts selling food items and avoid the whole kitchen and large staff headache. Another reason is that more brewpubs started packaging and selling beer off-site which moved them into the microbrewery category. Similarly, more microbreweries increased their sales volume and became regional craft breweries.

Cidery

A **cidery** is a production facility for making cider, also known as hard cider or perry, pear cider. Some cideries also own fruit orchards while others buy fruit and fruit juices. While cider associations do not have specific classifications, US law treats cideries like wineries and they can therefore have tasting rooms and restaurants depending on the zoning restrictions as well as state or local laws in the area.

Meadery

A **meadery** is a production facility that makes a fermented beverage, mead, from honey, also known as "honey wine." Like cider, mead is treated officially as wine but has different legal classifications in the United States. According to the US Internal Revenue Code of 1986, mead or honey wine is classified as an "agricultural wine."[3] Agricultural wine is made from the fermentation of an agricultural product other than the juice of fruit. Similar to cider, where zoning allows agricultural wine products, mead makers can have tasting rooms and restaurants.

Distillery

A **distillery** refers to a facility where alcoholic liquors are made. According to the American Distilling Institute, **craft spirits** are the products of an independently owned distillery where the product is physically distilled and bottled on-site with maximum annual sales of 52,000 cases.[4] A **craft blender** is independently owned and operates a facility that uses any combination of traditional or innovative techniques, such as fermenting, distilling, re-distilling, blending, infusing, or warehousing to create products with a unique flavor profile. Many craft distillers both distill and blend products and must identify themselves as such on their TTB profile.

While all legal distilleries operate as a **distilled spirits plant**, state and county regulations dictate whether or not the distillery can have a tasting room, bar, or sell off-site. These regulations vary dramatically from location to location. As states loosen restrictions, the brewpub equivalents are springing up for distilleries, such as CH Distillery, a Chicago distillery-bar pictured in Figure 2.5.

Cross Beverage Style Boundaries

Many craft beverage businesses are expanding their offerings to include other types of beverages under one roof. Some breweries are adding cider or mead to their line-up to attract women and health conscious drinkers, for example, and other demographic groups. In effect, there is very little additional investment for the business if it purchases fruit juice or honey and uses the same cellaring equipment. Widmer Brothers Brewing in Portland, Oregon, brought Square Mile cider into their operations, first with a contract brewing arrangement and later bringing cider production into the brewery.

There are also examples of brewery-distillery combinations since the distilled spirit can be made from the same base, the malt extract or "wash," with no need to boil it in a kettle prior to fermentation. For this combination, a still is necessary for the distillation step. For a spirits-focused business intending to make whisky, producing beer provides cash flow while the whiskey ages in barrels for several years. Similarly, a cidery-distillery combination creates an opportunity to make both ciders and fermented fruit juice-based spirits like eau de vie. These combinations benefit from shared-use equipment, including fermenters and mixing tanks, and barrel aging facilities. It must be stated that each individual beverage type requires its own license, and spirits require a designated space within any single facility.

©Photographee.eu/Shutterstock.com

FIGURE 2.5   Distillery-bar

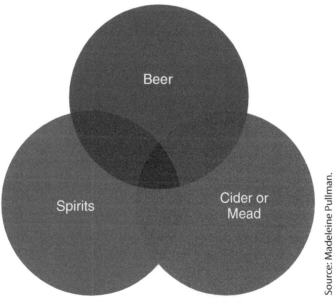

Source: Madeleine Pullman.

FIGURE 2.6   Crossing beverage style boundaries

Other Facilities Options

Contract

In a **contract arrangement**, a business, such as a Brewery A, hires another facility, Brewery B, to produce its product. Brewery A, the contract company, handles all the marketing, sales, and distribution of the beverage, while generally leaving the production and packaging to its producer brewery, Brewery B. Today facilities are being built and operating precisely to do this kind of contract production (cider, mead, or beer), sometime making multiple types of beverages under one roof for multiple brands.

Alternating Proprietorship

Another popular arrangement for "sharing" a business facility is the **alternating proprietorship**. According to the TTB, this term describes an arrangement in which two or more businesses take turns using the physical premises of a production facility.[5] Generally, the owner of an existing facility, the "host facility," agrees to rent space and equipment to a new "tenant." Alternating proprietorships allow existing production facilities to fill excess capacity while giving startup businesses an opportunity to begin on a small scale without investing in premises and equipment. In this arrangement, the tenant produces the product (for example, beer), keeps appropriate production records, labels the product with its own name and address, obtains the label and formulation approvals, and pays the tax when the product is removed from the host facility. The tenant has title or ownership of the product at all stages of the production process.

Mikkeller's Contract Brewing

Mikkeller, founded in Copenhagen, Denmark, distributes its beer all over the world, but does not own an official brewery. Instead, this company relies on contract brewing in collaboration with other brewers to create their signature experimental brews. Beginning as a home brewer, owner Mikkel Borg Bjergso stood out from the crowd at the 2006 Copenhagen Brewers Festival and landed an international distribution deal. His brand, Mikkeller, needed to increase production in order to meet the ensuing demand from the deal. Still a small company, the investment in a brewing facility and professional equipment was not in Bjergso's budget, so he rented the machinery and space from established brewers.

Mikkeller's main host brewery is in Belgium, but the company is also a tenant in Copenhagen, Norway, the United Kingdom, and the United States. Brew master Bjergso creates the recipes in his Copenhagen location while working with brewers around the world.

Mikkeller beers are sold in over 40 countries, and it has released over 800 beers, the majority of which are experimental. Bjergso has said that he finds inspiration in other brewers who are breaking all the rules with their beers. Most of his company's products are available in only select locations for a short period of time, but some are in constant production. It is still a challenge for Mikkeller to meet demand.

Packaging versus On-Premises Emphasis

One of the first concept decisions to consider is whether your business will be oriented toward **on-premises** consumption (taproom, pub, or restaurant), **off-premises** packaging and kegs for distribution, or some combination of the two. This section presents a continuum of choices depicted in Figure 2.7, explains the fundamental issues, and discusses the pros and cons.

Packaging

Kegs: A basic **packaging brewery** produces and sells kegged product, usually supplemented with an on-site tasting room wherever the law allows. Most microbreweries and some cideries and meaderies, start this way because it's relatively easy and straightforward. The upside of kegging is the simplicity since the new business only needs to buy or lease kegs, caps, and collar labels, keg washing equipment and a counter-pressure racking arm (filling station). However, there are several downsides of distributing only in kegs. Keg accounts are hard to get and keep, distributors have many brands already and, it is harder to expand beyond the local area. For each keg account the business needs almost five kegs (one on tap, one full at distributor, one empty coming back, one filled at brewery and one waiting to be filled). This quantity racks up the cost since kegs are expensive to own or lease. On the labor side, keg lines require steadfast cleaning and maintenance. Finally, kegs lack the packaging labels that convey the business story and brand directly to the consumer.

One success story for a basic keg concept is Boneyard Brewing in Bend, Oregon. Over a four-year period, the brewery packaged Boneyard Beer only in kegs and had a small tasting room where people bought growlers or pints. The brewery was able to grow from 500 to close to 18,000 barrels over that period predominately from the success of their RPM IPA. Other keg only producers include Mac & Jacks Brewery and Georgetown Brewing Company, both in the Seattle area.

Bottles and cans: Typically, packaging-oriented businesses will go on to add bottles and/or cans. Bottles and cans get much wider distribution and move into stores and restaurants. The package also becomes a mini-billboard for the product; consumers see the business branding, graphics, and story. The product is also transportable for consumers to purchase and bring home to consume when desired. The downside of this type of packaging is the cost that goes into labeling design and approval, labels, bottles, cans, boxes, and cardboard or plastic holders. Packaging also requires additional equipment or mobile packaging, a significant additional cost as well as a decent quality control

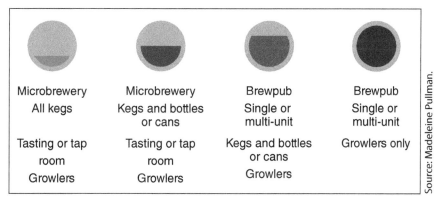

FIGURE 2.7   Packaging continuum

lab. Retail shelf space for packaged product is hard to come by and there can be problems with product stability and out-of-date product on store shelves.

Tasting or Taproom

The **tasting room** or **taproom** has become a significant element for all craft beverage producers. Most localities now allow tasting rooms to sell product rather than just give away small samples, which is itself a huge revenue opportunity. A tasting room is typically part of a packaging craft business because brewpubs and restaurants already have a sales outlet for their product. As detailed in Figures 2.9 and 2.10, if it costs $60 to make one keg of beer and the keg is sold to the distributor for $95, the business nets $35. But if the beer is sold in the tasting room for $5 per pint and there are roughly 120 pints (after some foam loss), then the revenue is $600. If the costs are $60 to make the keg and another $100 per keg for tasting room staff and overhead, then the keg nets $440. Many tasting rooms sell 5 to 10 percent of their packaging facility's product on-site but earn as much as 30 percent of their revenue from the taproom.

BEER PLANET
Beer Planet
www.BEERPLANET.be

©Christian Mueller/Shutterstock.com

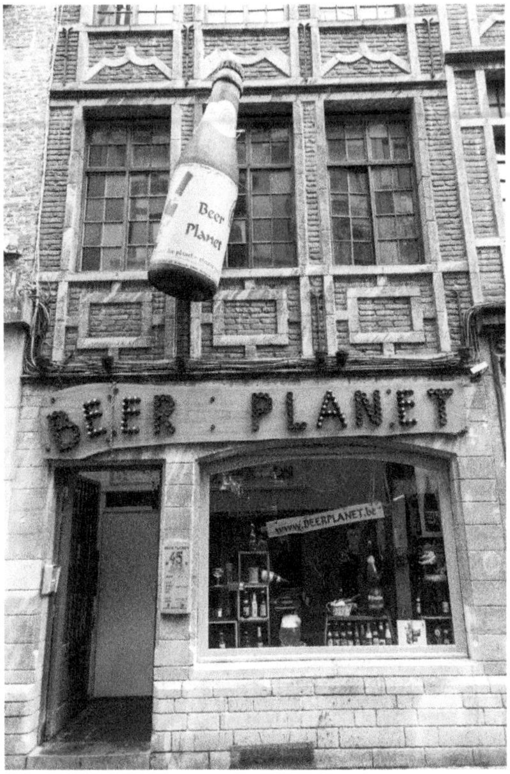

FIGURE 2.8 Off-site retail

Tasting rooms also become places to sell branded merchandise, including T-shirts and caps as well as growlers, bottles, or cans. Another redeeming feature is that the space allows the business to educate the consumer about the products and values of the business while becoming part of the local community. Consumers also provide rapid feedback to the producer about their perceptions of the product. While many bars around town may only carry a limited selection of the business's product line, the tasting room showcases its full range of products—and some have 20 or more beverages on tap at any given time. Often tasting rooms invite food carts to bring food to their facility so that patrons

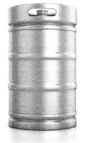

50 pounds base malt @ $.50
20 pounds specialty malt @ $.75
pound of hops @ $8
Labor and misc. $50/barrel
Taxes $12/barrel
Licensing $4/barrel
Rent and utilities $6/barrel
Total cost $120 per barrel or $60/keg
1 barrel of beer (31 gallons)

Source: Madeleine Pullman.
©koya979/Shutterstock.com

FIGURE 2.9 Cost of a keg

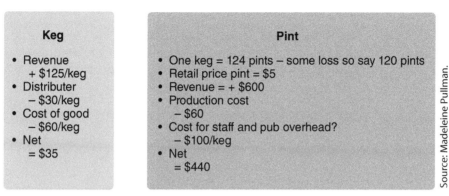

FIGURE 2.10   Keg versus pint economics

can eat and, as a result, stay longer and spend more. Following the wine industry's well-established tasting room lessons, businesses, like Green Flash Brewing Company in California, are investing significant sums building out tasting room facilities to enhance their overall customer experience.

Green Flash Tasting Rooms

Green Flash Brewing Company, one of the top 50 breweries based on beer sales volume and known for its hop-centric IPAs, operates two San Diego tasting rooms. Both are tourist destinations. The original tasting room on Mira Mesa has 30 taps, tours, a beer garden, and a food truck. In 2015 the brewery opened a new facility and tasting room in Poway, California called Cellar 3 (the original site is home to cellars 1 and 2). The new tasting room facility rounds out the brewery's portfolio by allowing for an expansion of their barrel-aging program as well as an opportunity to experiment with wild yeast. (Wild yeast projects require a separate facility from the original brewery due to potential cross-contamination.) Cellar 3 is also the name of the new beer series that includes the sours and barrel-aged beers made on-site. In essence, Cellar 3 provides more product experimentation and business growth while offering a singular tasting room experience for customers.

Green Flash CEO and co-founder Mike Hinkley wanted a new space that addressed brewers' needs as first priority, but the concept quickly evolved into a site for consumer engagement as well. Just behind the tasting room's bar, the new Cellar 3 space contains more than 800 barrels, fermentation and conditioning tanks as well as a cork and cage bottling line. Up to 155 customers can watch the brewery's barrel master work with the team while sampling the beers onsite, a boon for connoisseurs. Green Flash also runs hour-long educational tours of the facility covering wild yeast fermentation, barrel aging, and blending plus a guided tasting of four beers.

Inspired by craft beer as an art from, the design of Cellar 3 attracts consumers who enjoy the rare beer selections tapped on-site. Rotating curated artwork and a deco-inspired metal starburst facade behind the bar compliment the hand-crafted brews. The bar itself is situated among barrels and other production equipment. Each Cellar 3 bottle is artfully designed and is incorporated into the decor of the tasting room, creating an ever-evolving art installation that grows with each limited release. Much of the artwork displayed on the walls is for sale, making the tasting room feel like a gallery.

FIGURE 2.11   Tasting room

In today's market, a rotation of food trucks has almost become a brewery taproom essential, and Green Flash debuted its very own truck called Green Flash Gastro in 2015 at both taproom locations. A highly successful series of pop-up dinners in the brewery put on by Dave Adams, the Director of Beer Education, inspired the truck and its offerings of charcuterie, Italian sandwiches, and homemade jerky. There is also a lighted outdoor patio with benches where guests hang out. A program of special events, including live bands, reflects the connection between craft beer, art, and music.

Farmhouse Brewery

A **farmhouse brewery** is a concept that makes an explicit connection to the land, either by location or by state law. This distinction is important since some states give farmhouse breweries a formal legal definition that provides the entity with many of the privileges accorded to wineries. For example, the law might set a limit on production (say 15,000 barrels per year) and may or may not require it to be a farm as long as they use ingredients produced in that state. Or, the law may set in-state ingredient requirements such as 20 percent in-state hops and 40 percent other in-state ingredients (such as New York's Farm Brewery Law). Most farmhouse laws often allow on- and off-premises consumption and self-distribution similar to wineries—again depending on the state and county. Given the flexibility of some farmhouse brewery laws, the brewery could be located in a rural location such as Logsdon

Farmhouse Ales in Hood River, Oregon that has 10 acres of land growing hops and an orchard. Alternatively, urban farmhouse breweries such as the Bronx Brewery, buy New York-grown hops and other ingredients from community gardens and various New York growers.

Pub/Restaurant

Like the taproom, the **pub/restaurant** has all the advantages of selling product by the pint or glass and it can also deliver a full dining experience while appealing to all kinds of people. By offering food, customers stay on the premises longer than in a basic taproom and the average sales per person are much higher. Food also brings in families and groups. Many states and countries require that some percentage, say 25 to 50 percent, of all pub sales must be food. Traditionally brewpubs have offered standard fare like burgers, fries, and pizza. Increasingly, new brewpub concepts are diversifying into higher end and more original food ideas, such as Chinese street food, Southern-style barbeque, and local and sustainably raised meats and produce. The down side of having a pub/restaurant is that it requires a much different skill set: namely, producing food and running a profitable bar and kitchen. More about the interaction between food and craft beverages is covered in Chapter 18: Pub and Food Operations.

FIGURE 2.12   Facility comparison

Packaging	Pub/Restaurant
Small staff	Large staff
Product focus	Customer focus: interaction and full brand experience
Sales staff for retail growth	Food focus: profitable food service is key
Easy to expand	Hard to expand brewery other than multi-units
Lower rent and easier to find space in industrial areas	Smaller production requirements but harder to find appropriate space
Lower margin from distribution; high margin in taproom	High percentages direct sales to consumer means higher margins
Less experimentation other than for taproom sales	Opportunity to experiment more frequently with seasonals or one-offs
Source: Madeleine Pullman.	

Company Name and Legal Trademark

After you have determined your concept (including the product and business model), the next step is to determine the **name** of your entity and the imagery or brand around that name. Not only will the name and imagery have a major influence on the labeling, packaged product, and individual product names, but it will have an impact on the theming of the space where customers may also experience your brand—a tasting room, pub, or restaurant.

In the first wave of craft breweries during the 1980s and 1990s, most business names stemmed from geography, historic figures, and owner surnames; old guard names include Dogfish Head, Sierra

TABLE 2.2 Trademarking steps

Step	Activity
1	Identify potential names, images, and brand names. If the image is something like a red hat, then there could be an issue with conflict with products called "Red Hat" or using a red hat image if a similar company uses it.
2	Search Google and other search engines for potential users of that name.
3	Search beverage websites such as Beer Advocate, Rate Beer, Tastings, etc. for potential conflicts with other beverages.
4	Search US Patent and Trademark website.[6]
5	Hire a trademark attorney.
Source: Madeleine Pullman.	

Nevada, New Belgium, Widmer Brothers, McMenamins, and Sam Adams. The more recent wave of craft beverage names have more edge and are metaphorical, pun-based, and conceptual themes, such as Wandering Angus, Green Flash, Crooked Stave, Fat Head, Epic, and Dark Horse.

With thousands of craft beverage companies in existence and development, coming up with a unique name is extremely challenging. The name should be trademarked so that there are not conflicts with other products in the future. In order to receive a trademark, the name cannot be used by another related product (beverage or hospitality business in particular). Many conflicts arise from other breweries, cideries, wineries, vineyards, and even non-alcoholic beverages. But, hiring a good trademark lawyer to research and trademark the name is one sure way to avoid problems in the future.

Trademark: The trademark is applied to a word, symbol, or design that identifies the good or service. Company taglines or catchphrases fall under trademark law, such as Schaefer's "It's the One Beer to Have When You're Having More than One." As part of the consumer protection system, trademarks are under the jurisdiction of the US Patent and Trademark office. Owners of a federally registered trademark can sue for trademark infringement in federal court. This can prevent a business from selling the labeled goods or exporting/importing goods that display that trademark. Taking precautionary steps outlined in Table 2.2, early in the business development process avoids troublesome trademark issues down the road.

The United States Patent and Trademark website has a search engine for researching for images and words. For example, the search on the word "Dogfish Head" depicted in Figure 2.13 brings up various brands and company names all related to the brewery. A quick search under the websites image list brings up various label fonts and the brewery's branded image of the dogfish. Another beverage company wanting to put an image of the dogfish on their label would run into infringement problems.

Start List At: [   ] OR Jump to record: [   ] 23 **Records(s) found (This page: 1 ~ 23)**

Refine Search (Dogfish Head)[COMB] [   ] Submit

Current Search: S5: (Dogfish Head)[COMB] docs: 23 occ: 112

	Serial Number	Reg. Number	Word Mark	Check Status	Live/Dead
1	86726654	4926931	DOGFISH HEAD	TSDR	LIVE
2	86726553		DOGFISH HEAD DISTILLING CO.	TSDR	LIVE
3	86267656	4883850	DOGFISH HEAD	TSDR	LIVE
4	86141662		DOGFISH HEAD	TSDR	LIVE
5	86612171		DOGFISH HEAD 60 MINUTE IPA THE CONTINUALLY-HOPPED, INDIA PALE ALE.	TSDR	LIVE
6	86358612	4703658	DOGFISH HEAD	TSDR	LIVE
7	86182200	4622601	DOGFISH HEAD	TSDR	LIVE
8	86007778	4490909	DOGFISH HEAD 75 MINUTE IPA	TSDR	LIVE
9	85736702		DOGFISH HEAD BLUSH	TSDR	DEAD
10	85937005		DOGFISH HEAD	TSDR	LIVE
11	85673320	4385364	DOGFISH HEAD BOCCE BEER	TSDR	LIVE
12	85457455	4164234	DOGFISH HEAD	TSDR	LIVE
13	85457453	4164232	DOGFISH HEAD	TSDR	LIVE
14	85356704		DOGFISH HEAD TWEASON'ALE	TSDR	DEAD
15	78920608		DOGFISH HEAD RED AND WHITE	TSDR	DEAD
16	78920596		DOGFISH HEAD BLACK AND BLUE	TSDR	DEAD
17	78750962	3336614	DOGFISH HEAD ALEHOUSE	TSDR	LIVE
18	77587241	3622502	DOGFISH HEAD CRAFT BREWED ALES	TSDR	LIVE
19	77587316	3622505	DOGFISH HEAD BREWINGS & EATS	TSDR	LIVE
20	77587219	3622500	DOGFISH HEAD CRAFT BREWED ALES	TSDR	LIVE
21	77096021		DOGFISH HEAD VODKA EROTICA	TSDR	DEAD
22	76617326	3033850	DOGFISH HEAD JIN	TSDR	LIVE
23	76617325	3033849	DOGFISH HEAD TA-KEELA	TSDR	DEAD

Source: United States Patent and Trademark Office.

FIGURE 2.13   Dogfish Head trademark search

Important points to consider when naming your entity:

1. What does it infer about the story of your beverage?

2. What kind of image, personality, and brand does it convey?

3. How does it set the business apart from the pack?

4. What will the name mean about the stream of names for individual products as well as the business name?

5. Is the name and image "clean," in other words, no others are using it? Have you conducted an Internet and trademark search?

6. If the name and image are clean, how quickly can you trademark it? The first use must occur before one can formally apply for a trademark.

Copyright: A copyright protects original creative works, such as books, movies, songs, paintings, photographs, web content, and choreography. Anyone with a federally registered copyright controls how the work is reproduced, distributed, and presented publicly. Like a trademark, the copyright owner can sue anyone using protected material and prevent the distribution, importing, and exporting of the infringing product in federal court. For beverage producers, problems arise with using copyrighted art and photography on labels or songs used in videos or websites. Conversely, if the business develops its own content, that work should be copyrighted.

Trademark Troubles for an Oregon Brewery

Harvester Brewing, an established gluten-free brewery in Portland Oregon, was forced to change its name in 2014 when Hope Family Wines in California feared the brewery's name would cause brand confusion, even though it is in a different trademark class. The winery had a boxed wine called "Harvester" set for production. Harvester Brewing had no interest in a long and expensive legal battle with Hope Family, so the owners used the opportunity to engage with their consumers and reached out to gather new name ideas. The brewery strived to find a name in keeping with its existing tractor logo. The brewery settled on a fan's suggestion of "Ground Breaker." With the successful name change in place, this 100 percent gluten-free brewery, which sources hops and other ingredients from regional farms, is continuing to break new ground in the beer world.

SUMMARY

Starting a new business or building on an existing one requires a good understanding of the concept choices. From the initial stages of coming up with a beverage type, choosing the right concept for the market, designing the interior and exterior of the facility, and creating branding for the products—all of these must fit together into a coherent and compelling story. By looking at successful businesses, you can get a good idea of how well the pieces fit together. Having a good understanding of the legal aspects are also paramount. There is no use in choosing a concept that is not legal in your area or picking a name or brand image that has potential trademark conflicts. Many say that one of the hardest aspects of a startup craft business is trademark and naming issues. It pays to start on this process as soon as possible.

Base Camp Brewing Concept Design

Base Camp Brewing, located in Portland, Oregon, is a production brewery with a large tasting room and outdoor patio. Brewmaster and owner Justin Fay shares a passion for the outdoors and beer with many others in the Pacific Northwest, and he combined them to form his unique business concept. His dream for the brewery is for local outdoor enthusiasts come to plan their next adventure over a beer at Base Camp.

Base Camp built the brewery and taproom incorporating the outdoor adventure concept into every physical detail. Fay reached out to a logger contact to obtain wood for the tabletops and used boulders for table bases. Tap handles are decorated with carabineers, a canoe is strung from the ceiling, and nature and adventure photographs line the walls. Customers sip their beers on a patio seated around gravel fire pits. The plants on the property are all wild, native, edible plants and have small placards explaining their origin and significance. The

---

nature theme not only tells the brewery's story, but provides an educational component to the experience as well.

Another mission of the brewery is environmental awareness, so Base Camp packages in an unusual 22-ounce aluminum bottle instead of the standard glass bottle. The brewers believed that aluminum was better for the environment because it is lighter for transportation (requiring less fuel), is more likely to be recycled by consumers, requires less energy to produce, uses more recycled material in production, and does not include a paper label as most glass bottles do. In addition to these advantages, the aluminum bottle is also better for maintaining the quality of the beer since it protects the brew from light. The bottles are light, durable enough to carry in a backpack, and are therefore easy to bring on an outdoor adventure.

Consistency is key for any brewery—insuring that the beer tastes exactly the same every time someone drinks it—but consistency in messaging is also important to the brand. Fay strives for this brand coherence in all Base Camp products and publicity for visiting customers as well as those who have not visited the taproom. The brewery's flagship, In-tents India Pale Lager, was a play on words in reference to camping, and another signature beer is the S'more Stout with hints of marshmallow and graham cracker and a roasted marshmallow garnish. Base Camp also makes a location-specific series of beers inspired by the brew staff's favorite outdoor adventure spots. For example, the March 2015 Salmonberry River served to spread the word about watershed preservation in partnership with the Native Fish Society.

Beyond the brewery's decor and branding, Fay's team creatively targets the right customers, lures them in the door, and ensures they catch onto the theme. With the climbing gym a few blocks from Base Camp, there's a discount on beers for climbers. The brewery also hosts outdoor-related events such as a summer solstice party featuring many local outdoor companies, a speaker series with the Audubon Society, tastings on Mt. Hood après-ski sessions, and a partnership with the Portland Major League Ultimate team. Proving its brand beyond the tasting room décor is part of what Fay recognizes as "key in business."

LEARNING ADVENTURES

1. Describe a concept and story of a pub or taproom you frequent. Is the concept explicit or implicit? Who do you think this business's story resonates with and is it effective?

2. Create a concept and describe the story that accompanies the concept. Who is the target market for this concept and what is the size of this potential market in your area?

3. Do a trademark search on a name that you like (try Harvester if you want to read about a complicated situation). Summarize your findings and potential conflicts.

4. Create a vision for a concept. What would be the dream for this business 10 to 20 years out?

5. What trends to you see in beer, distillery, and cider concepts in your area?

ENDNOTES

1. Why We Brew (2016) Sierra Nevada Vision Statement. http://www.sierranevada.com/brewery/about-us/why-we-brew

2. Brewers Association (2015). US Brewery Count by Category.

3. TTB FAQs (2015) Alcohol FAQs: Honey Wine (Mead), Alcohol and Tobacco Trade Tax Bureau, last modified April 15, 2015, http://www.ttb.gov/faqs/alcohol_faqs.shtml#hw.

4. "Craft Certification," American Distilling Institute, http://distilling.com/resources/craft-certification.

5. TTB (2015). Alternating Proprietorships. http://www.ttb.gov/beer/alternating_prop.shtml

6. "Getting Started with Trademarks," United States Patent and Trademark Office, last modified September 28, 2015, http://www.uspto.gov/trademark.

CHAPTER THREE

Product and Process

Key Terms

angel's share
beer definition
beer process
beer tax issues
beer trends
blending
brew kettle
cider
cider process
cider tax issues
cider trends
distillation
distilled spirits
dry hopping

flagship product
heads
hearts
hops
lagering
lautering
malolactic
malted grains
mash tun
mead
mead production and taxes
mead trends
pasteurization
perry

pomace
portfolio
proof
proof gallons
seasonals
spirit production
spirit safe
spirit tax issues
sweat
tails
vatting
wine
wort

Overview

This chapter examines the main craft beverage product types and the production process involved. It covers the popular products, trends, and opportunities for innovative beverages as well as the relationship between product choice and process. The key ideas behind any product portfolio, the assortment of beverages offered by your business, will be an important addition to your business plan.

Learning Objectives

▶ Identify a product and define how the product is going to be different from the current products of that type and style.

▶ Understand consumer demand shifts between different products and categories.

▶ Appreciate the challenges for each beverage type and how ingredients and processes relate to tax and legal implications.

▶ Understand how the various products are made.

▶ Understand the basics of a beverage portfolio, a flagship product, and an initial portfolio for any beverage type.

▶ Explore the issues related to seasonality and one-off beverages.

Introduction

The craft beverage world is dominated by beer. Craft beer got a head start in the 1980s and, with beer being one of the most popular alcoholic beverages in the world, has grown exponentially in sales volume and number of brewing facilities. By 2014, the US craft beer industry produced more than 22 million barrels of beer from close to 3,500 facilities.[1] Other countries around the world are following suit with craft beer businesses taking off in Canada, most European countries, China, and parts of South American.

Cider has a long history in the United States and United Kingdom but was virtually abandoned in the United States from Prohibition until after 2000. The United Kingdom has maintained a solid craft and industrial cider market, as have historic cider making places such as France and Spain. But, the United States cider market has only recently taken off, growing rapidly, 73 percent production growth annually since 2008. In 2014 roughly 350 cideries produced over 54 million gallons of cider.[2] It is now slated to catch up within a few years to the United Kingdom in both production and demand.

Craft spirits came late to the game in the US, with only 50 distilleries operating in 2005 growing to more than 400 licensed craft distilled spirits producers by 2014. Craft spirits suffer from consumer confusion from pseudo craft producers—large industrial producers claiming to be "craft"—more than other craft beverages. Mead and alcoholic kombucha are gaining traction too, though are relatively small compared to the other beverage categories.

These newer craft products (craft cider, spirits, and so on) are nibbling away at the beer market as consumers explore new products and look for alternatives to beer for reasons including dietary concerns and variety seeking. As a result, some breweries are adding these other products to their beverage portfolios. For anyone interested in the craft beverage industry regardless of personal preferences, it is important to understand these different craft products, their attributes and trends, and the process for making them.

From post-Prohibition to early 1980s, beverage drinkers have gone from the *original* brewery styles (traditional lagers) through extensions of those brands with *exaggerated* styles (ice, lime, light, wheat) to the arrival of craft beers in the mid-1980s. At that point, the craft beer *revisionists* rolled out pale ales, IPAs, stouts, wheat beer, and the like—historic styles from the United Kingdom and other parts of Europe with an American influence. More recently, the craft movement has moved into the *extremist* phase: the United States has become world famous for highly hopped IPAs as well as sour, fruit-flavored, and barrel-aged beers. Other craft beverages like cider, spirits, and mead have adopted these trends and added hops, herbs and spices, different fruits, and barrel aging with all kinds of wood. Packaging and manufacturing processes have also gone in many new directions, including canning, larger format bottles, aging, lagering, and dry-hopping.[3]

As the consumer needs have shifted, craft beer is now marketed by style rather than brand (like the large industrial beers). The typical consumer looks at the style shelf first (for example, IPA) then selects a brand. Distilled spirits are also displayed by style but increasingly craft distilled spirits are separated out to their own category. Cider, mead, and others are currently considered a style and are not separated by flavor or sweetness. This could change as those beverages gain more market share. While consumers are very loyal to craft as a category, there is less loyalty to a specific beverage maker; rather, most craft consumers look for variety and adventure. They like to be educated and often try new things.

Beverages and Production

Beer

Beer is defined in different ways according to the country of origin. For example, the United States Internal Revenue Code (IRC) definition for "beer" is "beer, ale, porter, stout, and other similar fermented beverages (including sake or similar products) of any name or description containing one-half of one percent or more of alcohol by volume (ABV), brewed or produced from malt, wholly or in part, or from any substitute thereof." According to the Brewers Association, craft beer comes from a craft brewery (as defined in Chapter 2). Therefore, flavored malt beverages such as *Mike's Hard Lemonade*, are not considered beers.

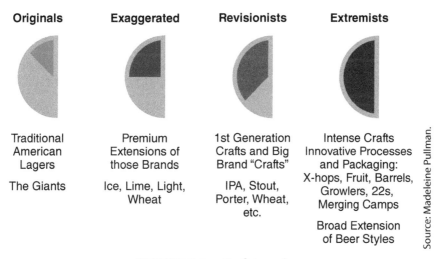

FIGURE 3.1   Craft trends

In Germany, according to the 1993 *Vorläufiges Biergesetz* (Provisional Beer Law), beer regulations differentiate between top- and bottom-fermented beers. Bottom-fermented beers (lagers) can consist of only water, malted barley, hops, and yeast; top-fermented beer (ales) can contain a wider variety of malt and other enhancers like pure sucrose and beet sugars. In addition to ingredient regulations, there are other process regulations. Other countries like Belgian have looser interpretations of all styles and minimal rules except for those designated as Trappist or certified Belgian abbey beers.

Beer process: Beer is typically made from **malted grains** (malted barley, wheat, or rye are common in the craft industry). Malted grains are grains that have gone through the malting process making it easier to extract sugar from the grain. At a malting facility, the grain is soaked in water to increase its water content. After the water is drained off, the grain is allowed to germinate and is kept under suitable conditions to convert its starches to sugars. At an opportune point, the germination is halted and the grain is kiln dried and sometimes roasted (for darker malts). Overall, malting provides the appropriate sugars, flavors, and colors for beers and spirits based on grain. Once the malted grain reaches the brewery, the rest of the process continues as shown in Figure 3.2.

The brewer designs a recipe of different malted and other grains (styles and roasts), which are put through a mill that splits the husk of the grain and exposes the endosperm's sugars and starches. The milled grain is then mixed with hot water in a **mash tun** where the malt's enzymes convert any remaining starches into fermentable sugars. The milling and mash step take a couple of hours. Afterwards, the liquid is separated from the grain and the grain is rinsed with more hot water, a step called **lautering**, which can be done with a specially designed mash tun or in a separate lautering vessel. The remaining liquid **wort** is drained into the **brew kettle** leaving the spent grains behind. The wort is boiled for an hour or so with hops added at specific points in the boil.

Hops are a bitter flower from the hops plant that add aroma and desirable bitterness to beer. They are grown predominately in the Pacific Northwest of the United States, Germany, Czech Republic, United Kingdom, and increasingly, China. Hops are harvested in the fall, dried, and either left whole or turned into compact pellets, which are easier to store and handle.

After the wort has finished boiling, it is cooled down via a heat exchanger to roughly room temperature and pumped into a fermentation tank with yeast. The whole process up to this point can take six to eight hours. The fermentation tank is kept at a steady temperature and the yeast works to convert the available sugars to alcohol and carbon dioxide. Depending on the fermentation temperature, the beer can take one to two weeks to complete its fermentation. Some brewers move the beer after the yeast settles out and continue a second fermentation in another conditioning tank, often adding more hops at this stage for enhanced aromas. This is called **dry hopping**. In any case, most beers move on to the conditioning tank with filtering along the way, if desired, and spend a week or so getting carbonated and chilled to the finished temperature. When the beer has reached the right temperature and carbonation, it is then ready to be served in a pub or tasting room, or packaged in kegs, bottles, or cans.

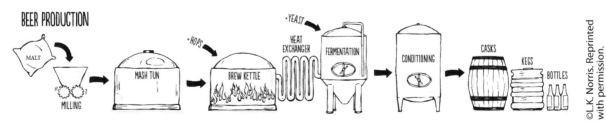

FIGURE 3.2   Brewing process

Beer tax issues: Small craft brewers benefit from lower production tax rates in the United States, paying $7 per barrel on the first 60,000 barrels and $18 per barrel after that up to 2 million barrels. Additionally, each state has a beer tax that averages around $6.20 per barrel.

Beer trends: At this moment, most popular craft beer style is India pale ale (IPA) followed by seasonal offerings. Almost every brewer feels compelled to create an IPA and different IPA versions continue to emerge and grow this market segment. While avid craft consumers seek interesting offerings, including highly hopped (and highly alcoholic) IPAs, Belgian sours, and farmhouse styles, the newest growth is in lower alcohol, easy-drinking styles like Pilsners and other lagers. One can expect the preferred styles to change over time.

The Resurgence of Craft Lagers

In the United States, lagers are often associated with the industrial beer giants, such as Budweiser, Coors, Pabst, and Miller, and craft beer drinkers have written this style off as cheap and tasteless. However, craft brewers are now discovering how lagers produced in the traditional way can create refreshing, distinctive, and flavorful beers that please their customers and round out their business portfolio.

Many factors distinguish an industrially brewed from a crafted lager. Where big brands rely on corn, rice and other sources of sugar, craft brewers use only water, barley malt, yeast, and hops and allow ample time for cold maturation, or **lagering**, which increases production costs. They also do not filter and pasteurize the beer for a longer shelf life like the major brands; craft lagers typically last for just 12 weeks in stores. Lager styles are characterized by a light hops flavor that show off the brewer's skills, since there's no opportunity to hide mistakes with an abundance of hops the way an ale-style can.

As the lager trend has grown with the universal popularity of craft beers, many craft producers are investing in the necessary resources, time, and equipment to include lagers. A brewery can make four batches of IPA in the time it takes to make a single batch of lager. Still, many craft producers are willing to address these costs in light of the demand for more sessionable options for those who want to drink a lower alcohol product in general and others who like to hang out at pubs over an extended period of time.

Cider

Similar to beer, **cider** has a legal definition or industry code of contact in the major cider producing countries (United Kingdom, Spain, France, and the United States). The definitions are similar except that the United Kingdom does not allow added alcohol. According to the United States TTB[4], the terms "cider" and "hard cider" refer to **wine** fermented from apples (including apple juice or concentrate). However, the terms have different meanings under the Internal Revenue Code (IRC) of 1986, as amended and the Federal Alcohol Administration Act (FAA Act). The FAA indicates that "cider" is a fruit wine produced by the normal alcoholic fermentation of the juice of sound, ripe apples. Cider

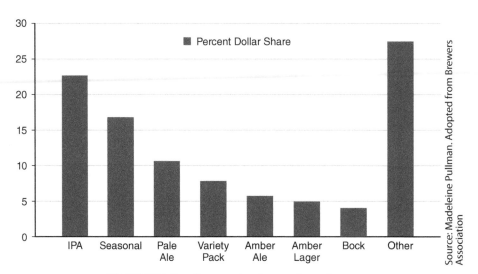

Source: Madeleine Pullman. Adopted from Brewers Association

FIGURE 3.3   Beer style share of market

must be derived wholly (except for sugar, water, or added alcohol) from apples. If made from pears, it can be called **perry** or pear wine. If the cider integrates other fruit, it has to be named accordingly. For example, a wine produced from the fermentation of apple juice and blueberry juice must be designated with a truthful and adequate statement of composition such as "apple-blueberry wine" or "blueberry cider."

Cider process: The cider-making process starts with late-summer or fall-harvested apples, typically either straight cider apples, dessert (eating) apples, or a combination of the two. The apples are harvested and then allowed to **sweat**, meaning they are stored for about one week to soften, and to

©Africa Studio/Shutterstock.com

FIGURE 3.4   Apple

lose excess water and increase sugar content. The apples are then washed and ground into a **pomace**, a mass of apple pieces. The pomace is placed in a press and pressure is applied to the mass to extract the juices. As an alternative to growing or buying apples and then pressing it, juice can be purchased directly. Regardless of the source, the juices are then put in a fermenter with yeast, and the simple sugars are converted into alcohol and carbon dioxide. Typically, ciders ferment at between 40 to 70° F (4 to 16° C) and can take up to three months to ferment at lower temperatures and only a few weeks at higher temperatures. Often, cider goes through a primary fermentation where it ferments to dryness and is transferred off the yeast to a clean vessel where it goes through secondary **malolactic** fermentation (lactic acid converting the malic acid to lactic).

After fermentation is complete, the cider can be moved to storage for maturation; it can also be aged in wood barrels. Depending on the desired flavor, maturation lasts from one to six months. Prior to packaging, other flavors such as cherry, blueberry, different apple juice, and acids may be added. Sparkling ciders go through sugar dosing and carbonation or forced carbonation. Finally, the finished product is packaged in bottles, kegs, or cans. To improve the shelf life of the bottled or canned product, a **pasteurization** step is needed. The cans or bottles are placed in hot water (160 to 185° F) for several minutes to kill any bacteria and yeast.

Cider tax issues: In the United States, cider incurs complex taxation laws. Cider is treated like wine and champagne rather than like beer, its apparent market partner, with strict limits on carbonation and alcohol levels. Over a certain level of carbonation, cider is taxed as champagne; over a certain ABV, cider is taxed as wine. Recently, the United States Association of Cider Makers won a major victory in changing the federal tax code to increase the levels of carbonation and alcohol in hard ciders to match current industry practices and international cider standards. As of January, 2017, if the cider is still or contains low carbonation (at or less than .64 g/100 ml CO_2), under 8.5 percent ABV, and only apple or pear juice, the TTB charges roughly $0.17 per gallon (with small producer credit) and $0.23/gallon (with the credit). On the other extreme, if carbonated (above 64 g/100 ml CO_2), the tax could be as high at $3.40 per gallon (the same as the champagne tax) depending on how carbonation is added. Anything less than or equal to 21 percent by volume and 64 g/100 ml CO_2 will pay taxes up to $0.67 per gallon ($1.57 without the credit) depending on the ABV rate and non-apple or pear juice content (higher alcohol and other juices raise the rate). Cider makers face similar tax and classification issues at the state level.

Cider trends: While cider is 20 percent of the United Kingdom's beer market, it makes up less than 1 percent of the United States beer market (3 percent of the craft market). The United Kingdom, France, and Spain have a long history of cider and have a significant export presence. In the United Kingdom, cider, with brands like *Strongbow*, was predominately marketed to and consumed by men. But that gender split is changing in most countries. Now women make up half the market compared to only 28 percent women drinkers in the craft beer market. The markets for cider are not

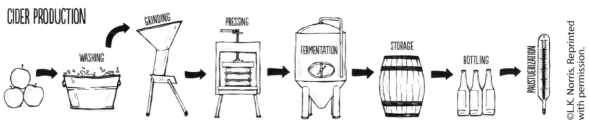

FIGURE 3.5   Cider-making process

only growing in the North American but also in Australia, New Zealand, and South Africa. In most cases, cider is taking market share from wine and beer. High-end ciders (produced and packaged more like champagne and fine wines) are gaining market share particularly among wine drinkers. The combination of fruit, sweeter ciders (pear, apple, berries, and flavorings), and novelty are also attracting younger drinkers (18 to 34 year olds) from both genders. Many popular cider brands are owned by multinational brewing companies who are jumping on the cider trend to expand their market as shown in Table 3.1.

TABLE 3.1   Big cider brands owned by breweries

Brand	Company
Woodchuck, Hornsby's and Magners	C&C Group (Irish maker and distributor of branded cider and beer)
Strongbow	Heineken
Crispin	Miller Coors
Jonny Appleseed, Michelob Ultra Light Cider and Stella Artois Cider	AB-InBev
Angry Orchard	Boston Beer
Square Mile	Craft Brewers Alliance
Source: Madeleine Pullman.	

Mead

According to the IRC of 1986, **mead** or honey wine is classified as an "agricultural wine."[5] Agricultural wine is made from the fermentation of an agricultural product other than the juice of fruit. The IRC does not allow for the use of coloring or flavoring materials (other than hops) in *standard honey wine*. Furthermore, wine spirits may not be added to standard honey wine, and standard honey wine may not contain more than 14 percent ABV. The IRC does provide for the production of wine specialty products that are made from a base of honey wine. These products are not standard agricultural wines, but are instead classified under the IRC regulations as "other than standard (OTS) wines." But the TTB labeling requirements allow the designation "mead" to be used in lieu of "honey wine" on labels.

Curiously, there is more naming flexibility with mead that contains fruit juices. A wine fermented from both fruit juice and an agricultural product does not fall within any of the standards of identity. This type of wine must be designated with a truthful and adequate statement of composition in accordance with the code of federal regulations (CFR), for example "cherry-honey wine" or "cherry mead." The wine also may be labeled with a distinctive or fanciful name, such as "Cherry Bee."

Mead production and taxes: Mead is relatively simple to produce and lacks strict legal definitions in most countries. Honey is added to warm water with any additional flavors and sugars. The mix is cooled and combined with yeast and filtered water in a fermenter. After fermenting the product for about one month, depending on the temperature, the product is moved (with or without filtering) into a secondary tank for further carbonation, then kegged or packaged in bottles or cans. Mead is taxed like cider (taxed like wine) by the US federal government.

Mead trends: Like cider and beer, mead is currently experiencing huge growth from a small base. Many existing breweries or cideries can easily add mead to their portfolio since it can be produced with the same equipment and helps attracts other segments of drinkers looking for variety that is lighter and gluten-free. Mead mixes well with fruits and spices, can be made in dry to sweet varieties, and fairs well with barrel aging.

Distilled Spirits

According to the TTB, **distilled spirits** are defined as a substance known as ethyl alcohol, ethanol, or spirits of wine in any form (including all dilutions or mixtures thereof, from whatever source or by whatever process produced), but not denatured spirits unless specifically stated.[6] The well-known craft spirits categories include vodka, gin, whiskey, rum, tequila (agave), moonshine, and brandy; other specialty categories include cordials, liqueurs, absinthe, and aquavit.

Spirit production: Spirits can be made with any fermented product. There are multiple routes to creating a spirit. One direct path used by spirit producers is to buy neutral alcohol or ethanol and redistill it with flavorings to create products like gin or vodka. Similarly, they can buy or produce a wine from grapes, other fruits, agave, or honey and distill those products for various brandies, liqueurs, tequila, and so on. Sugar can be mixed with water and fermented to create rum. The most advanced process is grain-based spirits.

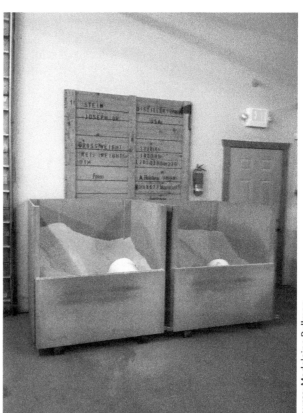

FIGURE 3.6   Ground corn and barley

Source: Madeleine Pullman.

Grain-based spirits like whiskey start out much like beer. Malted grain is ground in a mill, put into a mash tun with water until the starches are converted in to sugar, lautered to separate out the grain, cooled, and pumped directly into a fermenter with yeast.[7] The temperature can be considerably higher than other types of craft beverages—around 95° F, so that the product is fermented out in two or three days.

With a fermented product in hand, it is now time to move into the still for the **distillation** process. The still works by boiling the liquid and evaporating the alcohol. The alcohol re-condenses in a column with coils and is collected in a separate vessel. It comes out of the column in three phases: **heads, hearts**, and **tails**. The heads are the first boil from the ethanol, have off flavors, and are poisonous, the hearts or desirable liquid is found in the middle of the evaporation, and the tails are lower than desirable proof and also lack important flavor components. However, tails can be put through again for a second round of distillation. In traditional whiskey distilleries, the master distiller does the separation, analyzing the runoff through a **spirit safe**, a glass walled case which allows a distiller

SPIRITS DISTILLING

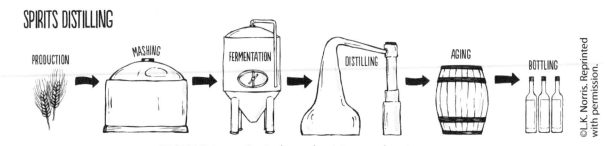

FIGURE 3.7 Grain-based spirits production

to analyze the spirit coming out of the still without coming into contact with the spirit itself, pictured in Figure 3.8.

The distiller may re-distill the first collection several times to improve the purity and smoothness of the product. Flavorings can be added during the distillation process (such as herb and spice mixes for gin) or after the product is completed.

Many spirits go from the still directly to a finishing tank to cool and package. Others go on to age in charred oak **barrels**. Distilled spirits are clear and those with color acquire that hue from barrel aging; they also pick up complexity and flavor in the barrel. Certain rums and whiskey spend several years in these barrels as well as some gins, such as Old Tom gin style. Usually the distilled spirit ends up as 70 to 80 percent ABV, which is too high for sitting in a barrel and will pick up harsh flavors. Before barreling, the spirit is typically watered down to 55 or 65 percent alcohol. During barrel aging, the spirit loses roughly 10 percent each year through evaporation known as the **angel's share**.

FIGURE 3.8 Spirits safe

FIGURE 3.9   Whiskey barrels aging

After aging, the spirit is often mixed with other barrels from the same production batch (**vatting**) or with different types of whiskey (**blending**). Before bottling, spirits are mixed with filtered water to get to the appropriate alcoholic proof. For example 55 to 65 percent ABV alcohol would typically be reduced to between 40 and 50 percent ABV, which corresponds to 80 to 100 Proof (1 percent ABV = 2 **proof**). Prior to bottling, some spirits are filtered to improve their clarity.

Spirit tax issues: Many countries tax spirits at a very high level, which is why spirits dominate duty free shops around the world. Taxes are the highest for spirits because many countries assert that spirits contribute to alcoholism. In Iceland, 90 percent of the consumer price for a liter of vodka goes to taxes in the form of a value added tax (VAT), alcohol duty, and the state monopoly liquor shop's cut. Many countries scale the tax to the alcohol level, or proof. In the United States, the federal spirit tax is based on **proof gallons** (as in, $13.50 per proof gallon). For example, if a brewery sells 10 gallons of 40 percent ABV (80 proof), then the tax is calculated as 10 gallons times 80 proof/100, which equals 8 proof gallons taxed at $13.50 or $108 dollars in federal taxes alone. Individual states add their own taxes too!

Spirit trends: For spirits overall, the highest sales come from vodka (about 40 percent), bourbon or bourbon blends (about 20 percent) followed by tequila, rum, scotch, and gin (each roughly 6 to 9 percent). Most craft spirit producers make multiple products, and nearly half make a whiskey that can take several years. Vodka, gin, and rum are increasingly popular to round out a producer's portfolio. And, many craft spirit makers are using nontraditional flavors like ginger, chocolate, and pepper in their clear spirits.

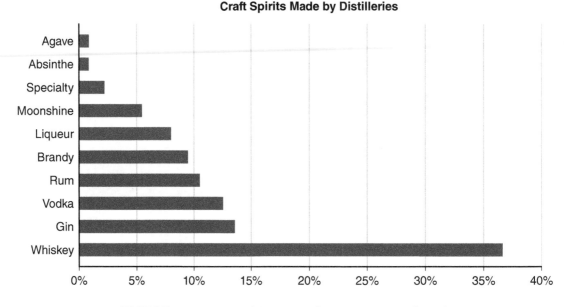

Craft Spirits Made by Distilleries

FIGURE 3.10   United States craft spirit type produced

The Flagship and the Portfolio

Most entrepreneurs start with an idea for the main beverage they plan to produce, a personal favorite or a perceived market opportunity. With any luck, this idea becomes the **flagship product** or the signature product the business is known for. The flagship puts the company on the map. For instance, when you think of New Belgium Brewery, Fat Tire, their amber ale, comes to mind; for Widmer Brewing, Hefeweizen; and for Sam Adams, Boston Lager. While these breweries make other beer styles, the flagship product generates the majority of their sales.

Some producers go into the market with several beers and one emerges as their flagship product. Other producers have a plan for a flagship or a set of flagships—a core group of products that will sell year round. Seasonal and one-of-a-kind beverages, called one-offs, surround that core. One of the vital considerations for creating a flagship product or set of products is knowing how many competitors are on the shelf or on tap in potential accounts and how well the proposed flagship can compete in that category. Today, flagship brands are becoming increasingly hard to grow with so much competition.

In the craft beverages market, there are so many choices and the general public is more aware and savvy than ever before. Target consumers, love variety. Often bar managers and consumers are willing to try a new product at least once if it's in an emerging or popular category. At the same time, there should always be something distinctive about the flagship in its market. For example, when the brewer at Lonerider Brewing Company in Raleigh, North Carolina was asked about his flagship choice of a Hefeweizen, he responded, "Funny how the style we like becomes the beer of choice. Seriously, besides that, we looked at the market and saw that nobody was brewing a German Hefeweizen locally as a flagship. We also saw how wheat beers, and session beers were becoming more popular. With the proliferation of great beers in the market we had to look for ways to differentiate ourselves."[8]

This quotation illustrates the key elements of selecting your flagship: understanding the market and where a demand is not being served; making a style that the company team likes, and thinking about differentiation.

A **portfolio** is the collection of beverages that a company makes. The portfolio should complement the flagship and appeal to the business's primary market; it should be coherent with the concept (both facility and image). For example, many distilleries want to produce a whiskey or another barrel-aged spirit as a flagship, but barrel aging can take anywhere from one to three years. So, in the meantime, they need something fast and easy to sell that builds the brand and generates cash. As a result, most distilleries produce vodka, gin, rum, cordials, and other products that can be quickly made and sold. The whiskey may end up being the distilleries' flagship but the portfolio of other products supports it.

When considering the initial portfolio, it is often helpful to think about rounding out taste and flavor profiles to create a sampler set (the four to six products that allow the consumer to taste your various products). A typical sampler set at a brewery includes a dark porter or stout, a light lager or pale ale, a highly flavorful beer like IPA, and perhaps a beer that might be new to the consumer. A cider set might contain a sweet, a dry, a berry or other fruit flavor, a hopped or spiced, or a single apple varietal cider. Product portfolios can and should change over time as new trends emerge and some products lose popularity. Finally, portfolios can make up a variety pack for the producer that is very popular with variety seeking consumers.

Portfolio and flagship design involves thinking about your primary market. If it is a resort town (beach, lake, or mountains), what will tourists want to take home? If it is a college town, what is the average cost of your products and are there enough people who are looking for more than Pabst Blue Ribbon or Keystone Light? As for the specific locale, what is popular in that region? Is there special ingredient availability like maple syrup in Vermont and Canada? Will people try the product if it is very distinctive? What about the weather, since people drink certain styles in hot versus cold places? Lagers and barrel aging will take longer and tie up available cash.

Photo courtesy of Madeleine Pullman. Reprinted with permission of Ale Apothecary.

FIGURE 3.11   Ale Apothecary portfolio

Seasonals: Seasonal products are the ideal way to try new recipes and ideas without committing to a big investment in labels and marketing. The business can get feedback from customers and make adjustments as needed. Seasonal and one-offs (products made for a limited time only) are easy to achieve in brewpubs since there are no packaging issues. These specialty items have gained importance for driving new and more profitable business since they are often higher priced (and often higher alcohol). Many breweries offer October, Christmas, spring, and summer seasonals. In production breweries, additional marketing effort will be required to get retailers' attention for the product. Since retailers have limited space, it has become a race for who can get their seasonal product out first. No one wants to be left with an Octoberfest or a Christmas beer months after the appropriate time period has lapsed, unless the producer had a real hit. Some cideries and distilleries make seasonal products based on the availability of certain fresh fruits or herbs. These can work off-season since they are not tied to a specific holiday or event.

Craft Breweries Get into Spirits

Many large, well-known craft brewers are opening distilleries as side businesses and dramatically broadening their portfolios. Dogfish Head in Delaware, Rogue in Oregon, and Ballast Point and Anchor Brewing in California are all dedicating time and money to craft distilling. While making wort is the first step of producing many spirits, the rest of the distilling process involves a learning curve and new skills for brewers. Nonetheless, established craft brewers are exploring with nontraditional ingredients. For example, Dogfish Head distills its gin with cucumber, coriander seed, and hops along with the juniper berries. Rogue produces a Chipotle Whiskey, Hazelnut Spice Rum, and a Bacon Maple Vodka. Ballast Point, which won an award for its whiskey, employs the same high-quality malted barley and yeast it uses for its beers. These breweries have an advantage entering the distilling market with a recognizable brand and established customer base. Currently, it is difficult to earn a profit in the craft distilling market due to high production costs and high excise taxes. The advantage for these well-known breweries is exemplified by Dogfish Head's experience: they moved their distilling operation to their production brewery in order to produce tens of thousands of cases and rapidly expand distribution.

SUMMARY

Many people come to the craft beverage world with an idea of what they want to make and the type of production that appeals to them. Along the path of developing a business and a concept, entrepreneurs realize that another product could make more sense to bring in cash or fit better within the local market. Understanding the different aspects of craft products and processes as well as consumer trends, ingredient availability and tax implications are important steps toward making crucial decisions and building an appropriate business model.

How an Irish Producer Built a Flagship and Portfolio

Dingle Brewing Company in Kerry, Ireland may be best known for making Tom Crean's Fresh Irish Lager, but the company's real goal has always been whiskey. On the site of a former creamery, the discovery of the working well inspired Dingle's owner Jerry O'Sullivan to create a craft whiskey. The trouble was Irish whiskey demands long aging time and O'Sullivan knew that it would be at least four years before any whiskey would be aged enough to sell. To resolve this dilemma, O'Sullivan determined to brew beer to keep the company afloat and chose to concentrate on lager. With the well on-site, the company already had the luxury of one of beer's main ingredients: an endless supply of pure water. Dingle purchased used brewing equipment with the exception of two tanks, which served a dual purpose as fermenters and conditioners.

In Ireland, stout is the national beverage and Guinness dominates the beer market along with Murphy's and Beamish. But for Irish youth, Guinness is their grandfather's beer, and European lager brands like Stella and Heineken have successfully targeted this demographic. In the emergent Irish craft market where brewers must decide how to position their products, many choose to brew American-style ales. However, ales have not seen the same success in Ireland as in the United States and England.

FIGURE 3.12   Dingle Brewing Company

Given that the market demand for lagers, when taking into account buying habits of college students and consumers in late-night bars and clubs and among college, nearly matched that for stouts, there was a real opportunity for Dingle's lager. O'Sullivan set out to produce a fresh, unpasteurized Irish-made lager on draft and capture a good percentage of the young Irish market. Through the years, there had been a decline in pubs with many closing their doors, and O'Sullivan wanted to lure people back to their local pubs with a local product. Hence, Tom Crean's was born.

Although the older population tends to be persistent in their beer choice, Crean's quickly captured the younger crowd as well as the tourists who visited southwest Ireland. Brand awareness came fast, and in short order Crean's became available in 92 pubs, including a few famous ones in Dublin on well-trafficked tourists routes. These visitors craved an authentic Irish experience, and so Crean's was not only domestically produced but proved to be very drinkable and refreshing. As for the locals, they enjoyed the fact that Crean's offered them something to drink after a full-bodied beer, since it was sessionable.

Part of the success can be attributed to the beer's namesake, local hero Tom Crean. Crean spent 27 years in the Navy, and more time in Antarctica than any other explorer. Crean was born in a town nearby the brewery, and the first pint of Crean's was poured at the launch party on his birthday. The logo of a compass with a tagline of "Discover Crean's" associates the beer with adventure and signifies that the beer is worth discovering.

As one of the most popular tourist destinations in Ireland, the village of Dingle receives dozens of tour busses per day and Dingle Brewing Company is one of the obligatory stops. The brewery now features a visitor center where tourists tour the brewery and distillery and enjoy samples in the tasting room. During the peak season, Crean's merchandise flies off the shelves.

In terms of international distribution, there are several challenges, not the least of which is that the units of alcohol measurements are different in each country. Quality is another. As a fresh lager, Crean's begins to deteriorate shortly after fermentation and has just a two week shelf life. Domestically, Dingle has dealt with these issues by educating pub owners about the lager's freshness and shelf life so that they don't over order six kegs once a month. Dingle's sales representatives also incentivize the pubs and make appearances at fairs to raise awareness of the Crean's brand and its freshness.

The Crean's recipe has been changed once and tweaked a few times, but O'Sullivan has no plans of changing the lager again or brewing other beers. Lagers are more expensive than ales to produce because they take more time and require cold storage. Dingle lagers Crean's for seven to 10 days, much shorter than the four to eight weeks standard for German lagers. But O'Sullivan tested different lagering timeframes side by side and could not tell any difference in flavor. Currently, Dingle brews about 160 kegs a week, brewing five days per week. Eventually, beer production in much higher volumes will take place at a new location. The original Dingle's facility, as dreamed, will be reserved for distilling and aging barrels and barrels of premium draft whiskey.

LEARNING ADVENTURES

1. Tour a facility of your choice and see how long it takes to make the product that you like. What are trickiest aspects of making that product?

2. Evaluate the portfolio of a craft beverage producer. What does each item contribute to the portfolio in terms of potential economic advantage and market appeal?

3. Look at your state's or country's tax policy for beer, cider, and spirits. How much does the production tax add to the overall cost of the product?

4. What are the best-selling items in your favorite pub? Find out by talking to a bartender and then try to determine what drives that popularity.

ENDNOTES

1. "State of the Industry 2015," Brewers Association presentation, https://www.brewersassociation.org/presentations/state-of-the-industry-2015.

2. Terry Bradshaw, "Hard Cider Production on the Rise, but Challenges Remain," *University of Vermont Outreach* (blog), May 21, 2015, http://learn.uvm.edu/blog-sustainability/hard-cider-production-and-cider-apple-yield.

3. "State of the Craft Beer Industry 2013," Demeter Group Investment Bank, http://demetergroup.net/sites/default/files/news/attachment/State-of-the-Craft-Beer-Industry-2013.pdf.

4. "Alcohol FAQs: Cider," Alcohol and Tobacco Trade Tax Bureau (TTB), last modified April 15, 2015, http://www.ttb.gov/faqs/alcohol_faqs.shtml#hw.

5. "Alcohol FAQs: Honey Wine (Mead)," TTB, last modified April 15, 2015, http://www.ttb.gov/faqs/alcohol_faqs.shtml#hw.

6. TTB Forms, http://www.ttb.gov/forms/.

7. Some distillers use straight grain, like corn, barley, or wheat, and add an enzyme to the mash to get a similar effect to a malted grain-based mash.

8. "Interview with a Brewer: Lonerider Brewing Co. in NC," *Monday Night Brewing* (blog), March 13, 2009, http://mondaynightbrewing.com/interview-with-a-brewer-lonerider-brewing-co-in-nc.

CHAPTER FOUR

Ingredients

Key Terms

bagged malt
base malt
basic
bins
cider apples
compressed hop pellets
costing
dessert apples
forward contract
fruit
fruit contracts
fruit delivery

fruit supply
grain silo
hop contracts
hop extract
hop supply
hops delivery
isomerization
leaf hops
lovibond
malt contracts
malt delivery
malt supply

perry
private versus public hops
proprietary hop
recipe
specialty malt
spices and flavorings
spot market
sugar
tote
water
yeast

Overview

Ingredients are the foundation of the craft beverage industry. This chapter delves into the strategic raw materials for beer, cider, and spirits: the grains, fruits, and hops, depending on the business concept. As one of the ways to differentiate your products from others on the market, ingredients are a principal part of product design. Insuring a supply of the strategic ingredients involves establishing relationships and creating contracts with the providers of these ingredients, and is covered in detail. This chapter also provides a recipe-costing tool for calculating ingredient estimates.

Learning Objectives

▶ Understand the strategic ingredients and average recipe needs for various craft beverages.

▶ Understand an ingredient contract.

▶ Identify trends in ingredients and implications for future needs.

▶ Differentiate between private versus public hop varietals.

▶ Understand the delivery options for ingredients.

▶ Calculate recipe cost based on ingredients.

▶ Apply recipe estimates to develop potential needs for one to three years.

Introduction

Craft beverages are predominately composed of ingredients that follow the agricultural seasons. As a result, they vary in supply and quality based on weather, demand, inventoried supplies, and many other factors. Following the laws of supply and demand, low supplies lead to higher prices and visa versa. For any craft beverage producer, buyers need to understand the factors that influence price as well as the strategic role that any given ingredient plays in the product line. If a product depends on a highly coveted patented hops or an unusual fruit like passion fruit or elderberries, then getting a stable and affordable supply of that ingredient is crucial. The ingredient buyer's toolkit must include a forecast of future needs based on product recipes, an understanding of factors that drive price changes, and the methods for reducing price and supply uncertainty.

Average Recipe Needs and Securing Ingredients

Each craft beverage recipe has a different set of foundational ingredients. Beer **recipes** use malt and hop varietals; ciders use dessert or cider apples as well as other fruits and sweetening ingredients; and spirits have an alcohol base or different types of sugar sources, grains, potatoes, and fruits. Other ingredients arc added such as yeast, acid, sulfur, yeast nutrient, finings, filtering aids, spices, and so on. So, it is important that beverage producers understand the sourcing issues and pricing for everything going into a bottle, serving tank, or keg. A general recipe for a craft beverage requires the estimated amounts of base ingredients outlined in Table 4.1.

While average recipes require these amounts, lower alcohol products may require less of some ingredients per barrel. For example, a light ale might have only 40 pounds of base malt. Some maybe diluted later to achieve the lower alcohol levels thus requiring less of the ingredients overall; often fermented ciders are diluted with apple juice or water to bring the alcohol down a few percentage points. Actual yields also depend on the amount of sugar extracted from the malting process or juices extracted during pressing.

TABLE 4.1   Base ingredient craft estimates

Beverage	Key Ingredients *Beer barrel (bbl.) = 31 gallons* *Whiskey barrel (wbl.)= 53 gallons*
Beer	Base malt: 50 pounds/bbl. Specialty malt: 20 pounds/bbl. Hops: 1.4 pounds/bbl.
Cider	Apples: 300-400 pounds/bbl.
Whiskey	Base malt: 1400 pounds/wbl.
Mead	Honey: 93-121 pounds/bbl.
Source: Madeleine Pullman.	

Hops

Hops are a strategic ingredient for beer, so what happens when it is time to open the pub and you cannot get the hops you need? Many suppliers require you to be in business before contracting with you. Increasingly, hops are also showing up in hopped products from both mead and cider producers. With few exceptions, all beer recipes contain hops. With India pale ales (IPAs) demanding more hops than the average beer and comprising more than 50 percent of craft consumer sales, the demand for hops is skyrocketing. This "hop craze" is worldwide, in every place where people produce craft-style beers. Aroma hops are the most favored by craft producers. However, due to the continued consolidation of big brewers who demand different hop varieties, aroma hops have lost significant acreage. Today, hops producers are scrambling to shift field cultivation to "hot" hops, but as it takes a few years to replant and get a hop vine into production, there is a lag time to meet the demand. Hops are the key ingredient to secure and maintain a predictable supply.

FIGURE 4.1   One brewery's annual hopsupply

Source: Madeleine Pullman

Hops can be purchased in multiple forms, detailed in Figure 4.2. In the conventional format, hop cones are picked from the vines and dried, compressed into bails, and sold as **leaf hops**. An alternative is to press the leaves into **compressed hop pellets,** which last longer and are easier to handle. Or, the essential aromas and bittering agents can be extracted from the hops into a liquid form, **hop extract**.

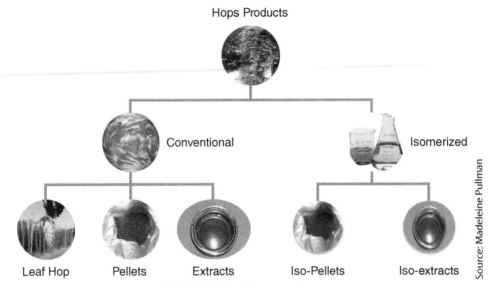

Hops Products

Conventional

Isomerized

Leaf Hop   Pellets   Extracts   Iso-Pellets   Iso-extracts

Source: Madeleine Pullman

FIGURE 4.2 Hops options

Another route for hops processing is **isomerization**, or converting a molecule into a different arrangement with the same atoms. This process changes the iso-alpha acids so that the hops are more efficiently used in the brew kettle. Isomerized hops come in both pellets (iso-pellets) and extracts (iso-extracts) and have an added advantage of conveniently adding more hop flavors during the conditioning phase of brewing.

Private versus Public Hops:

Major hop companies have found that it is advantageous to create patented or **proprietary hop** varieties. Grown in limited varieties (only authorized growers can grow the patented hop), they tend to be more expensive than the publicly available hops (any grower can buy the vine and propagate it). Of the top 10 most popular hops, four of them are private, and they can be challenging to secure since they are sold out several years in advance to contractual buyers.[1]

TABLE 4.2 Most popular hops for craft beer

Public	Private
Cascade	Simcoe®
Centennial	CTZ®
Chinook	Amarillo®
Crystal	Citra®
Willamette	
Saaz (Czech)	
Source: Madeleine Pullman	

Hop supply: As recently as 2007 and 2008, there have been severe hop shortages as well as boom and bust cycles, particularly with high alpha hops. When large breweries buy these hops on contract and warehouse the product, the hop supply gets out of sync with beer production. At this point, buying ceases, prices crash, and many farmers get out of the hop business. In 2007 and 2008, the poor growing conditions plus a warehouse fire that burned four percent of US hops supply, caused scarcity and sky-high prices. Today, most breweries buy hops on multiyear contracts. Given the current growth rate of craft beer and the limited production of hops, there are certain to be shortages in the years to come. Even as many hop farmers switch to growing aroma hops, thousands of new acres are necessary, as are investment in pelletizing and storage infrastructure. Many hop growers' facilities are too small to keep up with demand. According to estimates from the Brewers Association, 12,000 new acres need to be planted in order to produce 25 million more pounds of hops in the near future.[2]

Hop contracts: Hops can be purchased on the **spot market**—what is available at the price at that moment—or contracts. With a **forward contract** the beverage producer makes a commitment to buy a certain amount of hops from hops producers in the future. Larger breweries contract hops for four years or more at a time and have more ability to secure scarce hops in a tight market. Smaller craft producers secure hops by developing relationships with smaller scale growers and contracting for at least two to three years of supply. **Hop contracts** protect both the grower and the beverage producer. Since new hop vines can take up to two years to start producing usable hops, a contract gives the farmer enough leeway to plan for demand. On the brewer side, the brewer is guaranteed a supply of strategic ingredients. Key items for hops contracts are detailed in Table 4.3.

Hops delivery: Most hop companies hold hop products for the buyer in appropriate warehouse conditions (refrigerated and humidity controlled) and deliver them as needed. Whole hop cones are baled with burlap into 175–230 pound bales—great for buying freshly picked hops but challenging to move around once in-house. Alternatively, pelletized hops are vacuum-sealed in 11-pound (5 kg) or 44-pound (25 kg) pouches and boxed in a convenient form to measure and to move around.

FIGURE 4.3   Hop vines

TABLE 4.3 Contract items[3]

Item	Definition
Price and Payment	What is the agreed-upon price to pay for each variety or limits on the escalation of prices over the time period, terms of payment such as upfront money, money due at the time of delivery, and payment after delivery? This will vary between growers.
Quantity	What is the amount of each type of variety? Typically for a three year contract, one might contract for 100% of the next year, 75% of the following year, and 50% of the year after. Numbers should be updated every January to reflect updated forecasts.
Quality	Requirements stating the acceptable range of attributes, such as % alpha, % beta, and oil ml/100g (aroma, acidity, and oil content). Growers will have a target range for each variety. Only large breweries can specify quality levels.
Delivery Requirements	How will the hops be delivered, who pays for shipping, and when is the ownership or risk transferred? This can be negotiated with the grower.
Right to Inspection	Does the buyer have the right to inspect and reject or accept hops prior to delivery? Can the supplier solve the defective issue and resubmit?
Creditors' Rights	What will happen in the case of bankruptcy from either party?
Terms	What period of time is covered in the contract or is it open-ended? How can either party terminate the relationship?
Disputes	Does the contract define how a dispute should be resolved? Under what law (state) and forum (court or mediation) will disputes be resolved? Who will pay for damages and costs of the dispute?
Source: Madeleine Pullman	

Oregon Hophouse Cultivates Organic Hops Market

The Oregon Hophouse is a national leader in organic hop farming. Certified organic by Oregon Tilth in 2007, Oregon Hophouse was the first certified organic hop farm in Oregon. The farm has been growing hops for over 100 years, and is now run by the grandson of the original farmer, Patrick Leavy, who took over the family farm in 1978. Today, organic hops from the Leavy's farm are sold to breweries all over North America.

Hophouse refers to the picking machine and hop dryer on site, which can process tens of thousands of pounds of hops. Hop plants go through a three-story picking machine to strip the hops from their vine, sending individual hop cones down a conveyor belt. The majority of the hops are dried to less than 10 percent moisture in a drying kiln and are compressed into

200-pound bales for delivery. Fresh hops skip the drying process and are delivered in bags. This perishable ingredient must be used within a few weeks.

USDA National Organic Program agents inspect the hop farm annually, checking for fertility and pest management. Hops are a high-input crop, and the Oregon Hophouse uses a blend of natural fertilizers, including composted chicken manure, cow manure, cover crops, and other organic fertilizers with plant materials and minerals; it manages pests with a combination of natural predators and insecticidal soap. Leavy also has a hop-breeding program to develop patented pest-resistant hop varieties.

Prior to earning organic certification, the Oregon Hophouse provided hops to major brewers like Anheuser-Busch. In 2008 Leavy began growing different hop varieties for craft brewers, but he encountered a major hurdle: breweries could legally make certified organic beer *without* using organic hops because the weight of hops is so low compared to other beer ingredients.

With the help of other organic hop growers, Leavy formed the American Organic Hop Growers Association in 2009 and successfully lobbied the USDA to remove hops from the list of exempted products for organic beer certification, ensuring a market for organic growers. By 2014, the Leavy farm supplied both organic and conventional hops to 16 brewers in the United States and Canada. According to Leavy, the organic brewing market is still too small to focus on organic hop farming. Many breweries make a couple of organic beers, but only a handful are certified organic breweries.

With organic hops twice the price of conventional hops, brewers were initially reluctant to spend the extra cash especially since the organic varieties were less full flavored than conventional hops. In order to manage pests, possibly the biggest challenge in organic hops cultivation, growers were picking hops before they reached their peak. As organic pest management has improved however, organic hops now can be grown to their peak flavor.

The Oregon Hophouse cultivates seven varieties of organic hops with more anticipated through Leavy's breeding program. With a 20 percent growth in dollar volume during 2014, the organic beer market is expected to keep farmers like Leavy busy for years to come.

Malt

Malt is the foundational ingredient for beer and whiskey. Barley malt is made from processed barley, a weeklong process of sprouting barley seeds and then drying the seed once the essential starch altering enzymes emerge. Other grains (wheat, rye, millet) are also malted using the same process, but barley is the most common. Barley malt is categorized into two main types: **base malt** and **specialty malt**. Base malt makes up the bulk of the recipes for beer and whiskey and generates most of the fermentable sugars and main flavor. The malt is defined either by its barley varietal, process style, or wheat; the most popular are 2-Row, 6-Row, Pale Malt, Pilsen Malt, Maris Otter, and Wheat. Specialty malts go through more processes to develop different types of sugar profiles as well as darker roasted colors. The color rating system, **lovibond**, gives an indication of the color intensity from pale base malts (under 1.4–4 lovibond) and crystal specialty malts (15–150 lovibond) to chocolate or black roast specialty malts (300–550 lovibond).

Barley malt demands high-quality barley with a low protein content, which can be challenging to grow in less than ideal conditions. From a farmer's perspective, growing barley offers few advantages relative to other crops like wheat or corn, both of which are subsidized in the United States and other countries with well-funded research for developing higher yielding GMO crops. If a barley harvest does not achieve the necessary protein content or suffers from weather damage, it cannot be used for brewing and is sold off in low-priced animal feed markets.

Malt supply: Due to the challenges growing high-quality barley, United States and European Union barley acreage continues to shrink, losing out to GMO wheat and corn that offer higher yields and profits to farmers. In 2015, United States barley acreage reached an all-time low. With the growth of craft breweries and distilleries, demand is sure to outstrip supply. The main malt production houses are looking to increase capacity and exploring diverse areas for barley growing to improve the supply side. The United States relies on imported barley malt to fill its production gap. In 2012, 18 percent of US malt usage came from imports, up from only 9 percent in 2002. In the United States, organizations like the American Malting Barley Association are lobbying for research support and favorable federal farm programs, including crop insurance to reduce farmers' risks and policies that level the playing field with other crops.[4] Maltsters, small-scale artisanal producers, are slowly coming on line but they will not be producing enough malt to fill the gap for a long time.

The European Union is the largest grower and malting barley supplier today, but sells most of its production domestically, and production is projected to decline. Traditional producers like Australia and Canada have some barley surpluses available for export while new producers, including Argentina, Ukraine, and Russia, are stepping into the barley malt export arena.

Malt contracts: Similar to hop buying, beverage producers choose to buy malt on contract or spot market. And, given the increasing gap between supply and demand, contracting is a wise approach. The same types of contract items for hops apply to malt although malt quality specifications contain limits on protein and maximum moisture content, color range, and potential extract levels.

Malt delivery: Depending on the quantity needed, shipping distance and method, and storage space available, malt is delivered in

Source: Madeleine Pullman.

FIGURE 4.4 Grain tote

several different ways. Craft producers who buy small volumes of base or specialty malts use **bagged malt** in 50-pounds bags from US suppliers or 55-pound (25 kilograms) bags from European and Canadian suppliers. Bagged malt is shipped on pallets ordinarily holding 40 bags. The buyer pays the shipping fee as well as assorted other fees (fuel surcharge, hazardous materials, lift gate delivery, and sometimes other fees for challenging delivery locations). In most cases, it pays for the buyer to order more than what is immediately required since there is a volume discount and the other fees are one-time order fees (not based on quantity). Bags are easy to move around and store; plus they don't require special handling equipment. The next size up from bagged malt is the 2,000-pound **tote**, which saves between four and five cents per pound. The cost of shipping a tote is similar to a full pallet of bags. Totes require equipment for moving the tote into place and for moving the grain out of the tote, such as an auger or a gravity suspension sack structure.

FIGURE 4.5   Silo

Source: Madeleine Pullman.

As a beverage producer's demand for malt increases, a **grain silo** becomes the most viable and cost-effective option. A silo can take delivery of a full truckload of malt, 48,000 pounds in the United States, which cuts the malt price by more than half compared to bags. So, if a brewery produces 2,000 barrels per year and needs roughly 100,000 pounds of malt (2000 bbl. x 50 pounds base malt/bbl.), then taking delivery of full or half trucks quickly pays back the cost of silo infrastructure. This breakeven point is covered in Chapter 5: Equipment.

Overall, with malt demand growing and supply struggling to keeping up, it makes sense to contract for malt for businesses experiencing growth. Additionally, planning for deliveries of either bagged, tote, or truckloads of malt means carefully monitoring the economic implications of changes to the total cost of buying malt.

Fruit

An array of **fruits** is showing up in many craft beverages. From traditional fruits like apples, pears, peaches, cherries, and berries to other "fruits" like pumpkin (the family cucurbitaceae is considered a berry) to "vegetables" like rhubarb, fruit is expanding craft beverage portfolios. Producers choose to grow or buy whole fruits and extract their own fruit juice, such as pressing apples into cider, or they buy preprocessed fruit juice, purées, concentrates, extracts, and flavors. Of all these options, fresh fruit and juice is significantly more perishable than frozen purees or concentrates, extracts and flavors.

TABLE 4.4   Dessert and cider apple examples

Dessert Apples	Cider Apples
Pink Lady	Kingston Black
Golden Delicious	Yarlington Mill
Red Delicious	Esopus Spitzenberg
Jonagold	Dabinett
Granny Smith	Winesap
Gravenstein	Vilberie
Fuji	Crimson Black
Gala	Bramley
Honey Crisp	Newton Pippin

Source: Madeleine Pullman.

Traditional **cider apples** have a much shorter shelf life than dessert apples and are best used in season, creating a push to produce a lot of juice and process it in the fall. **Dessert apples** have a longer shelf life and can be stored for many months in appropriate warehousing environments. Cider apples ("bittersweets" and "bittersharps") tend to have more acid and tannins than dessert apples, which are sweet and less acidic. Generally speaking, cider apples make a more complex, flavorful cider and dessert apples less so, but the two are often blended with other ingredients to enhance flavor.

Fruit supply: Over the last 50 years dessert apples have taken over fruit orchards in countries like the United States, so cider apples are hard to find in these places. As the demand for cider grows, more cider apple orchards are being planted. In the traditional apple and pear cider-making countries like the United Kingdom, 95 percent of the cider fruit is either under 20 to 25 year contracts to other orchards or grown by major producers themselves. In the United States many of the cider producers are growing their own cider apples because so few are available to purchase, and **perry** (pear cider) pears are even more rare. Dessert apples as well as other types of orchard fruits and berries are readily available for use in ciders and other craft beverages. The large apple and pear processing businesses (in Washington state, Michigan, New York, and California) store fruit through the off-season, and the dessert apple juice culls (less attractive apples) are significantly less expensive than in-season fruit, often one-third of the price.

Fruit contracts: Fruit contracts are essential for anyone looking to buy cider apples or perry pears in any volume. As seen in the United Kingdom, cider apples are such a strategic ingredient for the major producers that they have extremely long contracts with apple and pear growers. As other countries follow suit, expect to see long contracts, especially as the emerging cider markets like the United States are dominated by a few big players. Fruit producers and brokers have payment terms similar to other ingredients, but typically offer 30-day payment terms to smaller businesses.

Fruit delivery: When buying fresh fruit in the volumes needed for pressing, the fruit is transported in fruit **bins** (800 to 875 pounds each for apples or pears). A full semi-truck can fit 48 to 50 bins. Bins require an appropriate storage place free of pests and a cool environment. Alternatively, pre-processed juice or purées can be purchase in all sizes of containers: tanker trucks with huge volumes, plastic totes (250 gallon), drums (50 gallon), bag-in-box treatments (multiple sizes), and plastic bottles (multiple sizes). Depending on the juice purchased, it can be pasteurized or shelf stable and therefore not requiring refrigeration.

Other Ingredients

Water: Often overlooked as an ingredient for all craft beverages, water is a significant ingredient. Good-quality water with appropriate mineral content can be a huge differentiator for beer. Water is also added to cider, mead, and spirits to achieve the desired alcohol content, and it needs to distilled or pure (bacteria and chlorine-free). Having an adequate water supply is key; during droughts, states like California have rationed water to breweries.

When selecting a site for production of a craft beverage, the water district can provide analysis of the local water. If water has too much sodium or chlorine, it may require additional treatment for brewing or creating wort for whiskey. Activated carbon filters remove the odor and taste of chlorine. The mineral makeup of water can change seasonally, so if brewers want a consistent product, then the alkalinity may need to be adjusted. High alkalinity produces dull-flavored beer

FIGURE 4.6   Boxes of apples

©Zoom Team/Shutterstock.com

and can be adjusted with food-grade lactic acid. If the water has low mineral content, then mineral salts can be added to adjust for specific beer styles. Some of the brewing water additions include salts such as gypsum, Epsom salt, calcium carbonate, and calcium chloride. Similarly, cider makers, who tend to like acid in their cider, often supplement the juice with sulfuric, malic, and citric acid.

Yeast: Every fermented beverage requires yeast. Beer makers have a wide range of beer-specific yeasts to choose from in the ale and lager families; other beverage makers typically use wine or champagne yeasts. Yeast is often available in both dry and liquid versions. Production breweries generally re-use ("re-pitch") yeast from one batch to the next or share yeast with other breweries so the cost is spread out over multiple batches. Production cider and mead makers tend to use dry yeast and do not re-pitch between batches in order to avoid potential contamination. Distillers use a wide variety of dry yeasts including high alcohol tolerant distillers yeast. Given that spirits are distilled after fermenting, the yeast has less of a flavor impact than in other beverages. There are many suppliers of yeast, and some of the strategic issues with yeast are managing the cost of ordering yeast (ordering in advance for many months can save money); limiting the varieties of yeast used in the facility to prevent problems and costs; and finding yeast flavor and performance characteristics that fit the operation and desired taste profile.

Spices and flavorings: Increasingly, spices are becoming very popular for use in craft beverages of all kinds. Craft breweries have a long tradition of spiced beers at Christmas, but increasingly, ginger is showing up throughout the year in all craft beverages. The more experimental producers are also playing around with exotic spices or flavorings, such as lavender, saffron, cinnamon, clove, nutmeg, cardamom, chilies, chocolate, coffee, raisins, and even flowers like rose hips and chamomile.

Some of the big malt distributors like Country Malt in the United States carry many of the ingredients; other sources include local farms, specialty spice stores, big grocery stores, and restaurant supply houses. Recipes that call for spices should be cost checked in advance (as shown later in this chapter) since large-scale use of exotic spices can be out of line with other ingredient costs.

Sugar: Different kinds of sweeteners are a vital part of many craft producer's tool kit, boosting the alcohol content and imparting particular flavors. Prior to fermentation, adding sugars will increase the alcohol content and add some flavor; when adding sugars after fermentation and maturing, sugars will add sweetness and different flavors such as caramel notes from brown sugar. Sugars are derived from all kinds of sources, including sugar beets (usually GMO), sugarcane, honey, maple sugar, brown rice, sorghum, and fruit concentrates. Sugar comes in many forms: syrup or concentrate, rock, moist, and other powders or crystals. It also ranges in color from clear or white to amber, brown, or dark brown. Most sugar products are widely available with relatively stable prices with the exception of honey and maple syrup. Both are more severely affected by weather conditions, and honey suffers from repeated bee die-off problems.

Locally Sourced Ingredients Distinguish Ale Apothecary

Ale Apothecary, a small brewery outside of Bend, Oregon, prides itself on creating an exceptionally hand-crafted product. Most recipes and production processes use natural and local ingredients produced with minimal contact with stainless steel. Mashing, open fermentation, conditioning, and dry-hopping all take place in oak barrels. The oak wood is porous, inviting the bacteria and yeast, which gives the beer its unusual and somewhat unpredictable character. The beer moves directly from the barrels to champagne bottles, unfiltered, with the house yeast culture and sugar added for secondary fermentation.

Ale Apothecary created its own lauter vessel out of a spruce tree for its beer, Sahati. Spruce branches line the vessel's bottom, filtering the wort through the needles. The brewery's annual fruit beer, Spencer, is aged for eight months with wild blackcurrant fruit picked from along the river near the brewery. The beer at Ale Apothecary is a reflection of its surroundings, incorporating ingredients unique to the area and creating a differentiated product in the ever-growing craft beer market.

Source: Madeleine Pullman.

FIGURE 4.7 Pine bough lauter

Basic recipe costing: The starting point for any recipe costing calculation is a recipe. If you do not already have a recipe, look online under beer, cider, mead, or spirit forums to find one. Many of those are for five gallons so it's important to scale it up to an appropriate size for an industrial application—at a minimum one bbl. (31 gallons) or one hectoliter for most ciders, mead, or beers and one wbl. (53 gallons or 200 liters) for spirits. Most equipment is sized in bbl., hectoliters, or liters. For example, brewing systems are sized based on the batch sized produced (mash tun/brew kettle capacity) and are three, five, seven, 10, 15 bbls., and so on. In this example, you will take a five gallon recipe and scale it up to one barrel as shown in Table 4.5:

TABLE 4.5   Scaled ingredients for American IPA for five gallons to one bbl

(A) Ingredients	(B) Weight (5 gallons)	(C)Weight (31 gallons=1 bbl.) Column B times (31/5)=6.2
2 Row Pale Malt	11.5 lbs.	71.3 lbs.
Crystal Malt 20 Lovibond	1 lbs.	6.2 lbs.
Light Munich Malt	0.75 lbs.	4.7 lbs.
Carapils	0.75 lbs.	4.7 lbs.
Torrified Wheat	0.25 lbs.	1.6 lbs.
Chinook Hops	1 oz.	6.2 oz.=.4 lbs.
Cascade Hops	5 oz.	31 oz.=1.9 lbs.
Willamette Hops	1.5 oz.	9.3 oz.=.6 lbs.
Source: Madeleine Pullman.		

The next step is to price the recipe. Prices for industrial-level production ingredients are significantly lower than the cost of the same ingredients at a homebrew shop or grocery store for fruit or juice. In this example, the prices will be in the ballpark for that product (without transportation costs) for purchasing in pallet volumes in the Northwest of the United States. Looking at the recipe below for one barrel of beer, notice that the grain bill comes to $52.82 and the hops bill comes to $21.15 with a grand total for $73.97 for one barrel (31 gallons) of ingredients. According to the recipe developer, this recipe on a homebrew scale costs almost $100 for five gallons, so there is a clear benefit to buying ingredients on a wholesale volume scale. Since this example is a hoppy IPA, there is a significant hop bill and more malt to balance the hops for an above-average malt bill.

TABLE 4.6 Recipe Cost for 1 bbl or 31 gallons

(A) Ingredients	(31 gallons = 1 bbl.)	(C) Price per pound	Cost for item (B) times (C)	Total
2 Row Pale Malt	71.3 lbs.	$0.56	$39.93	
Crystal Malt 20 Lovibond	6.2 lbs.	$0.79	$4.90	
Light Munich Malt	4.7 lbs.	$0.68	$3.20	
Carapils	4.7 lbs.	$0.78	$3.67	
Torrified Wheat	1.6 lbs.	$0.70	$1.12	$52.82
Chinook Hops	6.2 oz. = .4 lbs.	$8.75	$3.50	
Cascade Hops	31 oz. = 1.9 lbs.	$7.00	$13.30	
Willamette Hops	9.3 oz. = .6 lbs.	$7.25	$4.35	$21.15
Total				**$73.97**
Source: Madeleine Pullman.				

SUMMARY

As more competitors enter into each of the craft beverage business segments, producers are looking for new ways to differentiate their products through their choice of ingredients. For many years, hop varietals have been the main way to differentiate a craft beer, and more hops producers are working to breed new and unusual hops. But the use of craft malt has only begun to enter the recipes even though malt makes up the bulk of the ingredients in both beer and spirits. Craft maltsters are stepping up to produce local, organic, and unusual grains like millet, and custom malts that could make a big difference in the emergence of new products. Additionally, orchardists are planting heirloom and heritage cider apples and perry pears, but there is a lag time before these will become available, as trees need to mature and yield appropriate amounts of fruit. Those involved in the craft industry need to stay on the lookout for ingredient trends and opportunities to innovate as well as monitor factors influencing supply and demand of all strategic ingredients.

LEARNING ADVENTURES

1. Find a recipe online or through your existing collection and price the recipe with the available pricing that you can find online. Remember that if you use homebrew shop or grocery store prices, they are probably five to 10 times what industrial scale producers pay.

2. What are varieties of juice and cider apples available in your area? What can be purchased in juice form versus fresh apples?

3. Create a recipe for a barrel of cider and a barrel of beer based on recipes found through an Internet recipe database.[5] How do the recipes compare in price? What is the significant driver of cost?

ENDNOTES

1. Bart Watson, "Craft Brewing and Hops Usage," Brewers Association, http://www.usahops.org/userfiles/image/1422493631_Bart%20Watson%202015%20Hop%20Convention.pdf.

2. Ibid.

3. Marc Sorini and Beth Hatef, "10 Items to Address in Supply Contracts," *The New Brewer*, November/December 2012, 20–21.

4. "AMBA Overview," American Malting Barley Association, http://ambainc.org/content/8/amba-overview.

5. "Homebrew Forums: Recipe Database," Homebrewtalk, [is "Homebrewtalk" ok here or should be "Homebrew talk"?] http://www.homebrewtalk.com/.

CHAPTER FIVE

Packaging

Key Terms

brand name

can body

cans

capper

carriers

cartons

cases

class and type designation

closure

closures

COLA

cork

corker

costs

crowns

ends

fifth

fill

filler

flip-top

formula

graphics

grolsch

growlers

label

labeler

legal

mobile packaging

package stores

packs

product mixes

screw-top

seamer

TTB label approval and formulas

Overview

Many craft businesses bottle their beverages into packaging from start up, while others add packaged product at a later point in time. Beyond the actual liquid, the package is the major force behind brand identity. Packaging offers many different ways to engage with the customer: the customer can take the product home, learn more about the business from the packaging materials, and engage with the brand in a way that is not possible from a draft product served from kegs or directly from cellar room tanks in a pub or tasting room. This chapter details the many considerations involved in choosing packaging and designing various packaging elements. It concludes with a packaging cost calculation, building on the previous estimates of beverage costs conducted in Chapter 4: Ingredients.

Learning Objectives

▶ Understand the pros and cons of packaging.

▶ Identify packaging trends.

▶ Appreciate the types of boxes, bottles, cans, closures, and pack holder options.

▶ Understand label visual and legal issues.

▶ Know the process of label approval and formulas.

▶ Compare packaging equipment versus mobile packaging costs.

▶ Calculate packaged product costs.

Introduction

A pub or tasting room is the most direct way for consumers to get to know your brand. In that environment, the consumer can see the image your business is striving for, choose from of a full range of products, and learn the story of the brand. At some point, however, you may decide to stretch beyond the locale of your production site, and at this point, the packaged product becomes responsible for conveying the story of your craft business outside of the pub's doors.

Other than opening more pubs replicating pubs throughout a city or region, packaging is the only way to move beyond your home turf and for your business to grow significantly in size and revenue. Having a store presence contributes greatly to brand building and sales. Liquor stores and package stores are the preferred outlet for craft beverage purchases closely followed by grocery and convenience stores. As a businessperson, you need to understand the impact of different **product mixes**—the percentage of sales on-site, wholesale and retail keg and growler, and packaged products of various sizes—on your company's profits.

For distilled spirits, packaging is a given since these products are not sold in kegs and pubs are not a major aspect of product exposure—yet! In some states and countries, **package stores** (owned privately or by the state) are the only allowed outlet for spirits outside of bars and restaurants. The challenge for all craft beverages is getting shelf space in a store or on the bar shelves (for spirits) and then winning the consumer's attention enough to try the product amongst a sea of competitors. In this respect, you want to have a solid understanding of your particular consumer group so that the packaging you select resonates with their interests.

In a start-up business plan, it's important to include a graphic image of what the packaged product looks like to convey a sense of the brand, its potential appeal, and the target market. Typically, spirit and certain craft beverages produce a mockup of the bottle to show to investors. Starting early to think about graphics and other packaging elements is as important as making the product itself. This process can take time and requires legal approvals.

Trends: Today's craft consumer ordinarily knows what brand he or she will buy before going to the store. The great challenge for new brands is getting the consumer's attention in any retail environment. Interesting or attention-getting packaging attracts people's interest; thus many try for novel packaging such as custom or etched bottles, grolsch-style bottle closures (flip-top), unusual glass colors, and outlandish names and visuals. As high-end product growth accelerates in all beverage categories, packaging has to follow suit with special bottles, wax dipped or tied closures, high-end label paper and graphics, and other characteristics signaling quality.

For example, the oak-barrel fermented and aged, limited distribution beers from Ale Apothecary are sold in 750 milliliter (ml) champagne bottles with a champagne-style cork and a hand-tied string closure. The beers sell for $20–$25 per bottle. This specialty packaging reflects that price point well.

Beer and cider packaging has shifted from the standard six-pack to the 22-ounce or 750-ml bottle. More recently, cans have gained consumer acceptance and popularity. Large-format bottles like the 22-ounce or 750-ml bottle are an accessible way for a customer to try the product without committing to a full four- or six-pack. So these sizes tend to be a great entry point for startups or for companies entering new markets.

FIGURE 5.1   Fancy beer bottle

Photo courtesy of Madeleine Pullman. Reprinted with permission of Ale Apothecary.

Other packaging trends include eco-friendly and minimalist packaging. Refillables like **growlers** are well accepted, and some craft beverage producers have returnable or reusable bottles for retail. This practice is more common outside of the United States because it is challenging to implement a reverse supply chain without self-distributing or having a cooperative distributor. A producer can reduce packaging waste by avoiding cardboard cases, using four- or six-packs with recycled plastic can or bottle carriers, and shrink-wrapping groupings of four- or six-packs in cases or partial cases.

Container Materials

Bottles: Bottles come in various sizes depending on the business's location in the world as shown in Table 5.1. In the United States, the 12-ounce bottle is the gold standard. A 12-ounce six-pack not only takes up the most shelf space but also has the most competition within that space. The 22-ounce bottles are an advantageous starter size because they are relatively easy to fill and have a minimal shelf space footprint. The 750 ml (wine- or champagne-style bottle) is only slightly larger than the 22 ounce by 20 percent but looks much larger and has a more elegant, upscale look. These larger format bottles tend to do well in retail store environments since people can sample different products without buying multiples in a pack. For the consumer, the bigger bottles are generally a better value than a 12-ounce bottle and generate more profit for the craft producer.

While restaurants once resisted buying these larger formats, increasingly, they are selling them like wine where diners can share a bottle. This sharing format has allowed more people to try a wider range of beverages and increased impulse sales. Additionally, many of the craft beverages are higher alcohol (7 percent to 10 percent ABV), and sharing is a better way for consumers to try beers without imbibing excessive alcohol.

Bottles come in standard shapes and colors (brown, green, and clear) and can be purchased by the pallet or truckload from glass factories. For small craft beverage producers, group buying with other local breweries or cideries can bring the cost per unit below $0.20 per bottle depending on location. The 22-ounce bottle is double that price and a high-quality 750-ml bottle costs five to 10 times that price depending on the thickness of the glass, color, and other qualities.

FIGURE 5.2   Cans with plastic carrier

Photo courtesy of Madeleine Pullman. Reprinted with permission of Hopworks Urban Brewery and Eric Steen..

TABLE 5.1   Bottle sizes[1]

United States package sizes	Europe, Asia, and Latin America package sizes
11 oz. ("Stubby")	33 cl (11.2 oz.)
12-oz. bottles or cans	12 oz. (common in Asia and Latin America)
16-oz. bottles or cans	500 ml (16.9 oz.)
22 oz. ("Bomber")	1 imperial pint (20 oz.) in United Kingdom
750 ml (25.4 oz.)	750 ml (25.4 oz.)
Source: Madeleine Pullman.	

©Kondor83/Shutterstock.com

FIGURE 5.3   Spirits bottles

The price point for craft distillery products typically starts above US $20 for a 750-ml bottle (commonly known as a **fifth** in the United States); aged whiskey products sell for more than US $75; and craft whiskeys from Ireland and Scotland price upwards from there. As a result, the bottle has to be distinctive (often custom made) and look appropriate for its price point. Another consideration is how well any bottle grabs attention under light since spirit bottles are often displayed on illuminated bar shelves. Bottles such as these can make up 15 to 20 percent of the total cost of the final packaged product.

Closures: All bottles require some kind of closure that keeps air and bacteria out and product and carbonation (where appropriate) in. **Crowns** or caps make up the bulk of craft beer, cider, and mead closures. Crowns are low-cost solutions, and they can be made in a plethora of colors and have branded images on the top (logos, initials, and so forth). Depending on the amount of crowns purchased, they cost pennies each. Some beverage producers use a different color crown depending on the style of beer in the bottle. **Grolsch-** or **flip-top**-style bottle closures with a stopper and gasket were popularized by the Dutch brewery of the same name. Craft producers who have packaged in these bottles have found that capping the bottle first prolongs shelf life; the consumer can use flip-top after opening to preserve an unfinished bottle. **Cork** or synthetic cork closures are often used with the 750-ml bottles for a more elegant finished look. Finally, **screw-top** closures are used with cider or spirits in the larger format bottles. Depending on the volumes purchased, cork, synthetic cork, and screw-top closures may be as affordable as crown closures. Cork with additional treatments, such as a wood or synthetic top cap or glass "corks," are more expensive but add a distinctive and sophisticated closure for spirits.

Cans: Cans come in two popular sizes: 12 ounces for six-packs and 16 ounces for four-packs. Made of aluminum with a coated interior, compared to glass bottles, cans weigh less, use less packaging overall, and don't require labels or cardboard holders. As a result, many argue that cans are more sustainable than glass packaging. Also, transportation and refrigeration emissions are lower for beverages packaged in cans. Another benefit of cans is that the beverage is not exposed to light and less oxygen gets into the can. From a consumer standpoint, the can is ideal for summer outdoor rec-reation such as camping, fishing, boating, biking, backpacking, and more. While cans do not have the classy image that bottles offer, they do have a time and place in the craft consumer lifestyle. Increas-ingly, craft cider and beer producers are offering various products in cans as well as in bottles depend-ing on the particular brand and price point.

A can consists of two parts: the **can body** and the **end** (the top). The cost difference between an individual can with printing or one without is relatively close. The challenge with cans is that they need to be ordered in large fixed quantities, such as full or half truckloads, per design. The number of cans works out to roughly 1,400 bbl. of 16-ounce cans and 1,100 bbl. of 12-ounce cans for each variety. This quantity is challenging for most startups. Still, if purchased in these volumes, a can costs less than a 12-ounce bottle. As a result, some craft producers order blank cans and apply a sticker or labeled sleeve around the can rather than buying a pre-printed can (both of which add costs and have mixed results in terms of durability). Can **ends** also need to be ordered in large amounts; roughly 356,000 ends make up one pallet. Although the end sealant has a limited shelf life, the ends can be used for any product since they are typically not branded. Another option is a new can in the shape of a bottle (with a screw cap), which is novel but has the same purchasing minimums and quantity issues as the standard can.

TABLE 5.2   Container order quantities

Item	Units per pallet	Pallets per full truckload	Units per full truckload	Barrel equivalent per truckload
12-oz. can	8,169	25	204,225	618
16-oz. can	6,224	25	155,600	665
22-oz. Bottles	720	25	18,000	100
Can End	356,000	—		
Plastic Carriers	14,580	—		
Source: Madeleine Pullman.				

Packs or carriers: Customarily, smaller format bottles are grouped into packages: 12-ounce bot-tles or cans into six-packs and 16-ounce bottles or cans into four-packs. The bottles or cans are also grouped into half cases (12 units). Variations of other sizes also go into packs depending on the coun-try or producer preference. Packs have a carrying handle and are also known as a **carrier**. Aside from the consumer's convenience, carriers offer more real estate for brand messaging. Graphic artwork printed on the carrier is an opportunity to expand on the original brand or beverage style imagery on the label and provide more information about your business's story.

Carriers can be the single most expensive component of packaging. Some startups reduce this cost by using a plain or basic carrier affixed with things like stickers to differentiate between different products, rather than producing a unique carrier for each brand. But, if the carrier looks less profes-sional than the competitors on the shelf, stores may not accept it, or it may send an unfavorable mes-sage about the brand.

Plastic pack carriers: Plastic carriers are alternatives to the cardboard carriers. They either fit around the necks of the bottles or attach to the top of the cans. The cost for plastic is competitive with the cardboard carrier depending on the number of units ordered. In this case, the bottle or can label itself communicates the brand and style. This carrier type opts out of the opportunity for broader brand messaging of the cardboard carrier but eliminates the need and cost for different carriers for each brand.

Cartons and cases: All craft beverages require a carton or case for deliveries to stores and handling within the production facilities. Similar to the packs, the carton is another opportunity for branding. However, since the end consumer often does not see the carton in the retail environment, it is not necessary to spend a lot of money branding the carton. Using a standard case with the business brand and identifying

FIGURE 5.4   Six-pack cardboard carrier

©StudioOneNine/Shutterstock.com

the individual variety with stickers is one effective approach. Larger format bottles (22 ounce or 750 ml) standardly have 12 bottles in a case with dividers; smaller format bottles have 24 in a case with carriers or dividers, and cans have 24 on a tray. Most of the boxes are made from heavier duty cardboard to withstand the abuse of handling and truck delivery. In many instances, the bottle provider will deliver bottles in set-up cartons (with six-packs inside if needed) for bottling. This service can be very worthwhile for many craft beverage producers facing labor constraints.

Labels

The most problematic part of packaging is the label. Most countries strictly regulate labels for alcohol. Additionally, depending on the volumes produced, many governments require specific ingredient labeling. To make matters worse, many of the words craft producers want to use on their products are tightly regulated and have strict definitions.

Labels are made from a variety of papers or are etched on the bottle. Most smaller volume bottle packagers start with paper or synthetic labels that come on backing material similar to large stickers on a roll. As their volumes increase, a paper label with a glue attachment system becomes much more cost-effective. Generally, the small volumes of short run or seasonal product can really drive the price up. In limited runs, the prices can approach one dollar.

Graphics: The graphical imagery, fonts, and colors represent your brand and are a creative expression of each product's identity. Usually the business's marketing team works with professional graphic artists to design images that reflect the story and theme of the company. However, graphics cannot interfere with the legibility and legally required information printed on the label.

Legal: The legal requirements around labeling alcoholic beverages are complex. There are specific rules for different beverages and from different states and countries. While it is impossible to detail every possible rule, some of the highlights are covered. Most of the labeling requirements cited here are relevant to all crafts with the notable exception of cider and mead can have slightly different requirements if under 7 percent ABV.

Brand name: This is the name under which the beverage or line of beverages is marketed. If the beverage is not sold under a brand name, the bottler, packer, or importer becomes the brand name. The brand name must appear on the front of the container. The name, printed materials and graphic should accurately describe the product especially any content referring to age, origin, identity, or other characteristics of the beverage. According to the US government, all printed label content should contain a) nothing false or misleading, no statement or representation of analysis, standards, testing or product guarantee, nothing that disparages a competitor, no name or image of a public person that may likely cause a false association or endorsement, no misleading geographic reference, no United States government seal, stamp or flag, no United States armed forces emblem, seal, rank, or flag. For an exam-

FIGURE 5.5   Labels

ple of a label problem, a brewery labeled a product Holy Water and was forced to change the label to "Holy Water" (quotes added) with a disclaimer below it that read, "contains no holy water."

Class and type designation: The label identifies a specific class and/or class and type of beverage. Each class or class/type has a legal definition based on trade understanding of its characteristics. Many styles have a vague definition; for example Pale Ale is defined as a malt beverage containing 0.5 percent or more alcohol by volume. A malt beverage with a location-based designation like Dortmund, Belgium, or Munich must clarify that is a *dortmunder type* or *American dortmunder* (or with a prominent statement indicating where it is made somewhere other than Dortmund, Germany), *Munich style* or *Belgian style* if made in the United States.

Spirits have similar rules where the product is named in accordance with trade and consumer understanding. For example, whiskey cannot be called Scotch, Irish, or Canadian unless it is actually produced in those countries. Bourbon must be made in the United States with at least 51 percent corn aged in new oak charred barrels with very strict proof limits during production and bottling. For products like cider or mead (classified as wine) under 7 percent ABV, they must be designated with a truthful and adequate statements of compositions like "cherry cider" or "perry." Before designing the label for a product, refer to the TTB rules for that particular product to make sure that the class and type words are correct.

Name and Address: For domestically beverages, the name and address of the producer/bottler or packer must be provided. It can be modified with explanatory phrases such as "brewed and bottled by," "brewed by, or "bottled by," and so forth. Imported beverages require the same information with the addition of an explanatory phrase such as "imported by." A spirits label must show the state where distillation occurred.

Label War: Lagunitas versus Sierra Nevada IPA

In 2015 Lagunitas Brewing filed an infringement lawsuit in California against Sierra Nevada Brewing over a similarity to its trademarked logo and label design. Sierra Nevada's Hop Hunter IPA, a new beer about to launch out of its Chico brewery, displayed the label in contention. In the dispute between the two largest California craft breweries Lagunitas requested a restraining order to prevent Sierra Nevada from launching its new beer and unspecified damages.

Lagunitas claimed that the Hop Hunter label copied its IPA trademark with the elimination of a period between each letter and the slim spacing between the "P" and "A." It also claimed similarity in the slightly weathered look. Lagunitas had been brewing its popular IPA for over 20 years, and it accounted for 58 percent of the company's output. Lagunitas feared that the IPA label's similarity would create a perceived connection between the two beers and confuse its customers. In the lawsuit Lagunitas mentioned the potential boost in sales that Sierra Nevada might reap from an immediate consumer acceptance. They also claimed that the Hop Hunter label was unusual in comparison to other Sierra Nevada branding, leading consumers to believe it was a beer brewed in collaboration with Lagunitas.

This dispute quickly attracted a lot of attention from the beer-loving community, who were quick to express strong opinions on the lawsuit. Lagunitas's complaint infringed on the craft beer community's culture of working together for the love of beer. The public used Twitter to shame the company's decision to file a lawsuit and pointed out that the brewing company did not own the letters "IPA." (Lagunitas owns four federal trademarks for its IPA label, none of which claim its exclusive right to the "IPA" letters, only the logo design.) Some people asserted that Lagunitas did more damage to its brand by initiating the lawsuit than simply allowing the Sierra Nevada label to be sold. Others criticized Lagunitas for using the courts to defeat its competition rather than letting the product stand up for itself.

Craft beer drinkers announced their boycott of Lagunitas beer via social media and, as a result, public opinion proved its influence in the matter before the courts could pass judgement. After the social media uproar, Lagunitas founder Tony Magee later used Twitter to announce he was dropping the lawsuit. Surprised by the immediate backlash, Magee stated that the company had attempted to resolve the issue with Sierra Nevada directly before taking legal action. Meanwhile, Sierra Nevada released a statement noting that the brewery had been making IPA since 1981 and had no interest in confusing its products with other brands.

TABLE 5.3 Beer TTB label format requirements

Category	Definition	Examples
Net content statement	A statement indicating the amount of product in the bottle. Depending on the quantity must show the amount of fluid ounces, pints, quarts, gallons, liters, etc.	12 fl. oz. 1 pt. 355 ml 750 ml
Type size and legibility	All type sizes have minimums depending on the required statement. Type must be readily legible, appear on contrasting background, and appear separate and apart (more substantially conspicuous than descriptive or explanatory information).	Containers larger than ½ pint have 2 mm minimum; smaller ½ pint or less have 1 mm minimum. Alcohol content statement has to have same kind and size or lettering and a conspicuous coloring. Government warning type has specific minimums.
Alcohol content	Optional unless required or prohibited by state law. If used, should be expressed in percent by volume with specific formatting. Must be expressed to nearest 0.1% unless under 0.5% which may be expressed to nearest 0.01%. Spirits must have alcohol content.	4.5% ALCOHOL BY VOLUME ALC. 5.6% BY VOL. For Spirits: 44 % ALC BY VOL; 88 PROOF
Health warning statement	The government warning label must appear on all alcohol beverages for sale in the US containing not less than 0.5% alcohol by volume. It can appear on the front, back, or side of the container but must be one continuous paragraph with **Government Warning** in capital letters and bold type; the rest of the statement is not in bold type.	GOVERNMENT WARNING: (1) According to the Surgeon General, women should not drink alcoholic beverages during pregnancy because of the risk of birth defects. (2) Consumption of alcoholic beverages impairs your ability to drive a car or operate machinery, and may cause health problems.
Sulfites	Sulfite addition must be declared when sulfur dioxide or another sulfating agent is added.	"Contains sulfites" or "Contains sulfating agents" (usually applies to cider or fruit based products)

Source: Madeleine Pullman. Adopted from TTB guidelines

TTB label approval and formulas: Most craft producers must apply for Certification/Exemption of Label/Bottle Approval (**COLA**) for every label design through the TTB before bottling—with some exceptions. A COLA is needed if the state requires it or if you are shipping and selling over state lines. The purpose of the COLA is to prevent consumer deception or misleading statements. Label art and forms can be submitted electronically to simplify and speed the process. It typically takes about one month from when label materials are submitted to approval, but the TTB is required to process COLAs within 90 days. Packaged products cannot be sold without a COLA. On the upside, revisions to existing labels are relatively easy and some changes to not require going through the COLA process.

Cider and mead under 7 percent ABV do not require COLAs. Instead, they must comply with the FDA food labeling requirements including ingredient, nutrient, and allergen labeling (with certain exceptions for small producers). Cider with more than .392 grams of carbon dioxide per 100 ml must be labeled as "sparking" or "carbonated."

Certain kinds of craft products require **formula** approval from the TTB, essentially indicating the recipe and process used, before the product can be sold. This legal area is evolving as craft beverage producers continue to push the boundaries of creativity with unusual and non-traditional ingredients and processes. Products requiring formula approval must go through that step before the COLA application and formula approval can take several months Ciders with flavoring added may require a formula with unusual ingredients since they become "other than standard" wines. Similarly, beers that require formula approval are usually not traditional beer recipes. For example, formula approval is needed when adding:

▶   Flavors or other non-beverage ingredients (other than hops extract) containing alcohol

▶   Coloring, natural, or artificial colors

▶   Certain fruit, fruit juice, fruit concentrate, herbs, spices, or other foods

▶   Coconut

In the category of fruit, fruit juice, fruit concentrate, and so on, many ingredients are exempted, including apples, berries, pumpkins, citrus, cherries, and more, as well as most commonly used spices, chocolate, and coffee beans or grounds (not liquid). Beer or cider is allowed to have barrel aging or wood chip additions without a formula unless the barrels have discernable quantities of wine or distilled spirits.

Formula regulations and labeling requirements change frequently, so it behooves any craft producer to have someone in house who follows the legal issues and takes sole responsibility for applying for COLAs and formulas. The TTB has excellent resources on their websites and you should check them for each specific beverage during the planning stage of your business.

Typical Costs of Packaging Materials

The typical costs of packaging materials in the United States are shown in Table 5.4. They can vary depending on the amount of units ordered but printed materials will have a high setup cost for the artwork and the printing machines (labels, cans, and cardboard materials). The cost per unit drops as the volume increases. Premium labels with multiple colors, high end paper stock, gold or silver foils, and cutout areas drive up the cost of a label but may be appropriate for the brand and price point.

TABLE 5.4   Typical packaging material costs with volume orders

Parts	Range of costs for one ($)
Bottle	.16 (12 ounce) to $4 or more (custom)
Can and End	.09 to .15
Cap/Crown	.01–.02
Label	.02–1.00 (or more for super fancy and limited runs)
Six-pack or four-pack carrier (plastic)	.50–70
Six-pack or 12-pack (cardboard)	.40-.60
Carton (cardboard case w/dividers)	.85–1.00
Tray (cardboard)	.75
Source: Madeleine Pullman.	

Packaging Equipment

This section describes packaging equipment needs overall before taking up the mobile packaging option. There are three essential needs for packaging liquid product: 1) a device (**filler**) to get the product into a bottle or can, 2) a method for closing the bottle or can (**capper**, **corker**, or **seamer**), and 3) a method for applying the label if needed (**labeler**).

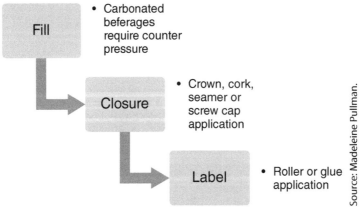

FIGURE 5.6   Packaging process

Fill: At the fill step, any carbonated beverage (beer or cider) requires counter-pressure so that carbonation does not escape during the filling process. This equipment has to operate quickly and have the ability to fill several bottles per minute (BPM), 40 BPM is a low baseline, in a sanitary environment. Spirits are generally filtered before going to a fill process, but they do not require counter-pressure and as sanitary an environment since the alcohol level is very high. Similarly, bottle conditioned cider and beer can be filled flat and augmented with sweetener. Then they require warm storage areas. As a result, the filling equipment for spirits and flat beverages is much less expensive.

Closure: Once filled, the package moves to the next step for closure. The capper places the cap on the bottle and presses down to crimp the cap into place. A corker presses corks into the bottle if that is the necessary closure. Corks can receive other treatments like wire closure, wax dip, foil enclosure. For cans, a can seamer attaches the lid or end to the can body by mechanically overlapping the two pieces.

Label: The labeler attaches the body and neck (if desired) label with roller and press mechanisms. Many labels

FIGURE 5.7   Spirits filling equipment

©Peter de Kievith/Shutterstock.com.

come pre-glued like a sticker and roll off the backing material right onto the bottle or can. The alternative is the paper label, which requires glue and a different style of labeling machine that applies glue to the label before affixing it onto the package.

Warehouse: The final steps are to get the bottles into packs, then cartons, and on to pallets either manually or automatically. There are machines available for every task from placing bottles into cartons, sealing the carton, stacking a pallet, wrapping a pallet in pallet plastic wrap, and moving the pallet into a refrigerated area. It goes without saying that in a smaller operation all of these steps are accomplished manually.

Costs: For many spirit startups, one person can run the packaging equipment. For breweries and cideries, very basic equipment and larger format bottles are a common starting place. An inexpensive or used automatic bottling line with counter-pressure starts at $60,000 but only handles 40 BPM. Other disadvantages of this caliber of equipment involve higher air levels in the bottle, leading to a shorter shelf life, and a tendency to waste product due to less precise filling and capping. Better

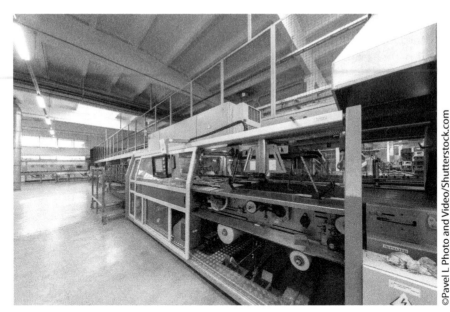

FIGURE 5.8 Packaging line

bottling equipment with faster speeds and higher quality performance runs well into the half-million-dollar-and-beyond price tag. Canning equipment costs start at three times the price of basic bottling equipment. Labor wise, most bottling/canning equipment will require at least three employees for packaging activities and warehousing.

Mobile packaging: Increasingly, mobile packaging businesses provide many packaging services to craft producers who chose not to (or cannot afford to) purchase their own packaging equipment. These businesses go directly to the production facility with all the equipment. Services include financing and holding cans or bottles for beverage producers, packaging the product in cans or bottles of various sizes, and running lab analytics on the packaged product. For canning operations, many of the companies provide the can ends since the minimum ordering quantity is so high and the shelf life of can end adhesive is a factor and ends are not usually branded materials.

Most of the services will have required minimums (for example, seven to 10 bbl. of product) and charge by the case (for example, $2.25 to $3 for filling a case of larger format bottles, $7 to $9 for filling if service provides large-format bottles, $3.50 to $6 for a case of cans if the beverage producer provides all the materials except for the can ends). For mobile packagers willing to finance and hold materials for the business, the charges reflect those services, and the minimums are typically higher (for example, 12 bbl. minimum for bottles and 15 bbl. minimum for cans). Prices run about three times more per case if the packager handles the materials.

Mobile packaging has been a boon to craft producers and frees up capital and other complications for startups. Packaging equipment demands an enormous amount of maintenance and troubleshooting; one employee must become the expert at keeping the line going. While mobile packagers come with a small crew, they usually expect the beverage producer to allocate employees to help with moving bottles and warehousing tasks, so there are still labor costs associated with mobile packaging.

Basic Package Costing

For pricing a package, you will need the product costs by the barrel (bbl., hl, or wbl.) from the exercise in Chapter 4: Ingredients. For example, if the liquid beverage cost came to $60.07 for a bbl., then looking at the conversion chart, there are 13.78 cases in one bbl. (12-ounce containers with 24 in a case). The cost per case for the beverage alone is:

$$\frac{\$60.07 \ / \ bbl.}{13.78 \ cases \ / \ bbl.} = \$4.36 \ / \ case$$

With four six-packs in a case, the cost estimate in Table 5.5 shows the cost of a case with labor as $11.59 (without is $11.09) and the cost of a six-pack is $2.90 with labor (without is $2.77).

TABLE 5.5   Package cost for case and six-pack of 12-ounce bottles

Packaging items	Cost per case	Cost per six-pack
Bottles (24)	$3.80	$0.95
Crowns (24)	$0.24	$0.06
Labels including printing and design (24)	$0.35	$0.09
Six-pack carriers (4)	$1.25	$0.31
Carton (1)	$0.85	$0.21
Pallet and pallet wrapping (1)	$0.24	$0.06
Labor bottling (ballpark estimate)	$0.50	$0.13
BEVERAGE COST	**$4.36**	**$1.09**
Total cost packaged *without* labor	$11.09	$2.77
Total cost packaged *with* labor	**$11.59**	**$2.90**
Source: Madeleine Pullman.		

TABLE 5.6   Package conversion factors

Production quantity	Package conversion factor to case
1 Barrel (bbl.)	31 gallons
	13.78 cases of 12 ounces * 24 units
	10.33 cases of 16 ounces * 24 units
	15.03 cases of 22 ounces * 12 units
	13.05 cases of 750 ml * 12 units
	3968 ounces
	248 pints
1 Hectoliter (hl)	.852 bbl.
	11.1 cases of 375 ml * 24 units
	11.1 cases of 750 ml * 12 units
	8.3 cases of 500 ml * 24 units
1 Liter	.264 gallons
1 Whiskey barrel (wbl.)	53 gallons (1.71 bbl. or 2.0 hl)
	200.24 liters
	267.12 bottles (750 ml)
	22.26 cases of 750 ml * 12 units
Source: Madeleine Pullman.	

In a metric example, one hl of the product cost 60.07 euros (€). To determine the cost for a case of 750 ml bottles, look at the conversion chart in Table 5.6 to see that there are 11.1 cases in one hl (750-ml containers with 12 in a case). The cost per case for the beverage alone is:

$$\frac{€60.07 \,/\, hl.}{11.1 \; cases \,/\, hl.} = €5.41 \,/\, case$$

With 12 750-ml units in a case, the cost estimate in Table 5.7 shows that the cost of a case with labor as €18.70 (without is €16.70) and the cost of a 750-ml bottle is €1.56 with labor (without is €1.39).

TABLE 5.7   Package cost for case and 750-ml bottles

Packaging items	Cost per case of 12 units	Cost per unit (750 ml)
Bottles (12)	€6.00	€0.50
Caps or corks and finish (12)	€3.00	€0.25
Labels including printing and design (12)	€1.20	€0.10
Carton (1)	€0.85	€0.07
Pallet and pallet wrapping (1)	€0.24	€0.02
Mobile bottling	€0.00	€0.00
Labor	€2.00	€ 0.17
Beverage cost	€5.41	€0.45
Total cost packaged product without labor	€16.70	€1.39
Total cost packaged with labor	€18.70	€1.56
Source: Madeleine Pullman.		

SUMMARY

Aside from the beverage produced, packaging is a linchpin of brand identity for any craft brewer and is one of the main ways that a consumer will find a new product on store shelves. As a craft beverage producer you must consider how package differentiates your product and tells the story of your brand. The label is highly regulated and all packaging material must conform to the legalities of the geographic area where it is produced. Many exciting options for packaging are coming online, and consumers have been more eager to try craft products in alternative packaging (like cans) than seen in the wine industry. Industry experts believe that bag-in-box packaging may be the next innovation for craft beer and cider. It pays for you as a craft producer to keep abreast of all packaging trends and consider where new ideas may fit into your business's product line.

Gigantic Brewing's Big Label Design Idea

Gigantic Brewing Company, a small-scale brewery in Portland, Oregon founded in 2012, brews many seasonal beers sold exclusively in 22-ounce bottles. Brewers and co-owners Ben Love and Van Havig are both industry veterans and have a simple goal of making one-off brews. Each beer is numbered with limited edition and collectible comic-style labels designed by a different artist. Gigantic allows complete creative freedom for the artists it works with, resulting in unique labels from one bottle to the next.

Gigantic rotates its one-offs, covering an expansive range of styles and unique ingredients. The beers remain on store shelves for three months until the next beer is ready for sale, each displaying its number on the bottle's label. Gigantic beers include ingredients such as plum, boysenberry, and black rice. Styles cover pale ales, wild ales, Vienna lagers, Baltic porters, and barley wines to list just a sampling. It offers only one consistent year-round beer, an IPA.

Love and Havig aim to match each beer to a particular artist. Gigantic's art director, Rob Reger, and friend, Matt Wagner of Hellion Gallery, curate a list of artists from Japan, Spain, Germany, and Australia. They launch new beers with the label artist's art show. Marketing wise, beer lovers become art fans while the followers of each artist become devotees of the beer—as well as the Gigantic Brewing brand in general.

Each label features attention-getting artwork under the Gigantic Brewing text. Along with a signature giant "G" on the side of the bottle, the artist selects a quote to be printed on the label. The only direction the artists receive is the proposed name and style of the beer. This is a distinctive approach compared to other brewers where they generally have an idea of what they want the final product to look like and direct the artist to render it. Customers can order any of the label designs poster form from the Gigantic Brewing website. Original pieces of the artists' other artworks are displayed in the brewery's small tasting room.

Love and Havig intended the name Gigantic to be ironic, since they had no intentions of growing a huge company. In this brewery's experience, the business name is reflective of the brand's gigantic presence rather than its physical size.

LEARNING ADVENTURES

1. Find a packaged beverage with a design you really admire. What makes this a strong package (the label or container, for example)? What does the package tell you about the brand? What type of consumer do you think this package is intended to attract?

2. Buy a package of your favorite beverage and analyze the contents of the label. How has the design integrated the essential elements? Does the package list alcohol content? If so, why is this included (legal, brand, or conveying something important like sessionability, for example)?

3. Cost out various packages (cans and bottles of various sizes) of your product (based on your recipe cost per bbl. from the previous chapters).

ENDNOTES

1. "Bottle Sizes of Craft Beer," *Craft Beer Restaurant.com*, http://craftbeerrestaurant.com/ Craft_Beer_Restaurant/Bottle_Sizes.html.

CHAPTER SIX

Kegging

Key Terms

cooperage

Hoff-Stevens

keg cap

keg collar

keg costing

keg float

keg logistics

keg rental

kegs (plastic)

kegs (stainless steel)

one-ways

pay-per-fill

Sankey

tap handles and lines

tap lines

velocity

Overview

Most craft beverage producers opt to keg some of their product. Even brewpubs using serving tanks also have kegs to sell their product to retail or wholesale consumers, or even just to empty a tank to make room for a new batch. Kegs come in several different sizes, and the retail consumer's preference for different sizes has changed over time. In addition, there are many keg services available that help producers finance and manage this important asset. This chapter covers the main issues around kegs and managing keg inventory and costs. It concludes with a keg cost estimation building on the previous chapters' estimates of beverage costs.

Learning Objectives

▶ Understand keg terminology.

▶ Recognize the different types of kegs.

▶ Compare the pros and cons of **plastic kegs**.

▶ Understand the other costs associated with keg management.

▶ Know the alternatives to owning kegs.

▶ Understand keg line servicing.

▶ Understand equipment needs.

▶ Calculate keg costs.

Introduction

Kegs and keg management are a crucial part of business in breweries, cideries, and meaderies, and increasingly with other beverages like wine and kombucha. As consumers look for methods to reduce packaging waste and sample fresher product, kegs are showing up in stores and restaurants that have never offered this kind of beverage container system before. New business models that support kegs are cropping up such as growler filling stations and tasting rooms.

The **Sankey** stainless steel keg is the most universally accepted style and the most highly recommended keg in the industry; **Hoff-Stevens** is an older style keg, and many people use them in their own brewpubs since they are commonly in circulation at lower prices. Each keg type has an appropriate coupler (such as the Sankey coupler) that connects it to a draft system with carbon dioxide gas (CO_2) going in to provide pressure and the liquid going out to the tap lines and tap. A bar or restaurant needs a keg and coupler for each individual product offered on draft.

The total number of kegs owned by any producer is called the **keg float**. Because stainless kegs are used multiple times, they become part of the overhead of the business and are not calculated as part of the cost of the beverage itself. **Cooperage** also refers to the keg float but specifically means a place where a cooper (barrel-maker) makes barrels.

Standard keg sizes are shown in Figure 6.1. For many years, the full keg, or 50-liter keg, was the industry norm. Today, as many retail outlets offer more beverage selections, smaller kegs have gained in popularity, especially the sixth barrel (1/6 bbl.) or 20-liter keg. Retailers can replace a full keg of one beer with two sixth barrels in roughly the same storage space, since they have the same height as a keg but almost half the diameter, to increase variety.

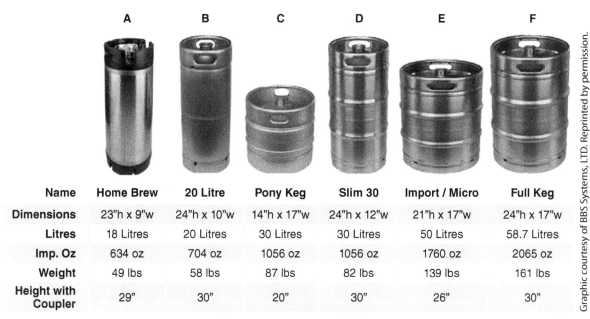

Name	Home Brew	20 Litre	Pony Keg	Slim 30	Import / Micro	Full Keg
	A	B	C	D	E	F
Dimensions	23"h x 9"w	24"h x 10"w	14"h x 17"w	24"h x 12"w	21"h x 17"w	24"h x 17"w
Litres	18 Litres	20 Litres	30 Litres	30 Litres	50 Litres	58.7 Litres
Imp. Oz	634 oz	704 oz	1056 oz	1056 oz	1760 oz	2065 oz
Weight	49 lbs	58 lbs	87 lbs	82 lbs	139 lbs	161 lbs
Height with Coupler	29"	30"	20"	30"	26"	30"

FIGURE 6.1 Types of kegs

Graphic courtesy of BBS Systems, LTD. Reprinted by permission.

Keg Materials

Compared to bottling, kegs require very little investment in ancillary materials and equipment but the kegs themselves are a substantial investment for startups.

Kegs (stainless steel): The stainless keg is the workhorse of the industry. Stainless kegs can handle high levels of pressure, have an easy surface to clean, and are highly durable. Durability is paramount considering how kegs are bounced around in breweries and on trucks, wheeled through bars, and stacked on shelves with other kegs on top. A full keg is quite heavy for one person to manage (about 160 pounds) and pallets of kegs (eight full kegs or 20 sixth kegs per pallet) add substantial weight to facility floors and delivery trucks. Moving full kegs off and on trucks or up and down stairs has caused many back injuries for beer producers and distributors over the years. When designing spaces for storing kegs, you need to consider the access issues for a pallet jack, dolly, keg lift, and other equipment that facilitates keg movement.

With stainless kegs costing between $100 and $200 each, owning hundreds of kegs can challenge any business's cash flow. And, at least 2 percent or more of the keg float is lost each year whenever kegs leave the facility. When producers expand production capacity and distribution range, keg flow expansion and loss rates need to be added into the financial projections. Several larger craft breweries have fallen victim to this issue and faced a multi-million dollar new keg bill for which the business had not budgeted.

Kegs (one-ways): description and cost, pros and cons: An alternative to stainless steel kegs are **one-way** kegs. Some are designed for single use; others, like Petainer (PET) kegs are refillable and shaped more like a standard stainless keg. One-way kegs have certain advantages and disadvantages. These kegs do not have the strength that stainless steel has in terms of durability but that may change over time. In particular, the low cost makes this keg an appealing choice for sending product to faraway locations for competitions, festivals, or export distribution. Along with these pros, some of the concerns with these kegs are detailed in Table 6.1.

FIGURE 6.2 Kegs

©Joshua Rainey Photography/Shutterstock.com

TABLE 6.1 One-way kegs pros and cons

Pros	Cons
► One-ways: they don't come back but some can be filled multiple times	► Disposal: many people see sustainability problems with a throw-away keg
► The cost is about less than half of stainless steel kegs	► Brand image: end consumer does not see it but the pub/restaurant staff does and they are opinion leaders
► No need to clean them since they come with clean plastic bladders	► Cardboard casing can get wet making stacking difficult
► Some breweries choose to use steel/traditional kegs in local markets, plastics for long distance markets like export markets	► Some require a special coupler for each account if not a sankey keg ($50 to $75)
► Bag-in-ball technology keeps propellant gas separate from beverage; can use air to push beverage which is a lot cheaper than CO_2	► Producers may need different equipment to fill kegs than their traditional equipment
► Lighter handling for people and that means cheaper transportation,	► If secondary fermentation is used, excess pressure can build up in keg with too much foam, leaking, for example
► Fully recyclable claims by manufacturer; it's not clear if that is the case if they don't get collected	

Source: Madeleine Pullman.

Photo courtesy of Scott Pillsbury. Reprinted with permission.

FIGURE 6.3   Keg collar and cap

Keg collar: Many producers use third-party-managed kegs that have limited brewery identification on the keg itself. Other producers have their brewery brand stenciled on the stainless keg but still need an identifier for the individual product. In both instances, customized keg collars are the solution since they serve as the keg's label. The collar is slipped over keg neck and contains the beverage style, brand information, producer address, government warning, fill date, and other required details for both producer and retailer.

Keg cap: The cap keeps the keg coupling area clean and protected during its journey from the filling station to the time it is attached to the coupler (when ready to serve). Keg caps are a simple, low-cost piece of plastic and can also have branding material printed on them.

TABLE 6.2   Typical keg costs

Parts	Range of costs
Stainless Steel Keg (½ bbl. or 50 l)	$100–120 (multiple uses)
Stainless Steel Keg (1/6 bbl. or 20 l)	$60–$100 (multiple uses)
Plastic Keg (1/6 bbl.)	$15–$30 (one time or limited use)
Keg Cap	$.05–$.10
Keg Collar	$.25–$.50
Source: Madeleine Pullman.	

Tap handles and lines: For each account, producers must provide a tap handle for every beverage style. The tap handle is a significant branding opportunity and should be designed with care and intention. In crowded markets, tap handles that stand out get the consumer's attention. In fact, attention-grabbing handles are getting bigger and bigger and can often interfere with the functionality of the handle or other handles. Besides size, tap handles offer imagery, descriptive material, or something unique or clever in the design. Handles are made of plastic, wood, metal, and many other materials. Plastic offers the opportunity to embed pictures. Many materials support three-dimensional designs. Most producers need multiples of each tap handle and the price of each handle tends to drop as the order size increases. Some of the other drivers of tap handle cost are complexity of design, materials like metal rather than plastics or wood, customization rather than stock shapes, and engraving. Typically, handle costs start around $10 each and climb from that point; most producers shoot for around $20 each for a solid design.

For those self-distributing, you many have to supply keg taps (connectors) for each account. Connected to the taps are the **tap lines** that supply product from the keg to the tap handle. Tap lines require regular cleaning and maintenance, and the responsibility for this job depends on the business location. In some states, the retail establishment is responsible for the lines and functionality of the draft system and in others, the distributor has that responsibility. In other states, either the distributor or the producer is responsible for the line maintenance. There are third-party

FIGURE 6.4   Tap handles

services that can be contracted to do this job. But, the producer should be clear on where the responsibility lies and also check on accounts to make sure that the job is being done well. Dirty tap lines can cause significant issues with the beverage that harm a producer's image. As a result, some producer's have contract clauses that address what happens if tap lines are not kept up to appropriate quality levels.

Keg Revenue Stream

Kegs outside of the brewpub or tasting room environment move from the producer to a distributor and into retail sites. A producer sells the keg to the distributor who marks the price up to the retailer who then marks the price up to the consumer. In the pattern of transactions, the retailer makes the best margin and profit from the keg.

In a hypothetical example, if a producer sells a keg off their dock (where permitted), they may charge $150 but when selling to a distributor, may get only $90. After accounting for the cost of the goods (not overhead) at $45, the producer clears $45 with a 50 percent profit margin. The distributor on the other hand, buys the keg for $90 and sells the keg for $125 thus making a 28 percent profit margin. The retailer who then buys the keg for $125 nets $600 (120 pints at $5 each). Thus, the retailer clears $475 or a 79 percent profit margin.

FIGURE 6.5   Keg margins

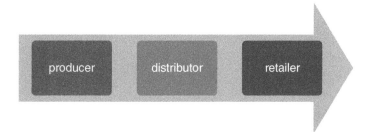

	Brewery/Cidery	**Distributor**	**Retailer (bar)**
Revenue (Rev)	$90	$125	$600 (120 pints @$5)
Cost of Goods (COGS)	$45	$90	$125
Gross Profit (GP)	$45	$35	$475
GPM= GP/Rev	50%	28%	79%
Source: Madeleine Pullman.			

On the other hand, if the keg goes directly to the producer's own tasting room or pub ($600 revenue on a $45 cost), the profit is $555, or a 92.5 percent profit margin—a very persuasive reason for having a brewpub of your own over distributing. It's no wonder that many producers want to go this route!

©Pavel L Photo and Video/Shutterstock.com

FIGURE 6.6   Keg storage

Keg Management

Keeping track of kegs is one of the major challenges for beverage businesses. For every keg customer, they need multiple kegs. In a distribution chain, more than half the kegs owned by any one business will be outside of its own facility either in a warehouse, at accounts, on a truck, or just sitting in someone's garage. As a consequence, kegs suffer from theft and other losses. As one Minnesota brewer commented, "When we send kegs to Texas, we are pretty much kissing them goodbye."

An individual producer needs four to five kegs for every sales account. How is this the case? First, the brewery needs a keg to fill and there needs to be a filled backup keg for each account, stored either in the account's walk-in refrigerator or in the distributor's warehouse (or in both locations). Then, there is the keg already on the retailer's tap, and finally, an empty keg in the distributor's warehouse or on its way back to the producer. If the producer is doing the distribution, there is tighter control over kegs, so four kegs per account can work, but otherwise five are required. So, if the producer has 150 accounts, then at least 600 kegs are needed at an average price of $112.5 for full keg and sixth barrel sizes for a total keg investment of $67,500.

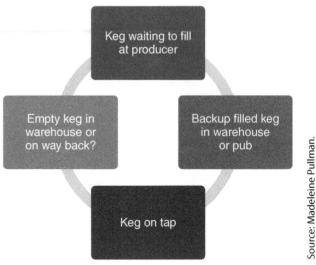

FIGURE 6.7 Kegs per account

Source: Madeleine Pullman.

Keg Services

Because of the potentially large investment in kegs and the high loss rate, third-party keg services have sprung up to manage kegs. Some services do **keg logistics** or **keg rental** such as MicroStar or Kegspediter in the United States. Upon contracting out these services, a producer either sells the existing float to the logistics company or does not buy kegs in the first place. The logistics company charges the producer on a per-use basis, depending on how many kegs are provided each month, where kegs are shipped to and how far. It does pickup and keg transfer and handles damaged kegs as well as keg loss. Typically, the services have a minimum of five-year contracts.

The payment for the services and activities takes several forms. In **pay-per-fill**, the service picks up all the kegs at distributors and the producer calls the service whenever they need kegs to fill. The producer may be responsible for washing the keg before using it. For example, a producer pays something like $10 for a sixth barrel and $12 for a full keg but is charged half that amount for in-house keg use (pub or tasting room).

FIGURE 6.8 Third-party keg management

In the rental scenario, the producer pays a deposit for a keg and a fee for each day of use (for example, $0.11-$0.13 per day). Both logistics and rental companies have minimum requirements to provide the service, such as using at least 150 kegs per month and distance limits (must be within 300 miles of the producer's distributor).

Distribution Revenue

Can a company survive on keg distribution alone without getting into packaging? This depends on how many keg accounts the producer can win and retain. Holding onto retail accounts is getting harder and harder since retailers are swapping out kegs all the time to give their customers new and enticing choices. There are very few producers that can survive on kegs alone other than those with a significant pub/restaurant presence. To understand the potential revenue from keg distribution, look at Table 6.3.

TABLE 6.3 Yearly revenue from keg distribution

Keg Price to Distributor	Yearly revenue forecast from keg distribution						
$90.00	Average # of kegs per account per month						
Average # of Accounts	1	1.5	2	2.5	3	3.5	4
50	$54,000	$81,000	$108,000	$135,000	$162,000	$189,000	$216,000
100	$108,000	$162,000	$216,000	$270,000	$324,000	$378,000	$432,000
150	$162,000	$243,000	$324,000	$405,000	$486,000	$567,000	$648,000
200	$216,000	$324,000	$432,000	$540,000	$648,000	$756,000	$864,000
300	$324,000	$486,000	$648,000	$810,000	$972,000	$1,134,000	$1,296,000

Source: Madeleine Pullman.

First, assume that the average full keg is sold to a distributor for $90. Second, estimate the keg's average **velocity**, the average number of kegs sold in each account per month (three full kegs in this example), and then estimate the average number of accounts that could be achieved, say 150 accounts. According to the chart, the total revenue is $486,000 per year based on the calculation in Equation 1.

EQUATION 1 Keg distribution revenue

$$price \times \frac{velocity}{month} \times 12 \ months \times number \ of \ accounts = revenue$$

$$\$90 \times \frac{3}{month} \times 12 \ months \times 150 \ accounts = \$486,000$$

Keg Equipment

Kegs require special equipment for washing and filling. While some equipment can handle both tasks, many producers prefer to separate them so that kegs can be washed as soon as they arrive back in house and old product does not sit in kegs for months on end, depending on the demand cycle. Keg washing is straightforward, and a machine usually has a fitting for introducing cleaning and sanitizing solutions inside the keg. In startup facilities, owners have modified sinks to handle this job at a very low cost. More efficient and effective machine costs start at $15,000 to $20,000 but can handle 20 to 25 kegs per hour; more expensive machines handling multiple kegs at even faster rates. Like the bottle filler, a keg filling machine must also have counter-pressure for carbonated beverages and can cost as much as a keg

©Dja65/Shutterstock.com

FIGURE 6.9 Keg

washing machine. Startups have come up with very inexpensive solutions to keg filling using modified keg connectors. Typically a keg should not take more than five to 10 minutes labor-wise to clean, fill, and store.

Basic Keg Costing

For pricing a keg, it is important to start with what the product costs to make by the barrel (bbl., hl, or wbl.) demonstrated in Chapter 4: Ingredients. For example, if the liquid beverage cost (without labor) comes to $60.07 for a barrel, one keg is a half barrel or:

$$\frac{\$60.07 \, / \, bbl.}{2 \, kegs \, / \, bbl.} = \$30.04 \, / \, keg$$

TABLE 6.4   Keg cost for full keg and sixth barrel

Keg Cost for Full Keg (15.5 gallons)	
Packaging items	**Cost per keg**
Keg Caps	$0.05
Keg Collars	$0.25
Labor Kegging (wash and fill)	$1.33
Beverage cost	$30.04
Total cost packaged beverage without labor	**$30.34**
Total cost package beverage with labor	**$31.67**
Source: Madeleine Pullman.	

The sixth barrel cost is:

$$\frac{\$60.07 \, / \, bbl.}{6} = \frac{\$10.01}{bbl.}$$

Keg Cost for Sixth Barrel (5.1 gallons)	
Keg Caps	**$0.05**
Keg Collars	**$0.25**
Labor Kegging (wash and Fill)	**$1.33**
Beverage cost	**$10.01**
Total cost packaged beverage without labor	$10.31
Total cost packaged beverage with labor	$11.64
Source: Madeleine Pullman.	

Compare selling a packaged versus a kegged product to see what makes the most sense (and cents!): the case of 12-ounce bottles cost $11.09 without labor and sells for about $26 to a wholesaler; so, $26 minus $11.09 equals $14.91 profit margin. One keg contains 6.89 cases. So, to equate cases to keg sales, 6.89 cases times $14.91 equals a profit margin of $102.73.

The keg sells for $90 to the wholesaler but the total cost is $30.34 without labor or $90 minus $30.34 for a profit margin of just $59.66.

Assuming that any labor or other overheard for bottling and kegging are roughly equivalent, selling the product in the equivalent amount of packaged goods brings in more profit margin than the keg. Granted, packaged goods have the added cost of mobile packaging or the capital investment in more expensive equipment than kegging. Just looking at the margins for the moment, there are clear bottom line advantages to selling packaged product. But, you need access to distributors and store placements to make this work.

SUMMARY

Kegs are an essential part of the craft beverage world and their popularity is expanding across all beverage types. Many consumers believe that draft products are far superior to bottled or canned equivalents. With the environmental advantages, kegs also avoid a lot of wasteful packaging. It is possible the future will bring even kegged spirits, that is, if governments can apply technology that monitors sales for tax revenue.

Boneyard Brewing's Keg-Only Business Model

Boneyard Brewing from Bend Oregon, is known for making hoppy beers, including a critically acclaimed IPA called RPM. The brewery gets its name from the "boneyard" of old equipment that owner Tony Lawrence collected while repairing brewery equipment around the country. Boneyard produced its first batch of beer in May 2010 on this second-hand equipment. The company has since replaced its original fermenters with new ones, completing a brewing system at a capacity of 15,000 barrels a year, and recently opened a brand-new production facility.

Boneyard distributes beer in Oregon and Washington, but is strictly a kegging, draft-only brewery. It does not bottle or can any of its beers. The owners have no stated interest in opening a brewpub or restaurant, and the brewery only offers samples and growler fills to customers.

The beer is unpasteurized and unfiltered, and therefore can be risky to distribute far from the home base where draft accounts may not treat the beer properly. The brewery's plan is to remain in Washington and Oregon with possible expansion to San Francisco. As the beer sells out in this territory readily, the owners feel that they do not need to risk beer quality in order to boost sales.

Boneyard is currently at capacity at its current facility, meeting the large number of keg orders from its distributor, Point Blank Distributing. With the list of draft accounts continuing to grow, it cannot produce enough beer to package. The brewery once owned a $35,000 canning machine with the intent of releasing 16-ounce cans, but sold it to another Bend brewery in order to concentrate on meeting keg demand.

Consumers looking to purchase six-packs of Boneyard beer are directed to the website, taplister.com, and the mobile application, Untappd, to search for Boneyard beers in nearby bars and restaurants. Boneyard focuses on making its RPM IPA and producing consistent beers year-round with other occasional beers in the rotation in limited quantities. A few of its hoppy beers, such as its double and triple IPA, are so sought after by Boneyard's fan base that they sell out almost immediately. These die-hard followers use social media to stay updated on local tappings, and the company's draft-only option creates a sense of urgency among the brewery's fans.

Generally speaking, it is hard for any business to solidify an identity and create brand awareness without standard packaging. Consumers do not see Boneyard's skull and cross bone logo while enjoying the beer in restaurants and bars. However, Boneyard Brewing's branding is prominent on its delivery trucks around the Pacific Northwest with uniquely designed images for each of its beer brands. Additionally, in keeping with the boneyard theme, the brewery crafts and welds signature tap handles using recycled materials. Boneyard also sells an abundance of merchandise in its brewery, including shirts, cycling socks, jerseys, and pint glasses. Boneyard also defies conventional marketing wisdom by not investing any resources in advertising, a remarkable and offbeat position in Oregon's highly competitive craft beer scene.

LEARNING ADVENTURES

1. Go to one of your local brewpubs and find out: 1) who is responsible for managing the kegging system; 2) how many kegs of a popular brand they go through per week on average; and 3) how does the demand for kegs change throughout the year.

2. Ask the manager at your favorite pub about the decision-making process to take on a new kegged product. What are the characteristics of products that become permanent fixtures?

3. Calculate the cost of a beer or cider keg based on your beverage cost recipe.

4. Determine the average wholesale and retail keg cost for a brand in your area by looking at brewery websites or visiting a local keg sales outlet.

CHAPTER SEVEN

Cost of Goods Sold

Key Terms

cost of goods manufactured	direct and indirect labor	taxes
cost of goods sold	high-gravity brewing	
dilution	ingredients and other materials	

Overview

The cost of goods sold, commonly referred to as COGS, is an important item for understanding the profitability of any beverage and has a significant impact on the business as a whole. At this stage in the book, you have accumulated the information necessary to compute the COGS of individual products—before tackling the entire overhead a beverage needs to cover with sales. We have covered the cost of the liquid and package as well labor that directly went into the creation of the filled package. We have yet to look at the cost implications of investments such as equipment, building, and the management team. For most producers, the cost of a barrel of product (case or gallon) decreases as the facility increases its production volume. This chapter investigates COGS calculations for producing a certain unit of product and compares this figure to industry averages.

Learning Objectives

▶ Understand the factors involved in cost of goods sold calculations.

▶ Know the difference between direct and indirect labor.

▶ Calculate cost of goods sold.

▶ Compare production brewery and brewpub cost of goods sold to industry averages.

Introduction

In the world of craft production, **cost of goods sold** (COGS) is the direct cost of making a beverage product. This chapter looks specifically at the COGS to produce one unit of product, such as a barrel or case. In a distribution model or in environments where the production side *sells* product to the pub/restaurant or retail side, COGS is what the buyer pays for a unit of product. For producers, COGS is the cost of creating the products that the company sells; therefore, the costs included in the COGS measure are those directly tied to the production of the products. In the beer market, COGS is usually expressed in barrels, and is often the same for cider. Alternatively, COGS can be expressed in gallons, liters, or case units.

There are two ways to determine COGS: either by directly calculating the cost of making the product or by tracking inventory at the beginning of a period, adding any materials purchased, and subtracting what is left at the end of a period. This chapter demonstrates the direct calculation method. It is important to bear in mind that this cost will not include any overhead that is part of the real cost of the product, such as facility, electricity, utilities, and other personnel, known as the **cost of goods manufactured**.

COGS: Direct Costs

Ingredients and other materials: All of the recipe ingredients used to produce a beverage are included in the COGS, such as malt, grain, fruit, hops, and yeast. By knowing the ingredient costs, it is possible—as illustrated in previous chapters—to calculate the cost of any recipe. During the production process, the batch may yield more or less than expected. So, it is important to keep track of exactly how many packages or kegs result from the recipe. If the yield is less than expected, the COGS will increase the liquid cost will now be more per barrel; if more then expected, the COGS will decrease as the liquid cost is now less per barrel.

Other materials that are part of the COGS include various brewing, cleaning and filtering aids, water adjustments, acids, yeast nutrients, and so on. Each batch of product may use a certain amount of filtering pads and that cost can be broken out on a per-barrel basis. Another item for consideration is barrels used for aging. If the barrel is used just once or twice, this cost should be assigned to the cost of making a barrel of product. For example, a twice-used oak barrel would have half of its cost assigned to each production lot.

Dilution: Some beverages have purified or distilled water or juice added to reduce the alcohol level or adjust the blend, and this, too, affects the cost of the final product. For example, most spirit producers sell their finished spirit at 80 to 88 proof (40 to 44 percent ABV). Whiskey makers put their product into the barrel aging stage at higher proofs (say 125 proof) so before bottling they need to add water to get it to a lower ABV level. The dilution formula is:

$$volume\ of\ water\ to\ add = \frac{alcohol\ \%\ existing - alcohol\ \%\ desired}{alcohol\ \%\ desired} \times existing\ volume$$

Example: You have 125 gallons of alcohol at 85 percent and you want to dilute it to 40 percent:

$$volume\ of\ water\ to\ add = \frac{85\% - 40\%}{40\%} \times 125\ gallons = 140.625\ gallons$$

In this example, the volume of water added to lower the alcohol level to 40 percent is 140.6 gallons with total finished gallons of 265.6 (the original 125 gallons of alcohol plus 140.6 gallons added water).

How will this reflect on the finished cost of the spirit? Assume that up to this point, the spirit cost is $22 to produce a gallon (125 gallons whiskey $22/gallon = $2750/batch) and you added 140.6 gallons of purified or distilled water at $1/gallon (140.6 gallons $1 = $140.60). As illustrated in Table 1, adding the water reduces the cost per finished gallon to $10.89.

TABLE 7.1   Cost of dilution example

Ingredient	Price/Volume	Cost
Spirit (85%) 125 gallons	$22/gallon	$2,750.00
Water 140.6 gallons	$1/gallon	$140.60
Finished (40%) 265.6 gallons		$2,890.60
Cost per finished gallon	$2,890.60/265.6 gallons = $10.89/gallon	
Source: Madeleine Pullman.		

Dilution is common for cider and spirits and for **high gravity brewing**, creating a beverage with a very high original gravity (OG) (above 1.075). OG is the measure of fermentable and un-fermentable substances in the liquid before fermentation. The difference between the OG and the final gravity measure after fermentation gives an indication of the alcohol level. Some producers increase their efficiency by creating a high gravity beer or cider and then diluting it down to a lower alcohol level with water. This approach will get more product out of limited equipment and potentially reduce the cost of the finished product.

Direct and indirect labor: There are two types of labor that apply to a product: direct and indirect labor. Direct labor is any labor you can trace to a specific production lot, such as the labor hours for the milled grain and for the brewed, filtered, bottled, or kegged batch. Conversely, indirect labor covers any labor that cannot be directly traced back to specific production units, such as accounting, production supervision, marketing, and other administrative tasks.

If hourly employees are involved in brewing, transferring, filtering, or packaging, then the sum of all of these hours is applied to a batch of product as follows:

$$\frac{labor\ cost}{batch} = \frac{brew\ time \times \frac{wage}{hr} + transfer\ time \times \frac{wage}{hr} + packaging\ time \times \frac{wage}{hr}}{Total\ batch\ yield(bbl.\ or\ cases)}$$

For example, assume the resulting batch size is 10 barrels and the average hourly wage for the employees is $18 per hour. If it takes six hours to brew and clean, four hours to transfer, filter, and clean, and two employees at six hours each to package or keg (12 hours packaging total), then the total labor per barrel is:

$$\frac{labor\ cost}{bbl.} = \frac{(6 \times \$18) + (4 \times \$18) + (12 \times \$18)}{10} = \frac{\$39.60}{bbl.}$$

The following examples for beer and spirits analyze COGS with and without labor. The tricky part of COGS is that direct labor costs may be challenging to separate out batch for batch. For example, in many production environments, the brewmaster, cider-maker, or distiller is in a salaried position, which is indirect labor. On the other hand, if using mobile bottling or canning, the cost of packaging can be easily applied to the COGS since this is not part of overhead and the cost is often quoted on a per package basis.

Taxes: State and federal producer taxes can also be considered part of the COGS, especially as we consider how many units it takes to break-even. But, for other purposes, like accounting reports, taxes are separated out. Also, it's a good idea to know COGS without taxes so products can be compared among brewpubs or facilities that may be in different locations.

Beer COGS Example

Based on the analysis in Chapter 4: Ingredients, a recipe for a beer has a cost breakdown with all ingredients and materials as illustrated in Table 7.2. In this example, the direct labor of making the beer is $50 per barrel so the total cost of the beer is $116.09 with labor or $66.09 without labor.

COGS for Beer Sold in Kegs (Half Barrel)

Once the product is put into kegs, the COGS of a packaged keg is $59.68 ($119.36 per barrel) with labor and $33.35 ($66.70 per barrel) without labor (one barrel equals two kegs), detailed in Table 7.3.

TABLE 7.2   Liquid costs per barrel example

Ingredients and materials	Cost/bbl.
Grain	$33.46
Hops	$14.62
Yeast	$0.03
Gases	$1.00
Cleaning	$1.50
Federal excise tax	$7.00
State excise tax	$2.48
Labor (brewing and transfer)	$50.00
Other (filtering aids)	$6.00
Total with direct labor	$116.09
Total without direct labor	$66.09
Source: Madeleine Pullman.	

TABLE 7.3   Total packaged cost for kegs

Packaging items	Cost per keg
Keg caps	$0.05
Keg collars	$0.25
Labor kegging (wash and fill)	$1.33
Beer cost without production labor	$33.05
Total cost packaged beer without labor	**$33.35**
Beer cost with production with labor	$58.05
Total cost packaged beer with labor	**$59.68**
	Per bbl.
Total cost packaged beer without labor	**$66.70**
Total cost packaged beer with labor	**$ 119.36**
Source: Madeleine Pullman.	

Industry Norms for Cider and Beer Production

Of interest to any producer is how their COGS compare to the national averages.[1] For beer, the average COGS per barrel for a production brewery with labor included ranges from $97.17 to $106.71 for a large (more than 15,000 barrels annually) to small (less than 1,000 barrels annually). For larger brewpubs (more than 1,000 barrels annually) to smaller brewpubs (less than or equal to 1,000 barrels annually), the averages range from $90 to $174.44 per barrel, respectively.

For cider in the Northwest US, larger producers (producing more than 100,000 gallons, annually) pay $1.44/gallon for juice while smaller producers (producing less than 100,000 gallons annually) pay $1.69/gallon; these prices including labor.[2] Packaging and kegging costs are similar to beer.

Larger production facilities can allocate less labor per batch since brewing time is the same but the batch size is larger and requires less labor and the packaging equipment is highly automated.

Spirits COGS Example

Assuming you know the cost per gallon to create the liquid, the next step is to include any barrels or other materials used for aging (shown in Table 7.4 as $1.50) and allocate the barrel cost over the batch of spirits.

To address the cost of packaging the spirits in cases of liter bottles with 12 bottles per case, the example in Table 7.5 calculates a COGS of $118.19, or $9.85 per liter bottle ($118.19 divided by 12) with all direct labor included.

TABLE 7.4   Spirits liquid cost

Item	Cost	Unit	Notes
Finished product cost (materials)	$12.28	per gallon	Distilled spirits cost after dilution for final bottling
Barrel	$1.50	per gallon	Cost to purchase each aging barrel divided by number of gallons produced assuming one use
Fed excise tax	$10.80	per gallon	$13.50 per proof gallon[a] 1 finished gallon at 40% ABV = .8 proof gallon
State excise tax	$0.67	per gallon	State tax[b]
Labor	$3.00	per gallon	Labor should include production and cellaring activities
Other	$0.00	per gallon	Additional ingredients or materials
Total with labor	$28.25	per gallon	Total with labor
Total without labor	$25.25	per gallon	Total without labor

[a] US Tax, see http://www.ttb.gov/tax_audit/atftaxes.shtml.
[b] OregonSpirits Tax used in example.
Source: Madeleine Pullman.

TABLE 7.5   Packaged spirits COGS example

Packaging items	Cost per case
Bottles (12 per case)	$24.00
Closure (12 per case)	$1.20
Labels, including printing and design	$1.20
Divider	$0.85
Carton	$0.85
Pallet and pallet wrapping	$0.24
Labor bottling	$1.00
Beverage cost (3.17 gallons per case of 12 liter bottles) using labor included beverage cost	$89.55
Total cost packaged without packaging labor	$117.89
Total cost packaged product with all direct labor	$118.89
Source: Madeleine Pullman.	

SUMMARY

The importance of understanding the COGS for each product line and package type cannot be underestimated. For the financial statement, the COGS is one entry where all the product types and package types produced during the recording period are pulled together. Business plans looking into the future must project the mix of different brands, packages and kegs for three years at least to get at the potential costs and revenues of the firm. After pricing the product and analyzing the potential sales, the business management can then see how well the margin (revenue minus COGS) covers all the other overhead items.

Tackling a Dilution Dilemma at 10 Barrel

In Germany, a radler (German for cyclist) is equal parts beer and sparkling lemonade. As a refreshing summer beverage, radlers have taken hold in the United States. Located in Bend, Oregon, 10 Barrel Brewing makes a radler-style beer called Swill—a light, summery beer, low in alcohol and easy to drink. But, it took the brewers a few years to get Swill just right. It also required a base beer, a special imperial Berliner Weisse, brewed deliberately strong at eight percent ABV. (Called German Sparkle Party, 10 Barrel also makes this beer into a few variations with other fruits, even cucumber.) 10 Barrel blends roughly 45 percent soda to 55 percent imperial Berliner Weisse for a final product of 4.5 percent ABV.

The big problem was that the original Swill was too carbonated. Excessively foamy, it occasionally exploded out of the bottle. Needless to say, Swill was recalled. The extra carbonation was caused by adding a sweetened juice to the beer containing live yeast. Since yeast actively consumes sugars, fermentation continued within the bottles. So, 10 Barrel's brewers had to be sure all the active yeast was killed off before bottling. They resolved the problem by adding a small amount of a preservative to the final product. Swill was originally a one-off beer that has now returned year after year propelled by the hugely positive response by 10 Barrel's consumers.

Here is the calculation for diluting the Weisse beer with lemon soda:

$$volume\ of\ juice\ to\ add = \frac{alcohol\ \%\ existing - alcohol\ \%\ desired}{alcohol\ \%\ desired} \times existing\ volume$$

$$volume\ of\ juice\ to\ add = \frac{8\% - 4.5\%}{4.5\%} \times 55\ gallon = 42.8\ gallons\ lemon\ soda$$

LEARNING ADVENTURES

1. Calculate the COGS for a packaged beer or cider using the approach from Chapter 4 (for the recipe) and 5 (packaged) or 6 (keg). Assess how it compares to industry norms.

2. Predict how the COGS might change as the batch capacity doubles or is ten times the size?

ENDNOTES

1. "New Brewery Operations Benchmarking Data," Brewers Association, https://www.brewersassociation.org/insights/new-brewery-operations-benchmarking-data/.

2. "Northwest Cider Survey," http://www.nwcider.com/news/2016/2/9/stateofcider2016.

CHAPTER EIGHT

Strategy

Key Terms

beliefs

core values

cost (price)

distinctive competence

distinctive competency

flexibility

innovation

mission

objectives

opportunities

policies

pub strategies

quality

strengths

strategy

sustainability

SWOT analysis

threats

vision

weaknesses

Overview

Before getting into big-ticket items like equipment, site, and employees, this chapter takes a step back and looks at the overall strategy of your business. The big picture decisions that you make at the outset will have long-term implications for your company. Generally, entrepreneurs and owners have a concept in mind before starting a business, but it is critical to consider how this concept is going to succeed in the marketplace now and in the future. The strategic plan you create will influence many other aspects of the business including operations, marketing, and human resource decisions. This chapter describes how to develop a solid strategic plan and how it relates to the other functional areas of your business.

Learning Objectives

▶ Identify the importance of strategy.

▶ Define and differentiate between the vision, mission, and core values.

▶ Understand how the strategic plan supports the vision.

▶ Examine how the strategic plan affects other functional area strategies.

▶ Understand and apply a SWOT analysis.

▶ Understand common business objectives and the trade-offs among them.

▶ Determine where the business currently is positioned and where it should go in the future.

▶ Demonstrate how the long-range plan for design and use of operations supports the overall business strategy.

Introduction

Strategy is the long-range plan for a business based on an understanding of the marketplace. The strategic plan stems from a vision of where the company aims to be in the future and addresses how the company will differentiate itself in a competitive environment. Additionally, the strategy creates a compass for the company used to align employee efforts as well as each functional area (marketing, operations, human resources, finance, and so forth) to accomplish the overall game plan. With a well thought out strategy, a company can make coherent steps toward achieving a goal and rather than jumping from idea to idea; it will act proactively instead of reactively to changes in the environment. Employees and functional areas will have a clear direction and can perform activities that support other functional areas and the interests of the firm.

Source: Madeleine Pullman.

FIGURE 8.1 Strategy and business plan

The first step toward strategy formulation is to state a **vision**. For some companies, the vision embeds their mission, values, and beliefs. The vision statement should follow the concept description in a business plan. Strategic elements play into every part of the business plan (shown in Figure 8.1) since each section needs to incorporate the long-term plan for the business.

The vision should define an optimal future state. It is usually inspirational so that employees can relate to the ideas and convey it to others. The vision is internally oriented and describes the purpose of the business, or why the owner(s) wants to be in this business. For example, New Belgium Brewery's vision statement includes the company's purpose, core values, beliefs, and mission. In reality, the vision and mission are two separate concepts but are closely related. Some companies, like New Belgium, have extensive lists of values that span from aspirations of quality ("producing world-class beers") to organizational behavior ("committing to authentic relationships and communications") to societal goals ("kindling social, environmental, and cultural change").[1]

Other businesses have shorter values statements, such as Lost Distillery's list that includes, "Fail quickly & learn," "Build powerful relationships," and "Create equitable wealth."[2] *Together, the vision, mission, and values set the foundation for the strategic plan.*

The **mission** is focused more on the current state of the business and should address what the business does, who it does it for, and how it does it. It also is internally oriented.

Champlain Orchards' mission is to grow a wide variety of delicious ecologically grown tree fruit while respecting the land, supporting our communities and surpassing customers' expectations.[3]

Off-centered ales for off-centered people (Dogfish Head Craft Brewery)

Core values and **beliefs** are useful concepts to include with vision and mission statements as they help employees and customers understand the desired culture of the company. These ideas can also help managers make decisions that align with the interests of the company. Some companies, such as New Belgium, have extensive lists of values:

1. Remembering that we are incredibly lucky to create something fine that enhances people's lives while surpassing our consumers' expectations.

2. Producing world-class beers.

3. Promoting beer culture and the responsible enjoyment of beer.

4. Kindling social, environmental, and cultural change as a business role model.

5. Environmental stewardship: Honoring nature at every turn of the business.

6. Cultivating potential through learning, high involvement culture, and the pursuit of opportunities.

7. Balancing the myriad needs of the company, our coworkers, and their families.

8. Trusting each other and committing to authentic relationships and communications.

9. Continuous innovative quality and efficiency improvements.

10. Having fun.[4]

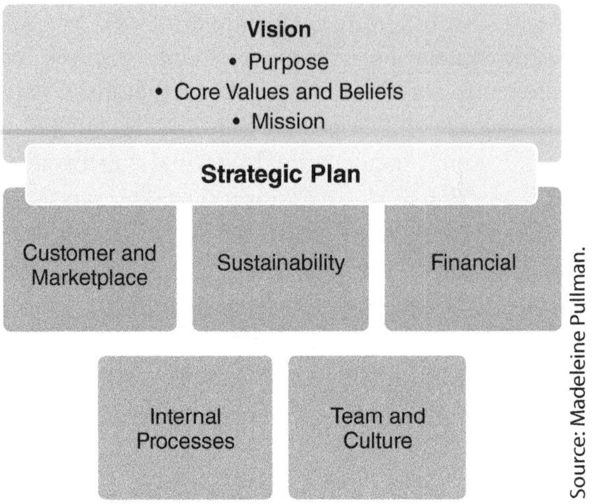

FIGURE 8.2 Strategic plan

Strategic Plan

Plans for the future should spell out how the company interacts with customers and the marketplace, how it makes products, how it hires and manages employees, and how it achieves financial goals. For example, if environmental and social sustainability are values and part of the mission and vision as seen with New Belgium, then financial decisions support those values; the brand is positioned with sustainability as part of its message to the customer and marketplace. Additionally, internal processes are designed to address those values, such as saving as much water as possible during production and donating to community and environmental causes. The employees are hired, trained, and promoted accordingly. At New Belgium, each employee receives an ownership stake in the company and a free custom bicycle after one year, an all expenses paid trip to Belgium after five years, and many other perks. Because of how this strategy plays out with human resources, this Colorado brewery is considered one of the best places to work in the US.[5]

Functional Strategy

The business strategy extends from the vision and other strategic goals, such as growth, into each functional area. For example, a strong sustainability element has a big impact on operations (the brewery, cidery, and distillery production) since this is the area where resources like water, energy, and production people are managed, and it is the source for the bulk of the waste.

Distinctive competence: A competency that a business is known for and which it performs better than others in the marketplace is a **distinctive competency**. The typical operational **objectives** for a distinctive competence include the following:

▶ **Cost (price):** Low production costs enable a company either to price product below the competitors or to generate a higher margin. The craft products sold by the big industrial breweries such as Blue Moon or Shock Top are good examples.

▶ **Quality:** Higher performance or a more consistent product can support a price premium. Producers with barrel aging, unique yeasts and ingredients, premium packaging, and special

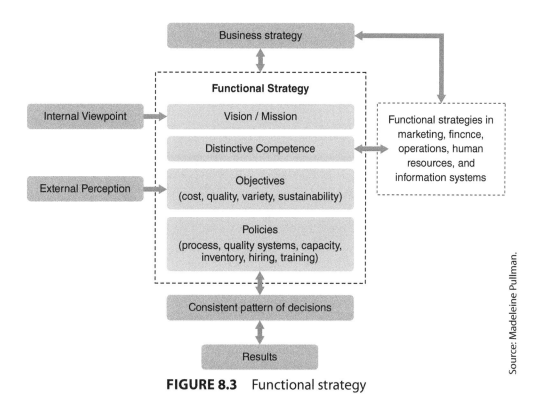

FIGURE 8.3   Functional strategy

processes fall under this classification. Whiskey producers with long aging processes and blending to create a premium product fall under this objective.

▶ **Sustainability:** Products that are produced with minimal negative impacts to the environment and society. They connect with consumers on social, environmental, and other values. The well-known sustainability-focused brewing companies are New Belgium, Sierra Nevada, and Hopworks.

▶ **Flexibility:** Choice flexibility (variety), interesting seasonal products, or a wide range of packaging options all represent this objective. Some producers constantly change their products and don't have a particular flagship. An example of this objective is Mikkeller, a famous Danish contract brewing company with a beverage portfolio including hundreds of products at any given time.

▶ **Innovation:** Products or processes that are produced or designed to be radically or incrementally different from others in their class. These companies adopt innovative packaging (Basecamp Brewery's aluminum bottle) or processes (Tilted Shed's January Barbeque Smoked Cider or Ransom's Old Tom Gin).

A company should clearly communicate its objective to the outside world. This comes through the marketing material and how well internal activities align with that objective.

How does the mission and vision translate into an objective? In the case of Delaware's Dogfish Head, the company's mission has led to decisions to make unusual beers and to invest in unique processes for making beers—an innovative objective and now its distinctive competency. Similarly, Sierra Nevada brewery developed a mountain and outdoors image; it translated that image into a compatible objective of sustainability. Today, relative to other producers, it is far advanced in sustainability efforts related to brewing processes. New Belgium has a distinctive competency in sustainable processes including some of the lowest water use per barrel produced, wastewater management that generates power through methane, investment in solar electric systems, and many other activities.

Differentiation the Dogfish Head Way

"Off-centered ales for off-centered people" is the motto and mission statement for Dogfish Head Craft Brewing based in Milton, Delaware. When brewer Sam Calagione founded the brewery in 1995, it was the smallest craft brewery in the country. Twenty years later it became one of the largest, renowned for making experimental ales with unordinary ingredients, often times inspired by ancient beer traditions. Many beers are high in alcohol and are aged in oak barrels.

An extraordinary opportunity arose for the company when a beer aficionado and flooring business owner named John Gasparine encountered "holy wood," or *palo santo* in Paraguay. Heavy, hard and oily, holy wood smells like sandalwood and is traditionally used to make bowls and utensils. When constructed into wine barrels, the wood's sweet smell is imparted into the wine, and this inspired Gasparine to suggest its use for Dogfish Head beers. Calagione agreed it would be a worthy investment since Dogfish Head has a goal of making potent, unique beers. He sent Gasparine back to South America to bring back enough *palo santo* wood to build a massive wooden barrel on-site.

That barrel, standing 15 feet high and 10feet in diameter, is housed in the main Delaware brewery. It was custom built by a father and son firm for a cost of $140,000—three times the cost of using oak. Still, the huge financial investment suited the brewery's mission to create one-of-a-kind beers, and the resulting essence from the *palo santo* wood paid off in the flavors of the beer. Calagione filled all nine thousand gallons the barrel holds with a strong brown beer to match the wood's intense aroma. The resulting brew, at 12 percent alcohol, was aromatic with hints of molasses, tobacco, black cherries, chocolate, and spice from the wood.

Dogfish has always brewed experimentally in small batches. Monitoring online beer sources such as RateBeer and BeerAdvocate, Calagione decides which beers are hits and should be brewed at the larger brewery. The decision to scale up recipes increases the cost of the beer's production, and the availability of unique resources is always a consideration. For Dogfish the financial risks have translated in huge success that keeps it on the leading edge of its competitors while keeping its faithful fan base interested and amazed.

A company could have a certain objective but how well it is translated into a distinctive competency depends on the execution. One thing is for sure, it is hard to do many things well and typically tradeoffs will be involved as shown in Figure 8.4. Having several objectives such as high quality and low cost simultaneously can be challenging to implement since high quality materials and processes cost more. Some of objectives can work well together; highly sustainable products and processes are often perceived to be better quality in the marketplace.

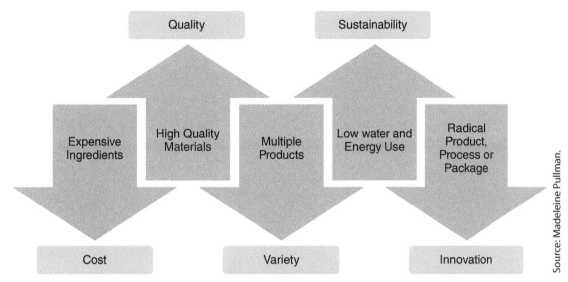

FIGURE 8.4   Objective trade-offs

Policies: Once you have determined your key objectives you develop the policies to implement each objective. Policies should address the long-range plan for the design and use of the functional area to support the overall business strategy and objectives. Table 8.1 presents examples of policies that are consistent with objectives related to production:

TABLE 8.1   Policies and objectives

Policy area	Examples of policies
Location, size and type of facilities	Cost focus: investment in low-cost buildings and locations Sustainability focus: investment in buildings where existing materials can be repurposed or building a LEED certified building
Worker skills and talents	Quality focus: continuous investment developing employees with high skill levels or hiring brewer or distiller with known reputations (medal winners, for example) Cost focus: developing a volunteer or intern program for help with bottling and tasting room
Equipment, technology, and processes	Innovation focus: investment in state-of-the-art equipment Quality focus: investment in packaging equipment to produce consistent products with longer shelf life
Controls for product and service quality	Cost focus: train people to control process quality Innovation focus: use equipment to control process quality
Source: Madeleine Pullman.	

SWOT Analysis

SWOT stands for strengths, weaknesses, opportunities, and threats. A **SWOT analysis** is a useful tool for evaluating how a chosen objective might work in the environment the business is facing. Once a business's objective is identified, the management team usually brainstorms to identify the internal and external factors that support and hinder the achievement of that objective.

Strengths and **weaknesses** are internal to the firm. For strengths, one should consider advantages and capabilities that the business has related to specific resources (money or land), assets (an existing building or cash) or people (one of the owners is a skilled brewer or cider-maker). The strengths may also be related to marketing abilities or existing brand awareness for an existing business looking to expand. Weaknesses are the flipside of these examples: lack of money or experience, poor brand awareness, supply chain issues related to ingredients, and other vulnerabilities.

FIGURE 8.5   SWOT analysis

Source: Madeleine Pullman.

Opportunities and **threats** are external to the firm. For example, from an opportunity perspective, the market may be underdeveloped for the business concept in different areas; a neighborhood with many people of the appropriate demographic may be growing; or there is potential for partnerships or contract production. Anything related to market or product development is an opportunity. Threats in the environment come in many forms: commoditization of craft by big producers, supply chain or retail lockout, legislation or regulation, competitive moves from others, market demand shifts to other beverages, labor availability, ingredient scarcity, and so on.

After evaluating the opportunities and threats relative to strengths and weaknesses, the team will have clear idea of whether the strengths are sufficient to counter the weaknesses and whether the opportunities are big enough to overcome potential threats. If not, perhaps a different concept or objective would be more appropriate.

For an example of applying the SWOT analysis, consider putting a small cidery in the rural Pacific Northwest near a tourist town. The cider would use all local ingredients and mountain hand-harvested fruits. The objectives would be quality and sustainability, since the fruit would be harvested locally and the business would contribute to the local community with employees and sales tax as well as provide a tourist activity. By conducting a complete SWOT analysis illustrated in Figure 8.6, the business owner(s) would have to decide if the strengths overcome the weaknesses and opportunities outweigh the threats.

Production Growth Strategy

A production beverage facility faces different strategic issues depending on its size. In the initial stages, the business is most concerned with raising funds, developing a brand, and deciding on the right business model (such as a tasting room, self-distribution, and/or buying club). Often, the busi-

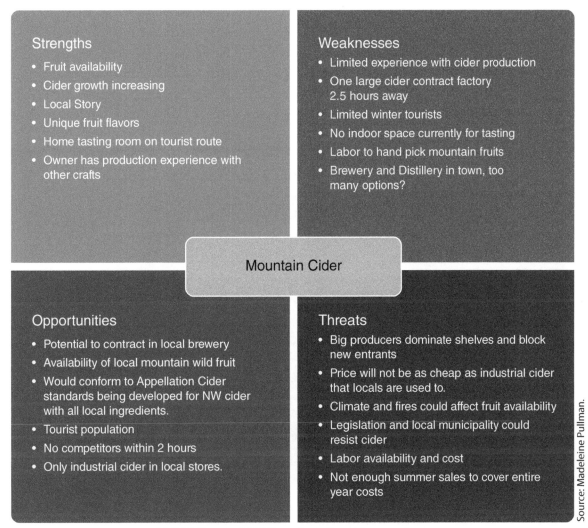

FIGURE 8.6   SWOT analysis for cider producer

Source: Madeleine Pullman.

ness is in a good position to experiment with products and get feedback from customers to establish a portfolio.

As the business grows, developing appropriate sales and marketing strategies and human resource strategies becomes more important. During this emergent phase, decisions about moving from self-distribution to a third-party distributor take on more significance since self-distribution becomes more challenging. The business may require more experienced employees; experienced brewers, cider or spirit makers will require better benefits and pay.

As the business grows to a large microbrewery, micro-cidery, or micro-distillery (but still under 15,000 barrels or the equivalent), the business model may need to change to remain competitive. Significantly more money and sophisticated financing is required for growth. The human resource strategy also becomes more sophisticated with career development tracks and appropriate retention incentives and benefits as well as finding appropriate skilled management from outside the company

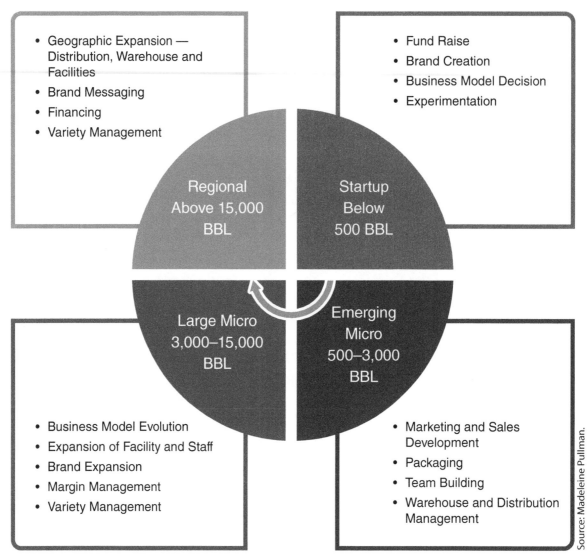

- Geographic Expansion — Distribution, Warehouse and Facilities
- Brand Messaging
- Financing
- Variety Management

- Fund Raise
- Brand Creation
- Business Model Decision
- Experimentation

Regional
Above 15,000
BBL

Startup
Below
500 BBL

Large Micro
3,000–15,000
BBL

Emerging
Micro
500–3,000
BBL

- Business Model Evolution
- Expansion of Facility and Staff
- Brand Expansion
- Margin Management
- Variety Management

- Marketing and Sales Development
- Packaging
- Team Building
- Warehouse and Distribution Management

Source: Madeleine Pullman.

FIGURE 8.7   Production strategic growth issues

for key roles. Managing the cost and revenues streams take on a big emphasis as does the role and dynamics of distribution.

As the business moves to a more regional distribution model and higher volumes of production, it faces fierce competition from more established players in the market. Retaining the brand's story and reputation is key, and the role of the distributors and financing relationships come to the forefront to cover the functional aspects of expansion. Operations and warehousing management and control systems in addition to strategic investments in information technologies are other significant areas that need to evolve.

Pub-Restaurant Strategies

In the craft business, another strategic decision is whether or not to include food. Some opt out and go for a tasting room model to reduce complexity and create higher margins. Other breweries start as a production site and eventually add food—and in some cases hotels, theatres, and music venues as in the case of McMenamins Breweries based in Portland, Oregon.

Key questions about adding food operations include the following:

1. Does food need to be part of the mix to have a retail sales outlet? Some localities require a certain percentage of food sales to operate as a brewpub.

2. If food is required, how will it complement the beverages?

3. Does food broaden or narrow the customer base? As a rule, food broadens the base by bringing in families, groups, and individuals that enjoy craft beverages or want hang out with those that do. Brewpub food is typically more affordable than fine dining. But bringing in families with small kids can conflict with the serious beverage aficionados, so the facility design should take each group into consideration, as shown in Figure 8.8.

4. How does the food strategy align with the beverage strategy? If the beverage is all about quality or sustainability, then the food must match that objective. Similarly with innovation, an innovative beverage producer should have a creative food program.

5. How can food contribute to differentiating the brand?

6. How will food impact the overall profitability of the business?

FIGURE 8.8   Brewpub with kid's area

Brewpubs are no longer novel in the beer world of beer. But for cider and spirits, the pub model has barely been scratched. Since the food in craft beverage restaurants over the past 20 to 30 years has tended to be very similar, customers are ready for concept innovation in this area. Also, in a saturated craft market, a neighborhood pub or a chain of pubs is one approach to avoid the crowding on retail shelves, especially if the developing areas of a city lack craft pubs.

McMenamins' Craft Beverage Empire

McMenamins defines itself as a "neighborhood gathering spot" that happen to exist in 65 unique locations throughout Oregon and Washington. Over the course of 30 years and employing 2,300 people, the company has built an empire encompassing a vast array of pubs, hotels, movie theaters, concert venues, spas, and event spaces—and all of them serving McMenamins' craft beverages.

Pioneers in craft brewing, the McMenamin brothers Mike and Brian opened the first post-Prohibition brewpub in Oregon in 1985. That same year, they were the first to incorporate fruit legally into brewing using raspberries in the company's Ruby Ale. In addition to beer, McMenamins produces wine, spirits, coffee, and cider. Kurt Widmer of Widmer Brewing credits McMenamins with making brewpubs and microbrews appealing to a wide range of people.

Distinctive venues are one of the company's major attributes that continue to intrigue a broad-based market. The first McMenamins' theater—and Oregon's first theater-pub—Mission Theater and Pub, opened in 1987. In 1990, the company entered the hospitality business with Edgefield, a 74-acre resort on an historic poor farm that includes lodging, golf, wine making, distilling, and gardening. The Crystal Ballroom followed in 1997 and hosts nationally recognized music acts in downtown Portland.

McMenamins locations are renovated historical properties including nine on the National Register of Historic Places. Venues include former churches, a former elementary school, a former brothel, and a pioneer homestead. McMenamins is a caretaker of these old buildings, restoring them and celebrating their history. Each location is quirky and eccentric, but consistently styled, from the décor to the menu, with the McMenamins brand.

The McMenamins brothers set the foundation for a new Oregon law, clearing the way for breweries to sell their own beer on-site, as well as allowing for one brewpub to brew for up to three separate outlets. This strategy enabled McMenamins to brew and distribute its own beers to its many locations, eliminating the immense cost of setting up new breweries at each place. Rather than sticking to one formula, McMenamins constantly creates innovative concepts for its span of businesses.

McMenamins pubs do sell other brewery's beers, but the majority of its pubs sales are McMenamins own. Along with the standard line of beers, the names of which are well known among Northwest beer drinkers, each location's brewer makes custom beers. Revenue from the pubs, hotels, theaters, music venues, golf courses, and spas exceeded $100 million as of 2015.

McMenamins' latest endeavor is a bottle shop in Northwest Portland, selling the multitude of goods developed over the years, including beers, wines, ciders, distilled spirits, merchandise, and other brewer's beers. McMenamins also recently took outside investment for the first time to fund a new resort in Washington and an expansion of Edgefield. Brian McMenamin explains their goal of constantly reinventing themselves in order to "avoid becoming a place your parents used to go." McMenamins not only lay the groundwork for Oregon brewpubs by pushing new legislation, but stays relevant in the competitive marketplace with eccentric neighborhood sites and excellent quality products.

SUMMARY

Strategic planning applies to either new or existing business. Some businesses hold quarterly or yearly meetings with staff and board members to talk about strategy. For others strategy is part of everyday conversations when management considers whether to introduce a new beer or cider or spirit product, when purchasing new equipment, or hiring a new employee. Successful business owners strive to understand the implications of different strategic decisions and make an appropriate choice based on current and projected market conditions.

Oskar Blues Growth Strategy through Craft in Cans

Oskar Blues, founded in Longmont, Colorado by Dale Katechis in 2002 is credited with pioneering craft beer in cans. The brewery's first cans were Dale's Pale Ale, named "Best Pale Ale" by the New York Times in 2005. By 2011, roughly 50 other craft breweries were canning beer, and grew to 262 breweries by 2013. Oskar Blues is the largest craft brewery in the United States to have never packaged its product in glass bottles. In doing so, this craft brewer helped to break the taboo against canned beer.

The decision to package in aluminum cans had its risks, given that canned beer was associated with cheap macro-beer brands at the time. However, Katechis believed canning was the superior packaging choice. Cans protect the quality of the beer, blocking out light. They are also lightweight, resulting in logistical cost savings. Canning craft beer has grown in popularity in recent years, and rather than being concerned with other craft breweries entering the canning market, Oskar Blues welcomes the widened acceptance that legitimizes the package and enforces the trend.

Initially, Oskar Blues was 100 percent self-distributed with Katechis himself bringing the beer to potential clients. Although it's common for craft breweries to establish their brand before warehouses pick them up, the decision to self-distribute was intentional for Oskar Blues. Early on, Katechis realized the need to educate retailers on the benefits of the can and to offer samplings of his beer. Eventually the brand was able to speak for itself, and the brewery captured the attention of many distributors that desired something slightly different in their portfolio.

Despite never having any trouble with distributors, Oskar Blues initially approached opening new markets cautiously, focusing on existing markets. In 2014, Oskar Blues quickly expanded into five new markets in the span of 60 days, partnering with family-owned distributors across each state and hosting launch parties.

Oskar Blues received a lot of media attention in 2010 when it was named one of the hottest brands by *Advertising Age*, listed as one of the fastest-growing companies by *Inc.* Magazine, and featured on the cover of *Market Watch* magazine. The brewing company landed back on *Inc.*'s fastest growing list in 2014 after having consistent double- and triple- digit growth for nine straight years, maintaining its spot in 2015 as well.

Once the Colorado facility had reached its limits, Katechis had to decide between building another facility nearby, adding on to the existing facility, or opening an East Coast brewery to save on shipping costs. The latter proved to be the right choice, given that 45 percent of Oskar Blues beer was sold in the eastern United States. Oskar Blues opened up its second brewery in Brevard, North Carolina in 2012. After only a few months of consideration, Oskar Blues closed on the new site in September and was shipping beer out of it by December. Initially producing 40,000 barrels, this second brewery has the potential to scale up to 85,000 barrels.

Other well-known craft breweries Sierra Nevada and New Belgium elected to build breweries in the area soon thereafter, enhancing an already thriving craft brewing scene. In 2015, both East and West Oskar Blues facilities expanded. The North Carolina facility added a second 50-barrel mash tun, and the Colorado site expanded by 60,000 square feet, adding oak aging and an event venue.

Over roughly 15 years, Oskar Blues rapidly went from a small pub, brewing in the basement, hand-canning, and self-distributing to production of 149,000 barrels between the two facilities. Katechis credits Oskar Blues' ability to make quick decisions and act fast to the fact that he's the only owner, and the company is nimble with limited financial debt.

After having raised enough cash in 2015, Oskar Blues acquired its first brewery, Michigan's Perrin Brewing, and has a goal of purchasing like-minded breweries in a variety of regional markets. In the fall of 2015 the brewery announced plans of opening up a 50,000 square foot brewing facility and music venue in Austin, Texas, bring it to three total facilities nationally.

Oskar Blues distributed to 44 states in 2015. Today it is one of the top 30 breweries in the United State and has plans to sell in all 50 states by mid-2016. The brewery's flagship pale ale still accounts for 50 percent of the brand mix.

LEARNING ADVENTURES

1. Find the vision, mission, core values, and beliefs for a company that you admire by searching online. How does this play out in in their strategic plan? What can you specifically see in their branding, marketing, and operational activities that illustrate the vision and plan?

2. Perform a SWOT analysis for your own concept or an existing brand in your area. What are your conclusions about the viability of this concept or brand in the long-term?

ENDNOTES

1. "New Belgium Brewing Purpose Statement," New Belgium Brewing Company, http://www.newbelgium.com/Brewery/company/history.aspx.

2. "Mission and Vision," Quest Brewing Company, http://questbrewing.com/the-brewery/mission-vision.

3. "Champlain Orchards' Mission, Value, and Vision Statements," Champlain Orchards Cidery, http://www.champlainorchardscidery.com/mission.

4. "Company Core Values and Beliefs," New Belgium Brewing Company, http://www.newbelgium.com/Brewery/company/history.aspx.

5. "7 Great Places to Work," *CNN Money*, last modified June 8, 2009, http://money.cnn.com/galleries/2009/smallbusiness/0906/gallery.best_small_companies.fsb/3.html.

CHAPTER NINE

Operations Plan

Key Terms

capacity
description
entire cycle
flagship

gantt chart
operational plan
production capacity
retail plan

startup
visual diagram of process

Overview

The operational plan is a major section of the business plan. This plan is highly detailed information that informs the reader (investors and staff) about the day-to-day tasks required for running production. How exactly is the product made and how much can be produced per month or year? Existing businesses use the tools of operations planning on a daily basis to schedule equipment and employees. It gives the production manager an idea of the current capacity of the facility and an opportunity to see how capacity might change with the addition of certain equipment or more employee time. With knowledge of future equipment and labor needs, the production manager can make decisions about the appropriate facility or make changes to a current facility, including hiring and training employees.

Learning Objectives

▶ Develop an operational plan.

▶ Draw a visual diagram of the process.

▶ Create a Gantt chart of beverage production processes from ingredients to packaging for startup and full production.

▶ Understand and calculate production capacity.

▶ Establish where expansion resources will be needed in the future.

▶ Determine a facility's and retail space's role in the business.

▶ Estimate the product projections for three years based on basic revenue estimates.

Introduction

The operations plan is the who, what, where, when and how of a business plan. With a vision in place, the plan indicates what the business proposes to make and how the business will accomplish this feat. Typically, a business should be planning at least three years into the future and addresses the roles for production, restaurant/pub or tasting room, and distribution where relevant.

Description: The operations plan covers every detail about how the business will make the craft beverage. For example, a cidery would address the following questions: Will the business have an orchard or will it purchase fruit to be pressed? If not, where will the juice come from and what type of juice will be purchased (from dessert or cider apples)? How long will the juice ferment and then condition? What kinds of additions are expected after conditioning and how will the product be packaged?

FIGURE 9.1   Operational plan

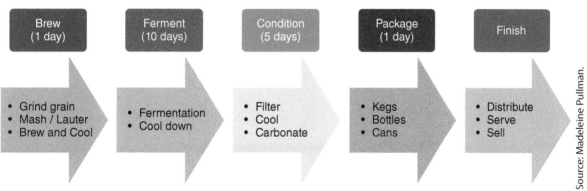

FIGURE 9.2   Visual diagram

Source: Madeleine Pullman.

Similarly, with a distillery, the plan would outline the production process from the raw ingredients and transformation to the finished product. If producing an aged product, like whiskey, then what other revenue source will carry the business through until the initial release (vodka, gin, rum, or cordials, for instance)? Finally, a brewery's operational plan, would address questions like, what will the predominant style be, what are the steps to achieving a finished product, and, how often will seasonal beers be introduced?

All of these production steps have implications for the cash flow and profitability of the business; for this reason, a business plan should spell out these details so that the financial implications are clear. Specifically, production volume, capacity, sales, and potential income from the particular production strategy should all be included for the three year period. In addition, the resources, such as equipment, space, people, and so on, required to get to each yearly production volume should be addressed in the plan.

Visual diagram of the process: To supplement the verbal description of the operational plan, it is helpful to provide a visual of how the process works. Potential timeframes specified in each production step help to emphasize the production cycle times and the areas that consume the most time, as shown in Figure 9.2.

Sample Process Descriptions and Visuals

This section provides brief overviews of a sample process description and a visual for a brewery and distillery. (These do not show capacity or estimated production volumes, which will be illustrated later in this chapter.)

Brewery: The brewery aims to produce a **flagship** and two additional beers (initially) of ale style. The business hopes to expand to four seasonal and other rotating beers on tap in the pub. The beer is made from regional local barley malts which are milled into grist in the first day of the cycle. The grist is then mixed with hot water in a mash/lauter and then the wort is transferred into the brew kettle. After boiling in the kettle with hops, the wort is cooled and transferred into a fermenter. Yeast is added and the beer ferments for 10 days. Afterwards, it is transferred to a conditioning tank for clarification and carbonation. After four to five days, it is ready to package or serve in the pub. The startup system can produce 12 batches per month (six flagship and three of each specialty).

BEER PRODUCTION

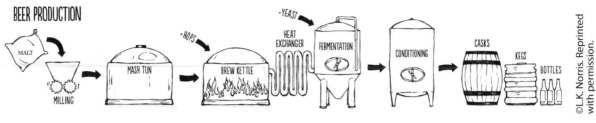

FIGURE 9.3   Brewery process

SPIRITS DISTILLING

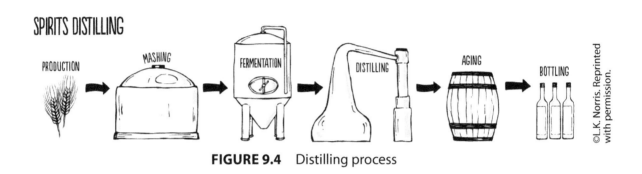

FIGURE 9.4   Distilling process

Distillery: The distillery plans to produce an aged whiskey (three years) from regionally produced barley malt. Additional products will be aperitif infusions from spirits with local herbs, botanicals, and fruits similar to products from European monasteries.

The local malt will be ground and mashed for a wash (one day). The resulting product will be rapidly fermented (three days) and distilled (one to two days). The spirit will go into barrel aging for whiskey (three years) or through a secondary distillation (one day) and infusion for the aperitif line (one month) prior to bottling. The distillery plans to offer four to six different aperitifs per year initially as well as a botanical gin. The whiskey will be released in three years and will be available each year after that.

Gantt Chart

The **Gantt chart** is a basic visual planning tool that shows the entire production cycle for a batch and helps determine the **capacity** of a system. The tool is also used to schedule products through the operation. This hypothetical example uses the production description from the brewery provided earlier. Beer is brewed in one day and transferred to a fermenter where it sits for seven to 10 days and is then transferred to the conditioning/brite tank for four to five days. On the last day, it is packaged or kegged. The day for each stage is at the top and the boxes are colored to indicate each brew going through the equipment; for example, the highlighted red color indicates one brew (perhaps an IPA) going through the system. On day 10, the brew leaves the fermenter and goes into a conditioning tank. It moves out of the conditioning tank on day 14 to packaging or kegging. Looking at the chart, you can see that the **entire cycle** for this hypothetical brew takes 14 days. Now, for some breweries, 14 days would be the absolute minimum and often they would age longer. Also, many specialty beers

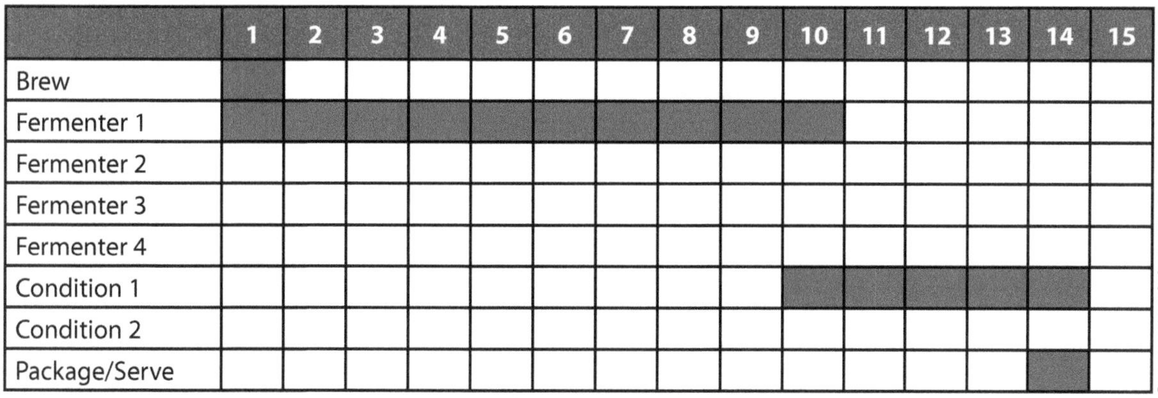

	1	2	3	4	5	6	7	8	9	10	11	12	13	14	15
Brew	█														
Fermenter 1		█	█	█	█	█	█	█	█	█					
Fermenter 2															
Fermenter 3															
Fermenter 4															
Condition 1										█	█	█	█	█	
Condition 2															
Package/Serve														█	

FIGURE 9.5   Gantt chart for one cycle

Source: Madeleine Pullman.

will take longer to produce so when planning production, make sure to allow for this "play factor." The example in Figure 9.5 uses 14 days to keep things simple.

For a **startup** brewery with the goal of having a variety of beers available on opening day, you can fill out the entire production schedule for a facility with four fermenters.[1] In Figure 9.6 each brew has a different color and is moved into an empty tank as soon as possible. With this schedule, eight brews are completed in 30 days. Note, this chart does not show the labor needed on each day but it is very easy to add the individual employees and therefore to see where there might be some labor constraints in achieving this schedule.

Once the facility gets beyond the startup phase you can see the actual output of a fully operational brewery with four fermenters and two conditioning tanks, presuming that every tank is refilled as soon as it is emptied in Figure 9.7. Notice that from day 31 to day 60, 12 brews came out of this system, so the capacity is 12 per month.

Calculating Production Capacity

Using the Gantt chart, you can visually understand the capacity of the system. You can also calculate what another fermenter or conditioning tank might offer if you had the opportunity to purchase an additional tank. Typically, the process that takes the most time dictates the capacity, so take a look at which stage takes the most time:

▶ Four fermenters with a fermentation time of 10 days. A batch will leave a fermenter every 10-days/four fermenters. So, a batch leaves the fermenter every **2.5 days.**

▶ Two conditioners with conditioning time of four days minimum. A batch will leave a conditioning tank every four days/two conditioners. So, a batch leaves the conditioning tank every **two days.**

▶ So, most time consuming is fermenters (**2.5** vs. **two days**).

▶ Assume 30 days/month.

▶ 30 days/ **2.5** days per batch = 12 batches per month maximum (as seen in Figure 9.7).

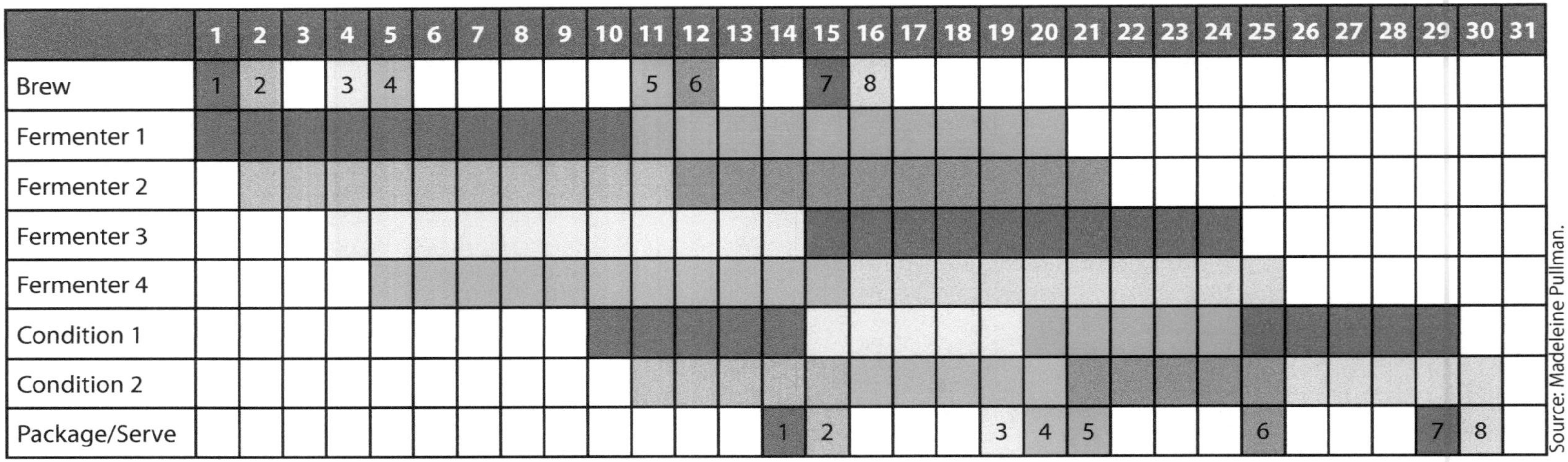

FIGURE 9.6   Gantt chart for startup month

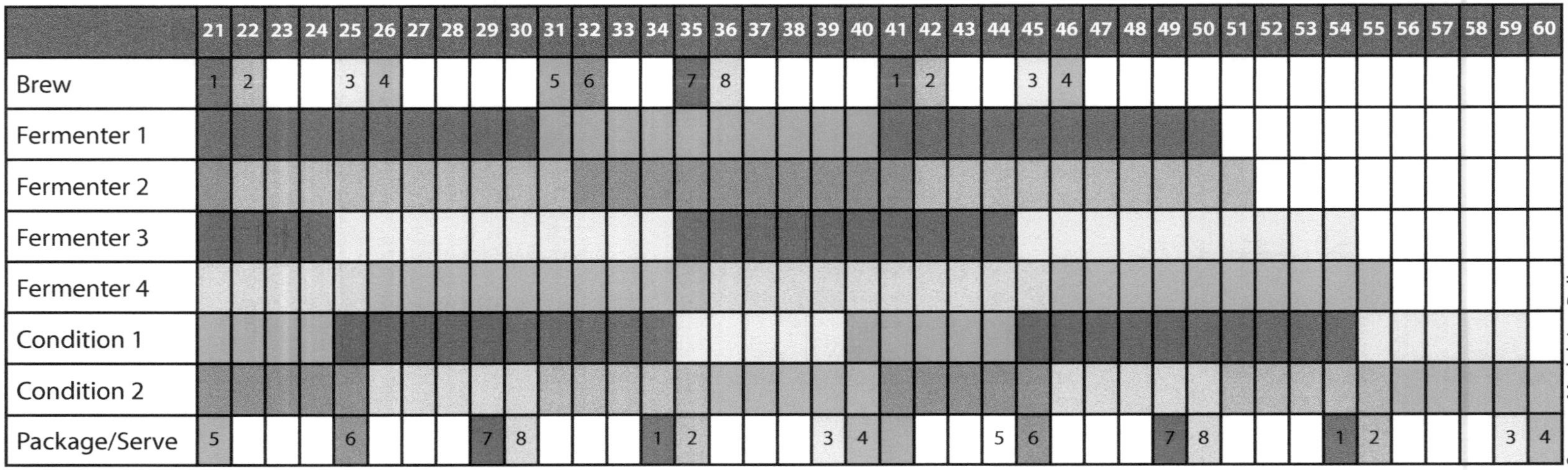

Source: Madeleine Pullman.

	1	2	3	4	5	6	7	8	9	10	11	12	13	14	15	16	17	18	19	20	21	22	23	24	25	26	27	28	29	30	31
Brew	1	2		3	4						5	6			7	8															
Fermenter 1																															
Fermenter 2																															
Fermenter 3																															
Fermenter 4																															
Condition 1																															
Condition 2																															
Package/Serve														1	2				3	4	5				6				7	8	

FIGURE 9.7   Gantt chart for full operations

Source: Madeleine Pullman.

	21	22	23	24	25	26	27	28	29	30	31	32	33	34	35	36	37	38	39	40	41	42	43	44	45	46	47	48	49	50	51	52	53	54	55	56	57	58	59	60
Brew		1	2		3	4					5	6			7	8					1	2			3	4														
Fermenter 1																																								
Fermenter 2																																								
Fermenter 3																																								
Fermenter 4																																								
Condition 1																																								
Condition 2																																								
Package/Serve	5					6				7	8			1	2				3	4				5	6				7	8					1	2			3	4

FIGURE 9.8   Fermenter additions

It is also important to know what the yearly amount produced on a brewing system might be. If this facility had a seven-barrel brew house with tanks of the same size, it could produce a little more than 1,000 barrels per year.

$$7 \; bbl. \; \times \; 12 \; \frac{batches}{month} \times 12 \; months = 1008 \; bbl./year$$

For a company with the goal to double that production for the second year, it could add two 15-barrel fermenters and one 15-barrel conditioner, brewing twice a day to fill the larger fermenters to 14 barrels, or two smaller tanks and more than double capacity to over 2,000 barrels per year.

- ► Two large fermenters (14 barrel) and four smaller (seven barrel) with a fermentation time of 10 days. A 14-barrel batch will leave the fermenters every 10 days/four fermenters. So, a 14-barrel batch leaves the fermenter every **2.5 days.**

- ► Two small conditioners (seven barrel) and one large (14 barrel) with conditioning time of four days minimum. A batch will leave a conditioning tank every four days/two conditioners. So, a batch leaves the conditioning tank every **two days.**

- ► The most time consuming is fermenters (**2.5** vs. **two days**).

- ► Assume 30 days/month.

- ► 30 days/ **2.5** days per batch = 12 (14-barrel batches) per month maximum.

$$14 \; bbl. \; \times \; 12 \; \frac{batches}{month} \times 12 \; months = 2016 \; bbl./year$$

TABLE 9.1 Equipment and labor capacity needs

	Production (bbl.)	Capital equipment	Brew house employees	Packaging staff
Year 1	1000	Start up package	Brewer and assistant	2 PT bottlers
Year 2	2000	2–15 bbl. fermenters and cond.	Brewer and 2 assistants	3 PT bottlers
Year 3	4000	Whirlpool, 2–4 fermenters and cond.	2 Brewers and 2–3 assistants	3 FT bottlers
Source: Madeleine Pullman.				

To double production again for the third year, the operation could buy a separate whirlpool, more fermenters/conditioners and brew four times a day to get to 4,000 barrels per year. In Table 9.1, the equipment strategy and **production capacity** is shown as well as the employee needs. Estimating employee needs will be explored further in Chapter 13: Entity and Team.

Plan Details for Production and Retail Facility's Roles

The operational plan should also contain more details about the production and retail space. When considering production, the plan should outline whether the business is producing for distributed production via packaging and kegging versus in-house (tasting room or pub) kegs sales and other in-house sales. The plan should provide an estimate about the number of products in the standard portfolio and seasonals.

For most businesses, the mix of packaged product to keg product will not stay the same through a three-year growth projection. In the example in Table 9.2, the year 1 packaged and kegged product makes up 20 percent and 80 percent of production volume respectively. The packaged percentage increases over time while the kegged percentage decreases. In year 1, the 800 barrels of keg product equals 1,600 kegs and they are split between in-house keg sales (pub/tasting room), retail keg sales from the dock, and wholesale keg sales via distribution.

The packaged product should also be delineated. In this example illustrated in Table 3, the in-house bottle percentage of total bottle sales decreases (even though the actual volume increases since total bottle production is increasing every year). The remaining bottles are projected to sell via distribution or the wholesale market. It is generally harder to expand in-house bottle sales relative to wholesale bottle sales over time.

TABLE 9.2   Kegged product three-year projections

	Total production (bbl.)	Production packaged (bbl.) 20, 30, 50%	Production kegged (bbl.) 80, 70, 50%	In house keg sales ($600/k)	Retail kegs dock ($130/k)	Wholesale kegs ($90/k)
Year 1	1000	200	800	1000	100	500
Year 2	2000	600	1200	1200	200	1000
Year 3	4000	2000	2000	1600	250	2150
Source: Madeleine Pullman.						

TABLE 9.3   Bottled product three-year projections

	Bottle production (bbl.)	In house bottle sales (bbl.) 25, 20, 10%	Wholesale bottle sales (bbl.)
Year 1	200	50	150
Year 2	600	120	480
Year 3	2000	200	1800
Source: Madeleine Pullman.			

After providing a volume estimate for channels (i.e., in-house versus wholesale), it is relatively straightforward to translate this into sales revenue with retail and wholesale package and keg price in the financial estimates.

For businesses with a retail aspect such as pub/restaurant, or tasting room, the **retail plan** should cover the role of the retail space in enough detail to get a sense of the following:

▶ What will the retail space offer? Food? Number of potential taps? Guest taps? Other alcohol and in-house beverages? Other products such as clothing, hats, growlers, glassware, and so on?

▶ How many seats will the retail space have? Inside seating? Outside seating? Lunch and dinner? Potential hours of operations per day?

▶ Are there other sales opportunities for the retail space? Private events? Tours and tastings for a fee?

©Anton_Ivanov/Shutterstock.com

FIGURE 9.9 Retail role

SUMMARY

An operational plan sets the stage for understanding the capacity of the production system, and hence the potential revenue that can come out of that equipment. A key thing to remember is that planned capacity might not end up as actual production. In the winter months, demand can be slow and any tank not filled leads to lost capacity for the year. An alternative is to produce and store product for the busy times. This strategy is really only feasible for products with long shelf lives. The plan will change over time and will be affected by the overall strategy, the marketing and distribution strategy, and of course, the available cash for purchasing equipment and hiring more staff. The Gantt chart is useful for many aspects of scheduling, such as ordering packaging or raw materials with enough lead time, figuring out if enough kegs are in stock to fill in the future, planning for seasonal releases and promotions activities, and creating an employee schedule.

Operations Overhaul at Reverend Nat's Hard Cider

Today, craft cider is where craft beer stood 20 years ago: on the cusp of staggering growth. As large brewing companies popularize hard cider among new consumers there is great opportunity for startups with distinctive handcrafted ciders to make a big impression in this niche. Reverend Nat's Hard Cider in Portland, Oregon is one such success story.

When Nat West (an ordained minister turned "cider evangelist") started making cider in his basement in 2012, he had no plans for retail sales. He sold the first keg of Reverend Nat's Hard Cider at a local cider shop, followed by the first bottles of Reverend Nat's as soon as they were ready. West self-distributed, personally introducing his product to retailers and pub owners, and he quickly had Reverend Nat's in nine establishments in the Portland area. With the flagship cider launched, West went to work on three other cider varieties and introduced them at summer craft cider and brewery festivals. The thirsty craft consuming public instantly recognized Reverend Nat's Hard Cider as an innovative and exciting cider brand, and it took off.

West thought about production methods for cider in two modes: either beer style or wine style. Beer style cider making was fast, involving a variety of apples or juice throughout the year to keep the production line flowing steadily. The shortest time from fruit to bottle was six weeks. On the other end of the spectrum, wine-style cider involved more expensive traditional cider apples from a single harvest. Slower paced, the cider spent more time in the tanks and bottle aging.

During the fall harvest season Reverend Nat's purchased Oregon apples while packing houses in Washington, New York, California, and Michigan filled in during the off-season. In 2012, the in-season mixed apple bins cost 30 cents per pound and juice culls averaged five to ten cents per pound. The apples came in cold, and Reverend Nat's turned them into juice as quickly as possible since they were more stable in that form, and the high sugar level yielded higher gravity and better flavor.

From the outset, the cidery invested in high-quality apple pressing equipment. With a Goodnature Squeezebox SX-200, it took two days to press a truckload of about 48 bins of apples running from 6 a.m. to 10 p.m. with two shifts of two people. One person operated the machine while the other unloaded apple bins, sorted apples, and kept the grinder running. Once they completed the juicing, the cleaning took another four hours. Cost wise, the company determined that pressing juice was cheaper than purchasing fresh juice.

West's original in-home production facility produced a 300-gallon batch of cider using an intermediate bulk container (IBC) and a 10-barrel brite tank from 3,200 pounds of apples. West chose plastic IBCs instead of stainless steel fermenters because plastic was inexpensive with a much quicker delivery time.

In addition to excellent apple-only ciders, West experimented with apricots, hops, pineapple, hibiscus, and even coffee. One his first hits was Hallelujah Hopricot, a cider brewed with apricot juice. Dry hopped just before bottling using whole-leaf hops rather than pellets, it had a robust aroma; "beer, cider, and wine all in one." This flagship product set Reverend Nat's apart and remains the company's best-seller with year-round availability.

Within months of its first sale, Reverend Nat's landed a distribution deal with Columbia Distributing. A large distributor with several well-known cider clients, it brought Reverend

Nat's a wide geographic reach within the Pacific Northwest, a great leg up for a startup. The challenge for the small company was how to fast track to commercial scale cider making.

West's first order of business was to increase speed and efficiency by investing in new and expensive equipment. Growth involved upgrades to the press and grinder, building out the new space, replacing the IBCs with stainless steel, additional employees, a cross-flow filter and a big pasteurizer. West had decided to pasteurize his cider for microbiological stability and to avoid the bottles from exploding due to active yeasts. Initially financed with personal credit cards and family loans, Reverend Nat's leased equipment from friends in the industry, and then turned to local investors. Final financing came from community development financial institutions (CDFI). The expansion also incurred more labor, including a production manager with a decade of brewing experience to oversee the staff.

The new cidery space dwarfed the original basement production facility by 2,000 percent. It offered plenty of room for new growth plus a public tasting room selling retail pints from Reverend Nat's growing portfolio of hard ciders plus special releases too limited for bottling. The taproom proved to be such a worthwhile investment for the company, West expanded its hours to host the public six nights a week, including specials before the nearby Portland Trailblazer's games as well as organizing an annual cider festival.

LEARNING ADVENTURES

1. Write an operational plan with an accompanying visual of the process.

2. Create a simple Gantt chart for one batch of product.

3. Create a startup Gantt chart using the "Scheduling for Opening Day" paper referenced in the endnotes.

4. Create an expansion growth plan with equipment and labor needs.

5. Create a keg or bottled project sales projection for three years.

ENDNOTES

1. Teri Farendorf, "Scheduling for Opening Day: Timing of Startup Beers," (2010), http//:www.terifahrendorf.com/Scheduling-for-Opening-Day.pdf.

CHAPTER TEN

Equipment

Key Terms

aesthetics	distillery grain system	pallet jacks
alembic still	equipment	point of sale (POS) system
auger	fixed costs	pot still
break-even analysis	grinder	press
brew house	heat exchanger	raw material handling
brewing system	hot liquor tank	right sizing
brite tank	hybrid pot-column still	sparge
cellaring equipment	intermediate bulk container (IBC)	steam heated
cider house	kegging equipment	variable costs
column still	lautering vessel	wash
conditioning tank	mash tun	wort chiller
continuous still	nano	
direct fired	packaging equipment	

Overview

This chapter surveys the production equipment required to start and grow a craft beverage business. The cost and size of equipment should align with the business's strategy and concept as well as the potential market demand. As a rule, production facilities are bigger than retail facilities like pubs-restaurants or tasting rooms since a production facility services many other outlets. The chapter also illustrates a break-even analysis to demonstrate how long it takes to pay off a particular piece of equipment or a complete brewing or distilling system.

Learning Objectives

► Understand a starting equipment package.

► Determine the equipment additions that are needed as production grows.

► Estimate costs of different equipment.

► Establish what size is right for the market and concept.

► Understand the difference between fixed and variable costs related to equipment use and investment.

► Determine a break-even point for equipment investment.

► Apply a break-even analysis to appropriate grain storage systems, packaging equipment, and the overall capital investment.

Introduction

Equipment is one of the biggest investments that a craft beverage business makes outside of a real estate purchase. Some entrepreneurs choose to rent buildings and, likewise, you can rent equipment from various services and manufacturers. Financial decisions about equipment at the startup and growth phase, as well as the replacement stage, have long-term implications for the business. Equipment choices impact not only the quality of the beverage but also affect things like product shelf life, appearance to outsiders, labor and utility requirements, and cash flow.

Seasoned beverage professionals agree that getting the best equipment possible makes all the difference in the world in producing a quality product. But money is always an issue, so it is common for businesses to start small with less than ideal equipment only later to invest in better equipment as cash flow improves. Another option to avoid the equipment and facility investment for startups is alternating proprietorships (AP) to rent use of an existing facility or contract from others to produce the product. Two advantages of an AP over contract arrangements include proprietary recipe protection and control of the process. Regardless, these arrangements are normally just starting points, and understanding the ins and outs of equipment costing is fundamental for all craft businesses.

Starting Small

One approach is to start small and build a market. A **nano** system is understood to mean a small **brewing system** but there is otherwise no consensus on the maximum size; it can range from a half barrel to 10-barrel system, referring to the batch size for a brewing setup. For the purpose of this discussion, a nano is considered to be sized at five barrels or less. Similar small systems can be purchased for distilleries; the yield for distilleries is closer to 10 percent of the still size; so, a one-barrel (31 gallon) still only produces a case or so of liter bottles. Besides the low cost, some of the advantages of nano systems are that they can fit into very small places and are often mobile, enabling the producer to roll the system out when needed and use the space for other activities when not needed.

FIGURE 10.1   Nano system

Source: Madeleine Pullman.

Many nano systems use standard utility voltage and water hookups, so they can fit into existing restaurants or a home garage without significant modifications. On the other hand, a nano system has very limited production. In order be profitable, almost all the product needs to be sold at retail full price rather than distributed at wholesale prices. So long as almost of the product is sold through a tasting room or pub, a business can turn a profit with 250 barrels per year for beer; the same is true of cider production on a small scale.

Major challenges for nano systems are the amount of effort required to produce a small amount of product. For example, to produce 250 barrels per year on a one-barrel brewing system requires 250 brew days. A 250-day brewing production schedule can quickly burn out brewers, especially considering how many other things that have to be done in a facility besides brewing. With a 10-barrel system, the equivalent amount is made in 25 days.

Similar problems happen with nano distilleries. Most nano systems are just a stepping stone to bigger systems; thus, the resale value of the small system is a consideration. If the equipment makers are backed up with orders and have long lead times, then equipment will hold its original value. That will not be the case if new and used equipment is easy to come by. Nanos are not an appropriate solution for seasonal markets, businesses with aggressive growth plans, and those that participate in distribution, festivals, donations, and other external events. The bottom line is that they simply do not have enough capacity.

Nano-Distillery Old Ballard Liquor Company

Old Ballard Liquor Company (OBLC) occupies just 750-square feet in a building on Seattle's old waterfront, but it fulfills a significant niche. OBLC introduced some of the first aquavits to craft spirits consumers in the United States. Lexi (who goes by her first name only) discovered aquavits while living in Sweden and now distills a short line of aquavits and a popular fruit-infused brandy called a bounce. Making as few as four cases from a 25-gallon still, Lexi has generated big waves for OBLC in the Scandinavian section of Seattle where she set up shop in the Northwest's cocktailing scene.

As the first nano-distillery in Washington state, OBLC makes the most of its still and tasting room space. Because aquavit demands only minimal aging, Lexi can keep production flowing to generate needed revenue. And, by offering a flagship line of aquavits plus many seasonal one-offs, Lexi always has new samples to offer her customers. Nano-distilling has given the business the ideal balance of production and innovation that has made OBLC a standout in its market.

Three aquavits—caraway, lemon, and dill, all based on classic Scandinavian libations—are the core of OBLC's portfolio. A stream of other creative, small-batch aquavits keep things interesting, while the cherry bounce and seasonal vodkas round out the company's offerings.

Lexi herself is equally renowned for her skills in educating customers about this novel product's history, production, flavorings, and customs—both inside the tasting room and in classes, workshops, and festivals. Notably, food pairing at tasting are increasingly important at these events.

Specialized, small, and seasonal are OBLC's strengths in a locavore culture like Seattle's. Its experience demonstrates how size has no bearing on brand impact when the concept and quality are high value. What remains to be seen is how Lexi copes with space and equipment needs as demand increases (including a recent distribution deal for OBLC aquavits outside of the Seattle area) and how OBLC will adapt to those changes.

From One to Five Barrels at Dragon's Gate Brewery

Starting small was a necessity as well as a strategy for Dragon's Gate Brewery owners Adam and Jennifer Gregory. They opened their farmhouse brewery, located near the wine-growing region on the Oregon and Washington border, using a one-barrel system. With other full-time jobs, a nano brewery fit their lifestyle and their mission to handcraft Belgian-style beers. On their 10 acres, the couple grew nine hops varieties, harvesting, processing, and hand selecting them for each beer. They brewed in 20-gallon batches and bottled unfiltered, unpasteurized, and bottle conditioned in 750-ml custom-made bottles with grolsch-style tops.

> The labor and attention to quality paid off in an unexpectedly huge following of beer adventurers who flocked to the brewery for a taste of these scarce libations. After three years and a solid customer base, it was time for Dragon's Gate to expand beyond a 40-gallon capacity. The Gregory's invested in a five-barrel system and a quantity of wine barrels for a barrel-aged beer program. Taking small steps has allowed Dragon's Gate the luxury of crafting beers by hand while expanding its product line and producing just enough quantity to offer distribution for the first time to its growing fan base in the Pacific Northwest.

Basic Startup Package

All craft beverages need equipment for handling raw materials, extraction of fermentable sugars and juice via pressing, mashing, or water addition, cellaring activities (fermenters and conditioning tanks or barrels), refrigeration, and packaging. Some of these activities can be subcontracted to others like mobile packaging and juice or wort purchasing. If a cidery purchases juice, most of the investment will go into cellaring equipment. Distilleries do not need a brew kettle; instead they need a mash tun/lauter if using grain and a still. Spirits are not currently packaged in kegs or cans so basic bottling equipment is the only packaging choice.

Raw material handling: A brewery or grain-based distillery needs a method to weigh the grain (scale) and feed it into a mill (**auger** or manually). Afterwards, the crushed grain needs to be collected into buckets or augered into a hopper or directly into the mash tun. After completing the mash, there needs to be a method to remove the spent grain from facility. For small producers, this is done with rolling carts or bins on **pallet jacks**. Designing and investing in appropriate handling equipment are

TABLE 10.1   Starting equipment

System	Raw Material Handling Systems	Extraction			Cellar				Packaging
		Mash and lauter	Heat exchanger (reduce wort temp)	Still or kettle	Fermenters	Brite tanks	Glycol system and other refrigeration	Kegs or barrels	– Kegging – Canning – Bottling
Brewery	Grain	X	X	Kettle	X	X	X	X	All possible
Distillery	Grain Fruit Wort Base Spirit	X (grain)	X (grain)	Still	X			X	Bottles
Cidery	– Fruit – Juice	Grinder and press for fruit			X	X	X	X	All possible
Source: Madeleine Pullman.									

often overlooked aspects of startups. Unfortunately, poor designs lead to back breaking work, frustrated employees, and a lot of wasted movement.

For cideries pressing their own fruit, apples and pears come in large bins. The fruit can be moved from the bin onto a conveyer or manually to feed the fruit into a **grinder** and on to a **press**. At the press, a handling system feeds the ground fruit or pomace in the press and another handling system moves the spent fruit out of the facility. Similar to beer production, spent pomace is removed with rolling cars or bins with pallet jacks.

Brew house: A turnkey brewing package has four components: 1) mash/lauter tun, 2) kettle/whirlpool, 3) hot liquor tank, and 4) wort chiller and pump. The **mash tun** is where the crushed grain is mixed with hot water; the vessel should be insulated to maintain constant temperature. In the lautering stage, the spent grain is separated from the extracted liquid and the grain is rinsed or **sparged** with additional water to extract as much fermentable sugar as possible. This can be achieved with a separate **lautering vessel** or with a combination mash tun/lauter vessel with a false bottom and fittings designed for sparging and recirculation. Smaller facilities typically start with a combination tank rather than two separate tanks.

FIGURE 10.2 Grain mill

FIGURE 10.3 Fruit pressing

Photo © Portland Kettleworks. Reprinted with permission.

FIGURE 10.4   Brewing system

The extracted liquid goes into the **brew kettle**. The kettle can be **direct fired** with gas or **steam heated**. Steam designs cost more to purchase but are usually less expensive to operate. The steam jacket heats the kettle up very fast and the liquid does not have a propensity to get scorched or caramelized, something that can occur with direct-fire kettles. When the hops have been added and the beer has finished the boil time, the hot liquid or wort goes through a whirlpool stage. In a whirlpool vessel, the finished brew is pumped in at an angle so the liquid starts spinning like a whirlpool. This effect causes undesirable spent hops and sediment to separate out from wort and settle in the middle, clearer product can then move to the fermenters. Again, small producers whirl the liquid in the kettle with paddles or pumps to avoid getting a separate vessel for this task.

In the last phase, the hot wort is pumped through a **wort chiller**, a **heat exchanger** that drops its temperature from boiling down to temperatures that yeast can tolerate, usually under 70 degrees Fahrenheit (21 degrees Celsius). Heat exchangers use city or well water to drop the hot wort's temperature; the hot wort passes through one side and the cool water passes through the other side. As the wort cools, the city water gains quite a bit of heat in the process and this can be collected in a **hot liquor tank**. This hot liquor tank is also used to heat water for the initial mash step whether it is this reclaimed water or initial city water that must be brought up to mash temperature.

Distillery grain system: A distillery that needs to extract sugars from grain needs a similar setup to a brewery except the brewing kettle. The basic parts are the mash/lauter, wort receiving vessel, hot liquor tank, and a heat exchanger to reduce the wort temperature. Distilleries can also purchase wort from a brewery or use juices, other non-malted grains with enzymes, potatoes, sugar, cane juice, honey, maple syrup, and other products with fermentable sugar. These may require a vessel for blending or temperature adjustments prior the fermentation stage.

Cider house: Since the cider house deals with juice that is already cool or at room temperature, the juice can do directly into a tank for blending or directly into the fermenter.

Cellaring equipment: The cellaring activities include fermentation, filtering, carbonating, aging or conditioning, and refrigeration. All beverages spend time in the cellar and some spend substantial amounts of time maturing in barrels, like whiskey. Fermentation tanks often have cone-shaped

FIGURE 10.5   Cellaring equipment

Source: Portland Kettleworks.

bottoms to collect yeast. After completing fermentation, beer or cider generally goes to a **conditioning tank** also known as the **brite tank**. Brite tanks can be equipped with carbonation stones to add carbonation before packaging or kegging. Typically cellar vessels are jacketed so that a refrigerated solution can pass through the jacket and keep the vessel cool. Glycol is the most common solution for refrigeration, and a glycol cooling system is used to chill both fermenters and conditioning tanks to thermostatically controlled temperatures.

Ordinarily, cellar tanks are made of stainless steel but increasingly, some cidery and distilleries are fermenting in plastic **intermediate bulk containers** (IBCs), a low cost solution. IBCs come in various sizes but are most common in 275 gallons or 1,040 liters. Smaller stainless tanks and IBCs have their temperatures controlled in walk-in coolers or rooms rather than with glycol jackets.

Still: Two still types are commonly used to produce spirits, the **pot still** and the **column still.** The pot still, also known as the **alembic still**, has a round shape like a pot or tea kettle and heat is applied to this pot. As the liquid boils, the vapor collects in a thin tube leading to a condenser. The condenser is

FIGURE 10.6   Cider-making with IBCs

Source: Cider Riot!

water cooled, which changes the vapor to a liquid state and the liquid is collected (the spirit). Pot stills are not particularly energy efficient and produce one batch per run. They do provide for a unique flavor especially if directly heated rather than steam heated. Many whiskey makers swear by the pot still.

The column still is also known as a **continuous still** since, as the name implies, it can be run continuously with more liquid added rather than batch to batch. The column produces a higher concentration of alcohol and a pure spirit. The column still is actually two or more connected columns with plates on the bottoms. The liquid or **wash** enters at the top and moves downward through each subsequent plate where the liquid is vaporized and rises up through the plates concentrating the alcohol; thus vapor is rising while the wash is descending. The final column, usually made of copper, collects the alcohol. Column stills are popular for vodka production and other spirits that require a very pure taste. Now, there are some **hybrid pot-column stills** that help craft distillers create a variety of products with one still. These can have a column added for botanicals (vapor moves through the herbs and spices) to make gin.

Stills are generally more technical than brewing or cidery equipment, and they tend to cost more, especially for a showpiece still with a copper pot and other

FIGURE 10.7   Still

©Joshua Rainey Photography/Shutterstock.com

copper treatments to the column. They are frequently purchased from European manufacturers and are the most expensive piece of equipment that a distillery will purchase. A comparison of the costs for different equipment of various sizes is shown below.

TABLE 10.2   Basic cost estimates

	Nano (3 bbl.)	Medium (15 bbl.)	Larger (30 bbl.)
Grain mill and grist case	$2,000–$4,000	$6,000–$8,000	$8,000–$10,000
Augers (each)		$2,000–$3,000	$3,000–$4,000
Turnkey brewing System (electric-steam)	$20,000–$35,000	$80,000–$90,000	$130,000–$150,000
Mash tun alone	$2,000–$10,000	$20,000	$40,000
Uni-Tanks (jacketed)	$7,000–$9,000	$10,000–$16,000	$18,000–$20,000
Brite or blending tanks	$6,000–$8,000	$12,000–$14,000	$16,000–$20,000
Stills	* range from $50,000–$150,000 depending on multiple factors		
Glycol chiller	$3,000–$4,000	Estimated cost = $1.4 x (bbl. capacity/year) + $5,150	
Accessories plus installation	Portable pumps, filters, hoses, fittings, clamps, IBCs, aging barrels, racks, fork lift, or pallet jack, and the like		
Source: Madeleine Pullman.			

There are several key things to remember when planning for equipment. First, a brewing system (mash, lauter, kettle, whirlpool) can fill a fermenter two to four times depending on shift length, labor availability, and the addition of a separate whirlpool tank to allow the brew kettle to empty quickly. For example, a 15-barrel brewing system can run two back-to-back batches to fill a 30-barrel fermenter in one day. Generally, brewpubs need one or two fermenters per brite/serving tank; packagers need three or four fermenters per brite tank.

Distillers will only end up with 10 percent of the fermenter volume, give or take, after going through the still. Subsequent tanks for blending spirits or barrel needs will be much smaller than the still and fermenter volume. Even though more product will be lost during barrel aging due to evaporation, some of it will be gained back with water dilution prior to barrel aging or dilution to final packaging proof strength (unless making some kind of highly alcoholic or full strength spirit).

The price for a complete production system adds up quickly. The brewery system outlined in Table 10.3 has all the essential items including a cold liquor tank as a place to store and chill water to drop the temperature of the wort faster through the heat exchanger. And, some places do not have cold enough city or well water to cool their wort to an appropriate temperature. The tank is not necessary in many locations. Overall, the system can run $125 to $350 per barrel of annual capacity until producing over 10,000 barrels of product where prices can drop to $75 per barrel. The greater the capacity, the lower the price due to economy of scale. As an example, the system in Table 10.3 is $153 per barrel ($230,154/1500 bbl.).

Packaging and kegging: Startup **kegging equipment** includes two main components, a keg washing and sanitizing setup, and keg filler. Keg fillers require a method for counter-pressuring the keg while it fills with carbonated product. Very simple systems can be made in-house for both filling and cleaning for under $2,000 but more advanced systems, which are able to clean and fill multiple kegs per hour, start at $40,000 and go up from there. Obviously, the more expensive systems do a solid job cleaning and filling and insure a longer shelf life for the product.

TABLE 10.3 Sample 10-bbl. system (yearly capacity 1,500 bbl.)

Item	Sample Estimate
Milling and grist case setup	$10,000
Steam brew house (10 bbl.) (hot liquor, mash/lauder, brew kettle)	$80,000
Cold liquor tank (20 bbl.)	$17,000
Heat exchanger and pump and manifold	$13,000
5–10 bbl. fermenters (uni-tanks)	$70,000
2–10 bbl. brite tank	$22,000
Glycol chiller	$7,194
Subtotal	$219,194
Total (add installation and glycol, clamps, carbonation stone, etc. ~ 5%)	$230,154
Source: Madeleine Pullman.	

Purchasing **packaging equipment** is required for startups that are not able to utilize mobile packaging services. Some small producers start with manual filling and hand label each bottle. Distillers, in particular, can get by with a manual filling station that costs under $2,000, filters the product prior to filling, and is perfect for limited release production runs.

Small-scale automated bottling and canning lines cost between $60,000 and $400,000 but can run from 50 to over 275 bottles or cans per minute, respectively. Again, better quality packaging equipment reduces the amount of contamination and air into the product, and thus extends the product shelf life and quality level.

Aesthetics: A final consideration when selecting equipment for a production facility is the aesthetic appeal. If the general public is never going to see the production area, then using old, recycled, or repurposed equipment may be just fine. In the Figure 10.9 photos, Tig Brich produces beer for their bar and has limited bottles for distribution in their town; they use repurposed dairy equipment and brew in an old shed behind the bar. Crean's, on the other hand, has many tours and will produce Irish whiskey as well as beer. They are looking to appeal to investors, build a high

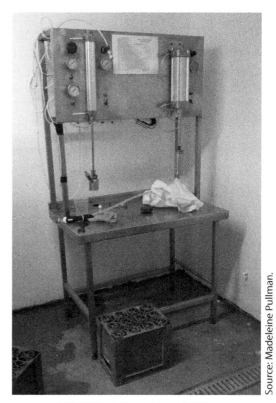

FIGURE 10.8   Manual filling

quality brand image, have their equipment in the public eye, and must invest in equipment that reflects a quality image. Copper vessels or cladding, polished stainless, and wood cladding all send a more impressive message than repurposed dairy equipment.

Tig Brich

Crean's

FIGURE 10.9   Aesthetics

Right sizing: In the startup phase, business owners need essential pieces of equipment. As cash begins to flow in and demand grows for the products, additional tanks and equipment are purchased to improve the efficiency and effectiveness of the operation. For example, when the facility is just producing for the local area, the shelf life of the bottle or can is not as important as when distribution begins and packaged product goes to faraway locations where the product may sit in warehouses and stores for longer periods of time. New producers can get away with simple packaging equipment and minimal filtering for local markets. When production volumes are small, buying grain by the bag makes sense since a full truckload of malt stored in a silo would take too long to use up and the malt quality would start to deteriorate. In short, there are equipment purchases that can be put off until growth kicks in as shown in Table 10.4.

It's always challenging to figure out what the right size is for the market and concept. Some of this decision calls for market research to determine the needs in the area. But the owners' stomach for risk as well as the starting budget are two other factors. A town with 20,000 people and minimal competition could be a great location for a pub or packaging facility. One might want to look at the retail store environment to see how a packaged product might fit into the mix. In larger areas, underserved neighborhoods are great opportunities for pubs and tasting rooms. Producers in tourist towns will probably require packaging so that tourists can take product home with them as souvenirs. Packaging will help level out seasonal fluctuations for pubs if they can distribute to other areas with less seasonality or counter seasonal markets (for example, Utah has skiing in the winter mountain towns and rafting and summer tourism in the desert towns).

TABLE 10.4 Scaling up equipment

	Brewery	Cidery	Distillery
Startup	Basic brew house 2–4 fermenters 1–2 Brite tanks Pump Kegging Simple or mobile bottling	Cider grinder and press 275 gal. IBCs Brite tank Pump Simple pasteurizer Simple or mobile bottling Kegging	Malt/lauter (grain) Blending tank 1–3 fermenters Still Finished product tank Barrels Simple bottling
Growth	Expand cellar Silo for grain Separate whirlpool and lauter vessels More refrigeration Use more of current space and shifts Better packaging line	Upgrade press and grinder Replace IBCs with stainless Cross flow filter Pasteurizer Better packaging line	Additional still Additional fermenters More barrels

Source: Madeleine Pullman.

Break-Even Analysis

The break-even analysis is a tool for critically examining major capital investments such as malt delivery (to purchase in bags, totes, or bulk truckloads), equipment upgrades, energy or water systems, facilities, or point of sale systems for a pub-restaurant. The tool can also be applied to make buy or lease decisions. For example, should a distillery invest in the equipment to make their own wort or should they purchase it from a brewery? Should a cider-maker press juice from apples or pears or should they buy the juice from others? Should the facility buy their own packaging line or use mobile packagers? At some point in any business's growth curve, it will make sense to go from one approach to another depending on production and purchasing volumes. Break-even analysis will illustrate the point where it makes sense to switch approaches.

Fixed versus variable cost: In order to apply a break-even analysis, you need to have fixed and variable costs data for each scenario. **Fixed costs** refer to the cost to purchase the equipment or product under each scenario. **Variable costs** cover the labor, utilities, and materials needed to make a unit of each product (COGS for a barrel, case, or bottle).

Framing the break-even scenario: One way to think of a break-even scenario is if you buy some piece of equipment for the fixed cost X and it saves variable cost Y on each unit used or produced, then how many units (U) need to be used or produced to equal the investment.

$$X = Y \times U$$

Another way to look at the problem is to set two scenarios equal to each other to determine when it makes sense to switch from one scenario to the next (solve for U).

$$X_1 + Y_1 \times U = X_2 + Y_2 \times U$$

Example: point of sale system: It costs $5,000 for a pub-restaurant to purchase a point of sale system (POS). The vendor claims that a POS system lowers restaurant costs by 3.5 percent. The restaurant costs include food, labor, and beverages so the savings is 3.5 percent times restaurant costs. Here the units are dollars of savings. When do the savings equal the investment?

$$Savings = investments$$

$$.035 \times restaurant\ costs = \$5,000$$

$$restaurant\ costs = \frac{\$5,000}{.035} = \$142,857$$

So, if the current restaurant costs are $50,000 per year, it will take:

$$\frac{\$142,857}{\$50,000\ per\ year} = 2.85\ years \cong 3\ years$$

Investing in the POS system will reach the break-even point in three years.

FIGURE 10.10 Silo, tote, and bags

Example: grain purchasing: For breweries and distilleries, there are several ways to purchase grain and some of the options involve a capitol investment or fixed cost. Purchasing grain in bags (50 pounds or 22 kilograms) will cost around $.56 per pound. Another alternative is to purchase the grain in totes (2,000 pounds) which drops the price to $.52 per pound but requires a tote handling system in house which costs $10,000. On the other hand, bulk truckloads of barley malt drop the cost to $.26 per pound if purchasing 48,000 pounds in a truck. In this case, a grain silo and grain handling system is required which could set the business back $20,000 to $30,000 in capital investment. This example illustrates the choice between bagged versus bulk grain with a $30,000 silo investment, setting the two scenarios equal:

$$\$.56 \times malt\ lb. = \$30,000 + \$.26 \times malt\ lb.$$

$$Savings = (\$.56 - \$.26) \times malt\ lb. = \$.30 \times malt\ lb.$$

$$Savings = investment$$

$$\$.30 \times malt\ lb. = \$30,000$$

How many pounds of malt does it take to pay off the investment?

$$malt\ lb. = \frac{\$30,000}{\$.30} = 100,000\ malt\ lb.$$

If a brewery uses about 50 pounds of base malt per barrel, then 100,000 pounds is divided by 50 pounds per barrel for a total of 2,000 barrels. Therefore, the silo would be paid off after 2,000 barrels. Since the barley is not stored in an airtight environment, it probably should be used within six months for optimal flavor and yields. So, if the facility can produce 2,000 barrels in six months, then the equipment will pay for itself in that time period.

Figure 10.11 plots all three options based on barrels of beer production. In all cases, the totes (at that price) do not make financial sense. The $20,000 silo system will break even at 1,333 barrels of product while the $30,000 silo system breaks even at 2,000 barrels. Note, these break-evens are relevant to the costs provided in the example and should be recalculated based on grain costs (including transportation and delivery) in your area.

Example: buy packaging equipment or go mobile: A cidery considering canning a product estimates the following costs: A canning line investment is $150,000, the labor involved is $.75 per

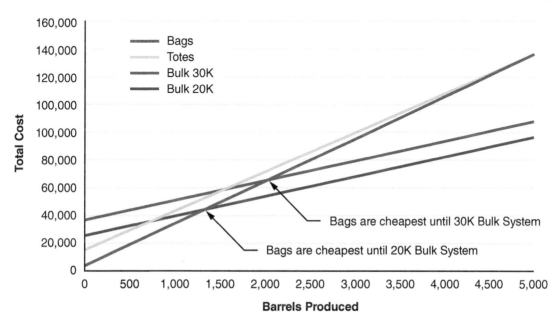

FIGURE 10.11   Barrel produced break-even analysis

Source: Madeleine Pullman.

case, and the lids cost $.25 per case. The mobile packager charges $6 per case of cans with lids. In both cases, the producer must cover the costs of the printed cans. The break-even is calculated by setting the two scenarios equal and solving for the number of cases.

$$\$150,000 + (\$.75 + \$.25) \times cases = \$6 \times cases$$

$$\frac{\$150,000}{(\$6 - \$1) \; per \; case} = 30,000 \; cases$$

In this case, a canning line would break even at 30,000 cases. If the producer packages 10,000 cans per year, the line breaks even in three years.

Example: break-even on all equipment: Finally, consider the big break-even, or determining when the equipment break-even if the user purchases a $500,000 distillery turnkey system (mash tun, still, fermenters, and simple bottling setup). The business sells everything to the state liquor business and makes $25 revenue per case after accounting for COGS. How many cases need to be sold to break even? If the business sells 2,500 cases per year, how many years does it take to break even? This break-even point is calculated by setting the profit equal to the equipment cost.

$$\frac{\$25}{case} \times cases \; sold = \$500,000$$

$$cases \; sold = \frac{\$50,000}{\$25 \, / \, case} = 20,000 \; cases$$

$$\frac{20,000 \; cases}{2,500 \; cases \, / \, year} = 8 \; years$$

Therefore, the business will break even on the equipment investment in eight years.

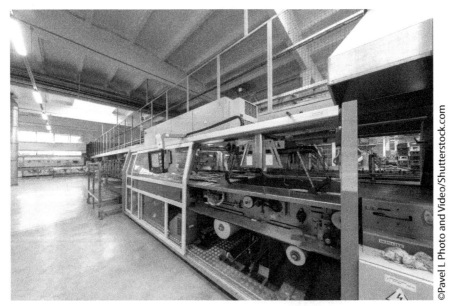

FIGURE 10.12   Packaging equipment

SUMMARY

Overall, a packaging microbrewery may require 3,000 to 6,000 barrels of production to be profitable but will have a much lower break-even point with a successful tasting room. Any facility that has predominately retail sales like a pub, will have a much lower break-even point for the production side, for example 300 barrels for a brewery. And the beverage brings up food sales by roughly 25 percent, which improves the profitability of the kitchen.

A cider facility is much less expensive to start since there is limited technical equipment and no energy required for boiling, only hot water for pasteurizing. Plus, IBCs are quite inexpensive and have become the workhorses of most contemporary cideries.

Distillers don't have to invest in fancy bottling equipment and need very few tanks, fermentation happens very fast (usually three or four days) and one tank is needed to blend or stage final product for bottling. On the other hand, stills are very costly and the resulting cost of a distillery equipment package can exceed the cost of a cidery or brewery.

For a business plan, a complete equipment list should be included with an estimate of total cost. Figure 10.13 is a template where you can enter all necessary equipment and fittings.

FIGURE 10.13 Equipment list template

Equipment Needs and Costs						
Input yearly capacity (bbl. or hl)		← For beer or cider- 31g bbl. or hl; For spirits- finished units (case or bbl.)		Equipment cost for category (* includes installation)		
		Size	Number	Brew house	Cider house	Distillery
Grinding/ milling	Grain mill*					
	Grist hopper*					
	Augers*					
	Fruit conveyer					
	Fruit washer*					
	Fruit grinder					
	Fruit press					
	Liquor storage or mixing tank*					
Brew house	Mash*					
	Mash mixer*					
	Lauter*					
	Kettle*					
	Whirlpool*					

		Size	Number	Brew house	Cider house	Distillery
	Control panel*					
	Hot water tank*					
	Cold water tank*					
	Heat exchanger					
	Pump					
	Control panel*					
	Piping*					
	Platforms*					
Still	Still*					
Cellering	Fermenters small or IBC*					
	Fermenters large*					
	Brite tanks*					
	Glycol chilling system *					
	Carbonation system					
	Control panel*					
	Filter					
Packaging equipment	Bottling/canning equipment*					
	Keg washer*					
	Keg filler*					
Miscellaneous	CIP system*					
	Steam boiler*					
	Forklift					
	Pallet jacks					
	Yeast tanks					
	Sanitary hoses					
	Stainless fittings					
	Walk in cooler*					
	Spent grain/pulp container					
	Quality control equipment					
	Pasteurizer					
	Miscellaneous					
Total equipment and packaging cost						
Cost per bbl. or hl						
Source: Madeleine Pullman.						

Two Oregon Coast Breweries Scale Up Fast!

On the tip of the Oregon coast where the Columbia River pours into the Pacific, two microbreweries have boomed in the gale force of demand for craft beer. Buoy Beer Company and its neighbor Fort George Brewery both launched with nano systems but very quickly scaled up and renovated spaces for housing their own signature taprooms and full-scale restaurants. Both businesses distribute their flagship beers while reserving one-offs and seasonals for taproom clientele only.

For Buoy Beer Company, the transition from a nano to a 20-barrel system for brewing its lager and red ale was lightening quick. Part of the challenge was the 60-day lagering that limited production when compared to a two week process for making a batch of ale. In consultation with Portland Kettleworks, the company designed the layout and equipment needs for its old cannery building property. Despite the condition of the building, the owners factored in the value of the building's community history, architectural features, and superlative waterfront view to the business. All told, it was less than a year between the time the company launched with a lager brewed in the three-barrel system in May 2013 to the full-fledged production on the new system in April 2014.

Buoy Beer Company still employs the three-barrel system for specialty beers. The 20-barrel system supplies its flagship European-style lagers and Northwest ales. Together the systems are able to produce close to 700 gallons at a time, which serves the taproom demands for growler fills as well as the distribution deal in 22-ounce bottles (with cans to follow) that includes a heavily populated region from Portland into southwest Washington.

As for Fort George brewery, which launched in 2007 with its own nano brewing system, the expansion was even greater. Within three years, the business relocated in a new brewing space featuring a 30-barrel system and a canning line as well as a taproom. Then, in May, 2015, Fort George added three more 120-barrel fermentation tanks along with another custom-fabricated 120-barrel brite tank. With the new total of eight 120-barrel fermentation tanks and three similarly sized brite tanks, the brewery has the capacity to brew 20,000 barrels a year. However, retrofitting equipment, upgrades to the boiler system, and new keg washing and filling equipment will be necessary to max out production. Nonetheless, the demand is relentless, and Fort George is striving to ramp up. Sagely, the owners anticipated a 15 to 20 percent growth per year with the goal of producing 18,000 barrels per year by 2016.

LEARNING ADVENTURES

1. Interview a beverage producer in your area to find out their basic startup equipment. In hindsight, which decisions were the right ones for the business and why? Which decisions would the producer like to remake and why?

2. Through looking online or talking to owners of existing facilities, come up with an equipment list for a startup facility and estimate the cost using the provided template in Figure 10.13.

3. Compute the break-even analysis for mobile bottling in 22-ounce bottles. Automated equipment costs $110,000 with in-house labor at $.75/case. Mobile bottling costs $3 per case. Assume that packaging is the same cost for both scenarios.

CHAPTER ELEVEN

Site and Facility

Key Terms

access
aging storage
agricultural zoning
assembly
barrel storage
build out
building codes
buying
change of use
chiller
contingency
electricity

facility
factory occupancy
floor to ceiling
functional space
industrial
industrial use
infrastructure
leasing
light industrial
loading and unloading
loading dock
natural gas

production space
pub or tasting room production only
retail space
retail/sales
setbacks
site
space requirements
storage
tenant improvements
water and sewer
zoning ordinances
zoning permit

Overview

This chapter delves into the considerable issues and research involved in site selection and facility design. Although this topic follows the discussion of equipment in Chapter 10, bear in mind that site and facility planning may happen prior to equipment decision-making or after ordering due to long lead times for both distillery and brewery equipment. Finding an appropriate and affordable site, either bare ground or with a building, for your business is a challenge all beverage business owners face. It encompasses nearly every aspect of business planning from infrastructure and production planning to access and zoning, to name a few. Most buildings are not move-in ready and require major modifications for craft production. As your business grows over time, you may need to go through this process several times. You may expand pub with multiple units within one city or throughout a state or country. In short, most businesses revisit this decision-making process more than once in their lifespan.

Learning Objectives

▶ Identify the challenges related to site and facility development.

▶ Determine which activities need to fit within the facility.

▶ Estimate the space for various activities within the facility.

▶ Understand the minimum resource and space requirements for the site.

▶ Develop a plan for facility access.

▶ Establish adequate utility infrastructure.

▶ Understand the pros and cons of leasing versus owning.

▶ Understand zoning, permitting, and building code requirements and how they are location dependent.

▶ Conduct a detailed estimate of potential costs for a site and facility.

Introduction

First off, it is important to differentiate between the site and the facility. The **site** is the piece of land where a building sits or will be constructed; the **facility** is a building designed and built or remodeled to serve a specific function. For craft beverage purposes, the facility houses the production and storage plus an optional tasting room or restaurant. (In some markets the production and **retail space**, like a tasting room or pub, are located in separate facilities.) There's no doubt that finding the perfect combination of site and facility is a daunting and costly task. It's quite common for startups to use an existing home with a garage or a separate building because it offers a convenient and low-cost choice. However, be aware that these arrangements put many constraints on the business: trucks cannot get into the driveway, there is not enough storage, the utilities are substandard for commercial production, and the business takes over the home space (with the potential to drive its residents crazy).

Within the industry, there are countless horror stories of the mistakes new craft beverage business people made during their site and facility selection phase. Unfortunately, oversights are very hard to correct in the first few years of the business. In some cases, a facility falls into a business owner's hands, as happened with one Irish pub. The owner inherited a multi-generational family pub with beer production space located above the bar. On the upside, the facility offered a great opportunity for a brewpub in a market without any other craft producers. The downsides were many, including the fact that everything—malt , spent grain, and other ingredients—had to be carried up and down the stairs, the ceiling height was too low for production, the floor leaked into the bar, and there was no additional space for storage or any other business activities.

At the other extreme, some business people build out beautiful production spaces separated from the pub or restaurant by glass walls or partitions. There are many unforeseen challenges with putting the production space on display including the need to keep the equipment (not to mention the employees) looking their best. When there are partitions, workers must take care not to inadvertently spray the customers with water or chemicals while cleaning.

Another common pitfall with facilities is that business owners do not plan for expansion. So, when they need new tanks that cannot fit through the space they are forced to cut through the roof and lower tanks into the production space with a crane. This process is a huge and costly hassle.

Other headaches stem from business owners not doing sufficient research on the site's zoning laws only later to find out that a retail space is not allowed or too limited in size, or that a silo cannot be placed outside. One brewery had to put its silo across the street and auger the grain under the road, another costly installation. All of these decisions affect costs and introduce inefficiencies into the business. In nearly every case, problems like these can be avoided with adequate planning both for existing demands and projected growth.

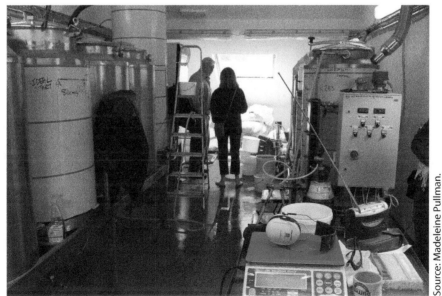

Source: Madeleine Pullman.

FIGURE 11.1   Site challenges

Site and Facility Space Requirements

The first step is to assess **space requirements** for the various activities of your business and then to determine where a facility with these activities is legally allowed to exist.

Production space: The space requirements are tied directly to equipment decisions. Depending on whether the facility is based on nano, 15-barrel, or 30-barrel capacity, the scale of the business (with a factor included for growth) will dictate the space requirements. For a production brewery or grain distillery, the packaging facility alone will consume at least 1.25 to 1.75 square feet (0.12 to 0.17 square meter) per barrel per year, not including a tasting room. And the space should have high ceilings to accommodate tank sizes and working on raised platforms.

For example, if you are planning on 1,000 barrels per year, your facility needs to be at least 1,250 to 1,750 square feet of space. Cideries can get by with about half as much space as a production brewery with mobile pressing equipment and bottling equipment. Distilleries require the same amount of space as breweries if they are producing the equivalent amount of wort from grain. But, distilleries that buy neutral spirits and run them through a filter and still do not need fermenters, mash setups, or other equipment that fills up space. They may only hold the spirits in house for a few days before storing it in barrels or packaging. For any beverage type, storage requires additional space, which is outlined later in this chapter.

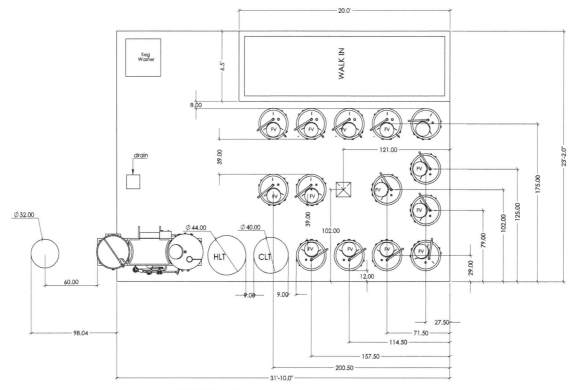

FIGURE 11.2 Space requirements

Source: Portland Kettleworks.

Figure 11.3   Tasting room

Pub or tasting room production only: For facilities producing only for retail in a pub or tasting room, the production area can be 0.6 to 1.00 square feet (0.06 to 0.10 square meter) per barrel per year. So, a 500-barrel facility needs as little as 300 square feet, especially if using a portable nano system rolled in and out when not brewing to use the same small space for other activities. For a cidery to fit in this same space, it would need to purchase juice or press it in another location and use stackable IBCs.

Functional space: Specific functions also require additional space, from retail, offices, and bathrooms to bonded areas for spirits producers. Retail space, such as a tasting room, should accommodate a bar area and good flow for guests. Tasting rooms are often quite large in markets where there is a high volume of visitors expected and a projected use for tours, merchandise, and special events. Overall, the trend is leaning towards increasingly larger tasting rooms. Green Flash built a 4,000 square foot tasting room and beer garden in San Diego; Port City's tasting room, in an industrial area of Alexandria, Virginia, is 2,000 square feet and accommodates a hundred beer lovers for music events and beer-yoga classes. At the same time, some producers like Old Ballard Liquor Company in Seattle fit an entire distilling operation and tasting room into 750 square feet. Clearly, their tasting room space has planned uses outside of tasting room hours.

Some facilities include space for a restaurant and other food production like catering for special events. Outdoor retail spaces for a beer or cider garden with seating areas for dining and picnicking is a big draw in most locations during warm weather months, and it can double sales. Some business concepts include a farm or orchard which requires even more space for fruit trees, grains, hops, produce, and more. There are even examples of full-service resorts with production facilities at their core. McMenamin's Edgefield compound, situated on 74 acres outside of Portland, Oregon, has a concert venue, multiple restaurants, hotel, gardens, cidery, brewery, distillery, and winery. The group has many other hotels and restaurants around the state of Oregon, each with its own brewing facility.

Unexpectedly Perfect Brewery Spaces

Large abandoned buildings and old factories can make perfect spaces for breweries. The high ceilings and open floor space allow for easy installation of brewing and packaging equipment. Flooring is able to endure the acid from beer spillage, impact shock, and temperature changes. These buildings often come cheap and are less expensive than building from the ground up. Typically located in industrial areas, these building's zoning laws might allow brewing but not retail or tasting room use. Older buildings may have environmental and historical barriers in repurposing the space. Neighboring communities often benefit from a brewery. Once-abandoned factories that have turned into brewpubs bring life to the area and instill a sense of community, making the area more attractive overall.

Dogfish Head Brewery Opens Hotel

Craft beer fans are also travelers, and their quest for great beer is combining brewing and tourism in a big way. While it is common for craft breweries have a tasting room and a pub, they don't commonly offer accommodations for their out-of-town visitors. When Dogfish Head Brewery surveyed its taproom customers, the business discovered that roughly half of its 1,000 weekly visitors preferred to stay overnight to make a weekend of drinking and enjoying the Delaware Coast.

As a result, Dogfish bought an existing hotel, the Vesuvio Motel, and renovated it to fit the brewery's brand. The Dogfish Inn opened in spring 2014. Located between the production facility and the pub, the hotel features 16 rooms and offers bikes so guests can check out the neighborhood scene, businesses, and beach. The Dogfish Inn does not serve its own beer, so as not to compete with the few nearby bars that do. Dogfish founder Sam Calagione received high praise from the local Department of Tourism, Governor's office and Economic Development Office in bringing visitors to other local businesses.

The potential for increasing the revenue of craft beverage businesses while boosting the local economy is a winning formula for craft distilleries and cideries as well. The Glenora Inn and Distillery in Nova Scotia has been producing single-malt whiskey for over 25 years on its 200-acre property. Guests tour the distillery, do tasting, and listen to live music throughout the day. A pub located adjacent to the distillery serves traditional English-style food during the day and switching to more elegant fare in the evenings.

FIGURE 11.4   Production storage

Storage: Without question, production facilities rarely have enough storage. All the ingredients as well as packaging materials, kegs, and finished products take up a surprising amount of space. A tall warehouse is very useful since tiers of shelving can be added to accommodate more products. Grain in sacks require about .25 square feet per barrel produced per year. When production is high enough to justify a silo outside of the facility, it frees up a lot of interior space (zoning laws permitting). As shown in Figure 11.4, production facilities generally end up with all kinds of items stored outside, if the weather and neighbors permit.

Aging storage: Because barrel aging is gaining in popularity for all craft beverages, businesses need dedicated space for **barrel storage** in a climate-controlled area. Wood barrels can be stacked end-to-end three high at the most; after that point the stress on the barrels causes leaking. A racking system (Figure 11.5) allows air circulation around the barrels and eliminates weight stress on the barrels.

Barrels have specific space requirements depending on whether you are using whiskey or wine barrels and horizontal or vertical storage positions. These are detailed in Table 11.1. Since barrels are heavy when filled with product, this table also includes an estimate for the volume and corresponding average weight per filled barrel. Furthermore, the floor needs to be able to support the weight of a stack of filled barrels.

FIGURE 11.5   Barrel storage space

TABLE 11.1   Barrel space requirements

Barrel Type	Volume (Weight)	Dimensions	Floor Space
Whiskey barrel	53 gallons (551 lb.) or 200 liters (248 kg.)	Height: 36 inch Top: 21 inch (diameter) Belly: 26 inches (diameter)	<u>Horizontal rack</u> 12 sq. ft. (1.1 m²) for 1–3 barrels <u>Vertical end-to-end</u> 9 sq. ft. (.82 m²) for 1–3 barrels
Bordeaux barrel	60 gallons (624 lb.) or 225 liters (279 kg.)	Height: 37.3 inch Top: 22 inch (diameter) Belly: 27 inches (diameter)	
Source: Madeleine Pullman.			

While a cement floor is usually adequate, other floors will need an assessment for appropriate engineering.

Access

For any facility and site, **access** refers to the ways or means of getting into and around various areas of the building. Planning for access involves addressing many questions about all of the different users and functions. Here are some questions to consider:

1. Can customers and suppliers easily access the building from highways or roads and is the site reasonably easy to find?

2. In terms of day-to-day operations, can employees get the necessary equipment and materials into the building? For example, is there enough room to bring in a tank and tilt it into position in the space?

3. When it comes time to expand later, will you be able to access unused parts of the building without moving walls or equipment?

4. Since raw materials such as grain, apples, and tanks of liquid will arrive on trucks with loaded pallets or bins, can large trucks or semis pull close to the building, preferably to a loading dock or large entry way?

5. Is the unloading spot as close to the final destination, such as the malt storage area or walk-in cooler, as possible? Is there room for a forklift or pallet jack to move objects from the truck to the final use area without obstruction?

Along with moving things into the building, outflow is equally important. Spent materials and finished goods such as kegs and pallets need a clear path to move them from the refrigerated area to

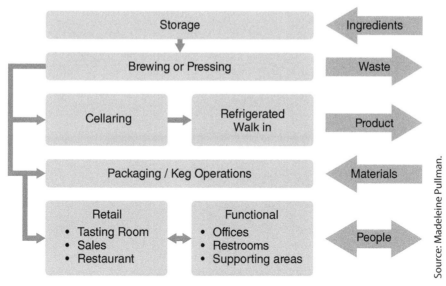

FIGURE 11.6   Access

Source: Madeleine Pullman.

trucks using a forklift or pallet jack. Hoses or other obstacles should not obstruct these paths. The spent material, grains, or fruits, need a place outside of the production facility where they can be kept until the farmer or disposal company picks them up. Often farmers do not pick up in a timely manner so spent grain can accumulate and get funky. Plan ahead for space for this accumulation and protection from weather and pests.

The main point underlying questions of access is minimizing the amount of time any material or product is being handled and crossing the path of other work happening in the production space.

Floor to ceiling: Starting at ground level, all craft production facilities need good drainage. The floor around the drain must be easy to clean and maintain a slope toward the drain. Existing buildings typically need to be modified to include a proper floor and drain; this step could involve cutting an existing cement floor and connecting to drainage. For a new building, a long floor drain constructed in the center of the production facility floor serves both the extraction side (brewing, pressing, and so on) and the cellaring area. There are many surface choices for production facilities from

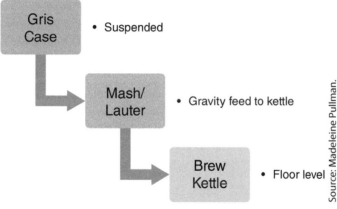

Source: Madeleine Pullman.

FIGURE 11.7   Elevation Setup for Brewing

©Mary Rice/Shutterstock.com

FIGURE 11.8   Loading docks

special paint and sealant to tiles, as well as other more expensive treatments. The floor of a craft production facility faces a lot of abuse, constant moisture, and cleaning, so it pays to invest in a good floor.

The ideal facility has adequate height to allow gravity to do some of the work rather than investing in augers and pumps. For example, in a brewery or grain distillery setup depicted in Figure 11.7, the milled grain is stored above the mash/lauter area and fed down. The mash/lauter is above the brew kettle on a platform so that it drains into the kettle using gravity. A two-story building has sufficient height for this arrangement, but a single-story building requires pumping and auguring, all of which adds another level of complexity and reduces efficiency for the business.

Loading and unloading: The primary goal when designing areas for loading and unloading is avoiding back-breaking activities. Many distributor employees have succumbed to back problems and the business has paid out worker's compensation claims because of poorly designed access for loading and unloading. Keeping everything on the same plane at a **loading dock** allows a truck to pull right up to the building with a pallet jack to load or unload pallets and avoids unnecessary lifting. For busy facilities (or once the business grows), separate loading docks for incoming and outgoing materials is the ideal set up to prevent conflicting activities from crossing paths.

Without loading docks, an electric or gas powered forklift (or even better, a super extending forklift that can move pallets up to second story storage areas) requires entryways with high doors. Tall garage doors enable the movement of several stacked pallets of kegs, containers, or malt bags. They also prevent pallet or forklift drivers from inadvertently ripping a hole in the wall or garage door, a realistic concern for all craft beverage businesses.

Infrastructure

When considering potential sites, conduct a thorough evaluation of the utilities for startup or current needs as well as for projected future growth. As the production level grows, water, gas, electric, and refrigeration needs scale in kind. Most utilities have different technical requirements for metering and operating at higher levels, and you should always check sites to make sure the utilities are upgradable.

Water and sewer: Any site and facility must have the necessary utilities to handle industrial level production. In short, are the pipes big enough? While some utilities like adequate electricity can be straightforward to modify with the utility company, some sites, particularly those in rural settings, often come with water and sewer shortcomings. Beer, in particular, requires adequate water quality and flow rates. In some settings, you may need to purchase water rights to get enough for production. Water quality significantly affects brewing and is modifiable with filtering and additives (for modifying acidity), but additives require a cold liquor tank for treating the water prior to brewing.

A typical brewery uses four to seven barrels of water for each barrel of finished product. Only the most environmentally conscious breweries like Sierra

FIGURE 11.9   Tall doors

Nevada and New Belgium have been able to get their water use close to four gallons per barrel of beer. Facilities with pubs use more water for the restaurant and bathrooms. Most of the water ends up going down the drain, and organic material and cleaning chemicals are damaging to septic systems. Those sites on city water and sewer do face scrutiny from sewage treatment officials for these same issues. Cideries and distilleries (without grain) use much less water and can get away with septic systems for spent water.

Gas: On an industrial basis, **natural gas** is used to heat hot water, boilers, and kettles or stills. A typical brewery production facility will use 1.3 therms of natural gas per barrel of beer. A grain-based distillery uses more since the still operates for many more hours than a brew kettle. As production increases, the gas pressure and volume must increase correspondingly. In most places, propane is more expensive by orders of magnitude than natural gas and is not viable for high-volume production unless it is the only available service.

Electric: Production facilities require **electricity** for numerous activities from basic lighting to running mills, pumps, and automated bottling lines. A typical brewery or cidery requires 10 to 15 kilowatt hours of electricity per barrel produced. A distillery does not require refrigeration so it uses half that amount per barrel of incoming wort or fermentable liquid.

TABLE 11.2   Utilities (based on brewing system production)

	Nano (< 7 BBL)	Medium (< 15 BBL)	Large (< 30 BBL)
Ideal space for production	2,000–5000 sq. ft. 20 ft. ceilings, dock	8,000–12,000 sq. ft. + outside storage high doors, dock	18,000–40,000 sq. ft. Multi-dock, high doors
Water meter	½ inch	1 inch	> 1 inch
Gas pressure	≤ 1 lb.	≥ 5 lb.	≥ 10 lb.
Electric (US)	400+ amp 3 phase	600+ amp 3 phase	2 kilovolt-amp 3 phase
Source: Madeleine Pullman.			

Chiller: Breweries and cideries also require a glycol chiller; a rule of thumb for a chiller is 8 to 20 Btu per barrel of product. The chiller is used for fermenters and conditioning tanks. The lower number applies to environments and products with low refrigeration needs (colder cellars and short cycle products). Long conditioning (ciders) or fermenting products (lagers) demand more chilling capacity as well as warmer cellar environments.

Table 11.2 provides the suggested capacities for brewery utilities and space.

An Australian Brewery Goes Solar

Bright Brewery in Victoria, Australia installed a 50-kilowatt solar system to supply the electricity to meet all of the needs of the brewing facility. The site contains a brewhouse as well as busy restaurant, and the solar panels meet 40 percent of the total electricity use. The brewery expects to save around $18,000 US dollars a year from the installation with a five-year payback. Once it has paid back the initial investment, Bright Brewery will be able to add more solar capacity and energy storage. The system of 192 panels takes up over 600 square meters on the roof. With a goal of becoming carbon neutral, the next project for Bright Brewery is to minimize the use of natural gas for its boiler. Much of the draw to Bright Brewery's area is the environment and outdoor adventure opportunities, and Bright Brewery has kicked off a national conversation on sustainability initiatives within the brewing industry in Australia.

Leasing versus Owning the Location

Most startups are strapped for cash and leasing is the only viable option. Others may have enough money to buy a location or own an existing location, like a farm or building, to convert into a production facility. Regardless, at some point in the business lifecycle, it makes financial sense for the business to buy a property.

Leasing: If you are leasing, you need to find out first whether the property owner and neighborhood is tolerant of an alcohol production facility and determine that it is a legal location for the business. Once that is settled, it is time to find out what the property owner is going to provide under the agreement. Typically, landlords pay for building out the site to your business's needs within reason; these improvements are known as the **tenant improvements.** Along with an allowance for the **build out**, a lease also includes **contingency** clauses that address costs above the allowance and identifies which party is responsible to pay for the difference. Other items to address in the lease relate to who is responsible for utilities, landscaping, maintenance, snow plowing, and waste collection. Some landlords have inadvertently included utility payments in brewery leases and lived to regret it. Generally speaking, landlords may pay for office utilities but do not cover the production side.

Buying: There are a number of considerations when purchasing a site with an existing building. First, is it the right space for the concept? Or, can it be modified into a production facility and retail space at a reasonable cost? Are the zoning and utilities appropriate? Does the building have adequate capacity for the long-term vision? Startups should determine whether buying a building is the best use of limited capital. A craft business needs a significant sum of money for buying equipment, setting up the facility, and paying operating expenses until sales reach adequate levels. Taking a hard look at the financial estimates for the future under the rent-versus-buy scenario helps to answer that question.

Legal Issues for Site and Facility

Depending on the location, legal issues related to the site and facility add complexity and headaches to the search for an appropriate site as well as substantial costs. Zoning dictates which areas are appropriate for production and retail; building codes regulate the construction and usage of a facility; and government agencies at the federal, state, and local levels mandate various permits for both the site and facility.

FIGURE 11.10   Zoning regulations

©Sved Oliver/Shutterstock.com

Zoning: Local governments design **zoning ordinances** to separate hazardous industrial areas from farming areas and residential areas. Materials considered hazardous may be cultural or physical. For example, most local ordinances stipulate that alcohol production or consumption be conducted at a certain distance away from schools and churches. Both distilleries and breweries use potentially hazardous materials. Ethanol, either produced or handled by distilleries, is highly flammable. The handling, storage, and milling of barley and wheat create flammable dust. In both types of facilities, the presence of open flames (gas), spirituous vapor, or grain dust are risks that could cause an explosion. Therefore, most zoning laws mandate that these facilities isolate dangerous elements.

Zoning regulates **setbacks**, or the distance the building must be away from the road and property lines. It also designates what materials can be stored inside and outside of the building, what kind of access the property has for trucks, pedestrians, and others, how much parking the site has, and how the business displays signs. Some industrial areas that are good locations for production have limits on the commercial use of the space. For example, a popular industrial area in Portland, Oregon restricts the commercial use space to 3,000 square feet. Any tasting room, pub, or restaurant that is part of a production space must fall within those limits.

Agricultural zoning and **historic districts** also offer surprising limitations. For example, in some agricultural zones, wineries (cideries or meaderies) are permitted tasting rooms but breweries and distilleries are not. Other places prohibit tasting rooms in either agricultural or historical zones; production facilities must be in areas zoned **light industrial** or **industrial**. States like Minnesota and Oregon have more progressive zoning laws that allow tasting rooms in properties zoned for commercial and traditional neighborhood uses.

Zoning laws change frequently; new zoning laws in locales around the country now allow production alongside pubs and taprooms. However, anyone interested in starting or expanding into a new facility should look closely at the zoning criteria for that area.

Zoning permit: If the area requires a zoning permit, you will need to file an application. Permit costs range from $3,000 to $8,000 depending on the location. This includes a survey of the land with the proposed building on it, building plans, planned use of the building, owner details, and other conditions specific to the area. In many cases, a public hearing is required, which could delay the building process. In this case, it is highly recommended that you get letters of support and arrange for "project friends" to testify at the hearing to emphasize the selling points of the project. This gives you an opportunity to respond to the potential negatives (odors, outdoor storage, public access, drunken or disorderly behavior, for example) and present plans for mitigation. Possible selling points include:

▶ Strength of the business as part of the community

▶ Statements from influential community members and neighbors to the site supporting the project

▶ Projections of revenue and new jobs to tourist and rural towns

▶ Storage plans, such as behind the building out of public site

▶ Public access description, such as between 4 p.m. and 9 p.m. at tasting room; no music or load noises

▶ Kettle steam operational plans, such as between 8 a.m. and 5 p.m. on weekdays; no odors outside of those hours

Building codes: Every facility must conform to local building codes; even basements and garage breweries face federal, state, and local provisions. Many locations allow home garage production as long as the building is separate from the home and has a separate entrance. Building codes focus on hazardous activities, structural elements, and classification of spaces. Different codes apply to "uses" or "occupancy types" as shown in Figure 11.11 where the uses are production, storage, and public space.

According to building codes, production places are classified differently from pubs. For example, a production brewery (with off-site distribution) is classified as **industrial use** and **factory occupancy**; a pub or place with a bar and seating area for on-site consumption is **retail/sales** and **assembly** use (for a restaurant).

Another concern is the previous use of the space. If the use is being changed, then you need to file a **change of use** form. For example, the previous site was manufacturing only and now you plan to add a pub (retail/sales use). This change may require costly construction such as seismic upgrades or installation of a sprinkler system. Not only do building codes have specific construction requirements but they also include specifications for paths and exit designs according to the specific use category. In General, change of use and building permits take a huge amount of time and building can not start without the permits.

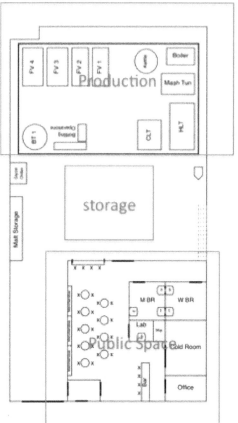

FIGURE 11.11   Building use criteria

Source: Madeleine Pullman.

Creating a Model of the Facility

The best advice is to plan the facility and equipment together to address the height and floor plan simultaneously. One way to get a visual idea of how the plan works with the equipment is to create a mock-up. Using foam board or Legos, layout the equipment to scale on a large sheet of paper representing the floor plan. Use plastic figures or fashion a person to scale with the foam board to see how well a person fits in the space. Do the same for a forklift or pallet jack. Examine how the flow will work with multiple activities going on, such as brewing or pressing, distilling, packaging, and deliveries.

SUMMARY

To facilitate the zoning and permitting process, hire an experienced contractor and equipment manufacturer. These individuals help you navigate through the hoops of securing a site and facility. Regardless, you should become familiar with the general zoning in your area before looking for sites. Plan for expansion to the site even if you start at the nano level, and think about your dream production area even if you are financially constrained at the outset. Finally, investigate legislation around regulations that impact craft production facilities, pubs, and tasting rooms. Get involved with lobbying efforts to improve these regulations so that they become more favorable to flexible facility use.

Epic Brewing Accommodates Utah's Zoning and Permitting Laws

Utah is known for its stringent alcohol laws. Even after Salt Lake City passed a law allowing direct sales of beer from a brewery, for many years they could not be over 4 percent ABV. Once it became legal to brew higher alcohol beers in 2008, they could not be poured on draft. All of this made business quite complicated for startup Epic Brewing, and that was just the beginning.

Epic Brewing opened with the idea of becoming a destination brewery. When it finally opened in 2008, Epic was the first in the state to brew higher alcohol beers. It started out selling 22-ounce bottles at the brewery, state-run liquor stores and in restaurants. Epic immediate success blew the founders' forecasts for its early years out of the water. As a result, they had not effectively planned for the growth.

In 2011, Epic proposed an expansion of its Salt Lake City brewery to rezone a space adjacent to the brewery from residential to commercial use. Epic's proposal to the city planners promised jobs, tax dollars and economic benefits from the expansion while keeping the existing neighborhood's best interests in mind. Epic encouraged its consumers to write letters and attend a planning commission meeting to address the rezoning request. Many fans of the brewery voiced opinions in support of the brewery expansion, but neighboring homeowners expressed concerns. Despite all of these efforts over 15 months, the planning commission voted a "no" recommendation to the city council. The Salt Lake City brewery's production capability was tapped out at 15,000 barrels even with the addition of tanks in 2012. In light of this obstacle, Epic's founders eventually set their sights on a new market, opening a taproom and brewery in Denver where they could sell Epic's higher alcohol beers on draft.

Epic's mistake was building the original Salt Lake City brewery without an expansion plan for the space and brewing systems. The business did not repeat this in Denver where the facility was designed with the ability to scale up readily should the new Colorado market take off. The founders made the investment early so that growth would be easier later on.

Denver had an established craft beer market when Epic arrived. Colorado's licensing laws are partially responsible for the explosion of breweries, since it allows new breweries to operate on-site tasting rooms without having to go through the local liquor license review process. It was a challenge for Epic to create brand awareness among all the other breweries. Epic's Denver brewery started distributing beers July 2013 throughout Colorado, and opened its 1,400 square foot tasting room to the public in September 2013. Expansion continued steadily into 2015.

The same year as the Denver launch, Epic revisited its original goal of being a Salt Lake City gathering place by opening a neighborhood pub. To comply with the laws concerning alcohol levels of draft beers, Epic served all of its beers out of bottles, even sample-sized bottles. Meanwhile, during the breweries fifth year of operations it experienced a 54 percent increase in sales, selling almost 17,000 barrels across its three breweries, and was in 19 national markets by the end of 2014.

In August 2015 Epic's management figured out a way to became the first Utah brewery to serve beers over 4 percent ABV in growlers: the growlers are prepackaged, must contain only the beer manufactured by the brewery, and are sold only at the brewery's location. Customers can purchase the returnable growlers with a small deposit fee and Epic rotates the beers offered in the growlers. Growlers are the largest container of beer legally allowed for purchase in Utah (kegs of any size are illegal for retail sale).

The next stage for this company is to open another Epic brewery in a new market, such as California. The co-founders are using the Colorado experience, not Utah, as the test case for their expansion plans.

LEARNING ADVENTURES

1. In your town or desired location, research the following details for leasing an appropriate space for a production facility: neighborhoods for industrial or industrial/retail, rental price per square foot (or meter) for the month, and other potential costs and benefits of a particular area. As an alternative, look into the cost of purchasing a building in that area through commercial real estate listings.

2. Evaluate an existing craft producer's site in your town or desired location. What are the pros and cons of that particular site? Looking at the interior and exterior, does the site allow for expansion of the facility? What would it take to add more tanks to this facility? For breweries or distilleries, does the site have a silo; if not, what are the challenges of adding a silo to that site? Is the storage adequate for bulk raw materials, finished product, barrel aging, and more? Are there any other concerns with growth at this particular site and facility?

FIGURE 11.12   Site and facility costing estimating sheet

Site and Facility Estimated Costs	< Quantity	Square footage required		Price per resource-unit
		Multiply factor x quantity	Factor	
Production yearly beer or cider (finished bbl. or hl) or spirits (pre-distilled 31 gallon bbl. or hl)				
Retail side: full restaurant and bar space only			< Input total space	
Retail side: pub space only			< Input total space	
Production side: space for in-house retail production only			.6–1 sq. ft./bbl. (not including pub)	
Production side: space for both in-house retail and wholesale packaging			Minimum 3 sq. ft./bbl. (not including pub)	
Production utilities (production just serves location needs)				
Water and sewer (multiply yearly demand by chosen factor and price/resource)			180–240 gal./bbl./yr	Cost per gal
Electricity (multiply yearly demand by chosen factor and price/resource)			10–12 kWh/bbl./mo x 12	Cost per kWh
Gas (multiply yearly demand by chosen factor and price/resource)			1.5–2.5 therms /bbl./mo x 12	Cost per therm

Production utilities (production serves location and packaging)		Price per resource-unit
Water and sewer (multiply yearly demand by chosen factor and price/resource)	180–240 gal./bbl./yr.	Cost per gal.
Electricity (multiply yearly demand by chosen factor and price/resource)	10–12 kWh/bbl./mo. x 12	Cost per kWh
Gas (multiply yearly demand by chosen factor and price/resource)	1.5–2.5 therms/bbl./mo. x 12	Cost per therm
Restaurant utility cost estimate /year		
Water and sewer	$0.20/ sq. ft./year	Based on average US restaurant costs or input in your area
Electricity	$2.90/ sq. ft./year	
Natural gas	$0.85/ sq. ft./year	
Leasing space cost estimate/year		
Pub and production facility lease (on-site serve only)	$6-$12/sq. ft./year	
Pub and production facility lease (on-site serve and package)	$6-$12/ sq. ft./year	Adjust to reflect your local sq. ft. price
Production facility only	$6-$12/ sq. ft./year	
Restaurant lease	$12-36/ sq. ft./year	
Buying Facility		
Land cost	Depends on area	
Pub/production build out	$400-$600 per bbl.	Adjust to reflect your local costs
Packaging only production build out	$150-$300 per bbl.	

Source: Madeleine Pullman.

CHAPTER TWELVE

Team

Key Terms

articles of incorporation
articles of organization
B corporation (B corp) or
    benefit corporation
B lab
benefits
bookkeeping
burden
C corporation (C corp)
capital contributions
company formation
compensation
contract
contract employee

cooperative (coop)
culture and fit
development
expectations
full-time vs. part-time
general description
general partnerships
hiring
job description
job title
joint ventures
limited partnerships
limited liability company
limited liability corporations (LLC)

management
operating agreement
organization structure
organizational chart
partnership
pay
pay and benefits
position responsibilities
profits, losses and distributions
S corporation (S corp)
sole proprietorship
startup team
transfers
turnover

Overview

Having the right team can make a business soar. Finding the best people and developing the skills and culture of your organization sets the
business on a positive course and makes life easier for everyone
involved. The alternative can mean day-to-day conflict, ruined rela-

tionships, and, in the worst case, the demise of the business. Team development starts with choosing the appropriate organizational structure, putting together complementary skills, planning for hiring and cultivating employees down the road, creating the business culture, and even planning for owner roles and responsibilities. This chapter addresses all of these complex points for creating highly functional organizations from the get-go.

Learning Objectives

▶ Understand the different organizational structures and choose the appropriate one for your business.

▶ Develop a startup team.

▶ Create an operating agreement.

▶ Create an organizational chart for startup and for the future.

▶ Plan for hiring, training, and developing employees.

▶ Define a pay and benefits package.

▶ Understand how to develop a business culture.

Introduction

In the startup phase, the initial team may consist of one visionary person, parents and their kids, a couple, old friends, or people who share a passion and perceive the opportunity for a craft product and concept. No matter who is involved, the first step is to hash out who is responsible for each activity. Most people come to the business with a resume of past experience and useful skills. It is important that each team member recognize his or her strengths and weaknesses. If you are working alone, be honest with yourself about weaknesses since these are the first areas for hiring. One person may know how to make the product and another person may have a business skill like marketing or sales, which is a clear division of responsibilities. In another case, a group of business people may get together without a clue as to how to make the desired beverage; the startup phase may involve contract production until reaching a certain size and then hiring a production person. Regardless of the composition, these details need to be spelled out in the business plan in the team section. The plan should also include the resumes and a short biography of each team member, stressing the strengths that they bring to the business and the proposed role for that person. Finally, the cost implications of salaries and hiring should also be part of the financial statement.

Organizational Structure

There are several different **organization structures** to choose from, and all have legal and financial implications as well as varying risks for the individuals involved. To make this decision, it is extremely important to consult with a lawyer and accountant before determining the appropriate structure for you. This section covers the legal classifications for the United States, which have parallel structures around the world. Regardless of your chosen structure, the name of the business should be a clean trademarkable name and having legal support on achieving this goal is well worth the money.

Sole proprietorship: The simplest organizational structure is the sole proprietorship. One person owns and runs the business entity and there is no distinction between the business and the owner. The business may operate under a fictitious name; thus, it will be required to file under this assumed name, "doing business as *fictitious name.*" Under this classification, the owner is entitled to all profits and is responsible for all of the business's debts, losses, and liabilities, including taxes paid just like other individual taxes. The advantages of choosing this structure are the simplicity of setup, complete control by the owner, and easy tax filing. On the other hand, alcohol is filled with liability issues, and since there is no separation between the owner and the business the owner can be directly sued and all business debts and obligations belong to the owner. It can also be hard to raise money as a sole proprietor and the individual is not only responsible for the success but the failure of the business.

Partnership: A **partnership** is a single business where two or more people share ownership. In these arrangements, partners contribute to the business in various, and ideally, equitable ways (cash, assets, skill, or labor), and share in both the profits and losses of the entity. Because more than one person is involved, individuals in this arrangement should create a written agreement covering a wide variety of issues such as how decisions are made, how profits and losses are distributed, conflicts resolved, and partnership exits accomplished. Partnerships can be **general partnerships,** operating similarly to a sole proprietorship except that the profits, liabilities, and activities are divided between partners; **limited partnerships,** limiting individual's exposure to liabilities as well as managerial input; or **joint ventures**, acting as general partners for one project or limited time periods. Partnerships have

FIGURE 12.1   Team as part of business plan

many of the benefits of sole proprietorships except that members benefit from complementary skills and shared resource input. The disadvantages include liability and debt exposure (although shared), profit sharing regardless of whoever is actually responsible for bringing in the profit, and partner conflict over decisions, a common occurrence.

Limited Liability Company: The rules for **Limited Liability Corporations (LLC)** differ state to state. Overall, the name should be unique within the state and followed by the designation LLC, and it cannot include certain words in the name like "bank." In this model, the business files **articles of organization** with a state organization (the specific submission entity depends on state such as secretary of state or another commerce organization) with the business, name, address, and member names. In the LLC, the business is not taxed; rather taxes pass through to the individuals who pay these taxes on their individual tax forms under a corporation, partnership, or sole proprietorship tax return. As the name implies, the LLC provides some protection from personal liability (debt or lawsuits) for the business actions. Profits can be distributed as spelled out in an operating agreement and the record keeping aspects are minimized relative to more sophisticated corporation categories. One of the biggest disadvantages of the LLC is the tax impact on the participants, as they must pay self-employment taxes, Medicare, and social security contributions for their share of the business income.

C Corporation. A **corporation**, also known as a **C Corp**, is a legal entity owned by shareholders with an IRS taxation structure that is specifically considered a unique entity separate from those who own it. The corporation structure shields the individual shareholders from liability and debts. But this shield comes at the price of complex administration, tax, and legal requirements. Similar to other structures, the business name is registered in a state with the words corporation, incorporated, or limited following the business name (depending on the state). The business files **articles of incorporation**, creates a board of directors, and issues stock according to the preference of the state. The corporation must pay state, federal, and local taxes and the individual shareholders pay taxes on the dividends from the business. The benefits of corporations are the limited liability exposure, ability to raise funds from stock sales, and lower taxation imposed on corporations than individuals. But, the complexity of corporation governance involves more administrative time, money, and headaches. Additionally, corporations face double taxation at the company level and the dividends to shareholders.

S Corporation. As another form of incorporating, the **S Corp**, avoids the double taxation issue. Profits and losses still pass through to the individual owner's tax returns but the business itself is not taxed; thus, the benefits include tax savings and business expense tax credits. These benefits come with certain bureaucratic hassles such as requirements for director and shareholder meetings with minutes, maintenance of records, bylaw adoption, and stock transfers. There is also a requirement for reasonable compensation to shareholders; high shareholder distributions (dividends) combined with low salaries to working shareholders can cause reclassification of the high distributions to wages by the IRS as it would appear to be a tax avoidance scheme.

Cooperative: Popular in agriculture, retail, and creative business, the **coop**, is an organization owned by and operated for the benefit of those using its services, namely the members. When the cooperative generates profits they are distributed among the members. Like a corporation, there is an elected board of directors and officers to run the organization. Other members also have voting rights to help direct the strategy and operation of the coop. The members buy into a coop and usually have equal voting rights. While this structure was once unusual for a craft business, coops are now starting to spring up for breweries and buying organizations for materials like bottles, malt, or fruit.

Community Owned Flying Bike Cooperative Brewery

Flying Bike Cooperative Brewery in Seattle, Washington is member-owned and democratically run as per the definition of a cooperative. Membership is open with a one-time $200 fee that bestows an equal ownership stake in the brewery. Members vote on which beers to brew and sell in the taproom, which can their own (scaled up) home brew recipes. Governance is by a member-elected board of directors plus one experienced head brewer who spent time at large Seattle breweries including Elysian and Pike Brewing Company. The board reviews the brewery's finances annually and determines how to split any profits among members. Members also receive discounts on beer, preferred access to special events, and bulk purchasing for home brewing ingredients.

After building its membership to over a 1,500 people over the course of five years, Flying Bike Cooperative Brewery opened a seven-barrel brew house to the public in August 2015. Prior to opening, the coop was active in sponsoring events and held home brewing competitions.

Flying Bike's mission is to educate the community on beer styles, beer brewing methods, and beer tastings. It invites people into the craft brewery world who would otherwise not be able to start their own businesses. One clear advantage of the coop model is that it guarantees a built-in customer base and strong advocates for the brewery who have an incentive to drink Flying Bike beer and to promote it over the long-term.

B Corporation: In certain states in the United States, the **B Corp** or **benefit corporation** is a new for-profit corporate entity that has a specific goal of including positive impact on society and the environment in addition to profit. B Corps are certified by the non-profit, **B Lab** when they demonstrate rigorous standards of social and environmental performance, accountability, and transparency.[1] Those with B Corp status register as a business under another IRS category such as S Corp for liability reasons but certify as B Corps to emphasize their sustainability efforts. Examples of craft beverage B Corps are Hopworks Urban Brewery (Oregon), Brewery Vivant (Michigan), Beau's All Natural Brewing Company (Ontario, Canada), New Belgium (Colorado), and Bison Brewing Company (California).

Overall, craft businesses should find a structure that protects the individual owners from liability as a high priority and pick an appropriate structure for the ownership group to retain decent financial and decision-making benefits. Cooperatives and B Corps fit the needs of certain organizations to promote personal values or benefit from group buying. Bear in mind that the structure can be changed in the future as needs evolve.

Reaching B Corp Status

From the get-go, Aslan Brewing Company in Bellingham, Washington made environmental sustainability a priority and applied for B Corporation certification. B Corporation status legally certifies a company to include stakeholder interests into their corporate responsibilities, redefining the business's bottom line. Where traditional businesses consider only shareholders, Aslan committed to its stakeholders' best interests, including those of its 50-plus staff, suppliers, community, and the environment. Aslan opened for business in May 2014 and achieved B Corporation status in January 2016 from the agency B Lab, meeting rigorous standards for very high levels of environmental and social performance. Aslan joins seven other breweries and 1,500 businesses globally as a B Corporation.

Owner Jack Lamb makes every business decision ensuring sustainability and diminishing the footprint of the business. For example, Aslan cans rather than bottles because cans are better for the beer, break less, have a substantially smaller carbon footprint, and are infinitely recyclable. As for ingredients, Aslan's beer is 100 percent USDA certified organic, using all organic ingredients and chemicals that have a low impact on the environment. Additionally, Aslan donated eight percent of its total profits to local non-profits and community organizations in 2015 and gives its spent grain to a local farmer to use for livestock feed.

Over eight months, Aslan renovated the historic building it resides in, creating minimal waste in the process and reusing as many materials as possible. Unused materials were sorted for recycling and green building saved the brewery tens of thousands of dollars. Efficiency was also of high consideration and Lamb chose LED lighting, Energy Star equipment, water recycling procedures, and a steam-fired brewhouse as opposed to direct-fire. The building itself is partially underground, so walk-in coolers were placed against the underground walls in order to maximize efficiency. Green Power Partnership Certification was awarded to Aslan by the EPA for being 100 percent wind powered as a Clean Energy Partner. In Partnering with Arcadia Power, for every kilowatt-hour that Aslan uses, a kilowatt-hour of clean energy is produced and released into the grid.

Brewing requires a huge amount of water from brewing to packaging to cleaning. Aslan has been active in working with the Washington Wild Brewshed Alliance to find solutions to cut water use. As an alliance, the breweries involved commit to choosing responsible cleaning methods, recycling steam, and utilizing closed-loop systems that allow water reuse for multiple purposes without contamination.

One of the biggest hurdles in achieving B Corporation status for Aslan was the requirement to be transparent concerning suppliers and its processes. For Lamb implementing the transparency requirements made the company more well rounded and allowed its mission to be accessible to a larger audience. Aslan incorporates its sustainability successes into its marketing efforts whenever possible, but is sensitive to oversharing and greenwashing. The brewery works hard to achieve the high standards of sustainability and knows its customers appreciate the accomplishments, but realizes that producing quality beer must come hand in hand.

Aslan has been a profitable enterprise since opening, exemplifying that product quality and economic success do not need to be sacrificed for sustainability. Aslan's business plan was built around quality products, organic ingredients, and sustainable practices, and is officially committed to these practices with the B Corporation certification. The Aslan team makes sure its margins stay strong while sticking to its low-impact priorities. Up next for Aslan is to incorporate solar power and local sourcing into its operation.

Startup Team and Future Needs

The **startup team** or individual comes with certain skills. Once a missing skill set has been identified, the team must decide how that void will be addressed and where the money will come from to pay for it. In some areas of the country, it may be relatively easy to find people with the desired skill sets while in others there is a dearth of skilled craft employees. This section looks at the various aspects of hiring team members.

Hiring: Many startups rely on volunteers or interns to help in the production and bottling side until they have enough cash to pay for full- and part-time employees. There are several problems with unpaid employees. First, production and packaging areas involve dangerous equipment and activities: kettles and stills have open flames and boiling liquids; cleaning chemicals can cause severe skin and eye burns; toxic levels of CO_2 can build up in tanks; bottling equipment can smash bottles and emit glass shards; packing equipment and heavy kegs can pinch body parts: and many other accidents are waiting to happen. Paid workers are protected by worker's compensation but volunteers are not. And while your spouse and father-in-law may not sue you, you should be aware of liability issues from others. Volunteers do not have the same level of commitment as paid employees and quickly burn out on the unglamorous aspects of the job such as pressing a full semi-truck of apples over 16 hours or working on a bottling line all day. Even with the incentive of taking home a case of craft beverages, the excitement wears off quickly.

Full-time versus part-time: Certain jobs are strategic to the business such as the brewmaster, distiller, or cider-maker. These should be full-time positions. For example, one full-time employee can handle all of the production for a decent sized brewpub without packaging and limited kegging. In some regions, seasonal cider making is the norm rather than year-round cider making and one cider maker could work part-time for several small businesses. However, this is not a workable model in breweries or distilleries with year-round production with daily activities. A business with a pub or restaurant also needs a full-time manager for that side of the business.

In the startup phase, the owners wear many hats, working in production, sales, bottling, and tasting rooms. To supplement the owners' time, part-time workers can support many of these areas until the business has enough cash to pay for full-time workers. All facilities need help with bottling, canning, and production activities like pressing apples in peak season or bottling off multiple cases of product.

Contract: A **contract employee** is similar to a part-time employee but works as an independent entity. Many producers hire professional services like accounting, legal, finance, or marketing to work for the business but not as an employee. Contract employees are a great way to try out various services to see how they might work on a long-term basis. For example, hiring a marketing service to develop the brand, label design, advertising, and so on makes sense for smaller businesses that may not be able to keep a marketing person busy throughout the year. Using a contract service is more economical than hiring a full-time person and provides access to top-notch talent.

Job description: Creating a **job description** is the first step in hiring a full- or part-time employee. First, a good job description provides a **job title** and commitment level (full- or part-time with the range of hours) as well as the reporting relationship. Second, it follows with a **general description** of the job objective and responsibilities. Third, it includes a list of desired skills, qualification background (for example, certificates or formalized training from a business, brewing, or distilling school) and desired years of experience. The description should provide the special requirements of the job such a lifting kegs or bags of grain, traveling throughout the region, for example. Finally, it outlines the specific tasks and responsibilities that the job entails starting with the most important and ending with the lower priority activities. This list also encompasses the majority of tasks required by the position. At the end, a salary range, benefits, and employer contact should be provided.

Sample Job Description

Job Title: Head Brewer—XYZ Brewing

General Description: We are a startup brewpub-in-planning located in ABC City. The potential candidate should be a people-focused leader with the experience to oversee all aspects of the brewing operations. We anticipate bringing on the Head Brewer by April 1, 20XX and we anticipate opening by June 1, 20XX. This will be an exciting opportunity for the right person as they will be working with ownership to install all brewing-related equipment and to develop and test recipes. The Head Brewer position has a competitive salary and benefits program. The ownership and management currently on the project are experienced in the craft beer industry and are opening a brewpub dedicated to artisanal, Belgian-style beers. We have purchased a new 20-barrel brew house, and anticipate producing near 2,000 barrels in our first year with room to grow up to 10,000 barrels in this location. The candidate will work with the Production Manager to ensure the reliability of all brewery and draft equipment, including brew house, cellar, packaging lines, utilities, and instrumentation.

Position Responsibilities:
► Contribute to a culture of open communication and mutual respect.
► Assist in the hiring, training and develop of other brewery staff.
► Assist in developing and managing a training program and safety program that is in line with company objectives and health and safety laws.
► Collaborate on brand development, expansion planning, and overall management.

► Create standardized operation and a quality assurance and control program.

► Manage all brewing operations efficiently and safely.

Job Requirements: Two to three years of professional brewing experience at a craft brewery or brewpub as well as recognized brewing education is preferred. The candidate should demonstrate strong leadership skills with experience in hiring, training, and management of all brewery personnel. The candidate should exhibit award-winning recipe formulation expertise as well as experience in brewing, yeast propagation, cellaring, packaging, quality control, excise tax record keeping, and project management.

Special Requirements: The candidate should have a demonstrated passion for craft beer particularly Belgian and innovative styles and commitment to grow craft beer in ABC City. The candidate will be expected to lift 50-pound grain bags and move kegs effectively.

Pay and Benefits: The salary will be commensurate with experience and will be supplemented with an incentive bonus for reaching target goals. Benefits include health, dental, retirement, starting three-week vacation as well as an employee stock-ownership plan. Please send resume and cover letter to SusyQ@ABCcity.com

Pay, expectations, and benefits: For startups, the ownership group should have a written agreement that indicates what stage the business must reach before owners are paid and, when that point arrives, an estimate of the salaries. For example, in Bend, Oregon, a brewery owner only paid himself enough to make ends meet until the business made a $50,000 profit then paid better salaries to the staff and added health benefits. After that point, the owner paid himself a modest salary until hitting the next $50,000 profit mark. For employees, the appropriate wages can be found through the various craft beverage associations. For example, the Brewers Association provides a salary report for the various positions in a brewery, and many of the brewery, cidery, and distillery business websites and blogs have ads with wages and benefits. Outside of the brewmaster, cider-maker, and distiller positions, many craft positions have similar activities regardless of whether the produce it beer, cider, spirits and even wine. Thus one can look at cellar and packaging positions for comparable wages.

Most craft producers provide incentives to keep good people from leaving. For example, some breweries pay for health and dental benefits, bonuses based on yearly output, and trips to the major industry conventions or more exotic trips to French cideries, Scottish Distilleries, or Belgium or German breweries for educational field trips. Companies like New Belgium, well known for great employee incentives, provides a personal employee bike, garden plot, dog day care area, community lunch, and many other lifestyle perks.

When determining the full cost of an employee, labor **burden** refers to the cost beyond the salary or hourly wage that must be included in the financial estimates. Burden can add 20-50 percent to the employee wage and includes any benefits that the company chooses to or must pay employees. Examples of burden costs include: payroll taxes, worker's compensation, health insurance, retirement benefits, uniforms, vehicle use, and training.

Source: Madeleine Pullman.

FIGURE 12.2   Culture and fit

Culture and employee fit: Every business develops their own unique culture whether it is designed intentionally or emerges on its own based on the leadership style, the team makeup, and incentive program. Ideally, a company culture stems from the mission and philosophy of the business. Each time a person is hired, the hiring team considers how the individual might fit into the culture that the company has or hopes to shape. At Hopworks, the culture is centered on sustainability and outdoor activities like biking. To align employees with the sustainability focus, they are given bonuses based on improving the sustainability metrics in their specific area such as water or energy use. Similarly, some businesses encourage loyalty and passion for the business through frequent events and hiring individuals who identify with the company values. The human resources people monitor **turnover** and work to hire and retain the right people. A high turnover environment is not only financially detrimental but can wreak havoc with employee morale and potentially affects service and product quality.

Development: Many employees enter into a craft business at an entry-level job such as working in the tasting room, bottling or kegging lines, or front-of-house servers. They have a passion for the industry and may have other long-term goals such as distilling or working in marketing or sales. Managers should pay attention to employee interests and look for ways to cultivate these people for other positions with more responsibility. Sending employees to certificate programs for food and beverage pairing, beverage business, or other technical skills is a good way to develop these interests and promote loyalty. Other activities include paying for employees to attend major festivals and conventions for the industry, which include learning sessions as well as opportunities to try other products from around the world.

Organizational Chart

All businesses create an organization structure formally documented in an **organizational chart**. For startup businesses, the chart should outline the proposed roles as well as additional strategic hires as

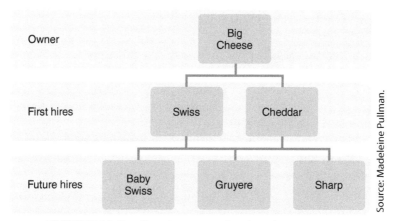

FIGURE 12.3   Starting organizational structure

Source: Madeleine Pullman.

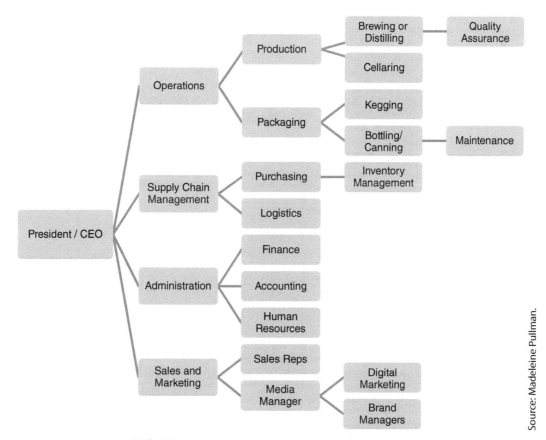

FIGURE 12.4   Future organizational structure

Source: Madeleine Pullman.

the business grows in the first three years as depicted in Figure 12.3. The organization's hiring plan should match the operations expansion plans for equipment and facility covered in Chapter 11.

In a fully developed business with more than 15,000 to 20,000 barrels of product, there are more defined roles and the organization chart has multiple tiers:

Estimating Team Costs and Future Needs

One of the best ways to estimate labor requirements and potential costs is to use the Gantt chart introduced in Chapter 9. Looking at each day's activity, you can estimate the amount of time a person needs to do the tasks for that day. For example in the startup cycle in Figure 12.5, for the first five days, one person, probably a brewer, can do this work since the brewing activity consumes most of the day. However, day 11 and day 15 demand 16 and 17 hours of work, respectively. While one person could do this work, it will quickly lead to burn out when the facility gets to capacity and those days are the norm. This would be an opportunity to hire or train a cellaring person to support the brewing days. The Gantt chart shows how to estimate the hours and the costs of the worker from average hourly wages for that job plus overhead (usually adding 20 percent or more to the hourly wage for taxes and benefits).

For future scenarios, you can use the Gantt chart with more equipment and bigger batches to estimate the labor requirements when production increases. Some employees will be salaried (often working more or less than 40 hours per week with more benefits) and others will stay at hourly depending on the job role (i.e., bottling line or bartender) and legal requirements of the area.

FIGURE 12.5 Gantt chart with labor hours

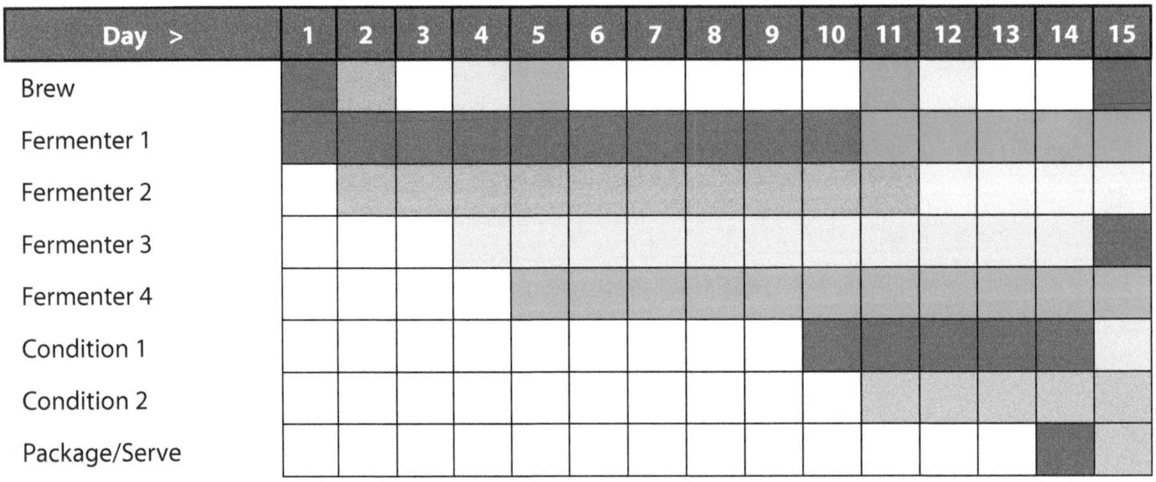

Labor Hours

	1	2	3	4	5	6	7	8	9	10	11	12	13	14	15
Brew	9	9		9	9						9	9			9
Ferm clean-sani	1	1	1	1						2	2			2	2
Brite tank clean-sani										1	1			2	2
Filtering										4	4				4
Kegging														4	4

Source: Madeleine Pullman.

Operating Agreement

Every organization forming an ownership team needs an operating agreement. This is one of the most important aspects of creating a partnership. Many individuals (the author included) have been swept into business arrangements with all the passion and enthusiasm for craft beverages but without a formal arrangement for getting out of the business or the compensation mechanism for selling out. There are operating agreements available online or through legal contract books. A good operating agreement contains the following elements:

Company formation indicates the type of organization (LLC, C Corp, or other structure) and how it was filed, along with company name and registered agent. The section should also cover how long the company will exist and what events will cause dissolution of the company or continuance of the company with voting rights. This section should also cover the purpose of the business, location of business, members of the business and whether and how additional members can be added.

Capital contributions include the amount of capital or assets contributed by each member and whether there are obligations to make additional contributions in the future.

Profits, losses, and distributions cover how profits and losses are determined and allocated (based on each member's relative interest in the company). There should be a clause that indicates how and when members will determine the available funds for distribution and how the distribution amount will be determined (after paying back certain loans, for example).

Management of the business addresses who actually manages the business and how the management team is created (via vote, for example). It should include a clause to indicate whether members should have any influence over the management team if they are not part of that team and other issues about the power of management (sale, lease, purchase of assets, borrowing, pre-payment, debt release, employment, and contracts, to name a few). This section would also include how liability is assigned to members, usually according to law. There could be a provision for a chief executive manager and member's requests for company information such as other member information, company tax returns, company operating agreement and other formation documents, financial statements, and so forth. In addition, managers generally want an indemnification clause or personal release from company liabilities.

Compensation covers what the managers will be paid for and what type of reimbursement of expenses are appropriate.

Bookkeeping addresses how the books will be maintained as well as members' capital input and distribution accounts. The section includes a clause about when the books are closed each year and how the members receive the financial information and materials for tax reporting.

Transfers concerns how a member sells, assigns, or disposes of his or her interest in the company. This section includes potential mechanisms such as an offer letter to other members and ideas for determining the price.

SUMMARY

This chapter has covered the main points of the creating a team to operate a craft business. Even companies that start with just one person end up with employees and perhaps other partners as the business grows. Depending on production, labor is not only a variable expense but is also a fixed expense for certain salaried or contracted positions. Overall, your plan should include team cost estimates for the first three years as well as a written description of the starting team and the addition strategy over the same time period.

FIGURE 12.6 Team costing estimating sheet

Team costs (include overhead/burden)			
Team classification	**Year 1**	**Year 2**	**Year 3**
Owner (s)			
Production head			
Assistants production			
Cellar staff			
Bottling/canning staff			
Tasting room staff			
Finance and legal			
Information technology			
Sales and marketing			
Other:			
Other:			
Other:			
Other:			
Total			
Restaurant/pub manager			
Restaurant/pub staff			
Kitchen management			
Kitchen staff			
Other staff			
TOTAL			
Source: Madeleine Pullman.			

Ninkasi Fosters Strong Company Culture

Ninkasi Brewing in Eugene, Oregon takes its name after the Sumerian goddess of brewing and beer. In 2014 the brewery earned a spot on *Outside* magazine's list of 100 best companies to work for two years in a row.[2] Ninkasi's core purpose is to perpetuate better living, and its core values are achieving quality output in everything they do, creative pursuit of mastery, integrity in its actions, and successful integration of work and life.

With over 100 employees, Ninkasi is a well-rounded organization overseen by a senior management team. The sales department and marketing department each have their own VPs. These departments are separate but with a lot of overlap. Accounting is handled mostly on-site. A supply chain staff is responsible for all ingredients that come in and flow through the organization. There is also a quality team, an operations department, and a facilities department to keep things running around the brewery. The tasting room crew interacts with the guests and gives tours.

Ninkasi offers many benefits for its staff, including insurance for full-time employees, paid time off, cellphones, merchandise credit for clothing and beer, and profit sharing. Managers also have a budget to reward departmental success with bonding experiences such as a rafting trip. The company prides itself in its fun environment that includes exercising together, dance parties, and home brewing with the brewing team. Each department holds a competition, such as cooking or costume contests, for team building. Ninkasi has bikes available for employees to ride around town, holds weekly runs, and fields various sports teams. Twice a week a masseuse visits the brewery. The dress code is casual and most employees wear jeans and Ninkasi gear. Weekly sensory classes are also held so that employees can advance their knowledge about beer.

Ninkasi completed a multi-year brewery expansion in 2014, including the hiring of new staff. Instead of building another brewery, the company focused on building company culture and on making quality beers. The new brewing space was built to grow; the 70,000 barrels of capacity can expand to produce up to 250,000 barrels. The new administrative space has a rock climbing wall, bars for the employees, heated bike parking, a pilot brew system, and even a recording studio.

The company describes its hiring process as "proactive," meaning that the brand and philosophy are well communicated, and it does not wait to recruit until positions are open. Ninkasi maintains a human resources staff, a recruiter, and organizational development staff. The company hires for culture first, and technical skills second.

New employees start by learning these values and are introduced into the company culture to create an immediate sense of belonging. New employees meet each member of the senior management team and conduct job shadows of positions in other departments for a full understanding of how the brewery operates to feel connected to the company's purpose.

Ninkasi's management dedicates a lot of time to regularly checking in with employees. Managers supply regular feedback and have measureable goals for each employee. When polled, 95 percent of Ninkasi employees stated that they knew what was expected of them, which keeps them motivated and engaged. There are many opportunities for employees to develop skills and for upward advancement. Positions at Ninkasi are competitive because of its reputation and culture and it attracts great talent.

Being a vital part of its community is of great importance to Ninkasi, both culturally and environmentally. Eugene is a small town, and craft products are a huge part of the town's ecosystem. Ninkasi has donated to non-profit organizations since 2011 through its "Beer is Love" donations program. Beer is donated to non-profit events and employees can take unlimited paid time off to volunteer in the community. Ninkasi hosts and plays a part in concerts, beer festivals, and many local events.

The brewery also has a strong relationship with local hop farmers and conducts many events at these farms. Sustainability is also a priority and the brewery makes its decisions in with an eye toward resource reduction and energy conservation. New facilities are LEED certified and solar panels contribute to the energy. Ninkasi realizes the value in making beer more efficient as ultimately better for bottom line, since the cost of input goods goes up even though the cost of a beer stays relatively flat.

Ninkasi's employee recruiting has strong ties to its marketing. The brewery's co-founders speak at events whenever possible and staff members are out in the community volunteering. The company upholds a reputation for being a fun and rewarding place to work with little employee turnover. Ninkasi employees are an important source for new recruits. They are encouraged to feel pride in what they do and, in turn, create more value as the company grows.

LEARNING ADVENTURES

1. Find an existing craft business, interview the owner(s), and determine the startup team's skills. How did they deal with a void in skills? What in particular has made the team successful in their human resource strategy?

2. Through looking at blogs and other craft industry job posts, determine an appropriate monthly salary and the burden rate in your state or province for a brewmaster, lead cidermaker, or distiller. Assume the person will have three weeks of vacation, $4,000 per year health insurance (unless provided in your location), retirement donation of 6 percent of salary, and appropriate payroll taxes for your area.[3]

3. Describe a craft business with a unique culture. What has the business done to cultivate this culture and how is it apparent to the consumers and visitors to the business?

ENDNOTES

1. "What are B Corps?" B Lab, https://www.bcorporation.net/what-are-b-corps.

2. "The 100 Best Places to Work in 2015," *Outside*, November 16, 2015. http://www.outsideonline.com/2032236/best-places-work-2015.

3. "How to Calculate Fully Burdened Labor Costs," *Houston Chronicle*, http://smallbusiness.chron.com/calculate-fully-burdened-labor-costs-33072.html.

CHAPTER THIRTEEN

Market and Concept

Key Terms

brand identity

brewers bond

client base

club buying

community-supported agriculture
(CSA)

competitive analysis

competitor matrix

consumer demographics

craft concept

demographics of an area

industry groups

key competitors

legality of concept

localism

market share

market size

product portfolio

projected trends

shared production facilities

subscription

Overview

There are many examples of craft brands that built a big presence over the years but then struggled to maintain market share as more aggressive upstarts did a better job of appealing to craft consumers. As the competition increases for all of the craft beverages, business owners need to stay on top of the game so that their new products succeed while their existing ones maintain, or preferably grow, market share. Understanding a particular market, how it may shift over time, and how the various brands and beverages fit into that market is a significant challenge—and a critical one—to insuring the life of your brand. This chapter describes how to research and determine the "fit" of your concept into an existing market.

Learning Objectives

▶ Create an industry overview and monitor trends.

▶ Understand how to differentiate a product from its competitors.

▶ Determine how a concept fits into a market.

▶ Locate resources for evaluating competitors.

▶ Understand demographics of craft consumers versus the potential market.

▶ Evaluate the legal environment and tax implications for a concept in a given market.

Introduction

The idea behind a **craft concept** and how it fits into a market can spring from several sources. You could be sitting in a neighborhood and realize that the area is really missing a good family-friendly brewpub. Or you could come up with a concept like a cider pub-restaurant and then try to figure out whether there is a market for such a place. Regardless of which came first, the concept or the market opportunity, you should understand how a startup concept fits into a particular market and the potential for it further down the road, including expansion into other markets. To set the stage for understanding the market, you should research the history of the industry and it has shaped your particular market. You should also investigate the **projected trends** for the market size and the beverage. If consumers are moving beyond IPAs and sweet ciders, what are they switching to? Who are the consumers ready for new ideas and where are they located? Once you understand the market and trends, you can then examine which businesses with similar products exist in your competitive space to assess the threat or opportunities for your concept.

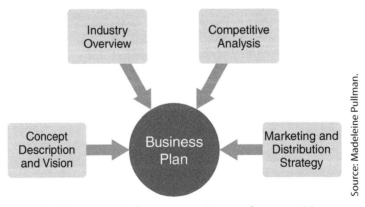

Source: Madeleine Pullman.

FIGURE 13.1   Industry overview and competitive analysis in the business plan

Industry Overview

Many craft beverage associations and guilds gather information about the current state of the industry and trends. Anyone in the craft beverage business should keep up on what's going on in the industry; some people try to keep up on other beverage sectors like mainstream beer and distilled spirits in general, cider, mead, and other potential competitors in the alcoholic industry space. For a startup plan, the websites for the associations and guilds are great sources of information of the historic and current status of the respective industries. While you don't have to go back to the beginning of time, the overview should cover the past five to 10 years nationally as well as at the state and town level. In the United States, the TTB and state licensing agencies also have information on the licenses, both those in place and pending, which will give you an idea of how many players are in the area. In other countries, similar government agencies exist for alcohol production licenses. The same **industry groups** can provide trend information on how product and style demand is changing. There are also other sources of data such as beverage style magazines and websites (Craft Beer Analytics, beverage marketing and consulting groups, national beverage sales data like Nielsen, among others). The industry overview should be comprehensive on all aspects of where the industry has been and where it's going in the near future.

Competitive Analysis

After understanding the industry, the next step is to gather information on competitive forces in your chosen market area. More specifically, you should answer the following questions for both your concept and beverage portfolio:

1. How will you differentiate your product from those competitors? What specifically do you offer that is better or different?

2. How does the concept and portfolio fit into the traditions of the field and the current movement in the industry?

3. What are the legal aspects in the city, county, state (country) that might affect your concept and products?

After addressing these questions, you should profile **key competitors** (typically three to five) and indicate the type of facility, types of products with average price points, **brand identity**, and what demographic groups are attracted to each product or concept. Numerous websites and aps exist to identify all the competitors and their offerings. While there may be national and international competition, a first step is to get a comprehensive list of everyone in your proposed local area.

Brewery competitor check: For example, imagine you wanted to open a brewpub in Chicago. Using a brewery locator website (craftbeer.com) and looking under the brewery locator for that area, you find 58 breweries. These can be mapped for a specific neighborhood or a large region as shown in Figure 13.2.

Some of the breweries are packaging only, some are pubs, and others are still in planning. By plotting all the breweries on a map of the city, you are able to see underserved areas, which may be areas of opportunity for a neighborhood pub. If you are interested in starting a microbrewery, you need to see how many competitors there are for taps in the retail spaces that might carry your prod-

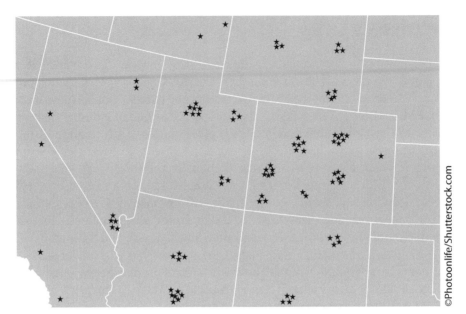

©Photoonlife/Shutterstock.com

FIGURE 13.2   Mapping of brewery businesses

ucts including restaurants, bars, growler filling stations, and so on. It is a good idea to do an informal investigation to determine how difficult it might be to get your product into those places or packaged product into area stores.

Distillery competitor check: For the same area, the Illinois Craft Distiller's Association shows 18 members with the majority clustered around Chicago and neighboring suburbs. There are even more in planning according to the Illinois State department that handles Class 9, Craft Distillers Licenses. In this case, distilleries are not going into every neighborhood like brewpubs, although Chicago does have one of the first distillery-pubs. Spirits have different consumption patterns than beer or cider but most distilleries still benefit from a tasting room or retail shop. In fact, it can help to have a group of distilleries closely located to each other. Portland, Oregon's distillery row has a collection of six to seven distilleries in a light industrial area. As a marketing group, they encourage tourism and tastings. Distilled spirit tourism and collective marketing has been very successful in places like the Scottish Highlands that has more than 200,000 people visiting single-malt whiskey distilleries every year, and the Kentucky Bourbon Trail Craft Tour® which has seven craft distilleries and more than 600,000 visitors to both the Craft and Kentucky Bourbon Trail Tour®.

Cider competitor check: For cider details in the United States, the United States Association of Cider Makers or cider information websites provide the best sources of information. In a recent search for the Chicago area, the site Cyder Market LLC (cydermarket.com) identified four cider producers and two wineries producing cider and apple wine.[1] Half are located in Chicago and the remainder in southern Illinois. While Illinois is not a major apple producer, it still has almost 50 orchards and large apple growers in the region (Michigan and Wisconsin) compete in the Chicago market. Therefore, you need to do extensive research to see what others are making in the general area and where the opportunities lie. As Chicago is a fairly strong beer and spirits town, your research should include identifying which Chicago bars, restaurants, and retail stores are carrying independent and local cider producers rather than just major brands owned by large breweries. Where are ciders doing well? Where are they not doing well and why? What is the popular local brand and how broadly is it distributed and accepted by consumers?

Game plan for further competitive analysis: After identifying the competitors, the next step is to visit each competitor to understand their concept and market niche. Ideally, this includes a facility tour and product samples, including food (if relevant). During this investigation, observe the market for this business and get a clear impression of its **client base**; why do customers choose to patronize this business or to purchase its beverages. (Equally relevant is to determine which type of customers are *not* supporting this brand by buying its products and why not.) Examine the **product portfolio** and identify the best-selling products. From looking at labels, tap handles, and identity merchandise like hats, T-shirts, and stickers, it should be clear what the brand conveys to the consumer. Further research involves identifying whether or not the concept is clear and how the business intentionally built its brand identity.

Competitor matrix: After completing this research, create a matrix of the key competitors to your concept. For example, for a startup brewpub in a certain neighborhood, identify other brewpubs and even pubs with craft offerings that compete with your concept. In Table 13.1 the five key competitors are categorized to identify their different brand identities and segment appeal. The matrix includes average beer and food prices (if your proposed concept will have a food-service component).

TABLE 13.1   Key competitors

Competitor	Type of Facility	Types of Products	Brand Identity	Appeals to
Spokeclub	Brewpub	Couple flagship products with 8 decent rotators —Food with local focus	Green, bicyclists, and community	Families and people who share those values
Old Pub	Brewpub	1 award winner and 5 rotating beers of high quality and unique —Minimal food	Classic, conservative, medal winning, elite	Beer nerds
The Playground	Brewpub	10 beers for non-discriminating craft drinkers —Pub food/kids menus	Fun, accessible, theme is dog, mountain, or historic site.	Families, business, and group gatherings
PBX	Micro	Solid IPA, others good decent	Non-conformist, rebel, edgy	Blue collar wannabes, motorcyclists

Source: Madeleine Pullman.

Trends Affecting Concept and Marketing

One of the current industry trends is **shared production facilities** (coops, joint ventures, contract, and brewing centers). Shared production facilities rely on good marketing to create a strong identity since brand identity is difficult to attach to a shared site. Another trend is **subscription** and **club buying**. In this model, the consumer pays in advance for the product and picks up the product yearly or seasonally at a designated location. Similar to community supported agriculture (**CSA**) models, the producer benefits from up-front payments and a simplified distribution model. The challenge is that the products are rarely in bars or stores so new customers must find the product through word-of-mouth or social media.

A Community-Supported Brewing Model

Begyle Brewing in Chicago, Illinois offers a community-supported brewery (CSB) membership for growler fills, operating much like a community-supported agriculture (CSA) farm subscription. Instead of paying for produce shares from a farm and receiving a weekly vegetable pickup, Begyle offers beer shares to its customers in six- and twelve-month increments. Pricing varies, depending on whether members choose one or two 64-ounce growlers, or even a 1/6 bbl. of beer per month. The discount is greater with the 12-month subscription and in the larger quantity. The growler is included in the membership price, and members receive discounts on merchandise as well as on additional beer purchases. Begyle also hosts CSB member-only events throughout the year. Membership sign-up periods are twice a year, in December and June, and are limited to 250 subscribers. Current members have the opportunity to renew their membership before new people can subscribe. The members themselves must pick up the beer, and beer fills do not roll over if they miss a month.

In this model, the business receives up-front cash with very simplified distribution. Customers prepay for beer, the brewery communicates where the money gets used, members have a vested interest in the business. For example, when Begyle wanted to expand its brewing facility, CSB membership program helped to fund the expansion. The CSA model also helps the brewery forecast for the year ahead.

Begyle had an established brand of bottled beer before selling its CSB subscription. But for a new brewery using a CSB-only model, the challenge is establishing a brand presence. If the beer is not available in stores, the business must work harder to attract the attention of consumers via word of mouth, social media, and other marketing strategies.

Another trend that will continue to be popular is **localism**, supporting the local or neighborhood community. As the big international brewers continue to buy up the larger craft businesses, the discerning craft consumer will look to support independent and local businesses. This trend is beneficial for small neighborhood producers. Their marketing messaging should emphasize the local attributes and ingredients like local craft malt, fruits, and hops, for example. As more people adopt localism as a brand attribute, expect to see people growing their own ingredients in order to be considered uber-local.

Growler filling stations, a newer concept, are cropping up not only in specialty shops but also in grocery chains and convenience stores. To sell in these outlets, conveying brand identity is key. This may require participating in tasting events at stores that allow it. Tasting events provide an opportunity for the craft producer to tell a compelling story about the brand and products.

Consumer Demographics

Another activity for investigation involves evaluating the demographics of the craft consumer and the demographics of your proposed market area. Generally, the historic industry analysis and trend information provides sufficient information on the demographics of the craft consumer. For example, according to the Brewers Association in 2001, the average craft beer consumer was 39-year-old white male with a relatively high income and education level. Today, that has changed. Young women between the ages of 21 and 34 now account for 15 percent of the

FIGURE 13.3   Growler filling station

total craft volume sales. The average consumer is now more diverse while still skewing towards higher social economic groups; 40 percent of craft volume is consumed by the bottom 60 percent of households by income.[2] Similar analysis can be found for other crafts products. The main demographic differences and trends for cider are that more women participate in cider by far; cider has close to 50 percent consumption by women. For distilled spirits, women are increasing their participation in whiskey and other brown liquor consumption. It pays to keep up on the trends to understand how these markets are shifting and to develop concepts and brands that address these shifts.

Cider Market Lures Longtime Brewers

From 2007 to 2014 sales of US-produced ciders have tripled and cider-only bars are more common. Oregon's Rogue Brewery recognized the resurgence in the cider market and a growing demand for gluten-free craft beverage options. After producing beer for over 25 years, Rogue released its first cider in 2014. Rogue's 20-acre orchard was brimming with fruit in 2014, so the brewery decided to celebrate by making small-batch cider. Rogue's 7 Hop Cider mirrors the brewery's popular 7 Hop IPA beer, and incorporates seven hops varieties all grown on its hop farm. Fruit Salad Cider, released soon after, features a fruit mix also grown on the farm. Rogue's president has stated that it's not actually cheaper to grow produce, but it upholds the company's "Grow-Your-Own Revolution." Rogue Ales established its brand around using its own farm grown ingredients, and making craft cider fits well under that brand, while helping to meet the rising demand for cider.

TABLE 13.2 Demographic comparison

Category	Boulder (103,166)	Pueblo (108,249)
Gender (% women)	48.4%	50.2%
Median age (years)	27.7	37.4
Median household income	$57,428	$33,784
Median rent monthly	$1,213	$716
Race majority	83.1% White	52.4% Hispanic
Source: Madeleine Pullman.		

Demographics of a chosen area: Once you understand the behaviors of craft consumers, the next step is to look at the demographics of an area to see how it matches up with consumer preferences. City government offices and demographic websites are the best sources for any area. Often it is useful to compare two locations to see how the demographics are different. For example, looking at Colorado on a demographic website (city-data.com) presented in Table 13.2 and based on 2013 data, you can see how the demographics for Boulder differ from Pueblo. While Boulder is an obvious choice for a craft beer business that is not to say that a craft business would not do well in Pueblo given the right brand and story. Boulder has considerably more competition in the craft market and more expensive real estate, which also factor into the analysis.

Legality of Concept in Location and Marketing Constraints

Similar to the discussion on site and facilities in Chapter 11, legal issues also come into play in your concept. It is only recently that many states have legalized taprooms and tasting rooms to sell product in their production facilities. Until that point, tastes could be offered to customers but not sold. The portion size of the taste was also regulated. Today, local authorities still may not allow certain concepts in specific neighborhoods. For example, a cider orchard business decided to set up a cidery in Mosier, Oregon, an area well known for fruit orchards and just outside of the popular windsurfing mecca of Hood River. After months of preparation, the business owners learned that their location was in a designated historic zone that did not allow a tasting room. These are the kind of surprises that no one wants to face.

Taxes are another issue affecting any concept in a specific location. Excise taxes change depending on the production level. In many locations, smaller producers pay less tax until they reach a certain production threshold. For example, in the US non-sparkling cider and mead (which fall under wine taxes) receive a $0.90 per gallon tax credit on their annual tax payments if they produce no more than 150,000 gallons annually. There are decreasing credit rates for a winery producing up to 250,000 gallons per year. Hard cider receives a credit of $0.056 per gallon, which is available for the first 100,000 gallons sold.[3] Excise taxes for beer in the United States have a similar structure. A producer pays seven dollars per barrel on first 60,000 barrels if the brewer produces less than two million barrels and $18 per barrel after the first 60,000 barrels. This tax structure could change as small breweries push for reform in the excise tax structure. In many places, state excise tax structure creates additional tax incentive programs for small producers.

Other taxes and required government payments creep in from issues like on-site production, wholesaling, private clubs, and bonds. For example, a **brewers bond** is required in advance of production, which is pegged to the expected production volume and filed to guarantee tax payments in the future. So again, it pays to stay on top of the legislative issues in your respective country, state, and local community. Great resources for regulations and tax information include the Alcohol, Tobacco, Tax and Trade Bureau (TTB), individual state liquor control boards or commissions, city and county zoning for alcohol and food businesses, local permitting agencies, and individual state and local alcohol laws.

SUMMARY

The success of a new business depends on a thorough understanding the market for the concept. One of the best ways to think about the market is to ask, what is the problem that needs to be solved? Some common situations are: there isn't a local cider or whiskey in the area; there is a surplus of apple and cherries in the town that cries out for a product; the neighborhood lacks a family friendly pub and "third place," a community space where people gather outside of work and home; no one is making sour or Belgium-style beers in the region; or, the town has a huge tourist population but no local beer, cider, or distilled spirits for people to buy. If the demographics and demand are present, there may be an opportunity for your concept. Just be sure that regulations allow for it first.

Market Fit for a Sour Beer Concept

Two industry veterans from craft's first wave in the 1980s, Art Larrance and Ron Gansberg, created Cascade Brewing in 1998 in Portland, Oregon. They produced well-balanced ales on a 10-barrel brewing system. However, in the Northwest's highly competitive craft brewing market, the pair quickly recognized the need to carve their own niche. Believing most beer styles were well covered already, they looked to sour beers.

Traditionally the sour taste in beer has been associated with spoilage bacteria, a mistake due to bacteria infesting a beer rather than being an intentional flavor characteristic. Today, sour beer is becoming increasingly popular as more craft breweries experiment with this novel style.

At Cascade's start, brewmaster Gansberg wanted to get out of the hops race among brewers and he rejected the "hoppier the better" core belief. Instead he sought a similarly intense sensory experience but with a difference. Once a winemaker, Gansberg was at home with barrels and fermenting fruits and saw sour beers as a blend of wine and beer making. Due to Portland's proximity to the Willamette Valley wine region, there was an abundance of wine barrels and a wide variety of local fruit. The use of regional fruits would become a key element to Cascade's style and reputation, unique both to the area and around the world.

For most craft breweries, the investment in heavy stainless steel equipment is huge. Larrance and Gansberg figured out that they could avoid these startup costs by using wine barrels, which would also add complexity to the beers. They were inspired by the centuries-old Belgian brewing traditions, but wanted to instill their own Pacific Northwest spin on the sour beer style.

In 2005 Cascade began creating base beers to age in barrels using the lactobacillus yeast to promote appealing sour flavors. Where traditional ales convert yeasts to produce alcohol and carbon dioxide, sour beers use bacteria to produce acids and the resulting sour flavor. Bacterial fermentation is a much slower process, requiring the beer to age and lending even greater complexity to the beer. The time spent on maturation varies depending on how much bacteria is present, or around four months for Cascade. A slow maturation in the barrels helps to age and mellow it over time. One barrel can lead to many different beers through blending, which means that recipes are not necessarily replicable. This uniqueness is also due to the fact that each year the fruit—and the barrels—are different. Cascade tries to make each beer better than the last, but also capitalizes on distinctiveness from year to year.

Larrance and Gansberg traveled to the Great American Brewers Festival in 2007 to sample other breweries' wood barrel-aged sour beers and left feeling confident that Cascade's sour would be competitive in the market. By 2008 Cascade had its first three oak-barrel aged and lactic-fermented Northwest style sour beers: the Kriek, Apricot , and Cuvée du Jongleur. The beers were hand bottled in 750-ml champagne bottles with a cork and sold for a premium price at the brewery's location. Soon the bottles were sold in other retail locations in Portland, as well as in Washington and California. The brewery won a bronze medal in the sour category at the 2008 Great American Brewers Festival, establishing a name for Cascade. The wood barrel inventory went from 60 to 150 oak barrels from 2008 to 2009, quickly growing to more than 1,300 by 2014. At the same festival in 2009, Cascade earned gold and silver medals for its beers, launching its barrel-aged sour beers nationally.

In 2010 Cascade opened up its second location near other craft breweries and distilleries, dedicated to making and serving its sour beers. In the 7,100-square foot building, formerly a produce warehouse, the pub occupies just over 2000 square feet. The remainder houses nearly 600 barrels for aging and fermenting, and is kept at the proper temperature for the cultivation of bacteria.

The new facility is similar to a Belgian blending house where all of the blending and aging takes place there. The building says "House of Sour" on it, a concept which wouldn't work just anywhere but was appropriate for a neighborhood dense with other craft breweries. The pub has 18 taps of Cascade's sours and ales, as well as two live barrels in the wall with unique blends. Every Tuesday night, a new one-barrel batch of a specially blended beer is tapped from the wooden barrel using a mallet. In a short presentation, brew staff talk about the beer as everyone in the barrel house samples it. In response to its popularity, Cascade moved barrel storage out of its blending house in 2015, with plans to expand the barrel house for retail and pub space.

The pub menu offers small plates, rotating cheeses, nuts, salads, and sandwiches with smoked meats. Each item pairs with a few beers on tap. Gansberg explains how everything in the cellar is like a giant spice rack and can be paired with food, bringing depth and complexity to a meal and vice versa. Cascade's beers highlight local produce and seasonality. Cranberry, for example, releases after Halloween, pairing well with the foods of the holiday season; Strawberry is aged until the following strawberry season.

Cascade distributes its bottles throughout Oregon, Washington, California, New York, Florida, Pennsylvania, North Carolina, and Massachusetts. Bottles are sold in the $20 range, a premium for beer, but reflect the time and cost required in creating a complexity comparable to wine. Gansberg explains how the beers broaden the flavor spectrum, capturing the interest of both wine and beer aficionados, a sort of middle ground. The brewery's creative blends and wide range of ingredients draw beer enthusiasts from all over the world who line-up at the door before the taproom is even open.

LEARNING ADVENTURES

1. For your state or town, map out all the craft businesses of a chosen beverage category (beer, cider, or spirits). Using the association or guild websites or the state alcohol licensing data research this question: Where are there obvious holes in the map and opportunities for a business location?

2. Tour one business (pub or production facility) and identify their client base and what attracts them to this business.

3. Make a competitor matrix for a product of your choice. What opportunities are missing in this market?

4. On a crowdfunding site (Kickstarter, CrowdBrewed, or another) find an example of a craft concept that found funding fast. What is the concept? How does it fit into their market and why do you think it succeeded? Alternatively, find a failed campaign and identify how the lack of "fit" in the marketplace contributed to the failure.

ENDNOTES

1. "Domestic Cider," The Cyder Market, LLC, https://cydermarket.com/Domestic_Cider.html.
2. Bart Watson, "The Demographics of Craft Beer Lovers, Brewers Association (2015), https://www.brewersassociation.org/wp-content/uploads/2014/10/Demographics-of-craft-beer.pdf.
3. "Quick Reference Guide to Wine Excise Tax," Alcohol and Tobacco Trade and Tax Bureau (TTB), [last updated November 26, 2014], http://www.ttb.gov/tax_audit/taxguide.shtml#one.

CHAPTER FOURTEEN

Sales Forecasting

Key Terms

baseline products

consumer-buying habits

expert opinions

growth pattern

monthly index method

off-site sales

on-site sales

patterns of demand

people's opinions

perishability limitations

product shelf life

qualitative methods

quantitative methods

seasonal pattern

seasonal products

Overview

After assessing the market for your concept, the next step is to get more specific and estimate how much product will sell in that market. This chapter describes the methods for estimating potential demand and shares tools for sales forecasting in different environments. Determining an estimate for an uncertain future is challenging enough when you have been in business for a while, but is certainly more difficult for someone in a startup situation or entering a new market. The trick is to thoroughly research your market and predict how different products and packages may perform in this market throughout the year. As a producer, you will need to recognize what your facility is capable of producing so that you can match capacity to demand throughout the year. It is possible to take a reactive stance toward demand and just respond to the market but only if your products are in high demand as in the case of some cult producers. More commonly, a proactive approach works on building demand in alignment with well-executed distribution and marketing efforts

Learning Objectives

▶ Understand active versus passive influence on demand.

▶ Evaluate the pros and cons of qualitative versus quantitative methods.

▶ Develop a forecast based on current market conditions.

▶ Understand different demand patterns and how to forecast under those conditions.

▶ Understand individual versus aggregate forecasts.

▶ Apply weighted average and monthly indices forecasting approaches.

Introduction

Every business plan requires both a forecast by month and annual sales projections over the next few years. For a startup business with no history in the market this activity can seem daunting. Will anyone buy this cider or beer? How many bottles of craft vodka will a typical bar go through in a month? What happens if your distributor gets your product into a chain store? Additional challenges stem from the fact that the demand for alcohol and its various styles fluctuate throughout the year. Like ice cream sales, beverage demand is weather and holiday dependent. In certain locations, tourists generate the biggest demand for craft products; this creates an environment with very high demand during certain months and very low demand in other months. These environments require creative strategies to raise low season demand, such as pricing and other marketing activities and distributing in a location with counter-seasonal effects. In spite of the challenges, every producer must devise a forecast for potential sales in order to create a production and employee schedule, to order materials, and to create a distribution plan. The forecast also influences cash flow projections, hiring, training, equipment purchases, expansion strategies, and many other areas of the business.

Main Types of Forecasts

There are two main ways to forecast and both are useful. **Qualitative methods** involve people's judgments, including **expert opinions** from industry leaders, associations, wholesalers, and trend watchers. Typically, the national craft beverage associations compile data of existing trends and share estimates of where they think sales are heading for the next year during their national conventions and in their publications. In addition to experts are other **people's opinions**, including your own, pertaining to customer tastes and changes in the market. For instance, if you are starting a cidery in a town, you might go around asking bar managers how many bottles and kegs of draft cider are typically sold per week and what kind of ciders their clients like to drink.

Quantitative methods are driven by data where you obtain historic sales data or commitments for the future from potential customers. For example, if a brewery had already operated for a year in a town and is considering expanding to another town in the region, it could assume that the same **pattern of demand** applies. **Seasonal patterns** of demand are generally consistent in terms of peaks and valleys, and the main forecasting adjustments are in the amount of growth or decline. This chapter introduces a variety of methods for using historic sales data to forecast the future. Generally, anyone who does forecasting should expect to use a combination of qualitative and quantitative methods because forecasting, which is both an art and a science, is never 100 percent accurate.

Forecasting for a New Business

As a new business owner, you have extremely limited knowledge to determine how much of your product will sell. Therefore, you must rely on the path of others who have blazed the trail before you to obtain the information and data to create your own forecasts. **On-site sales** are largely being driven by the location, quality of product, and word of mouth. For **off-site sales**, the biggest clues about the potential sales of a product come from competitors, package or bottle shops, grocery stores, bars, pubs, and restaurants in the same market. The first step is to figure out how many bars, pubs, and restaurants are likely candidates for your product. Any business selling alcohol is listed in the state's liquor licensing records. Be sure to note the type of license. If you produce spirits, there are specific licenses for businesses that can sell in this category. Similarly, beer and wine have different license categories.

FIGURE 14.1   Ask the bartender

In the next phase, it is important to identify which businesses lend themselves to craft products and which favor mass produced offerings. After determining a group of potential sales sites, visit a random sampling of them to ask how much craft product they move in a given time period. For example, as a craft gin producer you would go to as many craft cocktail bars as possible in different neighborhoods and, after having a nice drink, ask the bartender how many bottles of a competitive brand and style (say New Deal Gin No. 1) they might go through in one month. You would follow that up with a couple questions about how sales vary throughout the year as well as anything in particular that drives sales. Also, determine whether and how they might choose to pick up another craft style from a new producer.

After each visit, you estimate the probability of that establishment purchasing your new product. It helps to make a spreadsheet of all the potential buyers and give them a rating such as 10 percent: slim chance of purchasing; 50 percent: purchase could go either way; or 100 percent: purchase is assured. So for each place visited, you generate a probability of purchase and an estimate of monthly sales for a your different products.

Sales Estimate Example: Tinytown

A new distiller named Sue estimates that she has some chance of placing her product in 50 retailers in a place called Tinytown. After her casual research in Tinytown, she establishes a monthly estimate of one case of liter bottles per month per retailer. From these 50 retailers, she estimates the probability of purchasing in Tinytown as follows:

- ▶ 20 "for sure" retailers, 100 percent probability of a purchase (category A)

- ▶ 10 "maybe" retailers, 50 percent probability of a purchase (category B)

- ▶ 20 "wishful thinking" retailers, 10 percent probability of a purchase (category C)

Taking the average use per retailer (monthly volume) and multiplying it by the sum of each category's probability of purchase times the number of retailers in each category, Sue calculates the potential sales as follows:

$Monthy\ volume$

$$\times [(category\ A\ probability \times \#\ category\ A)$$
$$+ (category\ B\ probabilty \times \#\ category\ B)$$
$$+ (other\ categories)]$$

$$= \frac{1\ case}{month} \times \left[(100\% \times 20) + (50\% \times 10) + (10\% \times 20) \right]$$

$$= 1\frac{case}{month} \times [20 + 5 + 2] = 27\frac{cases}{month}$$

According to this formula Sue can expect to sell 27 cases per month to these 50 retailers. This estimate is for one style (say, gin or hopped cider) only. If she is producing other beverage styles, she needs to recreate this estimate for each style to find the total amount of her products' forecasted demand.

Patterns of Demand

Consumer-buying habits exhibit three basic patterns of demand, either individually or in combination as illustrated in Figure 14.2. First, if a product is something people consume regularly without any significant changes in behavior, the pattern of consumption is relatively flat with small fluctuations around a horizontal line. This holds true for beverages that people consume habitually like kombucha. The second basic pattern of demand is a trend where the product demand overall is growing or declining. This **growth pattern** can be seen year to year for any popular beverage company. Seasonal patterns, the third type, show similarly shaped peaks and valleys during the same points in the year. A craft facility in a beach or ski town has a peak season during the warm or cold months, respectively. Other seasons show less demand. Typically, ski towns might have another bump in the summer when tourists come for warm-weather alpine activities and beach towns might have extended shoulder seasons with dead time in the cold weather.

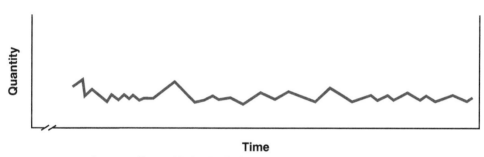

Time
Average: Demad is basically flat with random spikes and valleys.

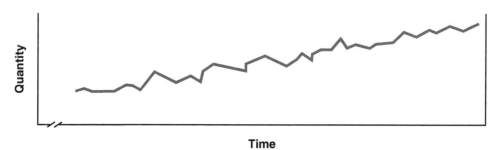

Time
Trend: Demand consistently increases or decreases.

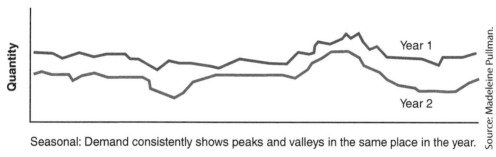

Seasonal: Demand consistently shows peaks and valleys in the same place in the year.

Source: Madeleine Pullman.

FIGURE 14.2   Patterns of demand

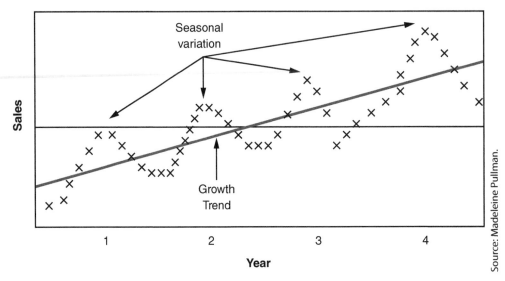

FIGURE 14.3   Seasonal and growth patterns

Most products experience some combination of these three basic demand patterns. For example, over a four-year period a product may show both general growth (trend) and seasonal growth. As illustrated in Figure 14.3, the peaks and valleys occur at the same times annually but amplify over time.

Beverage consumption shifts throughout the year depend on geographic location. Historically alcohol consumption has been higher during northern European winters than summers; the reverse is true in the United States where there is higher beer consumption in the summer than in winter. However, these patterns are undergoing change. While June through September in the US still have double the sales of other months, cold weather is no longer a signal for consumers to shift their overall consumption. Limited-edition seasonal flavors, such as those flavored with pumpkin and cinnamon, have increased fall beer consumption, while darker beers like stouts and bocks have increased demand in winter. Springtime offers a chance to consume more light, citrusy beers as well as shandies and radlers. Similarly, ciders have been associated with warm and fall weather consumption (apple harvest), but as styles branch out to include other fruits, spices, and barrel aging, cider has also become a cold-weather drink. Likewise, spirits have followed the same historic patterns as beer. Dark spirits (rum, brandy, whiskey) prevail in the winter or cold weather and light spirits (gin, vodka, tequila) in the summer or warm weather. But again with craft spirits and more unique offerings, you can expect shifts. The one constant among all beverage categories is the holiday consumption of alcohol, which is universally higher. Figure 14.4 demonstrates how beer consumption in the United States with average daily sales of several million cases soars to 10 times that amount during holidays. The peak holidays are the best times for spending marketing budgets on ads.

This information provides some clues as to how consumption might change throughout the year in a specific location. Most people in the industry are well aware of the high and low demand periods for their location and are good sources for pattern data.

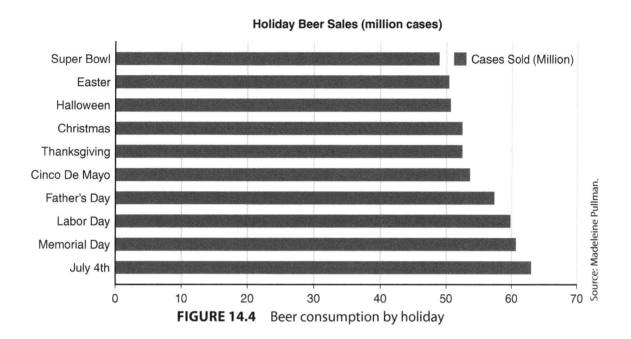

FIGURE 14.4   Beer consumption by holiday

Source: Madeleine Pullman.

Software for Forecasting

Software options now exist to help craft producers with the tough task of forecasting. These tools provide real-time analytics to help them plan their production schedule and manage their supply chain more precisely. Some packages (Orchestra Software) interact with the available distribution data (VIP Data Solutions.[1,2] Many of the available software options use seasonal trends so that producers can balance inventory throughout the entire supply chain and successfully get their beer to wholesalers on schedule. The software allows producers to get the freshest product to their consumers, while continuing to grow. Detecting short-term and long-term growth trends is very important for breweries to meet demand and grow sustainably.

Creating a First Year Forecast

After going through preliminary market research with retail sites, the next step is to figure out how average sales might change throughout the year. This pattern is of course, very location specific. Again, industry insiders (a distributor or bar manager) can provide estimates of how the average craft consumption rate changes throughout the year. Table 14.1 shows how the figures might be adjusted throughout the year for hypothetical *Tinytown* brand where the average craft keg consumption is two sixth barrels per month for a retail outlet.

TABLE 14.1 Adjusting average demand

Month	Average/ month	Adjustments and reason
January	2	-1 dead time
February	2	+.5 sports viewing
March	2	+.5 March Madness
April	2	
May	2	+1 getting warmer
June	2	+2 summer partying
July	2	+2 summer partying
August	2	+2 summer partying
September	2	+2 summer partying
October	2	+1 Oktoberfest
November	2	
December	2	+1 holiday parties
Source: Madeleine Pullman.		

After figuring out the monthly average demand per retail outlet, the number can be multiplied by the probability of sales estimates to get the overall demand as shown in the Tinytown sales estimate example.

During the first year of production, you should get feedback on how each of your products is performing in the market. Your own taproom or pub provides an opportunity for rapid feedback since you can observe sales and listen to customer feedback as it occurs. Distributors also provide solid feedback and can offer opinions about how your products might do in the forthcoming year. It is wise to start with a modest estimate of growth for the first few years, but if your business plans on aggressive marketing and produces a quality product, future growth can factor in these efforts.

Other considerations for first year and subsequent forecasts:

▶ How will **seasonal products** perform relative to **baseline products**? Will they potentially steal sales from your existing product line or build demand? Eventually, you will need to forecast for each product line separately and then aggregate all the forecasts into one.

▶ How will in-house sales compare to off-site sales? Again, these might need to be forecasted separately and then aggregated.

▶ How will the capacity of the production facility match up to the projected demand? An example later in this chapter and illustrated in Figure 14.6 looks at how to match up projections with capacity.

Working with Existing Sales Data

Once the business has collected sales data (usually based on the first year or two of sales), you can use different approaches to come up with future sales forecasts. The example is Table 14.2 displays two years of sales data.

Timing Seasonal Beer Releases

Figuring out the ideal time to release a seasonal beer can be tricky. Brewers strive to be the first to market with their seasonal beer and compete for shelf space in stores. The time is short to get customers' attention, since they do not buy seasonal beers after the corresponding season, and no one wants a surplus inventory of unsellable beer.

Each fall the most popular seasonal beer is pumpkin. Pumpkin beers even outsold IPAs during the month of October in 2013. In response, brewers are releasing their pumpkin beers earlier each year, competing for pumpkin beer sales and contributing to the phenomenon called "seasonal creep movement." Distributors and retailers are also pressuring breweries to deliver pumpkin beer early.

In 2014 one of the first pumpkin beers released was Southern Tier's Pumking, and the first bottles sold at the end of June. Southern Tier, located in New York State, bottled the beer on May 28 to prepare for an early release in nearby Pennsylvania. Given the increased demand annually this small production brewery has had to begin making pumpkin beer earlier each year in order not to run out of stock. Additionally, the brewery is trying to capture early demand, especially since there is a clear end to the time for pumpkin beer sales. So far, early pumpkin beer has received pushback from consumers who prefer to savor the summer months and its lighter style beers.

TABLE 14.2   Case sales for two years

Month	Year 1	Year 2
Jan	120	450
Feb	239	500
Mar	477	550
Apr	477	600
May	536	625
Jun	580	670
Jul	596	720
Aug	620	750
Sep	477	595
Oct	536	620
Nov	596	700
Dec	715	850

Source: Madeleine Pullman.

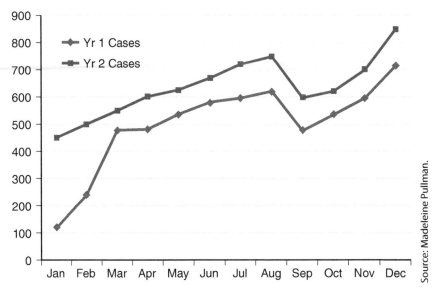

FIGURE 14.5 Plotted sales data for cases by month

The first thing to do is to plot data on a graph to look for obvious trends and patterns (Figure 14.5). In the plot, you can see that the product sales are increasing each year so there is definite growth. January sales in year one are low but are improving over time. There is a peak in demand in December each year and another smaller peak in July and August with a slow time in September and October. All of these patterns are important to know in order to plan for downtime, maintenance, and vacations during those slow times and then to build up inventory for the busy season.

Weighted average method: If there is no clear growth from year to year for a product, then the easiest way to forecast for the next year (if you have a few years of data) is to use the weighted average approach. With two years of data, you establish two numerical weights that add up to one. For example, if the recent year was more reflective of your expectations, then assign a higher weight (say 0.8) to the current year and the remaining weight (1.0 minus 0.8) to the previous year (0.2). Assign the weight for year one, $W_{year\ 1}$=0.2 and the weight for year two, $W_{year\ 2}$= 0.8. To forecast for each month of year three, use the following equation:

$$Forecast\ Year\ 3_{month} = (W_{year\ 1} \times Year\ 1\ Sales_{month}) + (W_{year\ 2} \times Year\ 2\ Sales_{month})$$

To calculate data for January for year three, compute the formula using the data from Table 14.2 as follows:

$$Forecast\ Year\ 3_{January} = 0.2 \times (120\ cases) + 0.8 \times (450\ cases) = 384$$

The result of this calculation for each month provides the completed year three forecast in Table 14.3.

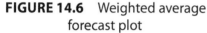

FIGURE 14.6   Weighted average forecast plot

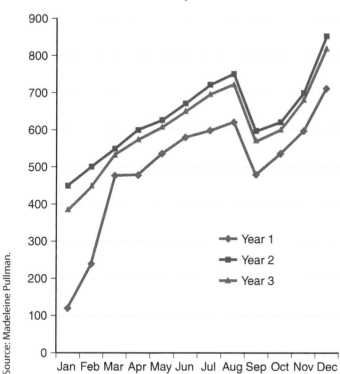

Source: Madeleine Pullman.

TABLE 14.3   Year three forecast with weighted average

Month	Year 1	Year 2	Year 3 Forecast
Jan	120	450	384
Feb	239	500	447.8
Mar	477	550	535.4
Apr	477	600	576
May	536	625	607.2
Jun	580	670	652
Jul	596	720	695.2
Aug	620	750	724
Sep	477	595	571.4
Oct	536	620	603.2
Nov	596	700	679.2
Dec	715	850	823

Source: Madeleine Pullman.

The plot of this forecast shows that year three is closer to what happened in year two shown in Figure 14.6. It reflects the lower demand of year one but is less than the demand in year two. The drawback of this method is that it does not reflect growth well and should be used with a product that is not experiencing growth in demand.

Growth: If you or your distributor has come to the conclusion that you will grow a certain amount for the next year, the best way to construct a monthly forecast is to use the **monthly index method.** This can also be broken down into weeks if weekly data is available from previous year(s). The index method can also be applied to a situation with only one year of previous data. Using the original data set in Table 14.2 add together both years' monthly demand and then divide it by the annual total for both year one and year two to get the percentage of the demand for each month (on average). Table 14.4 shows that January and December have 4.2 percent and 11.5 percent of overall demand, respectively.

If you estimate that your business will grow to 10,000 cases in year three, you multiply 10,000 by each month's percentile average to get a breakdown by month. This becomes next year's forecast by month detailed in Table 14.5.

TABLE 14.4 Monthly average calculation

Month	Year 1	Year 2	Sum of both years	% Yearly (Average)
Jan	120	450	570	4.2%
Feb	239	500	739	5.4%
Mar	477	550	1027	7.6%
Apr	477	600	1077	7.9%
May	536	625	1161	8.5%
Jun	580	670	1250	9.2%
Jul	596	720	1316	9.7%
Aug	620	750	1370	10.1%
Sep	477	595	1072	7.9%
Oct	536	620	1156	8.5%
Nov	596	700	1296	9.5%
Dec	715	850	1565	11.5%
TOTAL	5969	7630	13599	100%

Source: Madeleine Pullman.

Production Capacity and Perishability Limitations

When the forecasted amount and actual demand for certain months exceed the monthly **production capacity** there are two options. One option is to run short of the available product, which not only makes your customers and distributor unhappy but also costs the business in lost sales. Another option is to make product in advance during the slower periods and hold it in inventory. This option works so long as the **product shelf life** can hold through the typical sell cycle along with warehouse time. Take a look at the previous demand forecasts for year three in Table 14.5. If the facility has the capacity to make 1,000 cases per month then you can assume that with a 12,000 cases production capacity the business can handle 10,000 cases worth of demand. But, notice how the monthly demand plays out in the production schedule outlined in Table 14.6.

In this example, August and December require more product than the facility can produce. The August shortage of 7.5 cases can be easily handled during July's production. The December shortage of 150.9 cases requires increasing production as early as October. November does not have enough surplus capacity to make the entire production run needed and can only produce 46.9 additional cases. Therefore, October production needs to provide the remaining 104 cases to fulfill December's demand. It is important to insure that the pre-produced product is the first to move into sales channels so that shelf life limits are not exceeded at some point later in the season. Of course, this example is only valid for products that can be made within a month of the demand. Whiskey, aged cider and beer, or any products with long lead times need to be in production weeks, months, or years prior to the actual demand time.

TABLE 14.5   Monthly breakout for 10,000 cases

Month	% Yearly (Average)	Multiplied by 10,000 cases
Jan	4.2%	419.2
Feb	5.4%	543.5
Mar	7.6%	755.3
Apr	7.9%	792
May	8.5%	853.8
Jun	9.2%	919.2
Jul	9.7%	967.8
Aug	10.1%	1007.5
Sep	7.9%	788.3
Oct	8.5%	850.1
Nov	9.5%	953.1
Dec	11.5%	1150.9
TOTAL	1.00	10,000

Source: Madeleine Pullman.

TABLE 14.6   Capacity constraints and demand

Month	% Yearly (Average)	Year 3 Forecast	Capacity 1000 (Surplus or Shortage)	Make
Jan	4.2%	419.2	580.8	419.2
Feb	5.4%	543.5	456.5	543.5
Mar	7.6%	755.3	244.7	755.3
Apr	7.9%	792	208	792
May	8.5%	853.8	146.2	853.8
Jun	9.2%	919.2	80.8	919.2
Jul	9.7%	967.8	32.2	967.8 + 7.5
Aug	10.1%	1007.5	−7.5	1007.5
Sep	7.9%	788.3	211.7	788.3
Oct	8.5%	850.1	149.9	850.1 + 104
Nov	9.5%	953.1	46.9	953.1 + 46.9
Dec	11.5%	1150.9	−150.9	1150.9
TOTAL	1.00	10,000		

Making up for August

Making up for December

Still making up for August

"Enjoy By" Dates

Stone Brewing in San Diego is taking the concept of seasonal beer to the next level with its "Enjoy By" series of IPAs. Each beer's label is printed with its "enjoy by" date, generally a 35-day package-to-drink cycle. The expiration date creates a sense of urgency when consumers spot the date in large type. If any beer remains on the shelf after the expiration date it is to be immediately removed and returned to its distributors.

The idea is that consumers drink the beer at its freshest state, which can be important for an IPA with a big hop profile. Since hop flavor fades over time, beers brewed with a large amount of hops shine when enjoyed immediately. The brewery is challenged to bottle, keg, and ship the beer all in the same day. The "Enjoy By" series involves a great deal of additional work for the brewing, distribution, and sales teams.

The "Enjoy By" beer was first launched in 2012, and a batch of the beer was released into 11 different markets by early 2013. The beer is brewed only in small batches at a time and each one is distributed only to one or two distributors so different batches make it to different locations around the United States. The logistics of selling "Enjoy By" are complicated, and the distribution and sales teams must work closely with the wholesalers to be sure they understand the concept. CEO Greg Koch explained that they knew it would be impossible to release the series regularly to all of its markets without a mass awareness of the concept.

Stone has channels for consumers to communicate online to the brewery when they spot expired "Enjoy By" bottles on a shelf. Stone's reputation is on the line when the beer is expired since the taste is no longer at its best. Additionally, off tasting beer can reflect poorly on the retailer, wholesaler, and industry as a whole.

SUMMARY

There are many tricky aspects to matching the available supply to the unknown demand in the future through forecasting. The flagship product, as the most predictable in the portfolio, creates the least amount of forecasting headaches. Seasonals, on the other hand, typically have a limited-time-only appeal for customers (pumpkin spice beer or cider is not interesting after the fall season). It is best to pre-make seasonals and release early rather than having product left over after the season passes. When projecting aggressive growth in demand, the sales and marketing efforts and budgets should be commensurate with projections. Along the same vein, it is better not to oversell and under-produce product. Gauge production carefully and monitor your forecasting to see how well it matches what actually occurs month to month. If there are gaps, make an effort to understand why the projected forecast and actual demand are out of sync and recalculate your forecasts to reflect new information.

Crazy Mountain Brewing Manages Seasonality

Crazy Mountain Brewing is located near Vail and was founded by Kevin Selvy in 2010, coinciding with the boom in craft beer. Selvy not only loved the mountain-town lifestyle but also knew that Crazy Mountain could be the only production brewery within 100 miles, a rarity in Colorado. The flood of tourists during the winter and the summer guaranteed Crazy Mountain a ready market. Yet, for all of these advantages, opening a production brewery in the mountains was exceedingly difficult. Real estate is very expensive in Vail, manufacturing can be costly and unfavorable at cold temperatures, and transporting supplies and beer through mountain passes can be nearly impossible in some months of the year.

Selvy located Crazy Mountain Brewery strategically near a state highway so trucks only needed to drive 20 feet from the roadway to load and unload. Still, there was no way around the brewery's high elevation and extreme winter temperatures. Selvy planned ahead, contracting out two to three seasons for hops to avoid a shortage during a weather event.

The high cost of rent in Vail was compensated by the region's rich marketing opportunities and minimal local competition. Selvy learned that Vail had roughly 40 thousand year-round residents but 3 to 4 million visitors passing through for winter and summertime recreation. In recent years, enticed by Vail's tourism efforts, there were nearly as many summer tourists as winter, and the summer season was busier each year with many of the same people returning for both seasons. Crazy Mountain sales reflected this trend with 89 percent occurring during eight months of the year. Spring and fall were the slow seasons. As soon as ski season started, the brewery went from "zero to one hundred," in Selvy's words.

One of Crazy Mountain's key business strategies was to sell the beer to tourists and expose them to the brand. Visitors came to the brewery while on vacation and once back home, looked for the beer. This plan came true when Crazy Mountain started receiving calls from distributors all over the country. As the sole independent brewery in the area, Crazy Mountain Brewing found many untapped consumers. With just a handful of area brewpubs, Crazy Mountain garnered strong local support in the bars and restaurants. In addition, high-end restaurants in the mountain towns and high-volume restaurants on the mountain both served Crazy Mountain brews, helping to launch the brand.

Crazy Mountain Brewing began selling its beer in February 2010 and opened its tasting room by October. By the end of the first quarter, the brewery hit its third year sales goal and with a limited staff. Its first summer, Crazy Mountain employees were canning beer manually, filling just two cans at a time, to meet the explosive demand. In 2011, when the owner of one of the largest beer distributing companies bought a can of Crazy Mountain from his golf cart in Vail, Crazy Mountain landed its first distribution deal. Selvy raised half a million dollars in seed money from investors for an expansion that was completed in 2012. Crazy Mountain had a bottling and canning line as well as more tanks to increase production from 1,500 to 25,000 barrels. In additional to national distribution to 18 states, it also began distribution to Asia and Europe. To date, the company's second largest market outside of Colorado is in Scandinavia.

Three more expansions followed. In fall of 2015, Selvy announced plans to take over Breckenridge Brewery's facility in Denver to reach an even larger audience.

Early on, Selvy ran the business like a large brewery even when it was still small. He worked to set up a framework so that the business was ready when the demand came. Even so, the triple-digit growth in the first few years was difficult to manage. The tourism department of Vail tracked where guests visited from, and Crazy Mountain overlapped its marketing and distribution plans with these locations. Instead of starting locally and expanding to nearby states, Selvy targeted major craft brew markets, then grew towards them. Crazy Mountain also provided sales incentives, such as ski trips to Vail, to distributors, utilizing its location assets once again.

LEARNING ADVENTURES

1. Create the seasonal indices using the one year's worth of data provided in Table 14.7. Calculate the monthly demand for year two with a total production capacity of 15,000 barrels.

TABLE 14.7   Data for one year

Month	Year 1
Jan	120
Feb	239
Mar	477
Apr	477
May	536
Jun	580
Jul	596
Aug	620
Sep	477
Oct	536
Nov	596
Dec	715
Source: Madeleine Pullman.	

2. Conduct one interview with a bartender or bar manager to learn the basic demand for a product of your choice. How does it vary throughout the year? What drives sales in particular? How would this operation choose to pick up another craft style from a new producer?

ENDNOTES

1   Orchestra Software, http://www.orchestrasoftware.com/.

2   Vermont Information Processing, http://public.vtinfo.com/.

CHAPTER FIFTEEN

Marketing and Distribution

Key Terms

advertising
beverage tourism
brand
brand rights
cash on delivery (COD)
code dates
contract
distribution partnership
distribution plan
distributor's book
festivals and events
fit
franchise law
free house
freight on board (FOB)
houses
independent or specialty house

inventory
letter of intent
licenses
maintenance
major brand house
margin
marketing plan
markup
out of date (OOD)
places
positioning
price to customer (PTC)
price
producer
products
promote
promotional activities

pull
push
retailer
role
sales channels
self-distribution
shipping allowance
social media
target customer
termination
territory
third-party distribution
three-tier system
tied house
wholesaler
wine and spirits house

Overview

With your target market now clearly in mind, your next task is to figure out how to convey your story and product to these consumers. This involves creating both a marketing plan and a distribution plan that work in tandem. In the startup phase, you aim to sell as much product as possible on-site through a tasting room or pub. But, you will also want to build up off-site sales through distribution. Marketing efforts need to stay in step with the distribution strategy so that the vision and story—and the product, of course—connect with customers. This chapter describes the distribution methods for delivering your product into sales channels and illustrates how to calculate the potential costs and revenues.

Learning Objectives

▶ Understand how to reach the end consumer, retail store, or pub.

▶ Differentiate between marketing and distribution activities.

▶ Understand the three-tier system.

▶ Evaluate the pros and cons of self-distribution versus using a distributor.

▶ Understand the producer's relationship with a distributor.

▶ Differentiate and compute margin and markup.

▶ Understand the elements of a distribution contract.

Introduction

A great concept builds a **brand** with a story that resonates with the target audience. The challenge is getting that story in front of these consumers and the product into their hands. There are many different channels for reaching people with the product and the story. To succeed in this effort you need to have a well-thought-out plan. Some of the most prosperous brewing companies like New Belgium and Widmer Brothers Brewing started as small production facilities in the days when taprooms were not on the public radar. When Widmer Brothers started producing beer in 1984, they did not have their own pub (it opened in 1996) and began distribution using the brothers' small pickup truck. New

Belgium did not have a pub at their Colorado brewery either. Like other producers in those times, they had to find other businesses to carry their products. At the same time, they had to get the message out to consumers so that pubs and stores had reason to carry the products. Early brewpubs had a slightly different challenge; they faced the same marketing challenges as other restaurants in terms of finding a location frequented by their target market and creating good PR. Pioneers like Wynkoop (Denver, CO) and McMenamins (Portland, OR) renovated old buildings, often in edgy parts of town, and pulled the customers into those neighborhoods by offering craft beer and good food in a unique space. Wynkoop set the stage for converting the entire neighborhood into Denver's now-trendy LODO district of lofts, fine dining, and valet parking. The marketing and distribution challenges faced by those pioneers are quite similar to what you face today. One might argue that it is even more challenging for new businesses to get their messages to consumers amidst the "noise" of a substantially more competitive craft brewing world.

Marketing and Distribution Plans

Marketing and distribution plans are a standard component of every business plan but should also be a key part of your ongoing operations. The marketing plan identifies everything from who your target customers are and how you reach them to how you plan to retain existing customers and grow sales. The **distribution plan** covers the details of how you plan to get your product into those customers' hands. Clearly, these two plans are interwoven since distribution insures that the right product is on hand at the right time at the right price for each targeted sales channel and customer segment. Designed and conducted effectively, these plans are the roadmap to steadily attract customers and dramatically improve the success of your business.

Marketing Plan

The **marketing plan** builds on the concept, target market, and strategy covered in previous chapters. In addition, in order to match marketing to distribution efforts, it is useful to use the framework of the four Ps of marketing: price, product, promotion, and place. For example, if the business wants to sell growlers of product outside of the production location, it has to determine which **places** sell the growlers, how to **promote** the product in those environments, which **products** are best sold in a growler environment, and the appropriate **price** to sell the keg to the **retailer**. (Some of these decisions also connect to the distribution plan addressed later in this chapter.)

As a whole, a detailed marketing plan should address:

▶ The brand and story. How will the end user learn about your brand and story? Who is responsible for creating this? Who is responsible for educating others about the brand and story (sales people, distributors, pub staff, and others)?

▶ The **target customer** for the brand and sales channels. Sales channels are differentiated by the places the target customer consumes the product, off-site (purchased at a store and taken home) or on-site (imbibed on the premises at bars or restaurants). Different states have different laws for sales outlets which can add to the complexity of distribution. There are many different kinds of stores from craft-focused package stores to large chains and convenience stores. Similarly, there are many kinds of restaurants and pubs. Where does your target customer purchase beverages like yours?

▶ The money and time allocated to promoting the brand in various channels. On-site versus off-site channels require different types of promotion activities. A tap takeover of a pub is one kind of promotional activity and having a store tasting is another kind. Each requires time from certain staff people and varying levels of expense. A plan should address how money, time, and **promotional activities** might change over a three year period as the sales channel emphasis changes.

▶ If relevant, the plan should include details on the visitor experience to the business's physical site (pub, restaurant, tasting room, brewery, or taproom) as well as a description of how visitors engage with the product and brand during the visit.

Sixpoint Brewery's West Coast Laupnch

Sixpoint Brewery out of Brooklyn, New York, made the leap to the West Coast at the end of 2014 via Running Man Distributing. Sixpoint was founded in 2004 and sold in draft form only and began canning in 2011. Its branding is sharp and clean with packaging in a slim 12-ounce can. The brewery made a splash at a number of Portland's best-known beer bars through tap-takeovers. These launch parties featured co-owner Shane Welch who met with consumers and spoke to the brand. Most bars had five of Sixpoint's top beers on draft for consumers to try with cans available to take home.

Sixpoint also appealed to the local Portland consumers by collaborating with local companies on its new beers. Sixpoint's beer called 3Beans, incorporated Stumptown coffee beans and was available prior to its Portland launch. In May 2015, Sixpoint collaborated with Oregon's popular Jacobsen Salt Co. on a gose-style beer, an old German style sour and salty beer made with at least 50 percent wheat malt, just in time for the summer. Also in spring of 2015, Sixpoint and Running Man hosted a launch party for a new abbey style ale at a Belgian focused beer bar, Bazi, continuing to form relationships with new consumers. The brewery's aggressive launch into the already saturated Portland market was well worth the time investment. It received ample amount of press and created a presence for its beer.

Reaching the End Customer

The end customer is the person who drinks your product in a pub or purchases a bottle or six-pack at the store. But before they can become consumers, they have to learn about your product. Probably the best way to build a market for a startup craft product is to generate customer **pull**, meaning the customers hear about your product and ask for it in pubs and stores, thereby generating demand. The **push** strategy is more common with the big industrial breweries where the product is "pushed" to consumers through media marketing campaigns and promotional activities. The push strategy requires a significant amount of money for advertising and retail promotions. Regardless of the pull or push strategy, the product needs a distinct identity which is conveyed through stories, images, labels, tap handles, packaging, media materials, buildings, trucks, clothing—in short, everything designed for the business.

Table 15.1 categorizes the different ways customers find out about your product.

TABLE 15.1   Marketing to consumers

Method	Considerations	Cost
Social media: Facebook, beer rating sites, YouTube, Kickstarter, Twitter, and other similar social media venues	Very effect for reaching broad audience Videos and content needed constantly	Requires at least a half-time employee for content and updates
Advertising and traditional media	Effective for different audiences	Most expensive
Festivals and events	Target opinion leader Non-profits in sync with mission and story	Either money losers or break-even activities Consumes resources
Beverage tourism	Can be funded by state Cooperate with other businesses or organizations	Should make some money eventually
Source: Madeleine Pullman.		

Social media: Social media has become an effective way to build a brand and story even before opening the business. For example, Portland-based Ecliptic Brewpub had 2,000 Facebook "likes" before opening. During the initial stages of social media, Ninkasi Brewing in Eugene, Oregon built a local following through its pages on Myspace and Facebook with more than 8,000 fans before even selling its first bottle of beer. Long before other breweries caught on, Ninkasi had a presence on pho-to-sharing sites, posted daily on Twitter with a constant stream of commentary, special events, tast-ings, and promotions, and sponsored concerts with local bands. One band, Volfonx, promoted a free CD on Ninkasi's beer label to anyone who bought three bottles of the seasonal ale at a local bottle shop. The brewery quickly had more than 200 accounts in their own town.

Similarly, crowdfunding sites are another way to build an audience and create "pull" before open-ing the doors. The most successful craft beverage crowdfunding activity was Stone Brewery's cam-paign to raise money for its Berlin, Germany brewery project. The campaign, framed as pre-selling beer from the new facility, raised more than $2.5 million, well above the $1 million target. But beware: this is certainly not the norm; most craft beverage producers are lucky to raise $50,000. In marketing terms, it is not necessarily the money raised but the number of people who participate in the cam-paign and then become advocates for the business.

Today, proactive social media activity has become standard practice in the industry. It is an effec-tive method of reaching a broad audience but requires a constant stream of good quality photos, videos, and other content. A good estimate is one half-time employee to do this job plus the costs for quality video production, photography, and graphics. Alternatively, there are professionals for hire on a consulting or hourly basis.

Advertising and traditional media: Advertising comes in many forms today, from radio, Internet, and television advertising to print media and billboards. Your marketing team should be aware of the types of media most prevalent among your target market. While the popular craft food and beverage magazines or websites are obvious marketing opportunities, other advertising avenues better connect potential customers with the brand's story. For example, a brewery with a biking and environmental focus like New Belgium or Hopworks might advertise in local outdoors-oriented and biking publications. Similarly, Internet advertising can be easily connected to the target consumers based on their shopping history and other online behaviors. Craft **producers** have traditionally shied away from television advertising due to cost considerations and potential mismatch of the target audience. Increasingly, craft beverage businesses with the money are doing television spots. Or, delivery vans can be branded and are an effective mobile billboard for a brand. Overall, these types of promotional activities are the most costly.

An inexpensive alternative is to write educational articles for industry magazines and blogs. The Brewers Association and the various craft cider and distillery associations all publish newsletters and magazines that require content filled with hot topics in the industry. These outlets are a great way to contribute ideas to the industry as well as get your name and your company's name out. The only cost is your time and brainpower.

Festivals and events: In almost every part of the world where craft beverages are produced, festivals are held at the local, regional, and national levels. The Great American Beer Festival (**GABF**) is the biggest in the United States. In Europe Cannstatter Volksfestn and Oktoberfest have huge attendance rates. Cider and beer fests are cropping up in every state and country with enough producers to attract a good turnout. In some states, there are beer or cider festivals almost every weekend. The Great American Distillers Festival and other state's distiller festivals are rounding out the range of other craft beverage festivals.

As alluring as festivals are, every producer needs to be strategic about which festivals to attend. A festival requires adequate product, often a keg donation, and shipping fees, entry fees, and labor if the organizers request your staff rather than their own volunteers. Most nano producers do not have enough product to participate in more than a couple of festivals each year. Festivals are a break-even proposition at best so choose the festivals that will make the biggest impact. You should calculate all the relevant costs, the potential attendance, and know whether influential bloggers and other media writers will be attending. In the case of big festivals like the GABF, it can be very challenging since

FIGURE 15.1   Festivals

there are now more than 700 breweries represented with almost 4,000 beers. Given that the number of breweries in the United States far exceeds that capacity, booth spaces are assigned by a lottery based on geographical region.

Fundraising and other events for non-profit groups are another way to give your product exposure and show alignment with certain values. Start by researching non-profits that fit with your target market's interests such as sports, music, animals, environmental, community schools, or international disaster relief. Similar to the festivals, research the number and type of attendees to insure they match up with your target demographics and desired outcomes.

Finally, in-house events are a great way to generate interest from the public and raise money. Common events are barrel release parties, fresh hops, and charitable co-branding (for example, buy a beer and 25 cents goes to a fill-in-the-blank charity).

A Strategic Social Media Marketing Campaign

Social media is an important engagement tool for craft producers. Responding to a tweet, commenting on Instagram, or giving a "cheers" on Untappd all create conversation and meaningful customer experience with the brand. Since opening in 2012, Aslan Brewing in Bellingham, Washington has strategically used social media, specifically Instagram, to establish its brand among the area's young, adventure-loving target demographic. Initially, the company posted images of staff members enjoying Aslan beer in the Cascade Mountains and in other natural areas around Bellingham. Packaged in cans with a striking design of a lion's head in neon green, the beer conveyed the story of an outdoorsy and mountain-loving brand. Aslan took this campaign one step further in 2015 by holding an Instagram competition for followers to post photographs of Aslan beer in the great outdoors using the hashtag "#Aslanadventure." The prize was a growler fill and T-shirt package, but the brewery was the sure winner. The campaign resulted in crowd-sourced marketing material for the brewery to re-post and created a conversation on Instagram around its brand. It solidified Aslan's messaging that this beer was made to go on hikes, camping, and river and mountain trips—everywhere the brewery's customers yearned to travel.

Beverage tourism: Increasingly local, state, and countrywide tourism boards are promoting beverage tourism. Joining the local tourism or visitor association is beneficial to producers. Examples include the Kentucky Bourbon Trail Craft Tour, Portland's Distillery District, Nova Scotia Eat & Drink, Scotland's Scotch Whiskey tours and various cider tours in the United Kingdom and France. This kind of tourism relies on cooperation between the producers and tourism organizations to produce maps, articles, and websites to promote the regions through public relations. With beverage tourism other businesses support the tour, offering transportation, for example, while the producers provide space for the groups, employee time to provide tours, tasting materials, and so on. Fees are negotiated with the tour provider. Periodicals like Sunset Magazine, Destination Magazine, and other lifestyle magazines also promote food and beverage tourism by running stories about towns with a concentration of breweries, cideries or distilleries offering tours, tastings, or food and beverage events.

Distribution Plan

The distribution plan addresses the different sales channels and identifies the person in your organization responsible for getting product to those channels. On-site consumption is generally handled by a bar manager and production manager. An in-house distribution person or a third-party distribution company handles off-site distribution. Depending on how far away the product is distributed one producer may have several potential distributors throughout a state, region, or even nationally. Regardless of the distribution route, a business needs its own sales team to interact with the various channels. Your business plan should cover the following topics related to distribution:

▶ Self-distribution's role in the distribution strategy if relevant.

▶ Potential distributors for the product in the initial region as well as other regions as you expand.

▶ Cost (payment) to different players in the distribution chain.

▶ Percentage of product going to a distributor versus sold on-site over a three-year period.

▶ Planned incentives and promotions with the distributor as well as an expansion and sales growth plan.

Distributors' Role

While most people think the distributors' role is to support the sale of product and transport it to the pub or store, distributors perform several other valuable activities. First, they buy the product from the producer and store it, which generates both cash and space savings (such as reduced rent and walk-in space costs). Second, they help to market the product outside of the normal reach of the producer. Finally, distributors are required in many places around the world depending on local laws. Typically a distributor has exclusive rights, known as **brand rights,** to market a product in a specific area or **territory** such as county borders in the United States.

Source: Madeleine Pullman.
Image: ©robert_s/Shutterstock.com

FIGURE 15.2   Distributors activities

Three-Tier System

In many countries (and prior to Prohibition in the United States), breweries own or finance pubs and these pubs buy beer from the production brewery. This structure is known as the **tied house** or alternatively as the **free house.** *After* prohibition, the tied house arrangement was prohibited in the United States and **wholesalers** emerged to bridge the gap between the retailer and the producer. This is called a **three-tier system**. At the time, the three-tier system was appealing politically because it eliminated the dysfunctional system created by tied house arrangements. Also, wholesalers created thousands of jobs during the Depression.

The three tiers are the producer, the wholesaler, and the retailer. They function together to get product to the consumer. The producer and wholesaler have a contractual relationship protected under federal, and often state **franchise law**. This law protects the wholesaler against termination by the producer. The producer and wholesaler work together on marketing programs, pricing, and promotional activities for the retail channels. As an independent business, the wholesaler sets the price for the product to the retailer. While the producer can suggest a price to the retailer or price to consumer, neither the retailer nor the wholesaler is required to sell at that price.

Self-Distribution versus Third-Party Distribution

If legally permitted in your state, you may choose to self-distribute. Bear in mind, however, that self-distribution may become overwhelming after a certain point and you will need to call in a third-party distributor. In many locations it is legal to self-distribute, or in other words, for a brewery or cidery to sell directly to a licensed retailer. The laws around **self-distribution** vary among states so it is important to read your state's regulations to understand the ins and outs. In the United States, 16 states and the District of Columbia forbid self-distribution and instead use the three-tier system. Utah, for example, allows self-distribution from a warehouse on the brewery's premises as long as the

FIGURE 15.3   Three-tier system

brewer produces less than 60,000 barrels per year and sells to licensed retailers or for permitted events. Arkansas, on the other hand, only allows self-distribution to producers selling at least 35 percent of production within the state.[1]

Self-distribution helps small producers capture a bigger margin since the business earns the full retail price on the product instead of selling the product to distributors at a reduced wholesale price. By interacting directly with retail clients, the producer also has the opportunity to build strong relationships, convey the story of the brand, control pricing and promotions, and receive feedback. Additionally, the producer may do a better job managing the inventory, avoiding out-of-stock situations and keeping out-of-date product off the shelves since they only have to focus on their own products.

Conversely, taking on the distribution task adds many additional responsibilities and diversions for the producer. Running a craft production facility is demanding and time consuming alone, and so is the distribution job. In fact, many producers are ill equipped to become distributors not only in terms of resources and time but also skill sets. The distribution tasks require a sales staff, investment in vehicles and maintenance, costs of additional insurance and higher worker's compensation costs, distribution team management, and logistics. Unless a producer reaches a certain critical mass of customers with similar needs clustered within 100 miles of the production site, self-distribution can end up as a money-losing proposition.

Overall, self-distribution is a standard starting point for most craft businesses wherever legally feasible. It is one of the best ways for producers to educate themselves about the market, tell their story, and hear feedback, while learning the ropes of distribution. By going through a self-distribution phase, a young craft business can then build a market and become more appealing to potential distributors once a proven track record exists.

Third-Party Distribution

There are three main types of wholesale models or **houses**: 1) **wine and spirits houses**, 2) **major brand houses**, and 3) **independent or specialty houses**. Some of the key features to look for in any distributor are the structure of their draft department (how they takes care of kegs, tap handles, and draft line maintenance) and service to retail (such as merchandising and weekend support), chain store penetration, facilities (such as a warehouse), inventory management and delivery systems, fair contracts, and reputation.

Liquor and wine houses: These houses are a clear choice for spirits, cider, and mead but they do also carry brewery products. Southern Wine and Spirits dominates the US market and is as big or bigger than all beer houses on the market. Companies like this have operations in many states covering a broad territory, strong finances, consistent pricing, and solid inventory management systems. The sales staff is well trained and educated at "hand selling" specialty items and tends to have strong relationships with package stores, high-end restaurants, and grocery chains. If your craft beverage is a good fit for an outlet that sells lots of wine and cocktails, fine dining or specialty beverages, then the liquor and wine houses could be a good choice for your business.

On the other hand, this type of house generally does not service retail or draft environments as well as beer distributors. Wine and spirits historically have higher margins so beer and cider are less appealing to sell. These beverages tend to receive less attention from the house management and staff with a large portfolio of alternatives. Plus, **code dates** (indicating perishability) are not part of the wine and spirits world so the employees are not as sensitive to managing this inventory issue.

Major brand houses: Each market has a distributor connected to a major brand, for example AB-InBev. While there used to be three or four brand houses, the United States has one dominant company. AB-Inbev is the biggest beer wholesaler with a corresponding large sales staff and infrastructure. The company services all channels and has special departments for chain store management. As the biggest player in the market, it offers many advantages to producers: great sales and marketing data, coverage of virtually all licensed retail accounts, lots of money to support marketing efforts, financial stability, aggressive competitiveness, and skills at managing all things beer related such as draft accounts, code dates, out of stocks, and so forth.

But, a major brand house is always most loyal to its own brand and product portfolio. While historically brand houses have not been experts on craft beverages, this lack of expertise is rapidly changing as they bring in savvy sales staff to support their acquisitions of craft breweries and cideries. Given the choice of promoting someone else's craft product or their own craft portfolio, you can guess where the focus and incentives will go. With brand houses expect limited investment spending on other brands and promotions as well as push back on novel flavors, seasonals, and brand extensions.

Independent or specialty houses: Many startups and small producers are either unable to get into a major brand house or want more attention than those houses provide. As a result, independent houses are cropping up in many markets. These houses specialize in craft beverages and the staff is very knowledgeable about styles, flavors, histories, and techniques. Typically, these houses champion unique flavors, seasonals, and new products that interest the most sophisticated craft consumer. Their owners and employees understand the needs of draft accounts as well as special storage and shipping requirements. Additionally, they have the skills to monitor inventory issues like code dates and stocking product.

As these houses are highly specialized, they are better at building relationships with niche retail accounts than big chain stores and often do not have the skills or power to get products into national accounts or a wider variety of retailers. Because of their smaller scale and resources, the facilities, sales staff, inventory management system, and truck fleet may not be as new or sophisticated as the major brand houses. Financial stability of the company may also be a concern as well as its commitment to being a long-term player (rather than just building up a portfolio and selling the business to a major brand house).

Pricing and Cost of Distribution

Any brand strategy should define how the product is priced as part of the **positioning**, specifically the **price to customer (PTC)**. Both you and your distributor influence the PTC, and it pays to spend some time doing research on competitors' pricing in the stores and bars where you want your products sold. The distributor can help identify appropriate sales locations. After putting together a list of locations, identify the product leaders you plan to position your product against. You will be working backwards from this targeted PTC to figure out the distributor's price and your wholesale selling price. Generally 20 percent of all accounts represent 80 percent of the sales volume, so look hard at these key accounts since this is where you want to position your products.

Markup: This section provides formulas for calculating the price points for each player in the three-tier structure.

Mainly, retailers are concerned with markup or the percentage of profit based on cost.

$$Markup = \frac{PTC - Cost}{Cost}$$

So, if a retailer buys a case for $15 and the PTC is $20, then the retailer's markup is:

$$Markup = \frac{\$20 - \$15}{\$15} = \frac{\$5}{\$15} = .33 \ or \ 33\%$$

Alternatively, the retailer could have a standard markup for the craft beverage category, say 40 percent. If you know that your targeted price point is $18 to the customer, then you will need to "back out" what the retailer's purchase cost should be using the following formula:

$$Cost = \frac{PTC}{Markup + 1}$$

Example:

$$Cost = \frac{\$18}{.40 + 1} = \frac{\$18}{1.4} = \$12.86$$

Margin: Just to confuse things, wholesalers (distributors) tend to talk about margin for their cut of the pricing. Margin is the profit percentage based on sales price. In this case, the wholesalers' *cost* is what they pay the producer and their *price* is what the retailer pays the wholesaler or:

$$Margin = \frac{Price - Cost}{Price}$$

So, if the distributor is selling your product to the retailer for $12.86 and you sold them the product for $10, then their margin is:

$$Margin = \frac{Price - Cost}{Price} = \frac{\$12.86 - \$10}{\$12.86} = .22 = 22\%$$

The way it really works is that the wholesaler (distributor) dictates the target margin, generally in the 27 to 30 percent range for craft beer and cider, potentially more for spirits. So you figure this into your calculations to "back out" your selling price. This two-stage pricing markup calculation illustrates how much of a cut happens whenever products go through a distributor to a retail environment. Figure 15.5 shows the comparable margins for the producer, distributor, and retailer. It makes it clear why every new craft beverage owner now plans for a tasting room in which to sell their products wherever it is legal.

FIGURE 15.4   Three-tier economics

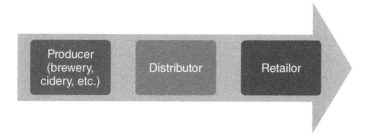

Measure	Producer (brewery, cidery, etc.)	Distributor	Retailer
Revenue (Rev)	$90	$125	$500
Cost of Goods (COGS)	$45	$90	$125
Gross Profit (GP)	$45	$35	$375
GP/Rev	50%	28%	75%
Source: Madeleine Pullman.			

Working Backwards at Ecliptic

Looking at their competitive set on the off-premise shelves, Ecliptic Brewery realized that that their core brands needed to sell for $4.99 per 22-ounce bottle. The retailers wanted a 30 percent margin while the distributor took a 27.6 percent margin for the core brands. John Harris, Ecliptic's owner, had to determine if the brewery could make enough profit in this setting. Working backwards, the distributor's price to the retailer (PTR) would need to be 70 percent of the shelf price (.70 * 4.99 = $3.49) so that a case of 12 bottles would need to be $41.88.

With the distributor's margin expectation, the brewery price to the distributor with all costs included or **laid in costs** would be (1-.276) or 72.4 percent of the wholesalers PTR or (.724 * $41.88) or $30.32. The wholesaler would pay the tax and shipping and handling which came to $1.32 so that the brewery would be paid $29 for a case or $2.42 per bottle. For the brewery, this price fell below their margin expectations. After negotiating with the distributor, they provided a $0.95 shipping allowance on each case taking it up to $29.95 for the brewery and meeting their target goals. To increase the profitability to the brewery, John would need to figure out how to drive down his Cost of Goods sold. Over the third year of operations, he purchased a grain silo to half the malt bill and next planned to bring bottling in-house to reduce the packaging costs per unit. For most producers, working on reducing the COGS is the name of the game when store pricing has limited flexibility.

Distribution Partnership

Distribution arrangements are contractual agreements, which are very challenging and costly to terminate. The franchise laws were set up to protect the distributors from producers terminating the agreement. So it goes without saying that choosing a distributor is one of the biggest decisions you will make. Like any potential long-term relationship, it is important to look at the fit between the producer and distributor, understand the respective roles of each party, and learn how to maintain a healthy relationship.

Fit: During the process of deciding on a distributor, the first thing to gauge is the fit between the two businesses, current life cycle phase, and long-term growth projections. A newer small producer with unusual products should consider a specialty craft house or wine and spirits house. Alternatively, a brewpub/packaging facility with solid name recognition in a region and an existing production rate over 5,000 barrels with plans to grow into convenience and grocery chains matches the services of a major brand house.

Other considerations are the cultures and personalities of the two businesses. A distiller may want to find a distributor that carries a book of wine and spirits with similar values in terms of premium and artisanal products. Cider makers may be more compatible with a distributor strong on draft beer and pub sales; if producing barrel-aged or single-varietal ciders with wine or champagne-style packaging they might seek companies serving specialty stores and fine dining.

You should also consider where your products might fit into the **distributor's book** of products in terms of range (number of craft products) and depth (styles and families of products). The producer should research each potential distributor to gain thorough knowledge of their different product attributes and processes as well as the personality and style of the salespeople. Other producers in the area are valuable sources of information on the reputation and work quality of potential distributors.

Role: One of the biggest misunderstandings among producers is the distributor's role in marketing their products. Distributors are very effective at moving, storing, and stocking product. But they cannot sell the product without the producer's commitment. As a producer, you need to get out into the field both on your own and alongside the distributor's sales staff to help score new accounts. You need to create and communicate the marketing and sales strategy so that the distributor can execute that strategy in a complementary way. Typically, the distributor will split the cost of marketing materials for promotions. In short, when you pick a distributor, you are not giving away the sales function; your business can now focus entirely on sales rather than delivering product. During the courtship phase, be sure to ask questions about distributor's draft service, call frequency to stores and bars, and other aspects of customer service.

Maintenance: The distributor represents many products. When producers feel like their products are not getting adequate attention it is easy for a producer and distributor to fall into an adversarial relationship. Be wary of this pitfall and remember that each entity needs to feel supported in its efforts. Distributor representatives respond well to positive feedback and incentives. Support for sales efforts with marketing materials and producer sales staff go a long way to building a supportive and trusting relationship.

Contract

The distribution arrangement is complex. The written **contract** is the main communication tool between the producer and distributor; thus it behooves all parties to have a well-written and legally researched document. As the producer, you should hire an experienced contract lawyer to help with this process, specifically someone that has worked with alcohol distribution law. Do not sign the first contract given to you by a distributor since there are many negotiation points. The resulting contract between both parties should be equitable and adequately address both parties' concerns. In the United States, state franchise laws trump the contract content so understand the requirements of those laws before signing. This section covers some of the key components and vocabulary of the distribution contract.

Letter of intent and licenses: After reaching a verbal agreement to work together, a typical first step is to issue a letter of intent to appoint (from the distributor). This document expresses an intention to enter into a contract. In the United States, this must be signed within seven business days and the distributor must acknowledge no intent to sell the brand or distributorship within the next 90 days. That clause is contingent upon the execution of the contract by both parties. Both parties must prove that they have the necessary licenses and permits to fulfill their roles in the contract.

Freight: The distributor maintains the territory outlined in the contract. Within that territory, the contract should specify how the distributor will get the product, how much it will cost to get it there, and who pays for those costs. The freight cost is typically called **FOB** (Freight on Board) indicating the point from which the freight is included in the price. For example, "$60 FOB brewery" implies that the cost does not include any shipping; "$90 FOB New York" means that the cost of the product includes the shipping to New York from the brewery. Recalling the discussion on markup and margin, the distributor marks up the product from the FOB price, so it is in both parties' shared interest to keep the shipping price as low as possible. In some situations, distributors offer a **shipping allowance** so that the producer can get an appropriate price on the retail shelf for locations out of their market.

Along these lines, there might be a minimum order quantity specified, such as a pallet of product, which indicates that it could be a mixed pallet of several products. The more product distributors can pick up in one truckload, the more they can reduce their transportation overhead. Minimum order quantities help keep the costs down for everyone.

Another freight issue is shipping problems such as breakage, invoice discrepancies, and any other cost-related shipping issues. The contract could specify how credits can address these problems.

Pricing and marketing details: The distributor will have a target margin typically dictated in the contract. The margin is applied to the FOB price and a price to retail can be specified. The bottom line with pricing and marketing details is to understand how much the distributor will invest against the brand. The distributor can help with different promotional activities like advertising, truck painting (logos on delivery trucks, and special events on a cost-sharing basis. The distributor could commit to appointing a brand manager and participate in special events. Another helpful issue to specify in the contract is the reporting of data when the producer gets sales data and who the contact person is for sales information.

Inventory: The contract should specify the **out of date (OOD)** product policy and responsibility of the distributor to manage perishability of the product. The product may require certain storage and shipping conditions, these should also be specified in the contract. If product needs to be destroyed, someone will be responsible for the cost of the expired product and for disposing of the product.

Sales commitments: In the contract, the producer can ask for certain commitments from the distributor. Examples of these commitments include sales goals such as on-premise (bars) and off-premise (store) activity such as the number of new keg handles or store or bar accounts each month.

Payment: The payment section would include terms of payment like **cash on delivery (COD)** in 30 or 60 days. Some states have COD laws for alcohol. If days are used, then the contract should specify if the day count starts at pickup from the producer or arrival at the distributor's warehouse. The method of payment may also be specified as cash, check, or electronic funds transfer.

Termination: All contracts should indicate situations leading to termination and the outcome of the termination. The contract should cover dispute resolution or the means of resolution such as non-binding arbitration or mediation. There should also exit clauses for each party. If a contract violation has occurred from the producer's perspective, the distributor should be allowed time to remedy the problem stated in a letter to the producer.

Additionally, the terms of a sale are part of this contract specifying some minimum multiplier (X) of the brand value for the producer to get out of the contract (the distributor is paid by another distributor or by the producer wanting distribution rights back). The brand value is based on the distributor's cost of a case equivalent sold by the distributor over the last 12 months. If the distributor sold 1,000 cases of product at $30 per case over the last 12 months, then the multiplier is applied to $30,000. The multiplier is challenging to determine and may be specified by the state. For example, if X equals five, then the distributor would be paid five times $30,000 or $150,000 for your brand. But, if another distributor purchases your distributor, then that purchase will nullify your existing contract.[2]

A Differentiated Distributorship for Craft Brews

Aaron Gardner created Point Blank Distribution in 2003 after working for a large distributor in Portland for 10 years. Gardner aimed to work solely with high-quality craft brands. With partner Scott Willis, the company grew from two employees to over 80 across Portland, Eugene and Bend, Oregon. Point Blank started with two craft brands and slowly picked up more, and the company's top brand has changed many times over the years.

The two partners quickly found that there were not enough distribution companies for craft brands. Point Blank found that there was an unfulfilled demand for 24-hour turnarounds to the marketplace, which was not done by larger distribution companies. Point Blank was hungry enough for business early on to take that demand on and to provide a very high level of service for their customers. Gardner admitted that occasionally the company lost money to make a customer happy.

In general, Point Blank likes to visit the local breweries in its portfolio once a week, or at least once a month, to check in. The best brand representatives visit often, retrieve weekly recaps and pick up samples to create relationships with customers.

When approached by a potential new vendor, Point Blank requests samples to make sure the product is high quality. Next, they look at packaging and assess how much effort was put into the brand. Gardner notes that many breweries skip this area or don't put enough time into it, stressing that packaging must tell a story. For Point Blank brands, volume expectations are dependent on what the brewery can provide. Gardner mentions that forecasting tools can be helpful to help decide what and how much to order, but that breweries should use it only as a guideline. Seventy percent of vendors will have annual or quarterly business meetings with Point Blank to set goals, learn how incentives work, find out what is selling well, and what the trends are.

Its minimum requirement on markups is at the lower end of the industry, at 25 percent of net, but 27 to 30 percent if possible. For Point Blank, the standard time frame is 30-day net, but they prefer 120. If the brewing company has a price in mind for the shelf, Point Blank can work backwards to figure out what the price that hits their dock needs to be.

Point Blank evaluates the brands in its portfolio each year, looking to see if sales or quality have decreased, or if there isn't a fit. Point Blank has been adding a buy-out clause to contracts in order to provide an "out" if needed. The company is not picky about who they sell to, but only aggressively seek customers who have a genuine appreciation for craft beer. Point Blank has made service its top priority and chooses to work closely with unique craft brands within the region.

SUMMARY

Distribution and marketing are tightly interwoven. The marketing team creates and schedules ads, social media, point of sale materials, coasters, packaging and label design, promotions, special events, and other public relations activities. The producer must count on employing a sales team to get and maintain accounts regardless of whether or not a distributor is used. The distribution arm must be ready to execute product according to the marketing schedule. When sales promotions are going to occur, the distributor needs adequate product in place to accommodate the sales as well as the point of sale material and any other print media that need to be at the retail locations. Overall, the marketing, distribution, and sales teams should be in constant communication and heading in the same direction to enable the success of the brand overall.

The Commons Brewery Self-Distributes

The Commons Brewery focuses on moderate alcohol and yeast-driven beers. The brewery presents itself as an alternative to the malt- and hop-forward beers that dominate the market in Portland, Oregon. After progressing up to a 15-barrel system with kegs and bottles, founder Mike Wright decided to continue self-distributing the beer locally. In Oregon, it is legal for breweries to self-distribute, and since The Commons grew gradually over five years, Wright never considered another distribution method.

Wright began by going door to door at potential buyers, which took a while to sell people and was a lot of legwork. However, once the beer was in a handful of places, it took on a life of its own, creating customer pull in restaurants and bars. Self-distribution allowed The Commons to keep every bit of income from sales as well as to get paid upon delivery. The company also maintained control of the beer all the way to the retailer, passing on the story of the brand and building relationship with retailers.

The Commons did not establish pricing controls. The brewery originally set its flagship beer, Urban Farmhouse Ale, at $7 per 750-ml bottle. Retailers marked it up to the level of other 750-ml bottles on the shelf. (Pricing would be more sensitive when the beer was being sold out of state because of the additional costs associated with transportation.) Wright found that he could persuade a retailer, but the brewery had no direct control over pricing. Over time, The Commons added a few employees to its brewery and distribution staff. It purchased two trucks for deliveries, and invested in storage space for the beer as well as cold storage to hold ready product.

As the logistical challenges mounted over time, The Commons finally handed off distribution to a third-party in February 2015 after considering that option for two years prior. Wright considered starting his own distribution company under a separate entity. However, after meeting with many distributors, he decided that distributors do provide a very valuable expertise. In partnering with a distributor, The Commons would to stay true to the creative beer business instead of diving into the distribution business. The brewery had just doubled its production capacity to 1,500 barrels annually by adding two 30-barrel fermenters. With the benefit of a sales army keeping in touch with retailers and facing at stores, The Commons staff could dedicate themselves to the sales and relationship side of the business.

After signing a distribution deal in 2013 for distribution throughout Oregon the distributor shortly thereafter was purchased by AB-Inbev. Out of concern that a large distributor might not best serve the interests of a small, independent craft brewery, The Commons backed out of the contract having worked with a good lawyer. By January 2014, the brewery was once again self-distributing.

Early in 2015, The Commons signed a new distribution deal with Maletis, a company focused on the Portland area and effective at growing a packaged beer brand, including expanding to out of state sales.

In hindsight, Wright recommends the experience of self-distributing while a brewery is getting up and running. Not only is it beneficial for the cash bump, but the brewery gains a storehouse of knowledge about the distribution process that proves useful when the brewery is ready to look for a distributor. In the case of The Commons, Wright knew where they needed help and how they could potentially shine with a solid working relationship with a distributor.

LEARNING ADVENTURES

1. Research the local distributors in your area that might carry your product of interest (beer, cider, spirits). How would you classify the house (big brand, independent, or specialty)? What kind of products do they carry? Which one do you think would do the best job for your chosen product and why?

2. Evaluate the trade channels in your area. What are the different types of chain stores, package stores, and smaller groceries serving your market? Detail the types of restaurants and pubs that are likely candidates too.

3. Given a product that you might be interested in selling, conduct a competitive analysis of the players in this segment. Come up with specific price points for your product line. Please provide reasons for your chosen PTC.

4. Go through the pricing exercise for a known bottle and keg product (find a product for which you know the PTC). Assume the store markup is 35 percent and the distributor markup is 25 percent. How much could the producer be selling the product for to the distributor? If the producer COG is $50 of their selling price, how much money are the producer and each of the other tier partners making in terms of profit margin?

ENDNOTES

1. "Self-Distribution Laws," Brewers Association, https://www.brewersassociation.org/government-affairs/laws/self-distribution-laws.

2. Laura Lodge, *Distribution Insight for the Craft Brewer*, (Denver, CO: Tatter Covered Press, 2012).

CHAPTER SIXTEEN

On- and Off-Premises Marketing and Distribution

Key Terms

above-the-line marketing (ATL)
below-the-line marketing (BTL)
bill backs
category captains
centralized purchasing
chain authorization
craft eccentric account
craft exclusive account
crafting account
date stamp
decentralized purchasing
domestic
domestic only account
facings

floor displays
front line price
incentives
inventory management
just-in-time (JIT)
kegs
marketing elements
off-premises
on-premises
out of stock (OOS)
packaging
pay-to-play
pint night
point of sale (POS)

promotional calendar
refresh
resets
rotating handles
round tables
sell by date
sell sheet
set
shelf-talkers
slims
suggested retail price
through the line marketing (TTL)

Overview

In today's beverage market, restaurants feature half a dozen craft brands, bars carry dozens, and stores stock hundreds. With such a bounty of choices in each of these settings, it is the producer's job to steer the consumer to the company's products through targeted marketing and distribution activities. The plans and strategies for marketing and distributing differ substantially depending on whether the retailer is selling product to be consumed on the premises or off the premises. The combined and coordinated efforts of the marketing and distribution team are necessary to support this goal. This chapter covers the different methods for addressing both on- and off-premises retail environments.

Learning Objectives

▶ Differentiate between on- and off-premises distribution and marketing methods.

▶ Understand different account classifications.

▶ Understand how to reach different customers and the potential resource requirements of the approach.

▶ Evaluate promotion and pricing strategies including legal and financial implications.

▶ Understand chain authorizations and the typical chain retail management.

▶ Comprehend the producer's role in effective on- and off-premise distribution.

Introduction

When consumers purchase beverages to drink on the premises in bars, pubs, or restaurants, there are many opportunities to learn about the brand and story. For most producers, these locations are crucial to building brand image. Interactions with the servers and visual cues like tap handles, coasters, glassware, and signage all support the brand image. Off-premises sales venues may have a knowledgeable beverage person who helps in the package aisles. But given the huge assortment of products, this person may be well informed on a narrow range of products. In the store environment there is very little room for brand messaging of any kind other than on the package itself. Additionally, the distributor has different tasks and issues to address in each environment, such as draft management in bars and promotional and pricing strategies in stores.

On-Premises

In well-developed craft markets, winning accounts—and keeping them—for kegged or bottled product in the **on-premises** environment is a gigantic challenge today. The best way for a customer to sample a craft product is in draft form for cider and beer or in cocktail form for spirits. The draft scene has become a retail space of **rotating handles**, meaning that when a keg runs out, that keg and tap handle are replaced by another brand. Most on-premises retailers want to have lots of variety and exciting new products to keep craft consumers engaged. National on-premises chain restaurants typically allocate handles to local craft beers and cider, but as competition increases locally, rotation is to be expected. Combining the effect of increased velocity of rotating handles with the decreased keg size (the traditional half barrel has switched to a preference for sixth barrels or **slims**) has led to reduced revenue per placement. Craft accounts have several distribution classifications as shown in Table 16.1 (the term **domestic** refers to the major industrial beer brands, such as Budweiser, Coors, Miller, and Heineken, for example). In most locations there are many potential on-premises accounts (close to 50 percent of all the accounts). But on-premise accounts make up only 10 to 20 percent of the overall sales compared to off-premise accounts. This is a major challenge for marketing and distribution activities due to the large number of on-premise accounts to visit but low sales per account. Chain restaurants offer bigger sales opportunities but can be particularly challenging for smaller producers to get into.

TABLE 16.1   On-premises craft account classifications

Classification	Description
Craft exclusive account	Accounts that only sell crafts.
Craft eccentric account	Accounts that focus on craft draft and domestic packages.
Crafting account	Accounts that are selling crafts and are moving to focus more on them.
Domestic only account	Accounts that do not and will not sell any crafts.
Source: Madeleine Pullman.	

On-Premises Marketing

Marketing efforts for the on-premises arena should focus on two areas: relationship building with key decision-makers and creation of visual materials to influence the customer. The **sell sheet** is a one-page document with the brand logo, brief story, key selling attributes and differentiating factors, and descriptions of the individual products as well at alcohol content (ABV) and other important details, such as IBUs for hopped products. This sheet supports the retailers selling efforts and is also used by salespeople in off-premises environments.

Other important marketing materials are branded items to use when serving your product or apparel worn by the staff. Glassware has a long tradition in Europe as a differentiating element. Creating an interesting branded glass for your flagship attracts attention. Coasters are also popular, and customers can take them away as a reminder of your products. Tap handles require a distinctive yet functional design to attract the eye. Other important items include signage, banners, posters, and

FIGURE 16.1 Glassware

clothing (shirts, hats, and so on). The investment cost for many of these marketing items can be shared with your distributor.

The producer supports marketing and sales in the on-premises environment by working with the staff, management, and other influencers. For example, they can visit accounts and provide education on the styles and flavors in their product line-up. The producer should do his or her homework and be knowledgeable about the account's menu and competitive offerings. This information can be used to provide suggestions on food and beverage pairings, cocktail ideas, information about upcoming limited editions and seasonal offerings, and specific details on the unique aspects of their production that could appeal to the business' consumers. Craft exclusive and eccentric account holders appreciate interactions with the head brewer, distiller, or cider-maker because of their unique abilities to provide technical details.

FIGURE 16.2 Food and beer pairing

FIGURE 16.3   Draft beer pour

On-Premises Distribution

The on-premises world involves rotating kegs and flowing draft lines. There is no better way to lose customers than to have your high-quality beer or cider travel through dirty draft lines. It behooves all producers to know their distributors' policy and procedures around draft line maintenance. Self-distributors also need to have a maintenance program in place for draft lines. Tap handles and kegs require deposits from tier participants such as distributors and bars; some tap handles cost as much as a keg. The producer and distributor should agree on the number of handles and accounts to target and they should monitor progress toward achieving a new handle account goals monthly. Tap handle costs can also be shared with the distributor.

    Incentives are very important—and the norm to the dismay of may craft producers—for securing and improving sales in the on-premises environment. Each state differs in what they allow for incentives and the monetary value. Particularly at issue is a concept called **pay-to-play** where large breweries offer as much as $10,000 per tap handle, free draft systems, free beer, and other incentives for tap handles to stay with their brand portfolio. However, in the United States it is illegal to buy accounts or handles in any form or fashion. How this plays out is that if a brewery gives a free or discounted keg to a bar then it has to offer the same deal to all other retailers. It is illegal to give free glassware to accounts to secure their business but the glass can be given away for free with the purchase of a draft at a **pint night** event. In Chicago for example, both illegal and legal incentives from big producers and distributors are effectively barring craft products from the market unless they can counter with incentives at high levels.[1] Many states have monetary limits on what producers and distributors can give away but the recipients of illegal incentives often set up alternative bank accounts to hide the money. Anyone found guilty of illegal activity can lose their license and/or be fined.

On-Premises Marketing Expertise from Left Hand Brewing

Dan Jennings who handles beer sales for Left Hand Brewing out of Longmont, Colorado emphasizes the importance of creating solid relationships with accounts, as well as providing thorough, explanatory product materials. Jennings makes a presentation for new accounts, telling the story of the brand, and highlighting good press coverage. Jennings provides sales decks to explain which beers are perennials, seasonals, 12-packs, and draft only, detailing release dates, too. He brings samples to all sales meetings and makes a good effort to get to know people, often buying lunch and trying to simply be friendly and humble rather than pushing for quick sales. He does make a point to follow up after each meeting. Educating the staff at a new account is also very important, and Jennings talks to servers about Left Hand's beer during a shift change or staff meeting. He provides sales sheets, stickers, and key chains to new accounts' staff in order to share the story of the beer.

Education of Left Hand's customer base is equally important as training bar and restaurant staff. Left Hand runs promotions and participates in beer festivals in order to establish the brand. Left Hand schedules campaigns around seasonal beers, for example, promoting its Milk Stout around St. Patrick's Day. Tap handles, pint glasses, and coasters are also provided to bars. Posters, table tents, shirts, wristbands, and beads related to the beer and St. Patrick's Day is handed out to customers. Left Hand's marketing team handles these seasonal promotions and follow up with a recap of numbers after a campaign ends. Left Hand keeps meticulous track of social media numbers and press hits for each event to measure effectiveness and assess the investment. Left Hand also participates in charitable events as a beer sponsor, including five different Bike for MS rides. The brewery tries to be a good community partner while reaping the publicity.

Off-Premises

The **off-premises** environment includes any place where customers buy packaged products to take away: supermarkets, drug stores, convenience stores, package stores, club stores, liquor chains and independents, military base stores, and even some hardware stores (depending on the state). Producers need to identify all potential accounts and prioritize them in terms of fit and opportunity. Like on-premises accounts, key accounts require frequent visitation to keep up with needs and changing priorities. The vast majority of sales is dominated by chains and requires **chain authorization**. In the initial stages, the chain buyers prefer to work with the distributors rather than the producer. The sooner you can be your own voice, the better, but that requires a solid relationship with your distributor and their buy-in. When a buyer for a chain or region of the chain authorizes you to sell your product there, you have received authorization. It entails two advance activities for the producer or distributor: a) getting an appointment with a chain buyer, and b) making a presentation to that buyer

FIGURE 16.4 Chain store shelf

with all aspects of your marketing program. The distributor and producer work together to insure that the marketing program makes sense and that the distributor can fit the product(s) into their product line-up within the stores.

Retail stores and chains have hundreds of new products pitched to them annually. As a result, getting an appointment with a chain buyer can be extremely difficult. Some chains have **centralized purchasing** with all decisions made at their headquarters. This requires traveling to the headquarters, but if accepted, your product could end up at all their stores. **Decentralized purchasing** chains require sales presentations and authorizations at each territory of interest, and the product does not receive support chain-wide. Most distributors know the chain's contact people and can support the producer in this effort. The producer should preview the presentation with the distributor so that it gets to the key points quickly and hits the appropriate selling points.

Once the producer receives authorization, more challenges emerge. Many chain stores have **category captains**, individuals funded by the powerful producers with the intention of maximizing profits for the retailer. The choice of products, called the **set,** and the display of products, called the **facings,** have an impact on every producer. For example, just one variety on a bottom shelf will definitely not perform as well as three or four varieties at eye level. Increasingly, some retailers are hiring their own category managers since there is a risk of the category captain representing their producer's brands at the expense of the store's optimal profit.

It is important that the producer stay involved with the retailer and category captain's meetings or **round tables** concerning shelf mix changes, also known as **resets** or **refresh** the category shelves. Anyone who does not participate in these meetings winds up on the losing end. Overall, startups will struggle to have a voice in chain store activities and should strive to build very good relationships with their distributor to have any chance of success in this particular retail world.

Off-Premises Marketing Program

The off-premises marketing program includes the following elements: who you are and what your brand is all about, promotional calendar, pricing and discounts, and description of marketing elements. Typically, the program is dynamic and should be flexible enough to respond to changes in the marketplace.

The **promotional calendar** is a planning tool that indicates the months of the year when promotions will occur for different packages and brands. The promotional calendar ties into pricing and discounts for both retailers and the distributor. The calendar covers every month (potentially broken down by weeks) and indicates promotions for a specific period of time.

Many types of promotion are possible and the type of promotion pricing strategy should be spelled out accompanying the promotion calendar for the distributor. The legality of certain pricing strategies depends on the state; for example, any promotion that looks like a gift of free alcohol from a wholesaler to the retailer is illegal in California.

When discounting occurs, it is important to participate in the retailer's ad space (newspapers flyers, for example). Alcoholic beverage space is increasingly shared by all alcohol groups (wine, spirits, beer, cider, and so on) as more states allow groceries, pharmacies, and other types of retailers to carry alcoholic beverages. All categories are getting more and more players and subsequently the bigger brands tend to dominate ads.

Marketing elements for advertising are broken into three parts. **Above the line marketing (ATL)** refers to marketing with broad scope and reach, such as television or radio campaigns, typically not used until the producer reaches a large size. ATL builds brand awareness. **Below the line marketing (BTL)** targets specific groups in a focused way with advertising and promotion. Doing events with specific groups, such as athletes or non-profits, or using targeted Internet ads are examples of BTL.

FIGURE 16.5 Promotional calendar: craft beer

STATE: X												
Promotion month:	**Jan**	**Feb**	**March**	**April**	**May**	**June**	**July**	**Aug**	**Sept**	**Oct**	**Nov**	**Dec**
Craft beer package:												
4/6/11.2 oz. bottles		3/5–4/7			5/7–6/2		7/2–7/28	8/27–9/29			11/19–12/31	
2/12/11.2oz. bottles–promo				4/2–4/28		6/4–6/30		8/6 - 9/1		10/1–11/3		
24/11.2 oz. cans–promo					4/30–9/29							
1/6 bbl. keg	Everyday Low Pricing (EDLP)											
1/ bbl. keg	EDLP											
Source: Madeleine Pullman.												

TABLE 16.2   Pricing for promotions

Pricing Strategy	Definition
By one, get one (BOGO)	This promotion means that two packages are sold for the price of one.
Volume discount/everyday low pricing (EDLP)	The buyer must commit to buying a certain quantity to get the price (10,000 cases, for example, will have the price dropped by 20 percent). This could also be known as every day low pricing that the buyer has one price for the year, assuming that a certain yearly volume is purchased. The producer needs to track this carefully to insure that the EDLP they receive is reflected in the desired retail shelf pricing since some stores have been know to pocket higher margins.
Discounting off the front line price	The **front line price** or **suggested retail price** (SRP) is the highest selling price to the consumer to which the discount is applied.
Mail-in coupon/rebate (MIC)	The coupon is a shelf talker item that the consumer can send to the producer for a cash rebate.
Instant rebate coupon (IRC)	Depending on state law, instant rebates are provided by the retailer to the purchaser of the product (with a coupon). The producer is then responsible for covering the rebate amount.
Post-off	A discount offered by the producer to the distributor for a specific time period. The distributor is paid back based on product sold through **bill backs** (credits to the distributor) at the end of the billing period.
False front-line pricing	The pricing scheme is similar like EDLP but the producer puts a higher front line price on the product while simultaneously running a post-off to the distributor, giving the illusion of a high front-line price.
Free cases based on buy-in	Buyers are given free cases based on a certain level of purchased product.
Source: Madeleine Pullman.	

Through the line marketing (TTL) is a hybrid of both ATL and BTL. Creating different YouTube videos that targeted videos to specific audiences, depending on where they live or their interests, can accomplish broad reach with a finite set of videos and promotions.

Point of Sale (POS) materials for the off-premises arena includes some of the same materials used in on-premises including sell sheets, signs, banners, clothing, and posters where appropriate and the store management allows it. More specific to this environment are **floor displays** and **shelf-talkers** (printed cards that can be attached to the store shelf to draw attention to the products or promotion). POS materials need to be provided to the distributor at no cost for basic things like sell sheets and negotiated cost sharing for more costly items.

FIGURE 16.6 Display

Off-Premises Distribution

New and smaller producers face the challenge of getting adequate attention from distributors since they carry so many products. Because there are so many retail accounts, both producers and distributor's sales staff have limited time to sell to retail and often just become order takers. Big brands have the staff and promotional clout to send representatives to chain stores frequently and end up controlling all the mindshare of the store decision-makers. To combat this problem, producers must be creative with new product offerings and promotions and supportive to the distribution team. Additionally, producers must insure the right product is on the right shelves at the right time when a customer looks for it. The right product is a high-quality product that remains in good condition and fits the retailer's target market.

Inventory management is key to supporting off-premises distribution. On a daily basis the producer should know what products the distributor has in the warehouse, what product is in retail inventory, the sales velocity, and generally how long the product sits on the shelf in various accounts. The retail accounts cannot run **out of stock** (OOS); on the other hand, neither the distributor nor the retailers want to carry large amounts of inventory. As a result, the producer will be asked to provide frequent supplies of product that are ordered **just-in-time** (JIT) to meet demand.

At the other end of the beverage supply continuum is the issue of too much product ordered or not moving off the shelves fast enough, leading to out of date product. Particularly with more perishable items like beer and cider, producers should package with a **sell by date** or **date stamp** on bottles, 6-packs, cases, cartons, and other packaging. It is the producer's responsibility to communicate the quality standards around product shelf life to the distributor and sales staff.

Off-Premises Sales Drive New Belgium

Off-premises sales drive 80 percent of Colorado-based New Belgium's incremental growth. As consumers become educated on New Belgium's various beers, they gravitate towards off-premise options. Because retail has become more creative in recent years in terms of packaging and promotions, breweries like New Belgium can now successfully build brands off-premises. In fact, a packaging re-haul gave New Belgium an eight point bump in 2014 and it became a stand-out brand on retail shelves. Sixty to 70 percent of New Belgium beers are sold in the package with the rest as draft sales. New Belgium used to survey every store it sold beer in but found that to be very inefficient and now demands account information from its distributors in order to see account level data weekly.

Since pricing strongly influences consumer purchasing decisions, the marketing team meticulously notes what the high and low prices are in different market places before setting prices on New Belgium beers. Price increases tend to happen in the spring and fall, except for price leaders such as Sam Adams, which does not need to follow the herd. New Belgium discounts through the use of promotions if they enter a new market at a higher price than competitors and need to bring prices down. In addition to discount promotions, New Belgium sees triple growth when the product is displayed in a store.

New Belgium has found that various beers have brand lifecycles, and that jumps in sales around new launches, eventually become irrelevant. Also, mixed packs of beer have proven to be extremely expensive for New Belgium. The boxes have to be hand-packed, stopping the line to switch styles, which is very inefficient. The brewery also found that is does not work to price it higher, and has to accept the lower margin on its "Folly Pack" variety pack.

Producer's Role

The producer is responsible for determining the unique selling proposition and conveying the product's price-to-value relationship. What really makes the product stand out from the competition and why is the product going to improve the seller's profit margins? If a bottle of beer or cider will retail for $20, why will customers want to spend that money? How will the product be positioned for success in the retailer's mix? The producer's should keep the sell sheet current for the sales team and provide advance information about the limited edition and seasonal products.

Additionally, the producer should have working knowledge of their 50 top on-premises and 50 top off-premises accounts. What does each of those customers need to stay enthusiastic about the products? By visiting these customers regularly (at least quarterly), the producer can stay on top of those needs and listen to feedback about how customers are changing as well as what is working and not working.

Finally, the producer must make a great product. A great product makes marketing and distribution efforts much easier while a marginal product will require huge effort and tons of money to put "lipstick on the pig."

Online Marketing Tools

Websites and apps are important conduits for connecting brewers with customers and creating word of mouth marketing. Ratebeer.com and BeerAdvocate.com are well-established online guides that offer beer enthusiasts popularity lists, forums, and information on craft breweries. Untappd is a mobile app where consumers rate beers, upload photos, tag the location, and share it through social media channels such as Twitter and Facebook. Craft breweries use this tool to see which of their beers are trending and to track their competitors. For brewers, it is important to monitor each of these platforms to make sure the right beers are listed and the information is up to date and accurate.

Hosting a blog on the company website is another avenue for customer engagement. Blogging builds a brewery founder's credibility, generates interest from themed content, such as how to brew beer and food pairing, and establishes the brand. Whether or not you choose to blog, it is important to connect with bloggers online, and even invite them to the brewery. Providing them with information, including a fact sheet, photos, and the logo can help to spread the word about the brewery in general, or to share new releases and special events and generate more excitement online that translates into more customers and sales.

SUMMARY

Overall, the producer needs to focus on distributing to all of the places where their potential consumers can find their product. Some of these are easier to get into relative to chain stores or restaurants. For example liquor stores, specialty grocery, and farmers' markets are great places to do tastings and get exposure to new customers. Depending on the state, tastings are allowed at many retail locations including club stores. There are many successful brands that invest long weekend hours sampling their products to club store patrons either with the producer's staff or an independent marketing firm. Marketing and distributing to on- and off-premises locations is complex, and it pays to have an experienced team member on the producer's staff who knows the lay of the land and all the players.

Baxter Brewing Builds a Brand Through Athletics

Many breweries participate in athletic events through sponsorship, but Baxter Brewing Company in Lewiston, Maine has taken the sports concept to the next level. Through its subsidiary, Baxter Outdoors, the company hosts a winter sports and a mountain bike series of races throughout the Northeast . Every entrant aged 21 and over receives a drink ticket to use after completion. Baxter runs the events and actually earns money while building its lifestyle brand. The company has expanded its consumer base well beyond beer drinkers to those who only participate in events and those who do both (as well as those who just drink) and in doing so has created a well-engaged community.

An Urban Grocery Buyer's View of Off-Premises Consumption

Green Zebra Grocery is a neighborhood convenient store for healthy, high-quality food in Portland, Oregon. The small store contains a deli, a coffee bar, a growler fill station, and a well-stocked beer and wine section. The beer, wine, and cider selection is curated by Steve Byers, Green Zebra's libations buyer. Byers describes regular customers as "ambidextrous," meaning that they drink a mix of beverage types and styles. They are also seasonally influenced, drinking darker beers in the winter months, lighter beers in the summer, and IPAs year round. Customers at Green Zebra appreciate having a steward at the shop who listens to their feedback and their requests and is able to bring in new product. Byers habitually tries out new products, observes how they sell, and when necessary, gives them a little push in the store with a display or a tasting. Green Zebra hosts regular Friday night tastings when customers can try something new each week.

When a brewer arrives at an authorization meeting, Byers expects a product sample, which is especially helpful if he has not tried the beverage before. A handout that details other important information, such as pricing, is useful as well. One of the most important factors when assessing a new producer is the willingness to commit to a good partnership. Byers can generally pick up on that quickly, based on how often and how long the visits last. Working with a self-distributed producer allows Byers to form a valuable relationship with the producers themselves. For example, when Cider Riot's representatives first came into Green Zebra, their excitement for product was contagious, and made the decision to sell the product an easy one. Byers describes his relationship with Cider Riot as a "win" because they are really nice people and the product is high quality and unique.

Green Zebra attempts a balanced variety of styles with seasonality in mind when stocking new products. The craft beer cooler is small, so Byers does not go over five SKUs of a one producer, and he tries to give smaller breweries a fair shake. As a case in point, Green Zebra consistently stocks five options from pFriem Family Brewers, which is in high demand. Shortages of pFriem beer occur, so the beer is viewed as rare and seems special to consumers. In Byer's view pFriem's pricing is honest, and the brewery could charge two dollars more for 16 ounces, but does not as a way of thanking local consumers.

The industry standard of pricing margins for craft breweries in most grocery stores is a 30 percent markup, and is closer to 20 to 25 percent at a large chain such as Walmart or 7-11. Many breweries keep a six-pack priced just under $10, but Byers believes that a price of $10.49 is what it should be. Green Zebra is checking out other comparable retailers frequently to stay in check with their pricing. Promotional deals are optimal for a retailer because it generates excitement in the store, and the brand becomes low hanging fruit. When a producer runs a promotion, Green Zebra places in-store ads and includes the deal in communications with customers. As a small store, Green Zebra does not have a lot of real estate on the floor for big displays. So, Byers generally chooses the product that is running a good deal to put on display.

Most grocers have a minimum pull through for SKUs in order to determine when to remove unsold products from the shelves. Byers creates a report of the bottom movers, products that have low sales over the past few months. If Byers has done everything he can in terms of shelf placement and promotion, the product is removed. Green Zebra has a backup plan beer on hand to fill in any holes if something goes out of stock. If Green Zebra needs to get rid of a beer quickly before its expiration date, the store will mark it down. Byers does not want Green Zebra to be responsible giving a poor impression because the product simply sat on the shelf for too long.

An additional opportunity for craft breweries to reach new consumers is through the in-store growler fill station. Green Zebra added a growler fill in the fall of 2013 when they were not as prevalent as they are today. Growler fills are a fun way for people to try different things. It may be a bigger investment for a consumer than one 22-ounce beer, but Green Zebra lets customers try samples of the growler options. The beer is fresh, and customers may be more apt to share their growler with friends, bringing in new potential fans.

In Byers' opinion craft breweries must make great beer and have a great story behind it to compete in the retail space. If there is a strong connection, the retailer can pass it on to customers. A good label speaks for itself too; if a consumer is holding up two similarly priced and styled beers, the label is a determining factor in the purchasing decision. Green Zebra has five rules for retailers: keep it fresh, full, cleaned, signed, and serviced.

LEARNING ADVENTURES

1. Create a sell sheet for an existing or potential brand.

2. Go to a popular bar and conduct an audit of promotional material from different brands.

    a. What do brands have in place?

    b. Whose coasters are offered on the bar?

    c. Who has done a successful job of placing promotional items in the bar? Calculate what the promotional cost per bar might be for the producer.

3. Look at a flyer for your favorite grocery store, visit the store and examine sales promotions there.

    a. Which products are in the flyer?

    b. Which products are on promotion in the store?

    c. What kinds of discounts are offered? Are any of those products perpetually on promotion and if so, what kind of producer fits into this category?

    d. How long does the promotion last?

ENDNOTES

1. James Ylisela Jr., David Sterrett, and Kate MacArthur, "Pay-To-Play Infects Chicago Beer Market, Crain's Investigation Finds," Crain's Chicago Business (2010) http://www.chicagobusiness.com/article/20101120/ISSUE01/311209986/pay-to-play-infects-chicago-beer-market-crains-investigation-finds.

CHAPTER SEVENTEEN

Inventory

Key Terms

continuous review

finished goods inventory

fixed time period approach

holding cost

ingredient prices fluctuate

inventory monitoring

lead times

opportunity cost

order cost

out of stock cost

periodic review

point of sale (pos) system

production cost

purchase cost

raw materials

setup cost

unpredictable demand

variety

volume discounts

work in progress (WIP)

Overview

Inventory is everything from grain and fruit to glass bottles sitting empty in your facility to finished product in your distributor's warehouse. It is not permanent, big-ticket items like equipment or furnishings, but includes everything your business needs to produce all of the beverages (and food) in your portfolio. Inventory eats up a ton of cash and requires constant monitoring. It must be accounted for in a business plan for both the startup and growth phases. Also, inventory is considered an asset and therefore must be detailed on financial statements. This chapter describes the ins and outs of inventory, the different classifications, the various purposes and systems for management, and the costing implications.

Learning Objectives

▶ Understand different inventory classifications.

▶ Evaluate starting inventory needs and costs.

▶ Consider various purposes of inventory.

▶ Compare different systems for monitoring inventory.

▶ Understand the hidden and clear-cut costs of inventory.

▶ Practice the method for costing different inventory strategies.

Introduction

To operate a beverage production business, you must constantly buy materials. Just to get started, your business needs recipe ingredients, packaging materials, and kegs. Additionally, there are basic items like cleaning supplies, printer paper, toilet paper, and other minor goods used on a day-to-day basis. And as soon as those items are used up, more need to be purchased. The day a beer is brewed or a cider goes into a fermenter, the **raw material** inventory is converted to a **work in progress (WIP)**, a different form of inventory. When the beverage is packaged and placed into the walk-in cooler, the product becomes **finished goods inventory**. From the WIP stage through the finished goods stage, federal and state agencies demand to know how much product with alcohol is sitting around in your facility so they can monitor and collect taxes on it.

Getting started requires quite a significant cash outlay for inventory. For example, most packaging producers need to invest in pallets of bottles or cans. Because the price per unit drops dramatically for volume purchases, this may mean purchasing an entire truckload of containers. The issue then becomes adequate storage for an entire truckload of bottles or cans. Similarly, the ingredients, labels, crowns, six-packs, and other necessary items require appropriate storage space that protects them from pests, moisture, theft, and other hazards. Cider producers who plan to press juice require a full truckload of fruit bins, which may have to be left outside or in a warehouse space prior to pressing.

Barrel-aging programs have become very popular. Barrel aging not only allows for spirits to mellow but also creates wonderfully complex flavors for many

FIGURE 17.1   Basic inventory

Source: Madeleine Pullman.

FIGURE 17.2 Cider apple bins

TABLE 17.1 Big versus small inventory items

Bigger items	Smaller items
Keg Float	Growlers
Barrels/Casks	Cleaners and sanitizers
Glassware	Water treatment minerals and acids
Keg caps and collars	Office supplies, printer ink, paper
Packaging	T-shirts and other merchandize
• Cartons	Tap handles
• 6-pack carriers (# brands)	Gaskets and clamps
• Labels (# brands)	Duct tape and WD-40
• Bottle crowns	Stickers
• Stretch wrap	Spent grain or pulp bins
• Artwork plates/label	CO_2 or O_2 tanks
• Bottle or cans	Hoses
• Grain, fruit, juice, concentrate, hops and other ingredients	Yeast

Source: Madeleine Pullman.

other beverages. But, barrel aging is a major cash drain when accounting for the cost of inventory, and those products should be priced to reflect the increased cost. Overall, inventory management is part of the business strategy since it has an impact on cash flow not only at the startup phase, but also in day-to-day operations and throughout future stages of growth.

Purpose of Inventory

Inventory serves a variety of purposes. First of all, most businesses face **unpredictable demand** for their products. For example, during one week in the tasting room, you might sell four kegs of IPA and two Pale Ales while the next week, only two kegs of IPA and two Pale Ales sell. Since demand varies, it is important to have backup kegs of various products. Second, most materials have **lead times** that vary from the producer or warehouse. The truck carrying the labels could get held up in a snowstorm or the packaging printer could have mechanical problems, so having a safety cushion of labels prevents losing a scheduled packaging day. Third, by having a **variety** of ingredients and packaging materials on hand, the manager has the ability to change the production schedule to another style if necessary. Not having enough kegs can cause major production dilemmas when a tank must be emptied in order for another product to move forward. Fourth, **volume discounts** exist for almost every inventory item. For example, buying malt or fruit in bulk amounts (by the truckload) generally cuts the cost of the product in half; thus, you end up with a lot of inventory but purchased at a reduced cost. Finally, **ingredient prices fluctuate** throughout the year and over time, so having the ability to buy significant amounts for low prices at harvest time (hops or fruit) is a wise decision.

Two Brothers Brewing and Hop Contracting

Based in Warrenville, Indiana, Two Brothers Brewing produces more than 40,000 barrels a year with a focus on European styles. The brewery is environmentally conscious, sources ingredients locally, and returns spent grain to local farms for feed. Two Brothers also purchases local hops to support the economy and to cut down on transportation. As a result, the brewery founders have learned the importance of hop contracting in order to ensure an allocation of the crop each year in a high demand and limited supply market.

With so many craft breweries on the scene, Two Brothers co-founder Jason Ebel recommends a five-year plan, contracting 100 percent of need for the first two years, 80 percent for the third year, 60 percent in the fourth year, and 40 percent in the fifth. Harvest patterns are hard to predict, so this plan allows for flexibility while demonstrating a commitment to a hop supplier. Ebel also seeks out new local hop farmers to find new hops varieties and to minimize the carbon footprint. After more than 10 years in this business, Two Brothers founders understand the necessity of hop contracting both for guaranteeing supply in a competitive market and for adhering to its mission of supporting local growers whenever possible.

Inventory Monitoring Approaches

In any business, someone's job is to monitor inventory so that there is a record of when to place an order and for accounting (both business and government). There are two ways to monitor inventory, **continuous review** and **periodic review**. Depending on the business concept, you will practice either one, or both, of these.

Continuous review: As the name implies, with this method the inventory item is monitored continuously and when a certain event occurs, such as the product falls below a certain level, a consistent quantity (Q) of product is reordered. For example, when the silo of base malt has 1,000 pounds remaining or perhaps just three pallets of bottles are left, the event triggers an order for another truckload of malt or bottles. In these instances a truckload is the consistent quantity, Q, ordered.

For a restaurant, the **point of sale** (POS) system can be tied to the inventory and order indicators. When someone orders a hamburger, the system automatically deducts one half-pound of hamburger from inventory numbers, and when it reaches a certain amount like 20 pounds remaining, the POS inventory generates a message to order another case of beef. Without a POS system, you can set up an excel spreadsheets that correspond to the production schedule and connects to ingredients used (based on standardized recipes) relative to when the last quantity arrived. You insert a visual trigger into the spreadsheet to tell the scheduler when to order more ingredients and packaging material.

Periodic review: Also known as the **fixed time period approach**, the inventory items are checked at

FIGURE 17.3   Base malt Inventory

regular periods (P), such as once a week or once every month, and an order is placed to bring the item's inventory back up to a baseline amount. In this approach the quantity ordered varies but the period, P, between inventory checks remains constant. In the craft beverage world, this approach is commonly used with retail outlets. You go to the store and see how much product remains on the shelf on specific days, and add product until it fills the allocated shelf (and backroom) space. The government alcohol inventory forms are also completed by periodic review, but rather than ordering anything, the business pays its excise taxes based on inventory that has been sold during the designated period.

General Costs of Inventory

Inventory costs have three key elements: purchase, holding, and ordering. The **purchase cost (C)** is the cost per unit whether referring to a growler, a pound of base malt or apples, or a case of bottles. This cost varies depending on the volume purchased. If the product is made in house and kept in inventory, it is called the **production cost** per unit. For example, making fermented spirit from grain or potatoes rather than buying pure ethyl alcohol has a production cost rather than a purchase cost.

The **holding cost (H)** is the actual cost of owning and keeping the item in storage. Holding costs include obvious expenses like the rent, taxes, and insurance for storage. It also includes hidden costs like breakage, theft, or damage along with paying people to handle and move the items in and out of the storage space. Another holding cost issue is the **opportunity cost** of purchasing inventory. Opportunity cost is the economic impact off the business choosing to buy something and store it rather than having that cash available for other investments. Each business has a cost of capital, so if the cash is not in the bank or other investments making a return then this is a lost opportunity. The holding cost includes all of these costs.

Finally, the **order cost**, also called the **setup cost (S)**. This cost addresses the fixed cost of purchasing an item that is not directly tied to the quantity ordered. For example, when you order branded T-shirts or caps, the screening company has a base setup price for any printing and then you pay per shirt or cap on top of that. Similarly, if you are shipping by a truck you pay for transportation regardless of whether the truck is full or less than full depending on the company and vehicle type. Other expenses that go into the order cost include employee time to place an order, which is independent of the order size.

Another cost, one that is much harder to quantify, is the cost of not having product available, or **out of stock cost**. Running out of product means lost customer sales, unhappy distributors and retailors, and potentially lost long-term customers because they

FIGURE 17.4   Barrel aging

Source: Madeleine Pullman.

switched to another product when yours was not available. This cost is important to consider but will not be included in the inventory costing due to the challenge of coming up with solid numbers.

Overall, the total cost of holding inventory (whether made in-house or purchased) is the following equation:

Total inventory cost = production or purchase cost + order cost + holding cost

Aging whiskey example: Whiskey is a classic example of significant inventory costs coming into play. Presume that it costs the distillery $1,000 to produce a barrel of aged whiskey (including ingredients, processing, energy, and labor).

$$C = Production\ Cost = \frac{\$1,000}{bbl.}$$

If the distillery has a brewery produce the wort then there might be transportation costs to bring it over (ordering costs). But assume for this example that the wort was made on-site. The holding cost includes the cost to store a barrel in a warehouse plus the opportunity cost of having $1,000 tied up for a number of years in a barrel of whiskey instead of as an investment.

$$H = storage + opportunity\ cost$$

What is the cost to store a barrel of whiskey? A barrel takes up roughly four square feet of space including stacking. Allowing for adequate circulation and movement space around it and a warehouse costs $1/square foot per month. The business estimates that it could earn eight percent interest on a typical investment; alternatively, eight percent could be the amount the business pays for working capital loans. Given these numbers, the storage costs are:

$$Storage = 4\,ft^2 \times \frac{\$1}{ft^2 - month} \times \frac{12\ month}{year} = \frac{\$48}{year}$$

$$Opportunity\ cost = \frac{8\%}{year} \times \$1{,}000 = \frac{\$80}{year}$$

Since the whiskey is stored for three years, the opportunity cost with compounded interest is $259.71, so the total cost of three years becomes:

$$Total\ cost = \$1{,}000 + (3 \times \$48) + \$259.71 = \$1{,}403.71$$

Thus, the cost of storing the whiskey adds almost 50 percent to the baseline costs. The selling price of the whiskey should increase proportionally to compensate for this cost increase.

Comparing Different Inventory Strategies

In the world of beverage production, volume discounts abound. It is always cheaper to buy more of an item in terms of purchase price, but tradeoffs exist when you consider paying for storage space and transportation as well. This section examines how to evaluate the purchasing options over a broader horizon. It considers what happens a full year. Here are some numbers that to know from your forecast and suppliers:

D = Annual demand for an item (this estimate should come from a forecast or previous year's information)

C = Cost per item under various volume conditions

S = Cost to place an order or setup an order

Q = Number of items in an order (order size usually related to minimums to get a price break)

H = Average cost to hold an item in storage including opportunity cost

In looking at the full year, there are three costs: annual purchase cost, annual order cost, and annual holding costs calculated as follows:

$$Annual\ purchase\ cost = annual\ demand \times \frac{cost}{item}$$

$$Annual\ order\ cost = annual\ number\ of\ orders \ \times\ \frac{cost}{order}$$

$$Annual\ holding\ cost = average\ number\ of\ items\ held\ \times cost\ to\ hold\ one\ item$$

To figure out the annual ordering cost you need to know how many times you will order during the year. If the forecast reports that you need D (the yearly demand for an item) and you have to order a minimum of Q (the order size) whenever you order, then the number of times you order is D/Q. Here is an example:

The estimated yearly demand for pint glasses is 1,000 (D=1,000) and one has to order a minimum of a full case of 100 (Q=100). Given those minimums, the number of orders needed to be placed is:

$$Number\ of\ orders = \frac{D}{Q} = \frac{1,000\ glasses}{100\ glasses\ /\ case} = 10\ orders$$

To figure out the holding cost, you need to know the average quantity of items being held. When the order first comes in, there are Q items but that will eventually get down to zero after using up or selling all the items. So, you take an average of those two points (Q and zero in stock) and get Q/2 as the average amount of product held. For example, when the bulk grain first arrives, there is Q in the silo. If you assume it gets close to zero before the next truckload arrives, on average you are holding Q/2 in the silo.

FIGURE 17.5 Number of cases needed

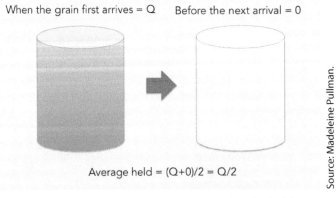

When the grain first arrives = Q   Before the next arrival = 0

Average held = (Q+0)/2 = Q/2

FIGURE 17.6 Average amount of grain held

For any item then, the total yearly cost is then:

$$Total \ cost = D \times C + \frac{D}{Q} \times S + \frac{Q}{2} \times H$$

Example Inventory Decision: Bulk versus Bagged Malt

To analyze the decision to buy malt in bulk versus bags from an inventory standpoint, assume that the company can rent space for bags or pay a lease for a silo for bulk malt. The company needs 96,000 pounds of 2-row malt for a year.

Bagged malt scenario: Bagged malt comes in 2,000-pound pallet loads and four pallets are ordered for a monthly order delivery. Buying malt delivered in this method and quantity has a cost of $0.55 per pound. The transportation cost is $240 for the four pallets (ordering cost) and the rent for warehouse works out to $0.24 per pound per year. With an opportunity cost of capital of eight percent, the holding cost for each pound is the rent plus interest:

$$Holding \ cost \ / \ lb. = rent + interest = \frac{\$.24}{lb. / \ year} + \frac{8\%}{year} \times \left(\frac{\$.55}{lb.}\right) = .24 + .044 = \frac{\$.284}{lb. / \ year}$$

The *yearly cost to purchase* the total demanded malt:

$$Yearly \ purchase \ cost = D \times C = 96,000 \ lb \times \frac{\$.55}{lb.} = \$52,800$$

FIGURE 17.7   Bagged malt

Source: Madeleine Pullman.

The *yearly cost to order* the malt (basically the transportation cost):

$$Yearly\ ordering\ cost = \frac{D}{Q} \times S = \frac{96,000\ lb.}{8,000\ lb.} \times \$240 = \$2,880$$

The *yearly holding cost* based on the holding cost per pound:

$$Yearly\ holding\ cost = H \times \frac{Q}{2} = \frac{\$.284}{lb./\ year} \times \frac{8,000\ lb.}{2} = \$1,136$$

The combined *total cost* to purchase, order, and hold is:

$$Total\ Cost = \$52,800 + \$2,880 + \$1,136 = \$56,816$$

Bulk malt scenario: In the bulk 2-row malt scenario, the minimum truckload is a half truck or 24,000 pounds for Q and the transportation price is $700. The bulk malt price drops to $.24 per pound. The rent for the silo works out to be $1.50 per pound per year. All other costs are the same.

$$Holding\ cost\ /\ lb. = rent + interest = \frac{\$1.50}{lb./\ year} + \frac{8\%}{year} \times \left(\frac{\$.24}{lb.}\right) = \$1.50 + \$.019 = \frac{\$1.519}{lb./\ year}$$

The *yearly cost to purchase* the total demanded malt:

$$Yearly\ purchase\ cost = D \times C = 96,000\ lb. \times \frac{\$.24}{lb.} = \$23,040$$

The *yearly cost to order* the malt (basically the transportation cost):

$$Yearly\ ordering\ cost = \frac{D}{Q} \times S = \frac{96,000\ lb.}{24,000\ lb.} \times \$700 = \$2,800$$

The *yearly holding cost* based on the holding cost per pound:

$$Yearly\ holding\ cost = H \times \frac{Q}{2} = \frac{\$1.519}{lb.} \times \frac{24,000\ lb.}{2} = \$18,228$$

The combined *total cost* to purchase, order and hold is:

$$Total\ cost = \$23,040 + \$2,800 + \$18,228 = \$44,068$$

In this comparison, the bulk malt total savings is almost $12,000 over the costs buying the malt by the bag.

Other volume discount merchandise: Many other items besides ingredients have volume discounts including packaging materials. The person in charge of purchasing in your business should look closely at different methods for purchasing bottles, cans, and other items that take up a lot of space. All printed goods from labels to T-shirts have volume price breaks too. It is essential to determine the storage space costs as well as the opportunity cost of investing in inventory.

FIGURE 17.8 Bulk malt

Source: Madeleine Pullman.

FIGURE 17.9 Packaging

Source: Madeleine Pullman.

A Can-undrum for Rockaway Brewing Company

Two surfers in Long Island City opened Rockaway Brewing Company as a nano brewery in 2012. Within three years, the brewery upgraded in stages to a 10-barrel system and was able to sell pints in its new taproom after the New York legislature passed a law allowing microbreweries to sell pints on the premises. The next step for the brewery was packaging its beer.

Rockaway raised $30,000 in one month in a Kickstarter campaign with a plan to produce four-packs of 16-ounce tallboys of ESB (extra special bitter), its flagship, for sale in bars and restaurants and at the brewery. The unusual 16-ounce cans would come from Crown, a popular supplier among craft breweries because of its smaller minimum order requirements of a half truckload or 12 pallets (100,000 cans).

In the same time span, Crown had added 350 new craft beer brands to its client list and experienced a shortage in the production of printed 16-ounce cans. This size became desirable for many craft brands as a way to differentiate their product from macrobreweries' standard 12-ounce cans. This demand led Crown to raise its minimum order up to a full truckload, a level that was out of reach for many breweries. Not only were the minimums more expensive, they resulted in too much inventory since empty cans and ends take up a lot of storage space and become unusable after a year or so.

Rockaway packaged about 6,000 cans a month and was unable to use the new canning equipment for its one-offs due to the shortage of 16-ounce cans. Simply switching to 12-ounce cans was not an option because the brand's labels were designed for the taller cans and new ones would require another COLA approval. Going forward, Rockaway was faced with the decision of ordering a full truckload of 16-ounce cans as the best business decision. The alternative was to order blank cans from Crown, as opposed to printed, and use custom designed shrink-sleeve wraps for the can artwork. The printed can has a better market image and longevity than the shrink sleeve so ordering a full truckload was the best option. Overall, strategic purchasing of materials including packaging would now become a priority for the brewery.

SUMMARY

As illustrated in the examples in this chapter, inventory involves some surprising costs. While whiskey distillers are generally well aware of the costs of holding on to product for a number of years before selling it, beer and cider makers who have taken to barrel aging with a passion may be unaware of its hidden cost overall. Another issue to consider when evaluating how much to order at any given time is the perishability of the materials. For the freshest malt, breweries may want to use up their malt supply within three or four months rather than buying larger amounts that last longer. Similarly, cans have a special lid sealant that can dry out with time. So, although it's tempting to order large quantities of generic can lids, this should be done with care not to exceed the recommended shelf life. Another concern is ordering too much specific packaging like labels or printed cans. At some point, you may decide to refresh the label design and do not want to be stuck with too many labels to use up. Therefore, you should look at how long a supply of product will be in house and adjust the chosen order size so that it will not exceed the recommended shelf life or usability of the product.

The Bruery's Barrel Aging Investment

In its first four years, The Bruery in Orange County, California experienced wild success with its barrel-aged sour beers. Barrel aging was this company's priority from the start in 2008, and it conducted one of the largest barrel-aging programs in the country. By end of 2012, The Bruery owned about 3,000 barrels and barrel-aged beer accounted for 40 percent of its production.

With an average aging time of 14 months, the choice to barrel-age was a large financial undertaking for the small-scale brewery. When CEO and founder Patrick Rue first started The Bruery, he released a few non-barrel aged beers in order to bring some cash in until barrel-aged beers were ready. The Hummulus Lager is still one of its most popular beers. The Bruery invested the time and money in barrel aging in order to differentiate the company from the beginning.

The Bruery does not brew any IPAs. CEO and founder Patrick Rue believes that the best beers for aging are barley wines, imperial stouts, and less hoppy beers with a higher alcohol content that smooths out after aging. This strategy and inventory investment paid off in the long run when The Bruery released its first aged beers. The Bruery's barrels include bourbon barrels, new American oak, new French oak, tequila, rye, and rum barrels. Rum barrels are rare and The Bruery had only one rum-barrel-aged beer while searching for a reliable source for more.

The Bruery's unique beers have attracted an immense following with sustained support through membership programs. The Bruery has three tiers of membership that often sell out. Members receive merchandise, discounts on beer, and access to special releases. The mid-tier level is the Reserve Society, whose members receive 15 percent off beer and access to limited release beers. The Bruery found its top customers in its Reserve Society and sent them invitations to its Hoarders Society, an invite-only group. These valued customers are able to buy very limited beers as a reward for being loyal supporters of The Bruery. This also allows the Bruery to make small batches to see how customers like it before making it in larger batches. While barrel aging can be somewhat of a gamble for breweries, the membership clubs offer some financial security to The Bruery.

In 2014 the Bruery invested 3 million dollars in more advanced production facilities and doubled its brewing capacity to 20,000 barrels a year. It opened up new locations dedicated to souring beer, and invested in a lot of new equipment. The risk that a souring yeast can contaminate a non-sour beer is high, so sour beers are fermented at a separate facility. The new farmhouse-style brewery produced beers under the slightly different name and branding of Bruery Terreux and included a tasting room.

Instead of focusing on flagship beers, The Bruery makes 70 to 100 different beers a year. About one dozen of these are distributed nationally and most are only available for short periods of time. The Bruery takes risks for the benefits of its customers who like to try new beers. With this focus on innovation, The Bruery has three year-round beers in addition to its original lager.

The Bruery positions its brand as higher end and charges a premium for its products. The value perception is enhanced by the 750-ml bottles and filled with a product that takes years, risk, and a real investment to produce well.

LEARNING ADVENTURES

1. Aged beer costing: Assume that you are going to age beer in a barrel for a year. You determine the cost of a 53-gallon barrel worth of beer to be $200 for the beer alone. The barrel costs $75 and you will only get one use out of it. Assume that the barrel takes up four square feet and that you pay $1 per month for a square foot in a warehouse. The opportunity cost for your business is 10 percent. Calculate the overall investment in this barrel-aged beer.

2. Ralph is considering ordering bamboo T-shirts for his cidery. The T-shirt company indicates that the cost to set up the silk screen, do an art check, and ship the shirts will be $200 regardless of quantity. The cost of the shirts is the following: $15 each for 100 shirts, $12.50 for 500 shirts, and $10 for 1,000 shirts. The holding cost is $.50 per year for each shirt and Ralph's opportunity cost is 7 percent per year. Ralph estimates that he will sell 2,000 T-shirts per year. What is the total cost of each choice and which should Ralph choose?

CHAPTER EIGHTEEN

Food and Beverage Operations

Key Terms

bikes and dogs
brand image
brewpub
comPASH
cover
food friend
food minimalist
food truck

happy hour
lighting
materials and fixtures
noise
pairing
party
pub food
revPASH

seat yield
serious food
table turns
tables
tasting room
zones

Overview

Running a retail environment with a production facility is a great way to build your brand while earning higher margins on beverages. A physical space created with a specific identity and theme engages customers in your story and invites them to learn more about your products. Tasting rooms have caught on as an important aspect of the production brewery space. The stereotypical tasting room has been executed as an uninviting warehouse atmosphere outfitted with picnic tables and food trucks. But increasingly, the newest tasting rooms are more pub-like with attentively designed interiors and activities that invite customers into the brand's story. As differentiation becomes ever more important in the competitive craft world, food offerings are moving beyond the traditional pub options of pizza, and burgers. This chapter investigates the trends in on-site pub and restaurant concepts carefully designed to build brand image and analyzes the importance of food in the whole craft beverage mix.

Learning Objectives

▶ Understand the importance of food and the trends in the craft industry.

▶ Compare beverage consumption patterns at different points in the day.

▶ Consider the pros and cons of outsourcing food service versus owning a restaurant.

▶ Understand the range of food and beverage concepts.

▶ Estimate the potential revenue from different pub configurations.

▶ Develop appropriate food and beverage matching.

▶ Understand the importance of pub and restaurant design elements.

Introduction

Most people find their way into the craft world because of their commitment to the beverages themselves and food is more often an afterthought. Some food and beverage entrepreneurs believe that pubs should stick with tried-and-true offerings originating with UK, Belgian, German, or American traditions. Others try to avoid food entirely and put a jar of pickled eggs, chips, peanuts, or beef jerky on the bar, and call it good. At the other end of the continuum are the entrepreneurs coming to the craft business with an idea for beer designed around the food. This is the new frontier: craft businesses that take food seriously as an integral part of their concept. Regardless of your own opinions about food in a craft facility, food service has a definite role to play in any beverage business, if nothing else, due to its profitability.

In a typical restaurant, food makes up the bulk of the sales followed by spirits (cocktails) as depicted in Figure 18.1. The remaining sales are nearly equally split among beer (including cider), wine, and non-alcoholic beverages. In a brewpub, the sales of alcoholic beverages can make up much more of the pie. Of course, food does not have the profit margins that alcohol does and a business can easily lose money if the food side of the business is not carefully managed. The important point

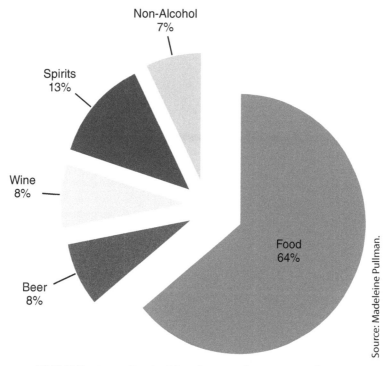

FIGURE 18.1   Typical food versus beverage sales

FIGURE 18.2   Spirits versus others

is that when a brewpub has no food available, only the most die-hard drinkers will stay in their seats for extended periods of time without leaving to eat.

While spirits do make up the majority of restaurant beverage sales, in terms of actual units (glasses) sold, beer and cider are not far behind spirits with 42 percent of all glasses sold versus spirits at 44 percent.

Alcohol Consumption Patterns

Typical consumers choose different alcoholic beverages as the afternoon and evening progresses. Beer and cider have their peak sales during the late afternoon and early evening hours, traditionally thought of as **happy hour** in the United States. Wine is the beverage of choice during dining hours, and spirits take off in the later evening and into the wee hours of the morning. Regardless, spirits sales dominate every time block due to their higher cost, not necessarily due to the number of glasses served. For the craft business owner, the challenge is to influence these classic patterns and expand consumption of your beverage type into other time periods. For example, cider can span both happy hour and dinner since many wine drinkers are attracted to cider. Large-format beer and cider, presented in nicely packaged wine- or champagne-style bottles, get consumers to think more about these beverages as a shareable dinner libation especially with more refined food selections.

Examining the relationship between food and beverages, there are many interesting phenomena. Whenever you have food and alcohol together on a check, the sum is greater than the parts. According to Figure 18.4, if a party has alcohol only, the average check is $20 and if they have food only, it is $26. But, the average check for parties with both food and alcohol is $73 with any beer, $86 with craft beer, and a whopping $150 with certain spirits (scotch, Canadian whiskey, or gin). Cider falls somewhere in between the pattern for craft beer and wine.

Clearly, people drink more beverages when they are eating too. This happens for a number of reasons. First, food extends the evening. What begins as a few drinks with friends turns into drinks and dinner once people are enjoying themselves. Second, since alcohol stimulates the appetite, when customers get hungry they do not have to leave to find something to eat. And third, food draws a broader demographic into the business. At any popular brewpub chain you will find business groups, families with kids, dates, mixed generations, and people from many walks of life. Many of the customers are not serious beer geeks but seek out casual dining with locally produced beverages. Parents enjoy brewpubs that offer spaces for kids to play. Most brewpubs strive to become the third place where people can kick back outside of home and work. So the design of the space is in often keeping with satisfying these needs, a topic discussed towards the end of this chapter.

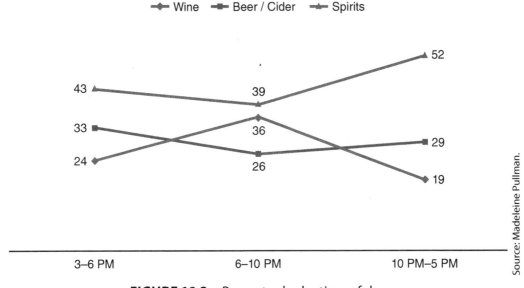

FIGURE 18.3   Percent sales by time of day

Avg Check

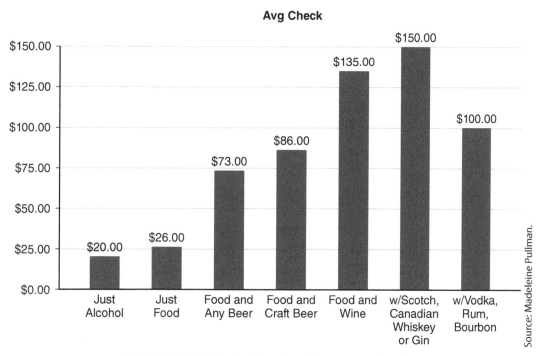

FIGURE 18.4   Typical food and beverage check

FIGURE 18.5   Brewpub as third place

Food Concepts and Menu Design

Food can be integrated into a craft concept at many different levels. For some business owners, dealing with *any* food seems overwhelming so they subcontract out the kitchen to other parties or bring in food trucks. Others want to control the full restaurant experience and go full tilt with a kitchen staff significantly bigger than the beverage production staff and bar personnel. This section outlines different food concepts and their potential pros and cons.

Food friend: On the simplest end of the food continuum is the food friend. By forming a symbiotic relationship with neighboring restaurants or food trucks, these parties supply food to the pub or tasting room. The menus are placed in the pub or tasting room and customers can call in a phone order and have food delivered. Alternatively, one or more food trucks pull up to the pub or tasting room and sell their products to the patrons outside.

Some business post **food truck** schedules for various days of the week. The upsides of the food friend model are the following: 1) the pub has food to offer which increases beverage sales, 2) the truck or vendor takes care of every food service detail and the pub only has to arrange clean-up of packaging or collecting baskets, and 3) different food trucks generate interest for trying new things. The down side is that the vendor or food truck will have limited choices and their business is not under your control. If a truck does not show up one day, the beverage sales could drop off by 30 to 50 percent. Your business will not have control over the food truck or restaurant's quality, customer service, schedule, and so forth.

Food minimalist: In this model, the pub offers simple in-house basics prepared by the bar staff or a single kitchen staff person. The patrons choose from a small collection of food items such as sandwiches, hot dogs or sausages, bar snacks, and a simple soup or chili. This model requires a space to prepare food that passes health codes. The upside is that now, your business makes all the profit from the food and you have control over the food service. The downside is that you do not make much profit with a very limited menu and it does not cater to a wide demographic of people. This model is especially limiting with the many dietary constraints that people have today, including gluten-free, vegetarian, local food only, or paleo, to name a few.

©CREATISTA/shutterstock.com

FIGURE 18.6   Food truck

FIGURE 18.7   Food truck schedule

Sunday	Monday	Tuesday	Wednesday	Thursday	Friday	Saturday
					12:00 P SXSW BBQ	12:30 P Sea ship 4:00 P Noodle
12:30 P Pizza Stone	Closed	4:00 P Phili Cheese	4:00 P Buenos Tacos	4:00 P Sams Subs	12:00 P SXSW BBQ	12:30 P Sea ship 4:00 P Noodle
12:30 P Pizza Stone	Closed	4:00 P Phili Cheese	4:00 P Buenos Tacos	4:00 P Sams Subs	12:00 P SXSW BBQ	12:30 P Sea ship 4:00 P Noodle
12:30 P Pizza Stone	Closed	4:00 P Phili Cheese	4:00 P Buenos Tacos	4:00 P Sams Subs	12:00 P SXSW BBQ	12:30 P Sea ship 4:00 P Noodle
12:30 P Pizza Stone	Closed	4:00 P Phili Cheese	4:00 P Buenos Tacos	4:00 P Sams Subs	12:00 P SXSW BBQ	12:30 P Sea ship 4:00 P Noodle
Source: Madeleine Pullman.						

©Mustafa Errrugal/Shutterstock.com

FIGURE 18.8   Simple food

TABLE 18. 1   Pub food

Country	Examples of pub food
United Kingdom	Fish and chips, steak (and kidney) pie, Irish stew, shepherd's pie, scotch egg, roast lamb and beef, bangers and mash, mash potatoes, welsh rarebit, smoked salmon, kippers, toad in the hole, sticky toffee pudding, spotted dick, trifle, and scones with strawberries and clotted cream.
United States	Chicken wings, nachos, peanuts in a shell, burgers, sandwiches, fries, pizza, hot dogs, bratwurst, Caesar salad, chili, chowder, chopped salad, ice cream, and cheese cake.
Germany	Pretzels and mustard, various sausages and smoked meats, pickles, sauerkraut and red cabbage, schnitzel, spaetzle, potatoes (salad, pancakes, fried, boiled and roasted) and apple strudel with iced or whipped cream.
Belgium	Mussels and fries, charcuterie, *carbonade Flamande* or Belgian beef stew, sausages, mashed root vegetables, waffles, and ice cream.
Source: Madeleine Pullman.	

Classic pub food: By far the most popular food concept for brewpubs is classic pub fare. Many customers expect this style of food; therefore some business owners feel that it is risky to deviate from this formula. On the other hand, the same old, same old food is not much of a differentiator in a competitive market. The classic pub offerings for beer-based concepts are tied to different countries of origin with the most popular menu items listed in Table 18.1.

While other countries have their own **pub food** (chicken feet for China), these are the main pub food styles. Notice that many pubs mix and match pub food from various countries on their menus. The one constant is french fries. In short, you cannot even think about *not* having fries on a decent pub menu.

Cider has its own food styles but cider-pubs are only now beginning to emerge. Historically, cider from the Normandy area in France has been served with crêpes both flour (dessert style) and buckwheat (savory style) and cheese dishes. The more astringent Spanish cider is served in bar environments with tapas, classic Spanish appetizers both cold and hot that range from the simple to the sophisticated.

Most people tend not to think about food that goes with spirits or cocktails other than appetizers. But the restaurant Ma'ono in Seattle pairs fried chicken with a huge whiskey selection while CH Distillery in Chicago offers nut mixes, cheese and fish dishes, oysters, and beef carpaccio.

Serious food: As the craft market matures and grows more competitive, new entrants are upping the game with novel food and craft beverage concepts. BTU Brasserie in Portland, Oregon entered the market with classic Chinese food and matching beers like their flagship Chinese rice beer. They quickly found themselves on the foodie website Eater.com as an interesting place to eat and drink.

Magnolia Pub & Brewery in San Francisco has long been recognized as a brewpub that takes the quality and sustainability of their food as seriously as their beers. The initial pub concept opened in 1997 with small-batch brews and high-quality food. Founder and owner, Dave McClean believes the food should be as good as the beer; the majority of the beer produced was sold through the pub until 2014.

©Nate Yovu. Reprinted with permission.

FIGURE 18.9   BTU Brasserie

Photo courtesy Dave McLean. Reprinted with permission.

FIGURE 18.10   Magnolia Pub & Brewery

In 2014, McLean opened a bigger production brewery next to their new Smokestack barbeque restaurant in the Dogpatch neighborhood. Again, buying sustainable pork, beef, and chicken from local farmers and the best quality food possible, the business produced smoked food on-site that paired well with their traditional UK-style ales. The brewery is so well regarded that when they launched a crowd-funding campaign on Bolstr, an online marketplace where entrepreneurs access capital from accredited investors, they raised $150,000 in less than 24 hours.

A **serious food** program like this brings higher revenues and a wider audience into the pubs. On the other hand, good food is not cheap and a higher bill can take customers with a pub-food-cost expectation aback. Additionally, high quality and innovative food requires talented kitchen staff and solid restaurant experience to deliver both quality and profits.

Photo courtesy Dave McLean. Reprinted with permission.

FIGURE 18.11   Smokestack BBQ

Pairing food and beverage: As food and craft beverage concepts break away from the traditional pub models, entrepreneurs are looking for menus to match their beers. Some pubs are specializing in pairing dinners and other suggesting pairings for certain menu items. One of the great advantages of pairing is that it gets people who default to IPA, for example, out of their style ruts. (In truth, highly hopped beers do not pair well with many food types!) Pairing suggestions lure customers into trying the pub's other beverage offerings that really shine when enjoyed with certain foods.

to begin
poached shrimp
confit pheasant
malheur brut, br. malheur, buggenhout, belgium

first
raviolo of winter squash, lacinato kale, farm egg, pumpkin brodo

tank 7, boulevard, kansas city, mo

second
duck breast, rooftop honey glaze, duck fat & arborio rice timbalo, winter chard

gift of the magi, lost abbey, san marcos, ca

to rest
black truffle sformato
2008 smoked porter, alaskan, juneau, ak

third
espresso creme brulee, vanilla tuile, smoked butter caramel
yeti, great divide brewing company, denver, co

Source: Madeleine Pullman.

FIGURE 18.12   Pairing menu

TABLE 18.2   Food and craft beverage pairing

Beverage Flavor	Match	Food
Bitter, sharp, or roasted from hops, malt, or alcohol	Balance	Sweet or rich tastes: barbecued meats and creamy desserts
Sweet from fruit, malt, or sugars	Balance	Sweet tastes like nutty cheese, desserts, and sweet vegetables and salad dressing; often good with spicy food.
Acidic	Counters	Salty and greasy foods like salsa and chips, corned beef, and pickled fish and vegetables.
Strong	Match	Strong flavors like oily fish, meat, and sauces.
Umami	Complements	Other funky flavors like cheese, aged foods, pâté, and mushrooms.
Source: Madeleine Pullman.		

Places like Monk's Kettle in San Francisco entice customers to pair a different beer with each course, which not only helps revenue but also educates the consumer. High-end pairings for a five-course dinner end up costing around $75 per person. A great source of information and training on this very topic comes from the Cicerone Certification Program, which offers training in craft beverage pairings. Table 18.2 outlines basic pairing principles.

Craft Beer and Distillery Pairings at StormBreaker

Stocking a full bar or offering other libations can bring important additional sales into a brewpub. StormBreaker Brewing in Portland, Oregon pairs all of their craft beer pours with spirits. Alongside the draft list, the menu at StormBreaker suggests a host of beer and spirit pairings—a half pint of any of their flagship beers complimented with a particular scotch of whiskey. There is also a full bar for customers to create their own pairings and cocktails as well as a full menu featuring regional ingredients, pickled vegetables, local meats, and cheese plates.

The pairings program at StormBreaker is a winning strategy, a unique offering for craft beverage fans that sets this brewery apart. In February of each year StormBreaker hosts "Brewstillery," a festival bringing together local craft brewers and distillers. Its first year included 12 distilleries and 18 breweries with 19 different pairings. The goal of Brewstillery is to create a more comfortable, intimate feeling in the brewpub during the winter months.

StormBreaker recently started bottling and distributing it beers to a handful of places in the city, which brought new people into the pub. However, the brewery is not very deep into distribution at this stage because they are selling so many pints at the pub.

Metrics for Measuring Pub Performance

In brewpub environments, the in-house beer is typically 35 percent of sales while food is 53 percent of sales. This is a higher proportion of beer sales than standard restaurants. The remaining sales come from guest taps (other brewery or cidery's products), other alcohol, and non-alcoholic beverages. In general, the percentages of costs in a typical restaurant are equally split between beverage and food cost, labor cost, and overhead cost. Keep in mind though; the cost for beer or cider produced in-house is 13 to 17 percent of its sales price while food cost is 30 percent of its sales price across an average menu. Pouring guest beverages in a pub will cost 30 to 32 percent of the sales cost, so the in-house produced beverages make a far greater margin for the business.

In restaurant lingo a **cover** is one guest or person who orders food and beverages. A group of covers, such as a couple or eight people, is called a **party**. While the pub or restaurant may have 150 available seats, all the seats may not be filled at any one time. The percentage used on average is known as the **seat yield**. At one point in any given evening every table could be taken, but the seat yield is less than 100 percent since a table that seats four may only have three customers and several tables that fit six people may have four-person parties. One way to improve seat yield is to have smaller combinable tables that can be configured for various group sizes or large communal tables that pack various parties together in the manner of German beer halls.

Another key concept is **table turns.** During a given night, such as from 5 p.m. to 11 p.m., a restaurant turns one table three times, meaning that three different parties used the table in succession. Clearly, the more table turns the better. Each turn has a time duration, which is printed on a quality POS system. Two business metrics that are useful to know are **RevPASH** and **ComPASH**.

$$RevPASH = \frac{time\ period's\ revenue\ from\ operation}{number\ of\ operations\ hours \times number\ of\ seats\ available}$$

and

$$ComPASH = \frac{time\ period's\ contribution\ margin\ from\ operation}{number\ of\ operations\ hours \times number\ of\ seats\ available}$$

While the business' RevPASH might look pretty good, the most important metric is ComPASH which tells you how well the business is actually doing.

Apple & Pear Cider-Pub: Example of RevPASH and ComPASH Calculations

Apple & Pear Cider-Pub has 40 seats and is open from 5 to 10 p.m. (five hours). The number of operations hours (five) times the number of seats (40) is 200 available seat hours. During a recent Saturday night, the pub sold $2,000 worth of food and beverages. Of that sales amount, $1,000 came from 200 pints of cider which retail for $5 but cost the business $1 to produce including labor (margin is $4 times 200 or $800). The 100 food menu items sold average around $10 but cost $6 to produce including food and labor (margin is $4) and made up $1,000 of the sales (margin is $4 times 100 items or $400). Therefore:

$$RevPASH = \frac{\$2,000}{200\ seat-hours} = \frac{\$10}{seat-hours}$$

and

$$ComPASH = \frac{\$400}{200\ seat-hours} = \frac{\$2}{seat-hours}$$

It is important to understand what could improve the ComPASH numbers. The cider margin could be improved by selling more cider, having a higher priced cider, and lowering the cost of production. On the food side, the menu should be designed to have a mix of higher-margin items and lower-margin items that pull people into the pub with a goal of higher margin overall for the complete menu mix. Similar to the cider margin, selling more food during the time period with higher prices and lower costs increases the margin. Perhaps, the early and later evening periods are slower. These are important times to promote specials to improve these metrics.

Estimating the Return on a Pub

When designing a pub, you can use statistics from the most recent Brewers Associations survey for US-based breweries to estimate revenues. These facts and figures in Table 18.3 show the average revenues per month for various kinds of seating and meals (lunch versus dinner). It also shows how many seats an average brewpub has versus a production brewery with a pub. Some noticeable differences for a brewpub versus a production brewery are the large difference in monthly revenue (production breweries typically have a much bigger brand presence) and the proportionally greater number of bar/lounge seats but fewer seats overall in production breweries.

If you are interested in estimating how a pub might perform, you count seats in the different areas (indoor versus bar/lounge) and multiply that by the average monthly revenue per seat. Outdoor seats may only be available during good weather in your community but you can assume that they earn as much as an indoor dining seat when they are open. The average checks reflect higher beer consumption at night.

TABLE 18.3 Pub statistics

	All breweries	Range*
Brewpubs		
Average monthly revenue per seat (indoor dining)	$506.26	$65.12 to $930.99
Average monthly revenue per seat (bar/lounge)	$702.36	$29.59 to $1,293.16
Average total seats per site	187	146 to 241
Percentage dining area seats	58%	52% to 71%
Percentage bar/lounge seats	17%	15% to 25%
Percentage outdoor seats	22%	14% to 32%
Average lunch check	$16.17	$14.86 to $18.78
Average dinner check	$21.35	$19.12 to $24.00
Production breweries with pub		
Average monthly revenue per seat (indoor dining)	$1,827.36	$1,228.27 to $1,818.24
Average monthly revenue per seat (bar/lounge)	$1,626.40	$699.60 to $2,069.06
Average total seats per site	176	55 to 279
Percentage dining area seats	52%	27% to 60%
Percentage bar/lounge seats	25%	18% to 82%
Percentage outdoor seats	23%	18% to 26%
Average lunch check	$15.95	$10 to $18.54
Average dinner check	$21.16	$15.50 to $22.68
*Range depends on bbl. production		
Source: Madeleine Pullman. Based on surveys from Brewers Association.		

Example: Wallowa Brewpub Revenue and Cost Estimate

Wallowa Brewpub has 150 seats: 50 indoor seats, 25 bar seats, and 75 outdoor seats. The outdoor seats are only available 40 percent of the year due to cold weather and snow. Based on the industry information in Table 18.3, the expected yearly sales are:

$Indoor\ seating\ revenue = 50\ seats \times \$506.25/seat - month \times 12\ months = \$303,750$

$Bar\ seating = 25\ seats \times \$702.36/seat - month \times 12\ months = \$210,708$

$Outdoor\ seating = 75\ seats \times \$560.25/seat - month \times (40\% \times 12\ months) = \$201,690$

$Total\ revenue\ from\ pub = \$303,750 + \$210,708 + \$201,690 = \$716,148$

According to brewpub averages, beer is 35 percent of the sales ($250,652), food is 53 percent of sales ($379,558), and the remainder is other products not produced in house ($85,938). Assuming a beer cost of 13 percent and a food cost of 30 percent, the beer margin is $218,067 and the food margin is $265,690. Of course, kitchen and wait staff labor could eat up 30 percent or more of the revenue in each of those totals. But theoretically there would be $338,630 to apply to profit and overhead from the in-house produced food and beverages.

Pub versus Production Design

Craft beverage facilities have become the third place the space in which community members gather besides home and work (although the coffee shop is also a contender). This dynamic presents new challenges and opportunities for what has traditionally been a factory environment and now has become a neighborhood hangout and tourist attraction. One of the biggest issues is trying to carry on routine production tasks with customers present. The focus becomes maximizing the usable space while reducing the conflict of visitors with production. The business should be laid out with separate space for customers (and potentially tours) from production, deliveries, and unsightly storage. There are several other specific design details unique to pubs.

Tables: Table configuration and layout is one of the primary areas of facility design. As mentioned in this chapter previously, combinable tables and moveable seating as well as communal tables make for more efficient use of the seating. In a craft pub, people tend to gather in groups of more than two so it's better to have four-tops (four person tables) to combine for larger groups. A pub does not need too many two-tops unless offering a fine dining experience.

People also like to be anchored against walls, hence the popularity of booths and banquette or bench seating against a wall. If tables are out in the open, it helps to use plants or partitions to create an anchoring effect. While wood and metal benches are nice for tasting rooms, for people enjoying an extended dining experience, upholstered furniture is preferred for comfort and back support.

Zones: Pubs benefit from having separate zones for different demographics. Single diners and pairs tend to sit at the bar. Areas for families with kids should be separated from other diners and especially the bar area. Consider adding private dining spaces for meetings and events as pubs are very popular venues for business and civic groups.

Lighting and noise: Lighting has a significant effect on the consumption of food and beverages. Consumption goes up as lighting dims, so the entire facility should have adjustable lighting to create the appropriate mood. Noise level is a complicated issue for pubs; increasingly they are designed to enhance noise so the energy level is more stimulating. Many would say that this trend has not been positive and that some places are way too noisy to carry on a conversation. The pub should be designed with noise dampening ability since music can always be added to increase the noise level.

Materials and fixtures: Everything that is placed in the pub, from the furniture to the art, should reflect the brand image and theme. The theme should be consistent throughout the entire facility including the outdoor seating and the server and bartender uniforms. And not to overlook the bathrooms, which have become interesting places to add items that reflect the theme. Breweries with a sustainability mission like Hopworks have used the bathrooms to show water-saving options.

Bikes and dogs: Many pub clients ride bikes. Adequate and secure bike parking is an essential part of the facility design. Similarly, a number of pubs encourage patrons to bring their dogs during nice weather. If this is the case, then places to tie leashes and water bowls should be conveniently placed outside and out of the way of other patrons.

A Brewpub for Dog Lovers

Lucky Labrador Brewing Company, located in several Portland neighborhoods, targets and draws in the dog-loving community. With the beloved Labrador as its logo, some Lucky Lab beers have dog-inspired names and the pubs are adorned in dog decor and artwork. Dogs are welcomed on the patio to hang out with their humans. Since the patios are covered and heated, dog owners can their enjoy beer and food outside with their four-footed companions year-round. Each pub has a full menu with twelve taps as well as an event space.

Lucky Lab hosts an annual event called Dogtoberfest with beer pours, live music, and a dog wash. The 21st annual event in 2015 results included 330 dogs washed, 42 dogs' nails clipped, and 18 units of human blood donated to the Red Cross. There were 16 vendors and the event raised more than $19,000 for the DoveLewis Blood Bank, providing enough blood for 600 small animal transfusions. Lucky Lab also hosts an event called "Dog Days of Summer" in which a Weiner dog race benefits the Oregon Dachshund Rescue. Combing canine love with Portland's love for bicycles, the company hosts an annual ride called ride "Tour de Lab," which tours multiple Lucky Lab locations and riders drink samples along the way.

SUMMARY

The food side of the pub business offers an opportunity for creativity and differentiation. Historically, there has been a lack of imagination with many brewpub food programs. Happily, many of today's entrepreneurs are recognizing how great food that helps draw in customers of all kinds and improves the bottom line. There is still a lot of untapped potential for great food and beverage combination ideas that would work well with cider, spirits, sour beers, mead, and other emerging craft beverages.

Ecliptic's Restaurant

When John Harris started his Portland brewery in 2013, he wanted to have a food program that was as strong as his beer program. With a sense that people like food more than beer, Harris felt that beer brings them in the first time, but food brings them back." Portland has become a destination food city in the United States, and in a market saturated with brewpubs with similar menus; he wanted a food program that matched the growing city's food culture.

Source: John Harris.

FIGURE 18.13   Ecliptic entrée

Early on, Harris decided against the popular tasting room concept and hired a restaurant designer to create an elegant astronomy-themed space. He worked with his chef to create a menu with seasonal entrée specialties (typically priced under $20) and high-quality pub offerings such as unique sandwiches, sides, and salads. Some of the entrées included pan-roasted rockfish, roasted chicken, and braised brisket. He also created a variety of unique vegetarian items such as a farro burger, beet melt, and a mushroom tart. While staying focused as a brewpub, Harris chose to offer craft cocktails, cider, and wine; these have grown to be a significant part of the revenue contribution. Running a full-service restaurant is certainly a more significant investment and management challenge than a tasting room, but it succeeds in drawing in a wider audience of people and potentially higher revenues overall.

FIGURE 18.14   Ecliptic interior and food

A Family Brewing Business Concept Brought to Life

Nestled in a popular waterfront district in Oregon's Columbia River Gorge, pFriem Family Brewers' brewery and tasting room opened in bustling Hood River during the summer of 2012. Using big brewery techniques on an artisanal scale, the family-run brewery sourced the best ingredients, hired a professional staff, and designed an inviting space. Founder Josh Pfriem's long-time love for Belgian beers inspired Pfriem's beer styles.

With an open brewery layout, pFriem's owners wanted each guest to feel like part of the family. The waiting area resembles a living room, and there are communal tables, a kids' play area, and an airy bar. The menu is European inspired with Northwest ingredients and every beer offered on tap is made by pFriem.

In pFriem's first year or two of business, wholesale was the driving force. The brewery was started on a shoestring budget and the founders did not anticipate the amount of business the tasting room would generate. In the first couple of years, pFriem had to sink every bit of profit from its tasting room back in just to keep up with business. As pFriem's brand became more popular, they began seeing more regular business throughout the year. After a few years of the tasting room being open, pFriem was at a point where profits from the tasting room were able to help fuel the growth of the brewery.

pFriem Family Brewers outgrew its brewing operation and restaurant almost immediately. Within six months, the brewpub added new fermenters, a kitchen expansion, a beer patio, a barrel-aging program, and additional keg storage. Production doubled with the installation of two new 45-barrel tanks, bringing their production to 3,000 barrels. Soon thereafter pFriem signed a deal with a Washington distributor followed by a distributor in British Columbia, Canada.

The tasting room opened with a full menu, although, pFriem refers to its restaurant as a tasting room rather than a pub. Since pFriem had a quality-minded goal for its beer, marketing, branding, and relationships, the food program had to be outstanding as well to elevate the beer experience. Taking cues from Belgium and Germany, pFriem developed its menu with European inspiration and regional Northwest ingredients while giving a nod to the thriving food scene in nearby Portland.

The pFriem team is continually massaging its menu to enhance the beers, maintain seasonality, and mature with the current food scene. Attempting those three things in high volume with high quality and local ingredients is a constant challenge. Sourcing locally is important, and pFriem buys bread for sandwiches from a local baker, purchases produce from the local Hood River farmers, retrieves hops for the beer from two hours away in Yakima, and brews with water flowing from Mt. Hood. pFriem has also partnered with local roaster Coava for a coffee beer, and with Jacobsen Salt for a gose-style beer.

As sales have grown, pFriem has increased staff and management, fixing bottlenecks, upgrading equipment, examining production flow, getting creative with the space it has to work with, and always trying to look through the lenses of its guests. pFriem's tasting room is busier than anyone imagined, and has been remodeled four times in less than four years and has now hit the zoning limit for its location.

Source: John Harris.

FIGURE 18.15   pFriem interior design

The design and fixtures within pFriem's tasting room and restaurant suit the brand, which Josh Pfriem describes as timeless with a post-modern feel of industrial chic. The bar, tables, and taster trays are built from rustic wood. The tap handles mirror old bourbon barrels with wood, steel, and large bolts. The walls around the brewery and behind the bar are worn wood, and giant windows look out onto the Columbia River waterfront.

The dining area in pFriem's tasting room is situated next to its brewing tanks, and the guests feel connected with the beer and the brewing process. pFriem has had challenges with expansions and setting new equipment in place while having the tasting room open. The cleaning regimen is adjusted around when the tasting room is open; for example, tanks are not cleaned during public hours.

LEARNING ADVENTURES

1. Go to a favorite brew or cider pub and after looking at the seats and menu, estimate the following:

    a. How many indoor table seats and bar seats versus outdoor table seats are available and how many months is the outdoor seating used?

    b. How much potential revenue can be made from each kind of seating in a year and the total revenue?

    c. Using average industry percentages for food and labor, how much does the business net in the year?

2. In your area, look at the menus of the popular brewpubs (either in person or online). What is the typical strategy for food? Has anyone done a food menu that is different and what in particular have they done? What is the risk of offering a menu like this?

3. Do a walk-through critique of what you think is a well-designed pub (cider or beer producer). How do different aspects of the design align with the business story? Are there elements that do not fit and why?

CHAPTER NINETEEN

Legal Issues

Key Terms

alcohol and tobacco tax and trade
  bureau (TTB)
bond
brewer's bond
brewer permit
brewer's notice application
compliance
conditional use permit

department of agriculture (DOA)
department of environmental quality
  (DEQ)
distilled spirits permit
distilled spirits plant (DSP)
federal alcohol administration act
  (FAA)
food and drug administration (FDA)

food safety modernization act
  (FSMA)
internal revenue code
national scenic area (NSA)
US federal distilled spirits permit
wine permit

Overview

Alcohol is a product ensnared in legal concerns and complexities. Every locale has a set of laws around alcohol production and sales based on its unique history and societal values. As societies and business models change over time, so do the laws—though rarely as fast as those in the industry would like. Previous chapters have covered zoning and building regulations and production taxes that are unique to each location and specific product. This chapter is an overview of federal and state agencies and permits and raises other legal issues for producers.

Learning Objectives

▶ Understand which regulatory agencies control different legal aspects.

▶ Determine the timeline of legal permit processes.

▶ Describe the US alcohol production permitting process.

▶ Understand how different state and provincial governments differ in regulations from location to location.

▶ Know the appropriate city government agency to contact for local regulations.

▶ Understand the Food and Drug Administration areas of concern.

Introduction

Before getting started in any business producing alcohol, you should familiarize yourself with the laws in your country, state (or province), and specific locality related to your product of interest. Each alcohol type has different regulations. Just because you see a wine tasting room down the street does not necessarily mean that it is permissible for you to open a tasting room for beer in the same location. In many states, different alcohol lobbies and industry histories have influenced each particular category's legal trajectory. Beverages with the same alcohol level and marketing channels have entirely different legal hurdles to be produced and marketed. The starting place for any potential producer is to read the federal alcohol laws to understand what can and cannot be done.

Federal Licensing

In the United States, alcohol falls under the **Federal Alcohol Administration Act (FAA)** and the **Internal Revenue Code**; the **Alcohol and Tobacco Tax and Trade Bureau (TTB)** administers the laws. Everyone must file an application with the TTB before producing *any* product. This means, no pilot brewing or production of any kind can occur until after choosing a site, building out a facility, installing production equipment, and receiving federal approval. It's a risky proposition since you want to be confident of receiving the permit after making an investment in a startup. The application process generally requires the following information:

▶ Who is the applicant(s)? Everyone involved with the business ownership must provide his or her legal history and eligibility. Often people convicted of a felony charge in the past will not be allowed to own an alcohol production business but this prohibition depends on the specific charge.

▶ What is the business structure (corporation, for example)? Articles of organization or certificate of organization are required to demonstrate the structure.

▶ What is the type of operation (brewery, distillery, winery, alternating proprietorship)? Each type of operation has a different application process.

- ▶ What is the description of the project, location, layout and security (to insure that the alcoholic product is protected). A physical address is required and the same address should be shown on all paperwork. A lease agreement or proof of property ownership is required as well as a diagram of the facility.

- ▶ What are the sources of funds? This requires documentation proving that adequate and legal funds are available for the project.

Additionally, the TTB requires a **bond** to guarantee that excise taxes will be paid. The bond is based on the production level and ranges from $1,000 to half a million dollars or more. For breweries, this is known as a **brewer's bond**. Each sector has a specific permit. Spirits apply for a US Federal **Distilled Spirits Permit**. In the United States, it is legal to own a still of any size for decoration, distilling water, distilling essential oils, and so forth. As long as it is *not* used for making alcohol, it does not have to be registered with any entity. But, as soon as you decide to make alcohol for consumption, you need a distilled spirits permit filing as a **Distilled Spirits Plant (DSP)**. Breweries apply for a **Brewer Permit** by submitting a **Brewer's Notice application.** Cider is legally categorizes as a wine and cider makers need to file an application with the TTB for a **wine permit** prior to producing, storing, blending, bottling or wholesaling cider. The TTB has online registration for all the alcohol permits.[1] Applicants improve their chances of success by providing accurate, thorough, and even excessive information. The applicant should indicate when the business needs to start producing product which may be well in advance of actually opening the doors for business. Also, the applicant(s) should use consistent names and addresses throughout the entire form. The TTB displays current application processing times for all beverage types on their website. Assume at least three months if the application is complete with nothing amiss but it is a good idea to allow for double that amount of time.

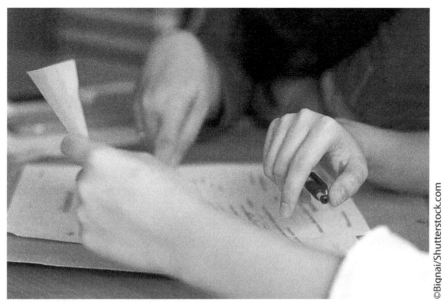

Figure 19.1 Application process

Compliance: The TTB has several methods to check compliance with alcohol laws and accurate taxation. Producers must file detailed reports (quarterly, monthly, or more frequently depending on the production rate). These reports balance the amount of beverage product in production, product in fermentation, aging or conditioning tanks, and amounts of barrels and packaged product to make sure that none goes missing and avoids a tax payment. Tax is paid on product that is packaged in kegs, bottles or cans. If product has to be destroyed for quality or past sell date reasons that loss must also be recorded but is not taxed. The agency has the right to drop by and check compliance with the actual product on location as well audit bottle fill and alcohol levels on retail shelves and marketing materials for appropriate claims.

State Liquor Control Boards

Each state and province establishes its own regulatory scheme. Most states will not provide a brewing or production license until the federal TTB permit is issued. In the United States, states vary on their sales and sampling laws (how they treat direct sales, packaging requirements and labeling, facility tours, tasting rooms, craft pubs, self-distribution, and craft production facilities) and excise taxes. The southern United States is more stringent than the northern and western regions of the county with regard to most alcohol laws. For example, the average US state tax on beer production is $0.19 per gallon, but Tennessee charges $1.286 per gallon while Oregon charges $0.0838 per gallon. Similar differences exist with spirits and cider or mead except when the state has an entrenched historic industry, such as whiskey. Washington state charges $35.22 per gallon while Kentucky and Tennessee charge $7.35 and $4.46 per gallon, respectively, reflecting the power of the whiskey industry groups to affect more modest taxes on spirits.[2]

Many states default to the three-tier system laws and require licenses to ship products into the state. Most require a state wholesaler's license to sell product off the premises as well as a licenses for on-premises sales.

In many locations, the production facility may be required to have a license from the state **Department of Agriculture (DOA)** to manufacture a product. For example, Pennsylvania DOA requires a Food Establishment Registration for manufacturing cider and a Retail Food Facilities license for selling or serving cider to consumers. In Oregon, a county health department license is required if the pub is over 50 percent of the business, but the DOA license is required if the brewery side is bigger.

Local Laws

More stringent local laws and codes trump state liquor licenses. Many cities have licensing requirements and additional regulations for production facilities that mimic the state and federal taxes. In many municipalities, there are regulations around resource and equipment use; stills and boilers, in particular, trigger intense scrutiny. All alcohol production facilities need to disclose their solid and liquid waste unless they are off the public sewer and water systems.

Some counties are "dry" and do not allow alcohol production or sales at all. Nearly half of the counties in Mississippi and Arkansas prohibit alcohol sales and almost half of the United States contain some counties preventing alcohol sales. BJs Brewpub chain once built a pub in a dry county and did not find out until construction was completed and learned that they could not brew. Other laws

FIGURE 19.2   No alcohol allowed

inhibiting alcohol include the ban on Sunday sales, restrictions on hours of sales, on-premises or off-premises sales, limits on the amount that can be sold on or off-premises at a production facility, limits on the amount of retail space allowed with a production facility, to name a few. These rules are typically found under local zoning ordinances and city alcohol licensing websites.

Food and Drug Administration

The Food and Drug Administration (FDA) is concerned with the food safety of commercially produced food and beverage products. For beer and spirits, the FDA typically leaves administration to the TTB with the exception of the **Food Safety Modernization ACT (FSMA)**. The FSMA is increasingly requiring stricter sanitation policies, regulations, and preventative controls to prevent unsafe product from reaching consumers. Generally this is not an issue for breweries or distilleries unless a routine TTB inspection finds product that is unsafe to consumers. Ciders face more scrutiny. The FSMA has regulations around pasteurization or filtering of cider. Additionally, the FDA imposes requirements about ingredients and product labeling for cider below 7 percent ABV (they do not regulate product at or over 7 percent). Small cideries (less than 100 full-time employees and less than 100,000 units sold in the United States) can apply for an exemption. Others must provide the following information:

- ► Name and place of manufacturer, bottler or distributor
- ► Net contents
- ► Statement of identity (for example, hard cider)
- ► Nutrition facts box (for example, serving size, calories, fat, and so forth)
- ► Food allergen labeling

©Rob Byron/Shutterstock.com

FIGURE 19.3   Nutritional label

Runcible Cider Presses On with Permitting

In 2010, Kelly McCune and Rob Miller purchased a 10-acre cherry orchard in the Columbia River Gorge area in search of interesting post-career endeavors. The orchard consisted of a shared well, a shipping container, wildflowers, and 400 ailing trees. Over the next few years of research and debate, the pair finally settled on getting into the burgeoning cider business by replanting the orchard with cider apple trees and producing hard cider on the farm. Since the land was in a beautiful setting in an agricultural tourism area, opening the place to visitors seemed like a great fit.

From the beginning, McCune and Miller knew they would be face challenges developing this piece of land. Zoned A2, small-scale agriculture, it required agricultural activity. But, the property is also in the **National Scenic Area (NSA),** a designation to protect the scenic beauty of the area. NSA status carries its own rulebook for development, interpreted and enforced individually by each county in the NSA.

In the fall of 2014, McCune and Miller took architectural plans for a house and "barn" (for production and office space) to their county planning department for permission to build. The application was approved for a house and "accessory structure." This designation meant that they could not do any processing in the buildings—including making cider in the barn— without a **conditional use permit**.

©Gary Gilardi/Shutterstock.com

FIGURE 19.4   National scenic area

At this point, the pair struggled to decipher which regulatory agency to appeal to next. They now had NSA and planning department approval for the structures and at some point would need approval from planning for making cider. Additionally they needed approval from Oregon Department of Agriculture (ODA) for processing safety, sanitation for septic and wastewater, **Department of Environmental Quality (DEQ)** for septic and water impacts, water-master approval for use of the community water, and then the TTB and Oregon Liquor Control (OLCC) for licensing.

After getting approval from the ODA, they submitted an application to the county for a conditional use permit. Only then did they discover that the NSA rules allow for a tasting room for wineries making "wine from grapes," but make no provision for "wine from apples." The county would not budge on the unclear definition so they applied instead for a farm stand, allowable on their land, where they could give "micro samples" of cider and sell packaged product.

The complicated conditional use permit approval was further delayed by complaints from a neighbor who worried that the cidery would bring unwanted traffic. To appease the neighbor and city, McClure and Miller wrote explanations of the process, water use, operations, schedule for sales, plans for the orchard, sound impact, volume of apples to cider, and more. Eventually, they engaged a land use attorney to help navigate the letter-writing and negotiation process. The resulting conditional use permit was granted in January 2016. However, it added unexpected restrictions on business activity such as a residency requirement and a stipulation that they use a certain percentage of their own orchard fruit in the cider.

Throughout this process these would-be cider makers also had to develop a wastewater plan, which is required by the DEQ, and thus is also part of the conditional use permit. They were asked to build a separate septic system for the cidery or drain into a holding tank, continually balance the pH, and repurpose the waste. Deciding on the holding tank, McClure and Miller were concerned that that it might prove challenging during the rainy production season. They also had to confirm to the regional water master that they would not exceed their water use allotment. At the end of the process, they realized that the correct order of applying for permits makes a big difference in how fast approvals happen since some permits build on each other. But because few people build cideries in the area, it was impossible to know which way to go prior to jumping into the whole process. Clearly, it took a passion for cider for these entrepreneurs to jump through all these hurdles.

SUMMARY

At the end of the day, dozens of licenses and permits may be required to operate an alcohol production facility in your area. It pays to do your homework in advance and go through every level of government to see where roadblocks might occur in your business planning and operations. Sometimes unexpected rules can appear that can seriously hamper the businesses operations and profitability. This chapter covered a number of regulatory hurdles, but alcohol production and sales also face label laws, city zoning, and building codes as well as other general business laws related to issues like labor laws. An experienced alcohol industry lawyer might be one of the essential ingredients and early investments for any startup as well as for those businesses in the growth phase.

LEARNING ADVENTURES

1.   For a beverage of your choice, look at the history of alcohol legislation in another country (for example, Iceland). What societal forces created the foundational alcohol laws and how have laws changed in the last 20 years?

2.   Go to the TTB or equivalent national alcohol regulation website and fill out an application (pretending that you are a real business). Where do you see potential challenges for a startup in this process?

3.   Go to your local city website and look at the alcohol licensing requirements for a production and bar facility. How many different permits or licenses are required? What is the estimated total cost of licensing in your location?

ENDNOTES

1.   Alcohol and Tobacco Trade Tax Bureau (TTB), http://www.ttb.gov.
2.   Samantha Jordan and Scott Drenkard, "Map of State Spirits Excise Tax Rates in 2015," Tax Foundation (2015), http://taxfoundation.org/blog/map-state-spirits-excise-tax-rates-2015.

CHAPTER TWENTY

Funding

Key Terms

accredited investor

angel investors

annual investor meetings

banks

break-even analysis

capitalization plan

cash flow

collateral

conflict of interest

credit history

credit unions

crowdfunding

debt

distribution of profits

enterprise zones

equity

equity crowdfund

grant programs

individual investors

institutional financing

investor communication

investor packet

line of credit

loan

management experience

matching grants

operating agreement

organizational documents

procedure for accepting offer

pro forma financials

quarterly investor updates

risk factors

securities regulation

security

small business association (SBA)

sophisticated investor

state and municipal development
     funds

stock

subscription/admission agreement

term sheet

traditional crowdfund

value-added producer grants

vendor and supplier financing

venture capital

Overview

As you've come this far, the question remains, how is this grand enterprise going to get off the ground and be infused with cash along its path? That is, of course, the million dollar question for every independently owned business. From using money from your own savings and assets to raising it from friends and family, to borrowing from banks or other formal investment arrangements, the bottom line is that most businesses require financing. While many people view non-traditional methods like crowdfunding as a potential method for funding, most new businesses will not attract nearly enough investment from this approach and need to rely on conventional avenues. This chapter surveys the sources for funding for an enterprise along with a discussion of the restrictions and the pros and cons of various methods.

Learning Objectives

▶ Understand different mechanisms for raising money for a business.

▶ Determine funding options from federal, state, local, and other funding agencies.

▶ Evaluate vendor and supplier financing options.

▶ Compare pros and cons of debt versus equity financing.

▶ Describe an accredited investor and sophisticated investor.

▶ Understand the basic requirements of institutional financing.

▶ Know the elements of an investor packet and Security Exchange Committee rules relative to equity investing.

▶ Compare a traditional crowd-fund to an equity crowdfund.

Introduction

The most obvious source of funding for any startup is using your own as well as friends' and family members' money. Some people have savings and other assets such as land and a building to bring to the business. The more cash and assets that you bring to the table, the easier it is to leverage other types of equity and debt financing. Money in hand, the bank and potential investors see that you have real skin in the game.

One common way to attract investment in your company is to offer shares or part of the company to someone in exchange for their cash, known as **equity**. Owners of the company typically get a large portion of the equity or convert it into other financial instruments like **stock**. With an equity position, there is typically not a specified time frame for repayment of the investment.

As an alternative to equity, **debt** financing does have a fixed time frame for repayment of the **loan** along with interest. The time frame may be short (less than a year) or long term (more than a year). With debt financing, the debt owner, for example, the bank, does not have ownership in the firm but the loan could be secured against the borrower's assets such as the business itself or another form of personal guarantee. In most cases, a business is financed by a combination of equity and debt.

Institutional Financing

Loans come from many sources, informally, through a note from friends or family, or formally, through institutional lending organizations such as **banks**, **credit unions**, and commercial finance companies. Small businesses can also access government guaranteed loans such as the **Small Business Association (SBA)** program in the United States. The SBA loans exist to encourage banks and other lenders to support small firms by guaranteeing part of the loan repayment to the bank. All businesses rely on banks for some of their funding whether it is a seasonal **line of credit** for buying materials and payroll needs or a loan that funds a large portion of the building, equipment, and startup costs.[1]

When applying for a bank loan either directly or through the SBA, the business must supply several key elements: proof of the ability to repay the loan, credit history, equity investment, collateral, and management experience. Proof of ability to pay comes from two main sources. First, as part of the **business plan's financial statements**, a **cash flow** analysis is created. This analysis will show the projected cash flowing into and out of the business over a three-year period (by month). These numbers come from forecast sales and operating costs as well as overhead and other costs. The cash flow statement is covered in Chapter 21. Second, a business can prove that it has assets to cover the business loan if the business goes under, called **collateral**. Collateral may be equipment, buildings, homes, and financial instruments such as stocks and bonds, and certificates of deposit.

As in any other loan application process, the loan agency examines the **credit history** of the applicant through credit bureaus that supply this analysis. Your personal credit history or score is based on your prior activity with credit cards, billing agencies, and other loans such as car, school, and mortgages. It is important to clear up any credit issues or errors on the report prior to applying for a loan.

The business **management experience** also sends a signal about the ability of the management and ownership team to create and operate a viable business. As part of the business plan, the resumes of each team member should reflect a history of experience related to running different aspects of a business. A strong team has complementary skills that illustrate experience in marketing, operations management, and finance. Experience in the craft beverage industry is also a strong playing card as are resumes for any hired talent in accounting or craft beverage production (brewmaster, cider-maker, distiller) or beverage business management (distribution, operations, marketing).

Most businesses are financed through both debt and equity. Financial institutions expect to see enough equity from the owner and shareholders to leverage the loan, typically a minimum of 20 percent equity and much higher depending on the perceived risk of the loan package.

State and Municipal Development Funds

In many locations around the world, governments create loan programs to revitalize certain locations undergoing tough economic times. Local governments as well as some non-profit foundations loan, give grants, or provide other incentives to businesses that locate to these neighborhoods and generate economic activity, especially jobs for people in underperforming areas. For example, **enterprise zones** in many states provide relief from property and other local taxes to businesses locating in those areas. These locations can be found by searching the Internet for your state and enterprise zones. For those situating in historic areas, there are often funds for restoration of historic exteriors to maintain a certain history and feel to a town. These funds generally come in the form of **matching grants** where the state matches the investment dollar for dollar.

FIGURE 20.1   Historic zone

Government Grant Programs

The federal, state, and local government offers **grant programs** for specific groups to develop businesses and for other activities within the business. These grants are targeted toward various groups such as women, minorities, and specific underdeveloped locations.[2] Other grants come from the Department of Agriculture (USDA) that funds **value-added producer grants**. For example, Cobbler Mountain Cellars and Foggy Ridge Cider in Floyd, Virginia received $200,000 each to create and market new products, expand operations, and support local and regional food systems.[3] For those producing barley, apples or other fruit, honey, or other beverage related crops, these USDA grants may be an entry point into the craft beverage industry. While applying for one of these grants may consume time, it could be well worth the effort.

Vendor and Supplier Financing

Today, many vendors provide financing or leasing arrangements for equipment. Brewing systems account for a large percentage of the brewery startup cost and many suppliers or third-parties now offer financing options. The collateral in this case is the equipment itself, so if the business cannot keep up with the payments, the equipment is repossessed. Other equipment that may qualify for financing are packaging lines, filtration systems, refrigeration systems such as glycol chillers, and kitchen equipment for pubs. On the one hand, financing equipment through the vendor allows businesses to open and expand quickly. On the other hand, if the equipment is repossessed, the business is no longer viable.

Another option is to finance through supply chain partners. Raw materials providers such as hops, fruit, or malt vendors may offer terms that allow you to commit to one year's worth of product but pay as you go. With this arrangement, the vendor stores your product for the year in their warehouse and delivers monthly or quarterly amounts of product, billing per delivery after the fact. The purchaser benefits from volume discounts and reduced storage costs while the vendor has a yearly commitment for product. At the other end of the chain, in many states, the distributor may loan money for order commitments or take an equity position in your company, not uncommon for many producer-distributor arrangements in newer markets with big opportunities.

Individual Investors

Outside of you and your business' partners, who are the most likely people to invest in your business? In most cases, these are your friends and family. For example, parents of many craft entrepreneurs fund newer beverage businesses with an equity position that is part of their retirement strategy or as a method for transferring inheritance to their children prematurely. On the positive side, friends and family are the easiest people to access and ask for money since they know you and are in your social circle. On the negative side, if things don't pan out with the business, you could end up with damaged relationships, so many advise to stay away from family involvement. So, it behooves you to consider the structure of the investment relationship and convey the risks of the business in a realistic way to all potential investors. Informally, friends and family can issue a note for the debt.

FIGURE 20.2 Investor group

Securities Regulation

The legalities around security regulations may seem boring but they are crucial to raising money today. Money spent on properly structuring these deals and insuring legal compliance is well worth it. Most investors want a **security** defined as stock, membership units, debt instruments, and right to acquire ownership. These investors are required to be registered unless they conform to specific exemptions of the Federal Securities Act. Registration can be a big headache for an investor and is most appropriate for institutional investors rather than individuals. But, each state has a specific version of securities law so it is important so look at your state's rules. To avoid registration, the sale of securities must comply with the Securities Act, Regulation D-Sale of Securities without Registration for Rule 506, Private Offering Exemption or Rule 504, Limited Offering Exemption. The business needs to file notice and comply with the fraud provisions of the Securities Act.

From the business perspective, the requirements for a Regulation D exemption have key features. First, you cannot advertise or generally solicit for investors, that is, you cannot post your investment opportunity on Facebook or any other media outlet, present to large groups, or do a mass mailing. You will need to meet with your friends, friends of friends, family, and so forth in small or one-on-one meetings instead and keep detailed records of these solicitations. Second, both parties should have a "reasonable" belief that the purchaser is purchasing for the purpose of investment and not for resale. Third, the business needs to file a Form D with the Security Exchange Commission (SEC) within 15 days after the first sale. Finally, the business needs to verify that the investor is **accredited** and/or **sophisticated** based on the following definition shown in Table 20.1.

Friends, family, friends of friends or family, and an individual's extended social network are all sources for accredited investors. Additionally, accredited investors are part of **venture capital** companies, groups of investors or financial investment companies looking for investment opportunities or **angel investors**, affluent individuals looking for business startups in exchange for debt or ownership equity.

TABLE 20.1   Accredited versus sophisticated investors

Accredited investors	Sophisticated investors
Must meet one of the following descriptions:	**Must meet the following criteria:**
• A natural person who together with his or her spouse has a net worth of more than $1,000,000 (not including the value of the primary residence).	• The investor is deemed to have sufficient investing experience and knowledge to weigh the risks and merits of an investment opportunity (often self-proclaimed).
• A natural person with an individual income of at least $200,000 (or joint income with spouse of $300,000) in each of the two most recent years and has a reasonable expectation of the same income in the current year.	**The investor has sufficient net worth and income:** • A net worth of $2.5 million or • An income of more than $250,000 in the past two years.
• A corporation or partnership not formed for the specific purpose of investing with assets in excess of $5,000,000.	
• Any director, executive officer, or general partner of the issuer (your business).	

For Rule 506 exemptions, the investment can have up to 35 sophisticated investors and an unlimited amount of accredited investors. State regulations can be preempted by this rule. For any sophisticated investors, the individuals must provide their financial information and must be provided with comprehensive investment information. Rule 506 Exemption is best if you have access to many accredited investors (a lot of wealthy friends or family). The Rule 504 exemption has a maximum offering price of one million dollars but does not have mandatory disclosures for the business or requirements for accredited or sophisticated investors. Advertising and solicitation is allowed if the offer is limited to accredited investors. But, state regulations cannot be preempted by Rule 504. This exemption is a good fit for businesses looking for less than one million dollars that have many potential non-accredited investors. An exemption is required for each investor.

The Investor Packet

In order to disclose all possible information to investors and protect the business from fraud claims, it is essential to create a comprehensive investor packet for potential investors to learn about the proposed business. In this packet, one should avoid a) material misrepresentations (non-truths), and b) omitting material facts that hide the truth. For example, if taprooms are not legal in a state and a business plan includes a taproom in the business model without indicating the legal status of taprooms, then this omitted material constitutes fraud. There are significant personal and professional repercussions for fraudulent investor information including liability, criminal charges, and problems with any future business investment activity. The basic components of the investor packet include the following details.

Business plan and pro forma financials are included so that investors can read about the business and the potential financial viability of the proposed business. Most of the business plan's content and financial materials are covered in this book.

Capitalization plan describes how much capital the proposed company has in place and what needs to be raised through the proposed investment offering. It should also cover when capital might be needed in the future and any proposed use of debt financing. This amount could be adjusted over time as investments come in, the business performance and cash flow change, and expansion plans come into play.

Organizational documents are paperwork like the certificate of formation or partnership certificate or agreements, limited liability company agreement, membership agreements and other documents defining the structure, governance, and members of the organization. Governed by the state's business laws, a lawyer creates many of these documents when forming the entity. Different documents are needed depending on whether the business is a corporation, partnership, or limited liability corporation.

Risk factors address the significant risks of the investment. Again, a good lawyer familiar with investment packages has the necessary language for this section. Some examples of risks include statements like:

- You should not invest unless you can bear the risk of losing your entire investment.

- There is no public market for the shares and no such market is expected to develop in the foreseeable future.

- No government authority has confirmed the accuracy or adequacy of the document.

- Investors are required to bear the financial risk of the investment for an indefinite period of time.

- These projections of future events may or not occur based on assumptions that may or may not prove accurate.

Procedure for accepting offer explains the terms with which the business entity will accept the investor's money.

Conflict of interest includes a statement of how the buyer might have some kind of conflict with the investment entity. Conflicts of interest are to be avoided. These conflicts could be related to the investor representing another entity that would have a conflict with the investment entity.

Term sheet is a simple document outlining the material terms and conditions of the business agreement.

Operating agreement is the agreement among those company members governing the business and the member's financial and managerial rights and duties.

Subscription/admission agreement covers the assurance by a company to sell a given number of shares to an investor at a given price. The investor agrees to pay that given price.

Investor Best Practices

To avoid potential problems with investors and the SEC, the business should follow investor best practices. Good communication with investors is the most important aspect of investor relations. For

FIGURE 20.3   Annual investor meeting

corporations, **annual investor meetings** are a regulatory requirement with an annual date spelled out in the company bylaws. Even if the business is not a corporation, annual investor meetings are highly suggested. During the meeting, the members approve the yearly financial report, vote on proposals, and elect members to the board of directors. The company keeps minutes on the activities at all investor meetings and those unable to attend have access to those minutes as well as ability to vote by proxy.

Another helpful tool for investor communication is **quarterly investor updates**. While these could have an informal aspect like interesting goings on at the business, new hires, new beverages, new projects, or updates on ongoing projects, it could include formal elements such as financial reporting and business strategy or concerns. There are other tools for **investor communication** such as emails, social media postings, and other ways to inform the investor of the business status.

Getting some return on the business besides free beer, whiskey, or cider is a major investor concern. The original investor packet should mention **distribution of profits**; it behooves the business to be relatively vague about distribution of profits in this document. As the business becomes financially healthy, it should create a policy that defines the parameters that calculate how much money is distributed and on what timeline to investors.

Finally, there are a number of issues that can create problems related to investors. Disregarding securities law is one way to get into big legal problems. The business could attract the wrong kind of investors for the craft beverage business; it's clearly not the same as a Silicon Valley technology business. Some investors expect a very high return and rapid payback of their investment, an unrealistic condition for a startup beverage producer. Additionally, investors may want some control, especially those buying a significant portion of the company. Owners need to be conscious of the amount of control they maintain without giving away too much. Although the business plan may seem appropriate at the time of conception, the plan could underestimate its capital needs, costs of doing business, and the time required to become profitable.

Crowdfunding

There are two types of crowdfunding, the **traditional crowdfund** and the **equity crowdfund**. Traditional crowdfunding platforms include Kickstarter, Indiegogo, and Crowdbrewed where the business posts a project with a monetary goal and offers rewards for different levels of cash contribution. The donors do not receive a share of the business, instead they get special offers such as discounts, merchandise, or privileges such as a brew day with the brewmaster. Some of the crowdfund sites give the business all the money raised in the campaign minus a fee while others have an all or nothing policy; if the project does don't hit the monetary goal, then it gets no money at all. On the upside, crowdfunding seems like a great way to raise money relatively easily. But, the incoming cash involves a lot of employee time, outflow of products, and correspondence for little money relative to other investment opportunities. For example, if a crowdfund campaign raises $50,000 for a taproom build-out, the host site takes five percent ($2,500) and the perks cost $10,000. Mailings, monitoring, and correspondence with donors takes 200 employee hours at $20 per hour. The business nets $35,000 but may have to pay taxes on the income reducing that amount to more like $25,000. While this brings the amount to half of what was expected, the campaign attracts many loyal customers to the business and acts as a marketing tool.

Crowdfunding as a Finance Strategy

Dean Howes from Salem, Oregon used Kickstarter to help launch Vagabond Brewing in 2012. For Howes, crowdfunding was a tool to build a community and raise money for the brewery while sorting out other financing. Vagabond's Kickstarter campaign was centered around Howes' team, some of them veterans, and building a brewery embodying their love of travel and adventure. Their Kickstarter goal was $25,000.

Vagabond's Kickstarter project page provided information about the brewery's team, detailing each member's education and brewing experience. Their Kickstarter video describes how they would use the money for startup costs such as legal fees, design, and a down payment for the hand-fabricated system, and for merchandise for the backers' rewards.

Howes had looked at many different loan programs, including SBA, county, state, federal, and veteran programs. The group decided to begin with a Kickstarter campaign and proved lucky with their social networks. Kickstarter was not free money, according to Howes, but the busiest 30 days he has ever experienced. It required a lot of time to reach out to their networks and ask people directly to contribute to Vagabond's campaign.

As is typical for Kickstarter projects, Vagabond set up tiers of rewards for backers. In Howes' view, this incentive was important not only for people to get something tangible for their contribution but it also helped them feel connected to the project. Rewards included the typical stickers, pint glasses, shirts, and hats. Each of these initial products ordered for the Kickstarter campaign were marketed as limited-edition merchandise. A medium-tier backer was rewarded with a "Mug Club" one-year membership, including a personally labeled stein. Howes highly recommends researching merchandise costs since the minimum runs for items like sweatshirts are costly. Additionally postage fees add up as does the time involved for shipping out rewards to backers.

The Vagabond team was creative in coming up with methods to attract bigger fish to its campaign. The team had to consider how to appropriately reward people for these larger donations and included the opportunity to come brew with the brewers, name a beer, and enjoy the personally made product over a special brewer's dinner. Vagabond also provided a contact on the campaign page to reach out to if none of the reward tiers were of interest and if a bigger or direct investment was desired. The same consideration of how to reward investors and loyal customers later carried into the business at Vagabond.

For Howes the flow of contributions from Kickstarter was nerve wracking in beginning. The team targeted anyone who related to the brewery and anyone who might identify with the brand, or lived in the area. Traffic to their project page spiked in the middle of the 30-day campaign and landed them a multitude of backers. Activity then died down, but the Vagabond team finished strong with a big social media push at the end. Vagabond's handful of biggest backers contributed $5,000.

The project brought in just under $28,000 within the month deadline from 319 individuals. Kickstarter takes five percent of earnings from its campaigns and Amazon takes 2.5 percent, so Vagabond ended up cashing in about $23,5000 from the campaign.

Still, it took Vagabond Brewing three years to raise all its required funding and opened in 2014. The co-founders settled on a seven-barrel system for the brewery. Vagabond also opened a taproom, going for the high margins from pint sales.

The Kickstarter money used for the brewing system's down payment helped the overall timeline of the project and avoided expensive delays. With other funds directed at construction of the taproom, the site was ready for move-in just as the hand-fabricated brewing system was done being built, thanks to that initial down payment funded by Vagabond's Kickstarter backers.

Having a good business plan in place with a little capital was the ideal starting point for Vagabond. When going to various lenders for the remaining funding, the co-founders were able to show that people were already giving them money through Kickstarter and that people were excited about their project. Successful crowdfunding made them attractive borrowers. It also provided good press for the brewery and brand exposure to the community at large.

The more recent phenomenon of equity crowdfunding exchanges funds for an ownership share in the business. The Jumpstart on Business Startups (JOBS) Act passed Rule 506c that allows equity fundraising online. This exemption allows general solicitation so that companies can publicly share their investment offering through social media and equity crowdfunding websites. At present, all purchasers must be accredited investors and the issuer must take reasonable steps to verify accredited investor status. The investor must also prove that they are accredited to participate in the investment. Third-party companies can provide proof of accredited investor verification. The investment offering must be through a registered broker or funding portal but cannot advertise terms of the offering. However, it can use advertising to direct investors to the broker or portal. The business must file with SEC (along with yearly financial statement filings) and must provide specific investment information to both the SEC and potential investors.[4]

SUMMARY

All but the wealthiest people require financing to start a business. There are many ways to finance a business and the chosen method depends on the overall cash needs and the lifecycle stage—a startup versus a mature operation. Most businesses keep a line of credit open at their local lender to cover fluctuations in cash throughout the year. Equity financing is better than carrying debt so long as the business can attract equity investors without giving up too much ownership stake or managerial control. Debt financing helps keep control in the owners' hands but requires significant cash outflow in loan payments each month. These are trade-offs that each business owner needs to consider in a financing strategy. **Break-even analysis** covered in Chapter 10 is useful for many financing decisions, including equipment decisions such as paying a mobile packager or a monthly loan for packaging equipment. Other decisions about debt versus equity depend on the business owners' tolerance for control by others, risk tolerance, and the ownership group resources.

A City Loan Revitalizes an Old Brewery

The oldest brewery in Michigan City, Zorn Brew Works, was revived after 77 years of closure by John Van Prooyen. In order to revitalize the history of the original brewery and introduce a new series of beers, he applied for a revolving loan from the city for restoring the historic building. The Michigan City Revolving Loan Committee has a mission of stabilizing and growing the employment opportunities and economy of Michigan City. It awarded the project a $260,000 loan to restore the brewery building and help with brewing equipment purchases. According to Van Prooyen the brewery planned to employ 25 workers and open a 44-room boutique hotel. With Van Prooyen's own $765,000 investment in the whole project, the city's loan helped support his decision to open a brewery in Michigan City and the city garnered a new historical attraction.

LEARNING ADVENTURES

1. Familiarize yourself with a few craft fundraising projects on the various websites (Kickstarter, Indiegogo, Craftfund, Fundable, Crowdbrewed, or others).

    a. Review a completed craft beverage project from a platform you like. Evaluate how the project fared and the potential pros and cons of the particular crowdfunding platform.

    b. Examine how much money the idea brought in and then estimate how much the campaign had to shell out to run it. In particular, estimate the cost to put together the video as well as the rewards. Remember some reward items require a minimum number of items to be purchased when you have monogrammed or printed items (T-shirts, glasses, for example). Also, analyze the fee structure for the crowdfunding site. Consider any other costs that this might entail (labor, postage, and time). What is your estimate of the net income that the project brought in (cash in-cash out)?

    c. When you look at a crowdfunding campaign, what do you think contributed to their success or failure? Would it have been better for the business to use a different crowdfunding platform?

2. Go to an equity crowdfunding website (AngelList, Early Shares, Fundable, Seedrs, Crowdfunder, or others). Find a craft beverage startup and write a brief summary of how the investment is structured (minimum investment, percent of company's financing, strength of business plan, ownership and governance, and so on).

3. Go to the Small Business Administration website (SBA.gov) and learn about its loan programs.

    a. Describe the four types of loan programs offered by the SBA. What is the purpose of each one? Which one would be most applicable for a startup beverage production facility?

    b. What are the requirements for eligibility for the 7(a) loan program? What type of businesses might not be eligible?

    c. What might a business expect to pay in fees for an SBA 7(a) loan? What is ballpark interest rate?

    d. There are specific rules around how 7(a) loan proceeds may be used. Describe how they can and cannot be used.

    e. The SBA considers the business' financial information as well as the business owners' personal financial information. In what way? Describe the personal information that must be submitted with a loan application.

ENDNOTES

1 "Borrowing Money for Your Business," U.S. Small Business Administration, https://www.sba.gov/content/borrowing-money.

2 "Federal Grants," http://www.federalgrants.com.

3 "Virginia Wineries, Cideries and Breweries Win USDA Grant Funding" [accessed 2/8/2016], http://vawineinmypocket.com/article/virginia_wineries_cideries_and_breweries_win_usda_grant_funding.

4 "Rule 506 of Regulation D," U.S. Securities and Exchange Commission [last updated 10/6/2014], https://www.sec.gov/answers/rule506.htm.

CHAPTER TWENTY-ONE

Financial Statements

Key Terms

accounts receivable

accumulated depreciation

administration expenses

assets

balance sheet

capital

cash

cash flow

cash on delivery (COD)

depreciation

earnings before interest, taxes,
    depreciation and amortization
    (EBITDA)

financing activities

fixed assets

intangible assets

interest expense

inventory

investing activities

loans

operating activities

operating expenses

marketing expenses

modified accelerated cost recovery
    system (MACRS)

net income

notes payable

paid-in capital

pro forma

pro forma profit and loss

rent

retained earnings

sales expenses

security deposits

Overview

Financial statements are at the heart of every business. They not only show a snapshot of the financial health of the business at a point in time but also project its viability. Startup businesses must include completed financial statements in their business plans. These are forecasts of the scenario you *hope* will occur in the future, so their creation is quite a challenge. The business team needs the assistance of an accounting or finance person to create these statements, but everyone in management and the stockholder or ownership group should have a solid understanding of what these statements represent. This chapter builds on financial calculations from previous chapters and pulls them together into profit-and-loss statements, balance sheets, and statements of cash flow. Along the way, it introduces other financial terms and concepts relevant to financial statements.

Learning Objectives

▶ Understand the three basic financial statements required in the business plan and for ongoing operations of the business.

▶ Determine yearly revenues and cost of goods sold.

▶ Understand depreciation and its impact on the income statement.

▶ Compare depreciation versus expensing kegs.

▶ Understand the difference between assets and liabilities.

▶ Know the industry averages for balance sheet items.

▶ Understand the relationship among the three financial statements and how changes in one area affect the other statements.

Introduction

There are three statements that make up a traditional financial package: profit and loss (P&L), balance sheet, and statement of cash flow. Most of this book has been building up the pieces of the P&L. For the P&L and the other two parts, we will have to apply a bit of conjecture about what will happen in the future with equity, debt, and other financial activities. Statements predicting future activity are called **pro forma**, indicated anticipated figures. Once a business is up and running, these statements cover past periods so the information is considerably more accurate and no longer *pro forma*.

Profit and Loss

The P&L statement, also known as the income statement, shows the projected income and expenses for a projected future period (for example, pro forma income statement) or for the past period (for example, a quarterly income statement). A **pro forma profit and loss** is an estimation of expected sales subtracting out any expenses related to those sales to come up with the resulting profit or loss.

Sales and Cost of Goods Sold

Based on the cost of goods sold (COGS) information in Chapter 7 for a beer example, you know the prices for selling to wholesale with a 25 percent margin with 1,000-barrel annual production as well as some retail sales on-premises in Table 21.1. In this example, the assumed breakdown of the barrels per channel/package is 60 percent wholesale (half to bottles/cans and half to kegs) and 40 percent retail (25 percent to bottles/cans and 75 percent to on-site keg sales and pints) based on yearly barrel production.

TABLE 21.1   Yearly wholesale sales and COGS estimate

Wholesale	COGS	Our selling price	Wholesale price to retailer 25% margin	Units	Sales = units x our selling price	COGS year = units x COGS
Packaging	Per case			Cases		
22-oz. bottles	$13.68	$30.00	$37.50	1803.6	$54,120	$24,680
4-pack (16-oz cans)	$19.24	$25.00	$31.25	1859.6	$46,485	$35,771
Kegs	Per keg			Kegs		
Draft kegs (1/2 bbl.)	$59.68	$90.00	$112.50	240	$21,600	$14,322
Draft kegs (1/6 bbl.)	$20.98	$55.00	$68.75	1080	$59,400	$22,656
				Totals	**$181,593**	**$97,439**
Source: Madeleine Pullman.						

With the retail sales, some kegs are sold from the dock and the remaining beer is sold through pints in the tasting room or packaged in cans or bottles to take off premises.

TABLE 21.2   Yearly retail sales and COGS estimate

Retail	COGS	Our selling price	Units	Sales = units x our selling price	COGS year= units x COGS
Packaged	Per case		Cases		
22-oz bottles	$13.68	$60.00	751.5	$45,090	$10,283
4-pack (16-oz cans)	$19.24	$40.00	518.5	$20,660	$9,936
Kegs	Per keg or pint		Kegs or pints		
Draft kegs (1/2 bbl.)	$59.68	$125.00	120	$15,000	$7,161
Pints sold	$0.48	$5.00	59,520	$297,600	$28,644
			Totals	**$378,350**	**$56,025**
Source: Madeleine Pullman.					

These numbers create the main part of the P&L statement for the first year as illustrated in Table 21.3.

TABLE 21.3   P&L example

	Year 1	% of sales	Per bbl. produced
Sales	1,000 bbl.		
Wholesale	$181,593.00	32.4%	$181.59
Retail	$378,350.00	67.6%	$378.35
COGS			
Wholesale	$97,439.26	17.4%	$97.43
Retail	$56,025.00	10.0%	$56.02
Gross profit	$406,488.00	72.6%	$406.49
Production administration and operating expense	$103,589.25	18.5%	$103.59
Retail administration and operating expense	$90,000.00	16.1%	$90.00
Sales and marketing expense	$33,597.00	6%	$33.60
Rent payment	$48,155.00	8.6%	$48.14
Earnings before interest, taxes, depreciation, and amortization (EBITDA)	$131,146.75	23.4%	$131.15
Depreciation	$(92,090.00)	16.45%	$93.09
Interest expense	$(30,383.00)	5.54%	$30.34
Net income (loss)	$8,673.75	1.55%	$8.67
Source: Madeleine Pullman.			

Expenses

A number of expenses are included in this category. In this example, they are broken down by production administration and operating expenses (the brewery side), retail administration and operating expenses (the tasting room side), sales and marketing expenses (for the whole business), and a rent payment, assuming that this business is renting space.

Administration and Operating Expenses

In this particular example, the production and retail **administration** and **operating expenses** are separated out but they could easily be combined into one category. The expenses would include salaries and benefits that are not part of the COGS labor. For example, the personnel from finance, management, and accounting, and potentially the operations manager (brewmaster), would be part of those salaries and benefits. Additionally, the supplies, utilities, maintenance, professional fees, and any other costs related to running the facility and tasting room would come under this total. Capital investments are not included in this total; these would include the equipment, building purchase and improvements, furniture, computers, and any deposits.

Sales and Marketing Expenses

Any materials, salaries, and benefits related to sales and marketing have a separate category on the P&L sheet, as do the materials related to promotion such as branded give-away items such as glasses, apparel, coasters, and signs as well as off-premises items like displays and store tags. This category also includes the cost of going to events such as festivals, competitions, tastings, and other promotions as well as any sales commission expenses and advertising.

Rent Payment

In the case where rent is paid for buildings or storage, this goes into the general expense category. If the building was purchased and has a mortgage payment, that particular item is an interest expense and, along with other debt, has a separate category and becomes part of the depreciation.

Depreciation

Certain expenses for purchased items are accounted for in COGS, and other expenses such as supplies, tap handles, and so forth are part of administration, marketing, sales, and operating expenses. But, other expenses of fixed assets must be recovered over a number of years through a concept known as depreciation. Depreciation represents the decrease in value of an asset over time as it ages; assets like buildings, vehicles, and equipment age over time and we can expense that decrease in value over time. Property that qualifies for depreciation must meet the following criteria according to the United States Tax Code.[1] This property must:

1. Be property that you own either outright or through financing.

2. Be used for the business or income producing activity.

3. Have a determinable useful life.

4. Be expected to last more than one year.

5. Not be excepted property (land, equipment used to build capital improvements, certain software, and other)[2].

Yearly depreciation amount is calculated based on the useful life of each asset. The cost of the asset includes the actual cost, sales tax, freight charges, installation, and testing fees. For many assets, the **Modified Accelerated Cost Recovery System (MACRS)** is most appropriate. The item or property must be classified as three-, five-, seven-, 10-, 15-, 20- or 25-year property or a non-residential real property (39 years). The IRS has determined the appropriate lifespan of many items. For example, cars, computers, office equipment have an expected life of five years; office furniture has seven years; a fruit bearing tree or vine, a single purpose agricultural structure; brewing equipment has 10 years or 17 years if classified under manufacture of grain products; and stainless tanks have 20 or more years.[3]

For an example of how depreciation works for a piece of equipment using a seven-year life MACRS table, assume half a year of use in the year it was purchased. The breakdown is shown in Table 21.4. If the business purchased a new filter at the beginning of July for $10,000, it shows a depreciation expense of $1,429 in the first year.

TABLE 21.4 MACRS for a seven-year asset

Year	Percentage recovery	Depreciation on a $10,000 asset
1	14.29%	$1,429
2	24.29%	$2,429
3	17.49%	$1,749
4	12.49%	$1,249
5	8.93%	$893
6	8.92%	$892
7	8.93%	$895
8	4.46%	$450
Source: Madeleine Pullman.		

Keg Dilemma

Kegs represent a problematic item for expenses, and no consensus exists on the best method for dealing with them. It boils down to two choices, expense the kegs or depreciate the kegs. Overall, lost kegs cost businesses more money than anyone realizes.

Expense kegs: For businesses that struggle to keep track of their kegs, it is permissible to expense kegs as incidental material and supplies. The benefit of this approach is that it is easy and provides a fast tax deduction early on in the business's life. But, the negatives of this approach are that the keg must also be reported on personal property tax returns, the businesses income looks low during the early stages, and keg deposits must still be tracked.

Depreciate kegs: If the business has a system for keeping track of the majority of the keg float, then the kegs should be depreciated under Food and Beverage equipment (Special Handling Devices). This rule allows three to four year life under MACRS method. The benefit of this approach is that the net income looks better for the first few years. But, the method requires fairly accurate tracking of the keg float and its age. This can become challenging when kegs get lost or damaged and, as a result, is often just an estimate of the float.

For a production facility, depreciation will include a purchased building, capital improvements to the building, all production equipment, forklifts, office equipment and furniture, computers, company trucks and cars, and many other items with a life longer than one year. This can add up to a significant amount each year as seen in Table 21.3 where the depreciation is more than $90,000 and reduces the taxable income substantially.

Interest Expense

Another element that appears on the P&L statement is the interest expense from taking on debt. Every time you make a loan payment, part of that is interest and another part pays down the principal or outstanding loan amount. For example, with a $100,000 loan at 5 percent, the total payments come to $8,000 per year. The first year, $5,000 is interest and $3,000 goes to loan or principal repayment. In subsequent years, the interest portion decreases while the principal increases.

TABLE 21.5   Interest schedule

Year	Interest rate	Beginning loan balance	Total payments	Interest paid	Principal paid	Ending loan balance
1	5%	$100,000	$8,000	$5,000	$3,000	$97,000
2	5%	$97,000	$8,000	$4,850	$3,150	$93,850
3	5%	$93,850	$8,000	$4,693	$3,307	$90,543
Source: Madeleine Pullman.						

The P&L sheet will reflect the amount of paid interest ($5000 in year 1) while another finance sheet, the balance sheet, will reflect the repayment of debt ($3,000 in year one) by reducing the amount of the loan.

EBITDA is an acronym that refers to earnings before interest, taxes, depreciation and amortization. This measurement is very useful to compare different companies' profitability and year-to-year performance. Every company may have different numbers for the interest, taxes, depreciation, and amortization based on how the business is structured, how much debt it took on, how much the taxes are in different localities, other factors affecting the business' taxes related to accounting magic, and the investment in buildings, equipment and other depreciable assets.

Net income reflects the amount left after accounting for the depreciation and interest. Since both depreciation and interest tend to be expenses (negative), they reduce the income overall. The net income is subject to taxation that depends on the federal and state taxation laws for the specific entity (corporation, partnership, sole proprietorship, for example).

In a business plan, a pro forma P&L, the statement is completed for three years in the future based on estimates of sales, expenses, additions of equipment, and other assets. Typically, the first year P&L is monthly.

Balance Sheet

The second essential financial statement is the **balance sheet**. This report shows the assets, liabilities, and capital at a particular point in time. It reflects changes in the P&L statement from a previous period (such as changes in overall assets and liabilities). As a shareholder or owner, this will highlight changes in equity and the relationship between what is owned versus owed. For many investors, this sheet has valuable information about the health of any business. The balance sheet has two sides, the assets side and the liabilities side.

Assets

Anything that your company owns that could bring future economic benefit is considered an asset. This includes land, buildings, equipment, cash, inventory, and accounts receivable (outstanding invoices owed to your company by others). Income is on the P&L statement, but that may not reflect the actual cash in the bank, raw materials siting in inventory, or outstanding invoices from the distributor or retailers. **Current assets** are assets that could be sold or converted to cash within one year.

Cash is whatever money is sitting in bank accounts at the end of the period. This may also include cash equivalents such as demand deposits, treasury bills, commercial paper (maturity of less than three months), checking accounts, savings accounts, and other short-term instruments on the cash side. Any other investments such as equity or debt held, which could be sold within a year, would fall under this category. They are reported at their market value at the time.

Accounts receivable represents invoices or money owed to the company by others for goods and services. They are expected to pay your business within the year. Notes receivable or debt with a short time horizon for money loaned to others also falls under this area. In the alcohol business, it is common for distributors or self-distributors to ask for **cash on delivery (COD)** thus reducing accounts receivable balances relative to other industries.

TABLE 21.6   Balance sheet assets

	Year 1	Year 2	Year 3
Current assets			
Cash	$72,324.00	$180,658.00	$463,066.00
Accounts receivable	$555,662.00	$611,228.00	$684,574.00
Inventory	$246,828.00	$271,512.00	$304,094.00
Total current assets	$874,814.00	$1,063,398.00	$1,451,734.00
Other assets			
Fixed assets	$1,500,000.00	$1,500,000.00	$1,500,000.00
Accumulated depreciation	$(20,400.00)	$(40,800.00)	$(61,200.00)
Net fixed assets	$1,479,600.00	$1,459,200.00	$1,438,800.00
Security deposits	$16,000.00	$16,000.00	$16,000.00
Total assets	$2,370,414.00	$2,538,598.00	$2,906,534.00
Source: Madeleine Pullman.			

Inventory includes any raw materials, bottles, cans, product in tank or barrels, finished goods and other supplies. These could be converted to cash in the short-term (under a year).

In this example, the business increases its current assets as the years pass due to improved income and expanding business in general (more inventory needed and more accounts receivable with more accounts).

Fixed assets are those assets that cannot be quickly converted into cash. These include the property, facility, and equipment. Many are depreciable items so the balance sheet shows the original value of all of those assets under fixed assets each year and then the **accumulated depreciation** that has been applied to the asset group. This goes up with time as more depreciation is applied to each asset and is cumulative. Remember, land is not depreciated so its value will typically not be reducing by the accumulated depreciation. Other fixed assets include things like **security deposits** and prepaid expenses such as rent, insurance premiums, and taxes.

Intangible assets are those assets that lack a physical presence but have economic value and advantages. Most startup businesses won't have intangible assets but any business with patents, copyrights, trademarks, goodwill, or brand value will report them. However, their value is highly uncertain.

Liabilities

Liabilities are your company's obligations representing either money that must be paid or services that must be performed. Similar to assets, they have current and long-term status.

TABLE 21.7   Liabilities

	Year 1	Year 2	Year 3
Current liabilities			
Accounts payable	$293,310.00	$184,984.00	$206,466.00
Total current liabilities	$293,310.00	$184,984.00	$206,466.00
Long term liabilities			
Notes payable	$68,000.00	$56,000.00	$100,000.00
Loan from partner	$224,000.00	$198,576.00	$180,884.00
SBA loan	$560,000.00	$474,000.00	$404,000.00
Total liabilities	$1,213,310.00	$969,560.00	$991,350.00
Paid-in capital	$1,081,800.00	$1,081,800.00	$1,081,800.00
Retained earnings	$(83,400.00)	$143,304.00	$543,238.00
Net income	$226,704.00	$399,934.00	$390,146.00
Total capital	$1,225,104.00	$1,625,038.00	$2,015,184.00
Total liabilities and capital	$2,370,414.00	$2,538,598.00	$2,906,534.00

Source: Madeleine Pullman.

Current liabilities are similar to the asset side. They are liabilities owed by the business in the short term (line of credit), wages payable, rent and utilities, notes, and dividends due in the short- term. Short-term liabilities are usually paid using current assets.

Accounts payable represents the bills owed to suppliers (for malt, hops, juice, fruit, and others), anything with short payment terms, such as due in 15 or 30 days. Accounts payable would match with expenses for the same period.

Long-term liabilities are those owed by the business for longer than one year.

Notes payable covers long-term loans (more than one year) for amounts that the company owes to a creditor along with interest expense. This might come from vehicle or equipment loans.

Loans (from individual or banks) include any other loans from partners, banks, or another financial institution with repayment terms of more than a year.

Capital

The concept of capital represents the owners' equity in the firm. After the initial investment (paid-in capital), the owners' equity amount changes based on yearly earnings. The equity or capital equals assets minus liabilities.

Paid-in capital is the capital provided to the business by investors through purchase of stock or ownership.

Retained earnings is the cumulative amount of net income over the years. In this example prior to year one, there had been a negative balance ($83,400) and that during year one, the net income was $226,704 so that the starting retained earnings in year two ($226,704 – $83,400 = $143,304).

Net income is the income from the corresponding year on the P&L sheet.

The following table shows the typical balance sheet average figures for brewpubs, small size producers, and medium size producers per barrels of production.

TABLE 21.8   Industry averages per barrel

	Brewpub $/bbl. all sizes	Production $/bbl. < 1,000 bbl.	Production $/bbl. 1001–15,000 bbl.
Total current assets	$342.98	$236.27	$92.06
Fixed or long-term assets	$958.79	$810.01	$303.14
Total assets	$1,278.88	$947.05	$384.22
Total current liabilities	$156.74	$203.87	$63.35
Total long-term liabilities	$524.82	$225.87	$174.39
Accounts receivable (days)	19.50	19.50	20.10
Equity	$608.82	$578.55	$177.78
Debt	$462.93	$221.15	$191.16
Source: Madeleine Pullman.			

Such data will soon be available for the cider and distilling industries, so stay tuned as these industries are quickly seeing the value of gathering industry-wide business statistics.

Cash Flow

The last financial statement required in the statement set is **cash flow**. The cash flow statement shows how a business' investing, operating, and financing activities impact actual cash available over a defined period (yearly, quarterly, or monthly). This statement will show how the company gets and spends cash, if there is enough cash produced from operations to keep the business afloat, if the company is able to pay off debts, why there are differences between the net income and cash flow, and whether the business will have adequate cash to invest in expansion or other opportunities in the future.

Operating activities show how much cash the core operation is generating. This could include sales from the production side, retail side, and any other activities generating cash such as selling apparel, tour fees or tastings, for example. Cash flow increases with sales revenue, interest, and dividends from other investments; it decreases from payments to suppliers, employees, lenders, government taxes, and any other payments for expenses. A non-cash expense is also shown which typically refers to depreciation expense.

Investing activities affect cash through dividends, interest, and the purchase or sale of any assets. Cash flow will increase with sale of any property, equipment, or facility; it will decrease by lending to others, purchasing any property, equipment or facility, debt, or security.

Financing activities change the cash position through raising money through the sale of shares (or buying back shares), or through taken on debt (or paying it back). Cash will increase with the sale of equity or the issuance of debt; it will decrease through paying dividends to shareholders or payment of debt or stock buyback.

TABLE 21.9   Cash flow

	Year 1	Year 2	Year 3
Cash flow from operating activities			
Net income	$226,704.00	$399,934.00	$405,346.00
Non-cash expenses	$100,000.00	$214,286.00	$200,572.00
Decrease / (increase) in current assets	$(283,814.00)	$(55,566.00)	$(73,346.00)
Increase / (decrease) in current liabilities	$54,600.00	$(108,326.00)	$21,482.00
Net cash flow from operating activities	$97,490.00	$450,328.00	$554,054.00
Cash flow from investing activities			
(Increase) in fixed assets	$(800,000.00)	$(60,000.00)	$(320,000.00)
(Increase) in investments	$-	$-	$(20,000.00)
Interest / dividends received	$-	$-	$-
Net cash flow from investing activities	$(800,000.00)	$(60,000.00)	$(340,000.00)
Cash flow from financing activities			
Issuance of equity	$100,000.00		
Bank loan received	$600,000.00		
(Repayment) of bank loan	$(25,166.00)	$(73,450.00)	$(101,146.00)
(Distributions) to partners			$(58,500.00)
Net cash flow from financing activities	$674,834.00	$(73,450.00)	$(159,646.00)
Net increase in cash	$(27,676.00)	$316,878.00	$54,408.00
Cash, beginning of period	$100,000.00	$72,324.00	$389,202.00
Cash, end of period	$72,324.00	$389,202.00	$443,610.00
Source: Madeleine Pullman. Based on Brewers Association survey.			

Relationship Between Balance Sheet and Cash Flow

Several things happen on the balance sheet that will affect the cash flow. First, look at that happens when assets change over time. If the accounts receivable amount is larger in year two than year one, some sales for year two have not been collected so we would see cash go down via that increase in current assets between year two and year one. Similarly, if inventory in the year two is more than the year one, then cash has been exchanged for inventory and we have increased the current inventory assets, decreasing our cash.

Second, current liabilities work in a similar way. If the accounts payable (our unpaid bills) increase in year two over year one, our stack or total of unpaid bills has increased. While we recognize the expense, we have yet to pay out for those bills in cash, so it is a positive adjustment to cash.

For an initial business plan, cash flow projections should be made for the first year on a monthly basis and for subsequent years on a yearly basis or monthly until positive cash flow status has been achieved. Once the business is in full operation, cash flow statements are an essential part of the monthly or quarterly statements and are part of the yearly budget to help anticipate potential problems.

SUMMARY

Each of the financial statements serves a specific purpose, but you should be clear on where important issues can surface. Finances can look wonderful on the P&L sheet by showing income or improvement in income over time. But, you may actually have all the cash tied up in equipment and inventory (bourbon-barrel aging your whiskey or beer, for instance) and not have enough cash to pay your employees. As you look into the future and envision an expansion of your facility and equipment, you will need to figure out the cash position along that path. Expansions not only require key production items but also packaging, kegs, more employees, and other cash outlays that will affect your financial position. This chapter is just a brief overview of the financial statements. It pays to have a finance and accounting person on your team to develop and maintain these statements as well as explain significant changes over time.

LEARNING ADVENTURES

1. From a list of equipment (Chapter 10) and site investments (Chapter 11), create a table that lists how each item is financed, which items are expensed and which are depreciated. Go to the IRS depreciation publication and determine the expected life of the depreciable items. [4]

2. Your business needs to buy 50 half-barrel kegs for $150 each and 100 sixth-barrel kegs for $100 each. If the three Year MACRS table has depreciation rates of the first year (33.33 percent), second year (44.45 percent), third year (14.81 percent) and last year (7.41 percent)—assuming half year convention. If your EBITDA is $100,000 before accounting for kegs, how will the net income look under two different scenarios for the first year: expensing kegs versus depreciating kegs?

3. Referring to Table 21.8, consider why these numbers for brewpubs and small versus medium production facilities might have such different average numbers for assets, liabilities, equity, and debt. State your reasons.

ENDNOTES

1. "Topic 704–Depreciation," IRS [last updated 12/30/2015], https://www.irs.gov/taxtopics/tc704.html.
2. Ibid.
3. "How to Depreciate Property, Appendix B: Table of Class Lives and Recovery Periods," IRS (2015), https://www.irs.gov/pub/irs-pdf/p946.pdf.
4. "How to Depreciate Property, Tables," IRS (2015), https://www.irs.gov/pub/irs-pdf/p946.pdf.

CHAPTER TWENTY-TWO

Conclusion

Key Terms

cause-based businesses
consolidation
cooperative
crowlers
diversity of flavors

diversity of styles
flavored malt beverages (FMBS)
for-profit
hard sodas
not-for-profit

process innovation
sharing economy
third place

Overview

This final chapter summarizes the current trends and opportunities facing professionals in the craft beverage industry. It examines overall trends in the craft beverage industry affected by the current environment and presents examples of existing businesses around the world.

Learning Objectives

▶ Understand how current trends create challenges and opportunities for craft producers.

▶ Consider the implications of raw material shortages on production and new product development.

▶ Evaluate the impact of consolidation on market access for all tiers of the craft supply chain.

▶ Compare pros and cons of changes to state and national regulations to the alcohol industry.

▶ Consider opportunities for mobile processes for your business or as a potential startup business.

▶ Evaluate the implications of the sharing economy on the craft industry.

▶ Understand the concept of social entrepreneurship.

▶ Determine possible opportunities for concepts and business models based on the various trends.

Geographic, Economic, and Political Trends

The craft beverage industry prides itself on having a strong local presence. Many producers and particularly pub/restaurants are an integral part of their own communities. In many parts of the world, the craft pub has become the **third place**, the space besides home and work that people frequent to socialize, have meetings, and feel part of their local neighborhood. It might compete with a coffee shop or diner for the role of third place. But, unlike those businesses, the alcohol industry sits in a unique legal and market context within a national and international web of societal views, politics, economics and agriculture. The United States and other countries have experienced how government policy like Prohibition killed off the alcohol industry for many years. Governments play a role in policies that reward certain agricultural products with subsidies, determine the competitive playing field for businesses, and tax alcohol products in different ways that help or hinder the industry growth. This larger national and global context sets the stage for challenges and opportunities for the industry as a whole.

Raw Material

All craft producers rely on a predictable source of agricultural products: barley, wheat, hops, apples, pears, and other fruits and grains. These products are subject to weather and with climate change, will be more susceptible with low yields occurring on a more frequent basis. Drought conditions not only cause low grain crop yields but lead to wildfires that destroyed many fruit trees in the northwestern United States in recent years. As government policies favor certain cereal grains (corn and wheat), essential craft crops like malting barley become less appealing for farmers to grow relative to those subsidized crops. The increasing demand for hops by the IPA producers has led to price increases and shortages of the most desirable varietals. Popular designer hops, such as Citra, Simcoe, Amarillo, and Galaxy, cannot be purchased by startup producers; these hops have multiple-year waiting lists. For producers, these pending shortages call for proactive strategies such as long-term contracts with suppliers, planting orchards, creating partnerships with farmers and orchardists to help fund the production of essential materials, and lobbying to change current government subsidies through guilds and associations. Currently, producers in the best position are distillers who use wheat or corn-based ethanol from the large conglomerates; this entire supply chain benefits from US farm and ethanol production subsidies.

FIGURE 22.1   Ethanol production

Market Access Trends

Consolidation of large brewers and wholesalers (retailers) is an ongoing concern and potential disruption to market access. In the United States, the required three-tier system allows for convenient distribution throughout the country. But many craft producers have reached a size where they could potentially distribute more effectively and efficiently through their own distribution system. With a single conglomerate, AB-Inbev, dominating the ownership of distributors and controlling accessing to off-premises and on-premises retail, many people are concerned that these channels will become nearly impossible to access. Along similar lines, there is increased retail chain store consolidation, such as a recent Safeway-Albertson merger, as well as many others in the United States. As stores consolidate, typically one decision-maker, a category captain, controls the purchase of beverages. If the store allows the largest producer (AB-Inbev) to control the shelves, then many fear that other competitors may be blocked. Recently, Washington State privatized liquor stores and big retailers and distributors appeared to benefit with more store locations and sales. Small producers and distillers in particular, were hurt since few of the big chain stores chose to carry their products and selected the major brands instead. Proactive strategies for craft producers involve active engagement with their guilds and associations to lobby for fair access. Business owners with on-premises pubs and tasting rooms are in the best position to counter the negative effects of blocked retail channels since they can sell a significant amount of product on their own premise.

Regulatory Environment

Increasingly legislators around the world are changing laws to encourage craft production. As of 2013 when Mississippi legalized home brewing, it was finally legal in all 50 states, but home *distilling* is still illegal in every state. A strong home-production culture leads to an enthusiast base with people willing to go to the next step of commercial operation. Many states have worked to modernize their

FIGURE 22.2   Spent grain

laws and taxation to encourage small-scale producers by allowing tasting rooms and pubs with pro-duction facilities, self-distribution up to certain limits, and farmhouse brewing and production. Many states have lower taxes for small producers relative to large ones. But, not all states are making things easier for producers. Many southern US states still do not allow breweries to sell packaged product directly to customers to take away. Georgia only recently permitted a "free souvenir" of 72 ounces of beer with a paid tour. Both Georgia and Alabama do not allow any self-distribution.

Many states and provinces have multiple regulatory requirements for craft producers. Some of these regulations exist to prevent excessive alcohol consumption but others benefit existing firms that gain from rules limiting competition (for example, distributors). Occasionally bills crop up that can cause problems for craft producers such as a recent Food and Drug Administration ruling that would require a written plan for minimizing contamination of spent grains for animal feed.

On the positive side, the United States recently changed the taxation laws so that carbonated cider would not incur the elevated champagne tax. Overall, regulatory changes both positively and nega-tively affect the craft industry in the state, province, and country. It is important for all producers to keep abreast of potential regulatory shifts so that their voices are heard during the legislative process.

General Business Trends

Many of the hottest business and societal trends also affect the craft industry and create great oppor-tunities for startups with limited cash (sharing economy and mobile processes) or for others with a mission to have a positive impact on society.

Mobile crossflow unit owned and operated by VintechPacific Ltd, in New Zealand. Reprinted wither permission of Guy Rutledge.

FIGURE 22.3   Mobile cross flow filter

Mobile Processes

Early on, small-scale wine producers realized that it did not make sense to own a bottling line when they only packaged 1,000 cases once a year. As a result, mobile bottling line businesses sprang up to serve the needs of that industry. Recently, mobile packaging businesses have arisen to serve the craft industry with both canning and bottling lines. The west coast and Colorado now have many mobile packaging companies while other states and Canadian provinces may have one company serving a large region. Following wine industry trends, other expensive equipment and challenging processes have also gone mobile, such a cross flow filtering, a filtering process which is expensive and challenging for a small producer. Particularly for small cider makers, mobile filtering allows them to use state-of-the-art technology in a pay-as-you-go model for better product clarity and shelf stability.

Beyond filtering and packaging, entrepreneurs are looking at going mobile with fruit pressing and small scale malting. Others are considering mobile brewing and distilling while still trying to work out the potential regulatory and technical obstacles.

Sharing Economy

Like cars and houses, production facilities can be established as a **sharing economy**, a market model where people share access to goods and services rather than having individual ownership. Given the high cost and economy of scale seen with large production facilities, sharing the equipment makes sense for startups. There are many ways to have a shared setup, from contract and alternating proprietorship to **cooperative** production. In the first two methods, one company owns the equipment and others either pay to have product made or rent use of the equipment. Many businesses have been started to serve the contract and alternating proprietorship market. For example, Kentucky Artisan Distillery was set up for entrepreneurs to experience spirits production and offers contract distillation.[1] The owners of Brewhub designed the business to handle contract brewing for breweries needing expanded capacity or startup incubation. With their first location in Florida, the company intends to add additional contract facilities throughout the country. LDB Beverage launched Jester and Judge, a cider, contract brewing, and bottling facility in Stevenson, Washington.

In cooperative arrangements, the production facility is member owned and operated. They have basic principles of democratic or collaborative management, member economic participation, voluntary and open membership, autonomy and independence, and a mission based on community and social values. Today, there are several brewery coops in the United States. For example, Flying Bike in Seattle, Washington now has more than 1,600 members with a production facility and tasting room. All members pay a fee to join and are included in decision-making; they can also participate in choosing recipes and making beer as discussed in Chapter 12.

Cause-Based Businesses

Cause-based businesses have a social or charitable mission. They can be **for-profit** or **not-for-profit** in structure but typically have collaboration between the social and moneymaking side so that all profits (non-profit) or a percentage of profits (for-profit) are allocate to the chosen charities.

An Italian Not-for-Profit Brewing Training Program

Semi di Libertà is an Italian not-for-profit organization founded in 2013 in Rome that blends artisanal beer production with inmate education and training. Meaning "seeds of liberty," the organization's mission is to provide inmates with the skills to become re-integrate into society while reducing the social and governmental costs of recidivism.

An advisory committee led by a president, a group of beer experts, and the inmate workers runs Semi di Libertà. The organization teaches the workers about craft beer making in a 300-liter microbrewery. The beer is bottled by disabled students in partnership with another organization. In 2015, the brewing involved nine inmates and eight students with the inmates themselves distributing the beer to retailers. The nine Semi di Libertà beers are sold in a handful of retail stores and pubs around Italy as well as in its own pub in Rome. The beer is also available through an online store that sells additional products made in the prison system. With names associated with themes of gaining freedom, some of the beers were developed in contests via social media, which engaged the public and garnered attention for the project. The organization sources beer ingredients that are fair trade and organic or come from other organizations that assist disadvantaged workers.

The president of Semi di Libertà originally proposed the organization to the Minister of Justice and Education for funding, and a school in Rome granted production space with equipment purchased by the Ministry of Education. In order to maintain support and approval of the stakeholders involved, Semi di Libertà must measure and report the program's benefits. Although easy to describe the positive impact on the inmates, it has proven difficult to quantify them in the short-term. The long-term benefits of the training and education that Semi di Libertà provides include employability, social inclusion, and reduced rates of re-incarceration.

Meanwhile, the brewery is also creating high-quality beer, and Semi di Libertà credits much of its successes to its networking efforts and relationships with other organizations within its supply chain.

Production Trends

Producers are innovating in ways that go far beyond traditional practices based in each beverage product category. Process innovations learned from other styles or industries are flowing across borders and unusual ingredients continue to appear in the recipes. Craft consumers have responded positively to these products and you should expect further innovations in the future.

Diversity of Styles and Flavors

With a crowded marketplace, craft businesses are looking to differentiate their products. What does a new startup offer that others cannot copy? The key differentiators will continue to be the story, unique local ingredients, or a business created by a unique group of people. A style that is not yet on consumers' radar can quickly be copied but could gain a competitive advantage as the first one in the market. Ale Apothecary in the mountains outside of Bend, Oregon, uses products that grow in their forest such as spruce tips and elderberries. The beer comes out of the mash tun and runs through a log filled with pine boughs. Not only does the brewery have a unique story but it limits production so that the products are rare and garner a cult following.

Brewing from the Landscape

Beers Made by Walking, created by artist Eric Steen, has a mission of connecting brewers to the land they live on through walks and nature hikes. The brewers create beers inspired by the hikes, often using out-of-the-ordinary ingredients such as herbs found on the walk. Wild yeast strains were collected from a Douglas Fir forest using fresh wort, and Burnside Brewing aged an IPA on blocks of cedar wood. Local environmental non-profits are involved in leading the hikes, and proceeds from the beer release events are donated back to the organizations. Originating in Colorado Springs in 2011, Steen organizes the program in parks and landscapes in several states and has worked with over a hundred breweries so far. Steen equates the process to a landscape painting where the resulting painting is a beer that brings together a greater community.

©hraska/Shutterstock.com

FIGURE 22.4 Wild berries

As consumers try new beverages of all kinds, there continues to be a push into **flavored malt beverages (FMBs)** or **hard sodas** with flavors like root beer, apple pie, French toast, strawberry, and ginger ale. While many hard-core craft drinkers frown upon these drinks, FMBs have grabbed market share from cider and other fruit or flavored beers. The jury is still out on how much staying power these hard sodas will have but the FMB, Mike's Hard Lemonade, is still a top seller in chains across the United States and has remained in a top position for many years. If you are a craft producer aiming for the cold shelf in grocery and convenience stores, you need to pay attention to any product that can take over that space.

Process Innovation

The craft world has borrowed ideas from other industry segments. Given the entrepreneurial spirit of the industry, **process innovations** have been the norm from barrel aging and super hopping to additions of ingredients across the spectrum. With small-scale pro-

©Hurst Photo/Shutterstock.com

FIGURE 22.5 Hard sodas

duction facilities, producers have the freedom to create new processes for dry hopping or adding other stages of fermentation and bacteria. Companies have invented small pilot brewing systems that conduct all steps at the press of a button for a gallon or two of test beer. But the innovations don't stop at the brewery door; many producers are working on new ways to deliver and pour draft product such as nitrogen-carbonation rather than the traditional carbon dioxide. Finally, there is new product development for take-away draft products such as growler filling stations that counter pressure fill with carbon dioxide or nitrogen to prevent oxidation and **crowlers**, cans filled to order like a growler. These innovations lead to other business opportunities in the industry and more sales opportunities for existing producers.

SUMMARY

Outside forces will continue to impact the craft industry. An agile business will figure out how to be both proactive in reducing risks of outside forces by joining with other producers and creating contingency plans. The craft industry has set a high bar for entrepreneurial activity and creativity. In this respect, the best players are positioned to not only adapt to the changing marketplace and regulatory environment, but to lead the charge in staying relevant to their consumers and community.

©zeljkodan/Shutterstock.com

FIGURE 22.6   Cheers!

The First Non-Profit Brewery

Ex Novo Brewing Company is the nation's first not-for-profit brewery. Located in Portland, Oregon, the brewery aims to blend great craft beer with positive social change by donating 100 percent of net profits to charity. Founder Joel Gregory, a former beer blogger, overcame many obstacles to become a certified non-profit and yet still does not have tax-exempt status with the IRS. The brewery is registered as a non-profit public benefit corporation (B corp) in Oregon, which makes it difficult to apply for loans and receive investments.

Gregory raised the money for his enterprise privately before launching Ex Novo as a 50-seat brewpub with artisanal food options. Brewing began in summer of 2014 on a 10-barrel system, resulting in eight taps by September of that year. The most popular beer is the Eliot IPA, named after the pub's neighborhood, and Ex-Novo regularly brews a fruit beer to showcase local produce. Gregory's goal is to make the best beer possible, establish a reputation and gathering fans, and then cut costs in production and operations. After reaching this stage, Gregory expects to have more funds to donate as well as to expand the brewery.

Photo courtesy Whitney Dawson. Reprinted with permission.

FIGURE 22.7 Ex Novo

Relying on social media and a grassroots approach, Gregory began spreading word of the brewery early, and was selling merchandise before the doors had opened. Gregory held events to create a community including a brew night at his house using hops from the neighborhood. The non-profit aspect is a forward focus on the website, but in the pub it is all about the beer and the non-profit mission takes a back seat.

The B Corp certification is a way to show Ex Novo's charitable giving in a transparent way and to emphasize the social mission to its audience. Gregory held sit-down meetings with each of its charities early on, and decided to split the contributions between four charities equally. Ex Novo has an application process for potential new charities to be selected by the board of directors. Many people around the country also contact Gregory to learn more about how to set up this novel brewing organizational model.

ENDNOTES

1. "About Us," Kentucky Artisan Distillery, http://www.kentuckyartisandistillery.com/#!about-us/c24mo.

GLOSSARY

Above-the-line marketing (ATL)—refers to marketing with broad scope to reach potential customers, such as television or radio campaigns, typically not used until the producer reaches large size.

Access—refers to the ways and means of getting into and around various areas of the building.

Accounts receivable—represents invoices or money owed to the company by others for goods and services.

Accredited investor—US government term defining an investor that has a certain minimum net worth or income that is allowed to invest in certain projects.

Accumulated depreciation—fixed assets that depreciate over time and accumulates with time as more depreciation is applied to each asset and is cumulative.

Administration expenses—these include salaries and benefits that are not part of the COGS labor. Additionally, the supplies, utilities, maintenance, professional fees, and other costs related to running the facility.

Advertising—marketing technique to bring awareness and visibility to a product through media sources.

Aesthetics—the look and feel of a space or item.

Aging storage—a climate-controlled dedicated space for tank or barrel aging.

Agricultural zoning—special zoning that benefits certain agricultural products such as wineries.

Alcohol and tobacco tax and trade bureau (TTB)—law regulation and administrators for alcohol related laws in the US.

Alcohol consumption patterns—patterns of consumption considering different variables—time of day, time of year, type of event, etc.

Alembic still—a commonly used still to produce spirits.

Alternating proprietorship—An arrangement in which two or more businesses take turns using a physical premises of a production facility.

Angel investors—groups of investors or financial investment companies looking for investment opportunities typically from small startups or entrepreneurs.

Angel's share—the percentage of alcohol that a spirit loses during barrel aging each year through evaporation (roughly 10 percent).

Annual investor meetings—A meeting for a company's investors that is a regulatory requirement with an annual date spelled out in the company bylaws.

Articles of incorporation—paperwork filed by a business and creates the board of directors and issues stock according to the preference of the state.

Articles of organization—filed by a business for a limited liability company.

Assets—anything a company owns that could bring future economic benefit including land, buildings, equipment, cash, inventory, and accounts receivable (money owed to the company by others).

Auger—a mechanism for moving grain.

B corporation (B corp) or benefit corporation—a new for-profit corporate entity that has a specific goal of including positive impact on society and the environment in addition to profit.

B lab—a non-profit organization which created and awards B corporation certification to companies that meet its criteria.

Bagged malt—malt sold in bags for those who need to buy smaller volumes of base or specialty malts.

Balance sheet—a report that shows the assets, liabilities, and capital at a particular point in time. It reflects the changes in the P&L statement from a previous period.

Banks—an institutional lending organization.

Barrel storage—storage of barrels during aging process.

Barrels—cylindrical container traditionally made of wood, used for holding beverages also refers to the measurement unit of 31 gallons.

Base malt—The foundational malt that will provide most of the enzymes to convert starches to fermentable sugars in a recipe.

Baseline products—the core portfolio of a producer, does not include seasonal or one-off product releases.

Beer definition—beer, ale, porter, stout, and other similar fermented beverages (including sake or similar products) of any name or description containing one-half of one percent or more of alcohol by volume (ABV), brewed or produced from malt, wholly or in part, or from any substitute thereof.

Beer process—the process in which beer is made.

Beer tax issues—small craft brewers benefit from lower production tax rates in the United States, paying $7 per barrel on the first 60,000 barrels and $18 per barrel after that up to 2 million barrels. Additionally, each state has a beer tax that averages around $6.20 per barrel.

Beer trends—consumer trends in the beer marketplace that change over time. Trends show shifting preferences for certain styles, alcohol content, etc.

Beliefs—useful concepts to include with vision and mission statements that help employees and customers understand the desired culture of a company.

Below-the-line marketing (BTL)—targets specific groups in a focused way with advertising and promotion.

Benefits—health, dental, retirement, vacation, and employee stock-ownership plans; perks offered by many employers.

Beverage tourism—local, state, and country wide tourism oriented toward interacting with beverages and their producers through events, tours, and other related activities.

Bill backs—credits to the distributor.

Bins—containers for fruit transportation. Also used to remove spent malt.

Blending—the mixing of a spirit or other product with other barrels from the same production batch, or with different types of products.

Bond—legal document required by the TTB to guarantee that excise taxes will be paid.

Bookkeeping—addresses how the books will be maintained as well as members' capital input and distribution accounts.

Bordeaux barrel—a barrel made of oak wood that typically holds 225 liters or 60 US gallons.

Bottles and cans—containers used for packaging.

Brand identity—how a business wants to be perceived by consumers including the name, logo, and other marketing activities to appeal to customers.

Brand name—name under which the beverage or line of beverages is marketed.

Brand rights—exclusive rights to market a product in a specific area or territory such as county borders in the US.

Break-even analysis—a useful tool for critically examining major capital investments to show the point where the business or decision element begins to pay for itself. This analysis is also useful for making decisions on operations, equipment, etc. indicating the point when a decision will make a profit.

Brew house—the equipment that produce beer (wort) prior to fermentation.

Brew kettle—a boiling device where wort is sterilized and hops and spices are added for flavoring.

Brewer permit–a permit to brew beer obtained by submitting an application with the TTB and gaining approval.

Brewer's bond—a government payment required in advance of production that insures that taxes will be paid on alcohol production.

Brewer's notice application—the application to apply for a permit.

Brewing system—the system that includes the brew house as well as the method for making product.

Brewpub—a restaurant-brewery that sells 25 percent or more of its beer on-site.

Brite tank—a conditioning tank where beer or cider is collected after fermentation is completed.

Build out—the process of creating the interior and exterior spaces for a production facility.

Building codes—set of construction rules that facilities must conform to depending on different state and local laws.

Burden—the cost beyond the employee's salary or hourly wage that must be included in the financial estimates to account for benefits and other employee related costs.

Business plan and pro forma financials—detailed plans about an intended or actual business and its potential financial viability.

Business plan—consists of key elements of the business including concept description and vision, industry overview, competitive analysis, marketing and distribution strategy, operational plan, the team, and financials.

Buying—purchasing a site.

C corporation (C corp)—a legal entity owned by shareholders with an IRS taxation structure that is specifically considered a unique entity separate from those who own it.

Can body—one of two parts of a can; the container part of a can.

Cans—packaging option for a beverage that comes in various sizes—12 ounces and 16 ounces in the US.

Capacity—the maximum or designed amount something can contain or process.

Capital contributions—the amount of capital or assets contributed by each member.

Capital—money or other assets owned by a person or organization.

Capitalization plan—plan that describes how much capital the proposed company has in place and what needs to be raised through the proposed investment offering.

Capper—a machine for applying a cap to a bottle.

Carriers—plastic or cardboard part that fit around the bottles or cans to group in 4, 6, or 12 packs.

Cartons—packaging for delivery of packaged beverages.

Cases—standard packaging for delivering bottles or cans. Larger format bottles (22 ounce) have 12 units in a case with dividers; smaller format bottles have 24 units in a case with carriers or dividers, and cans have 24 on a tray.

Cash—money that is sitting in bank accounts during a period of time. This may also include cash equivalents such as demand deposits, treasury bills, commercial paper, checking accounts, savings accounts, and other short-term instruments.

Cash flow—a statement that shows how a business' investing, operating, and financing activities impact actual cash available over a defined period (yearly, quarterly, or monthly). This statement will show how the company gets and spends cash.

Cash on delivery (COD)—a term of payment agreement where the product is paid for when it is delivered to the payee.

Category captains—individuals in charge of managing a category in a store with the intention of maximizing profits for the retailer.

Cause-based businesses—for-profit or not-for-profit businesses that have a social or charitable mission.

Cellaring equipment—the equipment used during cellaring activities (fermentation, filtering, carbonation, aging, conditioning, refrigeration).

Centralized purchasing—all decisions made at the headquarters.

Certified craft distilled spirit—craft distilled spirits that meet the certification standards of being run through a still of a certified craft producer, an independently owned craft distillery, small, and use traditional ingredients.

Chain authorization—the authorization to sell product in a chain.

Change of use—the process of changing the legal (zoning) status of a space from its previously used purpose.

Chiller—a refrigeration system used for cooling cellaring equipment.

Cider apples—apples with the appropriate levels of acids and flavor for cider, typically available in the fall with shorter shelf life than dessert apples.

Cider house—facility for producing cider.

Cider process—process of making cider which starts with late summer or fall harvested apples or with juice.

Cider tax issues—cider incurs complex taxation laws. Cider is treated like wine and champagne rather than like beer, its apparent market partner, with tax levels based on ingredients, carbonation, and alcohol levels.

Cider trends—consumer trends in the cider marketplace. Trends show shifting preferences for flavors, sweetness, and styles.

Cidery—a production facility for making hard cider, perry, and affiliated products.

Class and type designation—identifies a specific class and/or class and type of beverage.

Client base—a company's primary source of business.

Closures—all products require some kind of closure that keeps air and bacteria out and the product and carbonation in. Crowns, grolsch or flip-top, cork, and screw-top are all styles of different closures.

Club buying—a model where the consumer pays in advance for the product and receives some of the product yearly or seasonally.

Code dates—indicates perishability date or product age on the package.

COLA—Certification/Exemption of Label/Bottle Approval is required if the state requires it or if shipping and selling over state lines. The purpose of the COLA is to prevent consumer deception or misleading statements.

Collateral—assets to cover the business loan if the business goes under.

Column still—a type of still commonly used to product spirits.

Community-supported agriculture (CSA)—consumers pay for produce shares to a farm and receive weekly vegetable pickup.

Company formation—indicates the type of organization (LLC, C Corp, or other) and how it was filed, along with company name and registered agent.

comPASH—restaurant metric which is the periodic total contribution from operations divided by (number of operations hours times number of seat places for guests).

Compensation—what the managers will be paid and the appropriate reimbursement of expenses.

Competitive analysis—identifies competitors and outlines their concept and market niche relative to the focal business.

Competitor matrix—a chart detailing the key competitors, their product offerings, type of facilities, brand identity, and segment appeal.

Compliance—the act of complying with the law, in this case the TTB which has forms and potentially audits insure that alcohol sales and activities are measured and taxed correctly.

Compressed hop pellets—a compressed form of leaf hops that lasts longer and is easier to handle than leaf hops

Concept—describes what a business determines to do, the overall idea that shapes the business identity, and the model for making money.

Conditional use permit—a zoning exception that allows the property or building owner to use the property in a way not otherwise permitted by a particular zoning district

Conditioning tank—tank where beer or cider is collected after fermentation is completed.

Conflict of interest—a statement of how the buyer might have some kind of conflict with the investment entity.

Consolidation—the act of combining or buying up other entities to create one single or dominant company.

Consumer demographics—characteristics of consumers in different market areas or segments.

Consumer-buying habits—exhibited patterns of buying behaviors by consumers.

Contingency—a clause used to address costs above the allowance and identifies which party is responsible to pay for the difference.

Continuous review—a method for reviewing inventory where inventory is constantly checked or whenever a sale occurs.

Continuous still—the column still—it can run continuously with more liquid added rather than batch to batch.

Contract arrangement—a business hires another facility to produce its product.

Contract employee—similar to a part-time employee but works as an independent entity.

Contract—the business and legal agreement between the producer and distributor.

Cooperage—a place where a cooper (barrel maker) makes barrels. Also refers to the stock of kegs and barrels owned by a business.

Cooperative (coop)—an organization owned by and operated for the benefit of those using its services, namely the members.

Copyright—laws that protect original creative works like names, books, movies, songs, paintings, photographs, web content, and choreography.

Core values—useful concepts to include with vision and mission statements that help employees and customers understand the desired culture of a company.

Cork—style of closure often used with 750-ml bottles for a more elegant finished look, made of natural or synthetic cork or plastic.

Corker—a machine for closing a bottle with a cork.

Cost (price) strategy—low production costs enable a company either to price product below the competitors or to generate a higher margin.

Cost of goods manufactured—cost of product made including facility, electricity, utilities, and other personnel costs.

Cost of goods sold—the direct cost of making a beverage product only.

Costing—calculation of costs for a recipes and other resources used in production.

Cover—restaurant term for "one guest or person" who orders food and beverage.

Craft beer—beer produced by a craft brewery.

Craft beverage—an alcoholic beverage made by a small, independent, and typically traditional method producer, not industrial or mass-produced.

Craft blender—independently owned and operates a facility that uses any combination of traditional or innovative techniques such as fermenting, distilling, re-distilling, blending, infusing, or warehousing to create products and must identify themselves as such on their TTB profile.

Craft brewery—a small and independent producer of craft beers.

Craft cider—a beverage made from fermented apple, made in small batches by independent producers.

Craft concept—the concept developed for the craft business such as pub with certain style beers or a distillery that focuses on certain types of spirits.

Craft eccentric account—accounts that focus on craft draft and domestic packages.

Craft exclusive account—accounts that only sell craft beverages.

Craft spirits—the products of an independently owned distillery.

Crafting account—accounts that are selling some craft beverages and are moving to focus more on them.

Credit history—an examination of a person or entity's past credit activity.

Credit unions—a non-profit organization with functions similar to a bank.

Crowdfunding—the practice of funding a project by raising many small amounts of money from a large number of people, typically through a website.

Crowlers—a can that is filled on demand with beer or cider from a tasting room or pub.

Crowns—a common closure for bottles also known as a cap.

Culture and fit—a unique culture either designed intentionally or emergent based on the leadership style, team makeup, and incentive program.

Date stamp—a purchase by date or date of production stamped on a package.

Debt—financing that has a fixed time frame for repayment of a loan along with interest.

Decentralized purchasing—purchasing is done by region or localities rather than one centralized entity.

Demographics of an area—characteristics of potential consumers in a specific geographic area.

Department of agriculture (DOA)—government agency that monitors agricultural activities and requires permits and licenses for certain alcohol activities from agricultural products.

Department of environmental quality (DEQ)—government agency that permits and regulates production dealing with safety, sanitation, wastewater, etc. from production facilities

Depreciation—a concept where fixed assets that must be recovered over a number of years. It represents the decrease in value of an asset over time as it ages.

Description—details in the operations plan about how the business will make the craft beverage.

Dessert apples—sweeter, less acidic apples with longer shelf life and can be stored for many months in appropriate warehousing environments.

Development—cultivating and promoting talent so that people have opportunities for growth.

Dilution—the addition of purified or distilled water or juice to reduce the alcohol level or adjust the blend.

Direct and indirect labor—two types of labor that apply to a product. Direct labor includes hourly employees and other employees that can be directly tied to product production. Indirect labor includes managers and other employees that can not be directly tied to product production such as accounting and marketing.

Direct fired—heated with direct heat such as gas.

Distillation—the process for purifying or extracting a concentrated liquid by heating and cooling.

Distilled spirits permit—US TTB issued permit to run a distilled spirits plant.

Distilled spirits plant (DSP)—an establishment licensed by the TTB which is qualified to perform any distilled spirits operation (produce spirits using a still, brew wort or mash, mix ingredients, etc.).

Distilled spirits—a substance known as ethyl alcohol, ethanol, or spirits of wine in any form (including all dilutions or mixtures thereof, from whatever source or by whatever process produced), but not denatured spirits unless specifically stated.

Distillery grain system—a system for extracting sugars from grain (malted or not).

Distillery—a facility where alcoholic liquors and spirits are made.

Distinctive competency—a competency that a business is known for and which it performs better than others in the marketplace.

Distribution of profits—profits from a business that are allocated to shareholders.

Distribution partnership—contractual agreements which are very challenging and costly to terminate.

Distribution plan—covers the details of how a business plans to get their product into the customers' hands.

Distributor's book—a book of products with range (number of craft products) and depth (styles and families of products).

Diversity of flavors—a choice of flavors, typically innovative flavors previously not seen

Diversity of styles—a choice of beverage styles, typically innovative styles previously not seen.

Domestic only account—accounts that do not sell any craft beverages.

Domestic—refers to the major industrial beer brands, such as Budweiser, Coors, Miller, and Heineken, for example).

Draft lines—lines that run between the keg and tap handle.

Dry hopping—the process of ,adding more hops during secondary fermentation for enhanced aromas.

Earnings before interest, taxes, depreciation and amortization (EBITDA)—a useful measurement to compare different companies' profitability and year-to-year performance.

Electricity—power for basic lighting, running mills, pumps, and automated bottling lines.

Ends—the top end of a can.

Enterprise zones—specific zones encouraging business development through grants or reduced taxes in order provide relief from poverty or encourage economic development in general.

Entire cycle—the complete process time from start to finished product.

Equipment—machinery and other materials needed to start and grow a business.

Equity crowdfund—a crowdfunding option that exchanges funds for an ownership share in the business.

Equity—ability to offer shares of the company in exchange for cash from investors. With an equity position, there is typically not a specified time frame for repayment of the investment.

Expectations—opportunities and/or prospects.

Expert opinions—a qualitative method involving the collection of opinions from leaders, associations, wholesalers, and trend watchers.

Facility—a building designed and built or remodeled to serve a specific function.

Facings—the display of products.

Factory occupancy—a building classification code for industrial use.

Farmhouse brewery—a concept that makes an explicit connection to the land, either by location or by state law.

Federal alcohol administration act (FAA)—US government agency that administers alcohol laws and regulations.

Festivals and events—gatherings held at the local, regional, and national levels with public attendance and many participating producers.

Fifth—a common and known name for a 750-ml bottle.

Fill—a process where equipment operates to fill bottles or cans with the product.

Filler—a device used to fill the product into a bottle or can.

Financing activities—activities that change the cash position by raising money through the sale of shares (or buying back shares), or through taken on debt (or paying it back).

Finished goods inventory—product that has been completed.

Fit—the process of finding a partner or distributor that aligns with the needs of both parties.

Fixed assets—assets that cannot be quickly converted into cash, such as property, facilities, and equipment.

Fixed costs—the cost to purchase the equipment or capitol investments that are not directly tied to the unit of production.

Fixed time period approach—inventory items are checked at regular periods, such as once a week or once a month.

Flagship product—the signature product that a business is known for.

Flavored malt beverages (FMBS)—new beverages created from a malt base with added flavoring such as alcoholic root beer, lemonade, ginger beer, etc.

Flexibility—choice variety, or wide range of options.

Flip-top—a style of bottle closure with a wire attached to a stopper.

Floor displays—a method of displaying products.

Floor to ceiling—evaluation of facility production height needs from ground level up.

Food and drug administration (FDA)—US government agency concerned with the food safety of commercially produced food and beverage products.

Food friend—a symbolic relationship with neighboring restaurants or food trucks. These parties supply food to the pub or tasting room.

Food safety modernization act (FSMA)—an act intended to improve food safety in the US by is requiring stricter sanitation policies, regulations, and preventative controls to prevent unsafe product from reaching consumers.

Food truck—a truck that prepares food for consumption, a mobile restaurant.

For-profit—a business structure with a mission to make a profit.

Formula—the recipe and process used for beverage products.

Forward contract—a commitment by the producer to buy a certain amount of ingredients from another party in the future.

Franchise law—a state law that protects the contractual relationship between the producer and wholesaler.

Free house—a pub or restaurant is free to sell whatever beer (or other beverage) that is choses and is not tied to a specific producer.

Freight on board (FOB)—product cost indicating the point from which the seller pays transportation of the goods.

Front line price—the highest selling price to the consumer to which the discount is applied.

Fruit contracts—forward contracts for buying fruit.

Fruit delivery—the delivery of fruit in bins.

Fruit supply—the amount of available fruit to purchase for cider production, increasingly demand is not keeping up with supply.

Fruit—producers grow or buy fruits, extract their juice, and create a craft beverage.

Full-time vs. part-time—jobs strategic to the business are typically full-time positions. Part-time is less hours and jobs may be seasonal.

Functional space—useful and efficient space.

Future needs—employment needs in the future due to business growth or shrinkage.

Gantt chart—a basic visual planning tool that shows the entire production cycle for a batch or batches of product and helps determine the capacity of a system.

General description—summary or overview of the job objectives and responsibilities.

General partnerships—operating similarly to a sole proprietorship except that the profits, liabilities, and activities are divided between partners.

Gluten-free—free from any type of gluten-containing grain (barley, wheat, rye, or crossbreeds of those grains).

Grain silo—a cost-effective grain storage option for beverage producers.

Grant programs—money from federal, state, and local government offered for specific groups to develop businesses.

Graphics—the graphical imagery, fonts, and colors used to represent a brand and product.

Grinder—a piece of equipment that grinds or chops fruit or grain into smaller pieces.

Grolsch—a style of bottle closure using a flip-top.

Growlers—eco-friendly refillable packaging.

Growth pattern—a basic pattern of demand where the demand overall is growing or declining.

Guilds and associations—state and national organizations that work to promote the interests of different craft beverage producers as a state Brewers Guild or a regional Cider association.

Happy hour—a period of time during the day when some food and beverages are typically discounted.

Hard sodas—a malt beverage with flavors like root beer, apple pie, French toast, strawberry, and ginger ale (see FMBS).

Heads—the first stage of extraction from a still, exhibiting off flavors and toxic characteristics.

Hearts—extraction from a still which is the desirable liquid found in the middle state of the evaporation.

Heat exchanger—equipment that changes the temperature of liquid by running hot liquid on one side and cold on the other side so that the hot decreases temperature while the cold increases temperature.

Height considerations—assessment of proper height needs.

High-gravity brewing—creating a beverage with a very high original gravity (above 1.075).

Hiring—employing workers and compensating them.

Historical districts—a zone with historical classification.

Hoff-Stevens—an older style keg.

Holding cost—the actual cost of owning and keeping the item in storage.

Hop contracts—a forward contract for hops between a brewer and hop producer.

Hop extract—a product consisting of the essential aromas and bittering agents extracted from the hops into a liquid form.

Hop supply—the amount of hops in the world at anytime. There have been severe hop shortages as well as boom and bust cycles, particularly with high alpha hops.

Hops delivery—most companies hold hop products for the buyer in appropriate warehouse conditions (refrigerated and humidity controlled) and deliver them as needed.

Hops—a bitter flower from the hops plant that add aroma and desirable bitterness to beer.

Hot liquor tank—a tank for storing hot water.

Houses—wholesale distribution models that usually refer to the focus of the business such as wine and spirits houses, major brand houses, and independent or specialty houses.

Hybrid pot-column still—a still that can help craft distillers create a variety of products with one still.

Incentives—cash or other monetary equivalents used to secure and improve sales in the on-premises environment.

Independent or specialty house—particular focus of a distributor indicating that they are not tied to a major producer or focus on specialty products.

Independent—craft brewer where less than 25 percent of the craft brewery is owned or controlled (or equivalent economic interest) by a beverage alcohol industry member who is not themselves a craft brewer.

Individual investors—outside investors who put up cash for a business and receive shares in the company in return.

Industrial use—a building code classification for production or factory use

Industrial—area of production such as factories.

Industry groups—a classification method for individual stocks or companies usually grouped based on common industry interests.

Industry history—the history of a particular industry group and its development locally, nationally or internationally.

Infrastructure—the basic physical elements needed for a building including the space, physical access and utilities.

Ingredient prices fluctuatation—throughout the year and over time price variances can occur, so having the ability to buy significant amounts of hops or fruit, for example, for low prices at an optimal time (harvest time for example) is a wise decision.

Ingredients and other materials—all of the recipe ingredients used to produce a beverage (malt, grain, fruit, hops, and yeast).

Innovation—products or processes that are produced or designed to be radically or incrementally different from others in their classes.

Institutional financing—loans from lending organizations like banks and credit unions.

Intangible assets—assets that lack a physical presence but have economic value and advantages.

Interest expense—an item that appears on the P&L statement that represents the cost of taking on debt. Every time a loan payment is made, part of that payment is interest and another part of that payment pays down the principal (outstanding loan amount).

Intermediate bulk container (IBC)—large plastic containers uses for storing and fermenting liquids

Internal revenue code—US government agency that develops rules and collects money from taxes.

Inventory management—management of all inventory including the policies for order quantities and frequency.

Inventory monitoring—the monitoring of inventory so that there is record of product going in and orders going out.

Inventory—all raw materials, work in progress, products in stock or in the facility.

Investing activities—events that affect cash through dividends, interest, and the purchase or sale of any assets.

Investor communication—updates to investors that outline what is going on in the company, new projects, financial reporting, strategies or concerns.

Investor packet—a comprehensive packet of information for potential investors.

Isomerization—the process of converting a molecule into a different arrangement with the same atoms.

Jacket—a metal jacket or sandwich that wraps around kettles or tanks for heating or cooling the side surfaces. For brew kettles, a steam filled jacket will heat up very fast and avoid scorched or caramelized wort issues.

Job description—provides a job title and outlines the commitment level as well as the reporting relationship. It also provides a general description of the job objectives and responsibilities.

Job requirements—expectations and duties for a specific job.

Job title—name designated for a specific job role.

Joint ventures—acting as general partners for one project or limited time periods.

Just-in-time (JIT)—frequent supplies of product that are ordered just in time to meet demand.

Keg cap—a cap that keeps the keg coupling area clean and protected.

Keg collar—a keg's label that identifies the beverage style, brand information, producer address, government warning, fill date, and other required details for both producer and retailer.

Keg costing—what the product costs to produce various sizes of filled kegs .

Keg float—the total number of kegs owned by a producer.

Keg logistics—a process for producers to manage kegs—the producer contracts services and either sells the existing float to a logistics company, or leases kegs from the providor.

Keg one-ways—an alternative to stainless steel kegs with the design intention of traveling one-way from producer to retailer. Some are designed for single use and others are refillable.

Keg rental—the producer is charged on a per-use basis each month for the number of kegs and where they are shipped to and how far.

Kegging equipment—includes two main components—one for washing and sanitizing setup, and the other for filling the keg.

Kegs (plastic)—keg made out of plastic or other composite materials.

Kegs (stainless steel)—keg made out of stainless steel.

Kegs—a container of half barrel size or 15.5 gallons by volume or more generally referring to a metal or plastic bulk container.

Key competitors—companies in the same line of business that offers similar product or service.

Kombucha—a fermented tea-based beverage.

Label—sticker or etching on the bottles or cans of the product that identifies the product.

Labeler—a machine for applying the label on the bottles or cans.

Lagering—cold maturation.

Laid-in costs—the total cost of placing goods in inventory including the invoice price, freight or shipping, and related purchasing taxes.

Large brewery—a brewery with an annual beer production over 6 million barrels.

Lautering vessel—an insulated vessel where spent grain is separated from the extracted liquid and sparged.

Lautering—separating of the liquid from the grain, and the remaining grain is rinsed with more hot water.

Lead times—time that it takes from order placement to order delivery.

Leaf hops—conventional format of hops that are picked from the vines and dried, compressed into bails, and sold in these bails.

Leasing—contract renting land or facilities.

Legal—refers to the legal requirements around labeling alcoholic beverages. There are specific rules for different beverages from different states and countries.

Legality of concept—legal issues related to a concept such as a tasting room that has different rules depending on the state and county.

Letter of intent—a document describing agreements or the terms of a deal between parties before the agreement is actually finalized or an agreement to agree.

Licenses—legal documents or permits from a government or authority group authorizing the ownership, use of something, or activity to take place (such as selling or producing product).

Light industrial—a building code classification referring to less capital intensive and more consumer-oriented industries rather than business-to-business industries.

Lighting—the design of lights in a space. The amount of light has a significant effect on the consumption of food and beverages; consumption goes up as lighting dims.

Limited liability company or corporation (LLC)—a US government defined business classification which limits the liability of the company and avoids double taxation to the owners.

Limited partnerships—limiting individual's exposure to liabilities as well as managerial input.

Line of credit—a program from banks or credit unions with open access to funds for buying materials, payroll needs, or equipment that needs to be repaid and usually with interest.

Loading and unloading—refers to proper access for loading and unloading materials.

Loading dock—a raised dock that allows a truck to pull right up to the building for loading and unloading at the same level.

Loan—money from individuals or banks or any other financial institution with repayment terms for more than a year.

Localism—a popular trend that focuses on supporting the local or neighborhood community.

Lovibond—the color rating system that gives an indication of the color intensity from pale base malts to chocolate or black roast specialty malts.

Maintenance—efforts to support and provide adequate attention to the producers (from distributors).

Major brand house—one of the three main types of wholesale models where a large brand is the focal point of sales.

Malolactic—a secondary fermentation (lactic acid converting the malic acid to lactic).

Malt contracts—malt purchased on contract with quality and/or quantity specifications.

Malt delivery—the malt delivery depends on the quantity needed, shipping distance, method, and storage space available. Malt is delivered in several different ways.

Malt supply—the amount of malt available to purchase in the world. High quality barley acreage continues to shrink, losing out to GMO wheat and corn that offer higher yields and profits to farmers at the same time demand is increasing for malt-based beverages.

Malted grains—grain that has been sprouted and kiln dried so that sugars are converted to fermentable forms.

Management experience—management skill set and knowledge.

Management—the team who actually manages the business.

Margin—the profit percentage based on sales price.

Market access trends—developing patterns in relation to convenient distribution and market access.

Market share—the portion of market sales controlled by a particular company or product.

Market size—a measurement of the total volume of a given market.

Marketing elements—advertising broken into three parts—above the line marketing, below the line marketing, and through the line marketing.

Marketing expenses—any costs for materials, salaries, and benefits that are related to sales and marketing.

Marketing plan—a plan that outlines the concepts, target market, and strategy for sales of a product. The plan uses the framework of the four Ps of marketing—price, product, promotion, and place.

Markup—the percentage of profit based on cost.

Mash tun—equipment where the malt is mixed with hot water so that the malt's enzymes convert starches into fermentable sugars.

Matching grants—in certain situations, government programs offer funds matching the business' investment dollar for dollar.

Materials and fixtures—items in the a retail space such as decorations, furnishings, and signage that reflect the brand image and theme.

Mead production and taxes—mead is simple to produce and lacks strict legal definitions in most countries. Honey is added to warm water with any additional flavors and sugars. The mix is cooled and combined with yeast and filtered water in a fermenter. After fermenting the product for about one month, depending on the temperature, the product is moved (with or without filtering) into a secondary tank for further carbonation, then kegged or packaged in bottles or cans. Mead is taxed like wine by the US federal government.

Mead trends—consumer trends around mead in the market place. Currently experiencing growth from a small base, mead has gained popularity with the rise of other craft beverage styles.

Mead—a fermented honey beverages, and the oldest alcoholic beverage; honey wine classified as an agricultural wine.

Meadery—a production facility that makes a fermented beverage, mead, from honey.

Microbrewery—a brewery that produces less than 15,000 barrels of beer per year, with 75 percent or more of its beer sold off-site.

Mission—the intended focus of the business which addresses what the business does, who it does it for, and how it does it.

Mobile packaging—provides many packaging services to craft producers who chose not to (or who cannot afford to) purchase their own packaging equipment.

Mobile processes—mobile processes for canning, bottling, and many other beverage activities used by small-scale producers that allows them to use state-of the art technology in a pay-as-you-go model rather than owning the equipment themselves

Modified accelerated cost recovery system (MACRS)—a system for determining estimated depreciation amounts for assets.

Monthly index method—a method used to construct a monthly forecast based on previous historic patterns.

Naming—identity given to a business.

Nano—a small brewing system.

National scenic area (NSA)—areas designated to protect the scenic beauty of an area.

Natural gas—gas used to heat water, boilers, and kettles or stills.

Net income—the amount of income left after accounting for the depreciation and interest.

Noise—the acoustic quality and level in a space. Pubs are increasingly designed to enhance noise so that the energy level is more stimulating.

Not-for-profit—a type of organization that does not earn profits for its owners.

Notes payable—covers long-term loans for amounts that the company owes to a creditor along with interest expense.

Objectives—the goals of a company.

Off-premises—locations where customers buy packaged products to take away: supermarkets, drug stores, convenience stores, package stores, club stores, liquor chains and independents, military base stores, and even some hardware stores (depending on the state).

Off-site sales—sales activity where consumers buy product to take away from the place of business.

On-premises—locations where customers buy products to consume on-site such as bars and restaurants.

On-site sales—sales activity where consumers buy product to consume on the premises.

Operating activities—a financial statement entry that show how much cash the core operation is generating from sales from the production side, retail side, and any other activities generating cash.

Operating agreement—the agreement among those company members governing the business and the member's financial and managerial rights and duties.

Operating expenses—supplies, utilities, maintenance, professional fees, and other costs related to running the facility.

Operational plan—a major section of the business plan that details information that informs investors and staff about the day-to-day tasks required for running production.

Opportunities—external situations or openings for a company.

Opportunity cost—the economic impact off the business choosing to buy something and hold it rather than having that cash available for other investments.

Order cost—the fixed cost of purchasing an item that is not directly tied to the quantity ordered such as setup cost or fixed transportation cost.

Organization structure—the legal and financial structure of an organization.

Organizational chart—an outline of roles within an organization.

Organizational documents—an organization's paperwork like the certificate of formation or partnership certificate or agreements.

Out of date (OOD)—product that has gone beyond its sell by date.

Out of stock (OOS)—when retail accounts run out of product.

Out of stock cost—the loss of customer sales due to running out of product.

Package stores—state-owned or privately owned stores that sell alcoholic products, especially spirits outside of bars and restaurants. In some states and countries, these stores are the only outlet allowed to sell spirits outside of bars and restaurants.

Packaging brewery—a brewery that produces and packages product in kegs or smaller packages.

Packaging equipment—equipment for canning or bottling product.

Packaging—beverage containers and cartons including bottles, cans, packs, and cases.

Packs—smaller format bottles grouped into packages.

Paid in capital—capital contributed to an organization by investors by stock purchase from the corporation (not from the open or stock market).

Pairing—combining food and beverage that complement each other.

Pallet jacks—a machine used to move pallets around a facility.

Partnership—a single business where two or more people share ownership.

Party—a group of covers, such as a couple or eight people.

Pasteurization—a heat immersion process which kills most bacteria to improve the shelf life of the bottled or canned product.

Patterns of demand—trends where demand overall is growing or declining.

Pay and benefits—the salary or wage and additional perks offered to employees.

Pay-per-fill—a service picks up all the kegs at distributors and the producer calls the service whenever they need to fill.

Pay-to-play—situation where breweries offer money or equivalent to secure a tab handle. Incentives include free draft systems, free beer, and other items for clients to stay with their brand portfolio.

Pay—salary or wages.

People's opinions—refers to customer tastes and changes in the market.

Periodic review—a method for monitoring inventory where it is checked at regular intervals such as once a week or month.

Perishability limitations—the shelf life of a particular beverage where the product is considered drinkable up to a certain age.

Perry—a fermented beverage (cider) made from pears.

Pint night—a promotional incentive event where pints are sold at discounts.

Places—locations businesses identify to sell the products.

Point of sale (POS) materials—materials for the off-premises arena include some of the same materials used in on-premises—sell sheets, signs, banners, clothing, and posters.

Point of sale (POS) system—a system used to track sales and inventory for a company.

Policies—long-range plans and processes for implementing objectives.

Pomace—a mass of apple and other fruit pieces.

Portfolio—a collection of beverages that a company makes.

Position responsibilities—duties and expectations for specific jobs.

Positioning—an element of branding which indicates how a product will be sold relative to its competitors.

Pot still—type of still commonly used to produce spirits.

Press—equipment used to squeeze out juice out of ground fruit.

Price to customer (PTC)—the price the customer pays for a product—influenced by the producer and distributor.

Price—cost of product on the shelf.

Private versus public hops—major hop companies have found that it is advantageous to create patented or proprietary hop varieties. Grown in limited varieties (only authorized growers can grow the patented hop), they tend to be more expensive than the publicly available hops (any grower can buy the vine and propagate it). Of the top 10 most popular hops, four of them are private, and they can be challenging to secure since they are sold out several years in advance to contractual buyers.

Pro forma profit and loss—an estimation of expected sales subtracting out any expenses related to those sales to come up with the resulting profit and loss.

Pro forma—statement predicting future activity and indicate anticipated figures.

Procedure for accepting offer—a document that explains the terms with which the business entity will accept the investor's money.

Process innovation—creative ideas applied to process activities such as barrel aging, dry hopping, and additions of unusual ingredients to beverages .

Producer—maker of the product.

Product mixes—the breakdown of sales on-site, wholesale and retail keg and growler, and packaged products of various sizes.

Product portfolio—the collection of beverages and packaging types that a craft business produces.

Product shelf life—the maximum time a product can be stored before quality is significantly affected.

Production capacity—the maximum amount of product that can be produced in a given time.

Production cost—the cost to produce an item.

Production space—space for various production activities.

Production trends—patterns and demand have producers go beyond traditional practices; examples are innovative processes, diversity of styles and flavors, and a unique company story drive production.

Products—goods produced for sale.

Profits, losses and distributions—covers how profits and losses are determined and allocated.

Projected trends—current or predicted trends for different styles or packing in the industry. Can include projected growth trends for the market.

Promote—methods used to market the product using advertising, social media, etc.

Promotional activities—plans, events, and campaigns to promote and market your product.

Promotional calendar—a planning tool that indicates the months of the year when promotions will occur.

Proof gallons—equals one gallon of spirits that is 50% alcohol at 60 degrees F.

Proof—indicates the amount of alcohol. 1% alcohol equals 2 Proof.

Proprietary hop—patented variety of hop grown in limited varieties and only authorized growers can grow the hop.

Pub food—the type of food that is typically served in a pub. While other countries have their own pub food (chicken feet for China), there are common items offered that are the main pub food items. Many pubs mix and match pub food from various countries on their menus. French fries have become universal.

Pub or tasting room production only—refers to facilities that produce beverages to be consumed on the premises predominately.

Pub strategies—long-range plan for a pub based on an understanding of the marketplace.

Pub/restaurant—a facility that sells product by the pint or glass and also offers food.

Pull—when customers hear about a product and ask for it in pubs and stores and thereby generate demand.

Purchase cost—the cost to purchase an item.

Push—a strategy common with big industrial breweries where the product is pushed to consumers through media marketing campaigns and promotional activities.

Qualitative methods—a method used to forecast future sales involving people's judgments including expert opinions.

Quality—high performance or more consistent product.

Quantitative methods—a data driven method where historical sales data or commitments are used to predict future sales.

Quarterly investor updates—communication updates to investors that outline what is going on in the company, new projects, financial reporting, strategies or concerns.

Raw material handling—the system for handling raw materials in a production facility.

Raw material—typical agricultural products such as barley, wheat, hops, apples, pears, and other fruits and grains. Natural weather occurrences (drought, wildfires, etc.) and shortages affect the supply of raw materials. Materials that have not been processed such as ingredients.

Recipe—list of necessary ingredients and process steps for creating a product.

Refresh—the changing of the look of a product or product category on a retail store's shelves.

Regional craft brewery—a brewery that makes between 15,000 to 6 million barrels per year.

Regulatory environment—a culture of changing laws initiated by legislators to encourage or discourage craft beverage production and consumption.

Reinheitsgebot beer purity law—a German law permitting beer to be made with only barley, hops, and water later including yeast and wheat.

Rent—payment for buildings, storage, or other facility is considered a general expense category.

Resets—the rearrangement of a product category on retail store's shelves.

Retail plan—a detailed outline of the business plan for companies with a retail aspect (pub/restaurant, tasting room) to include the role of retail.

Retail sales—sales of product to locations where customers buy the product for off- or on-premise consumption.

Retail space—facility space for direct interaction with customers such as a pub, tasting room, restaurant, or gift shop.

Retailer—businesses that sell product directly to the customers.

Retained earnings—the cumulative amount of net income over the years.

revPASH—a restaurant metric defined as the periodic revenue from operations divided by (number of operations hours times number of seat places for guests).

Right sizing—determining the essential pieces and sizes of equipment needed to operate efficiently at each stage of a businesses development.

Risk factors—a list of all potential issues that may put the investors money at risk.

Role—a description of the functions one expects from a product or person.

Rotating handles—the act of changing to a different brand when a keg runs out. Both that keg and tap handle are replaced by a different brand.

Round tables—meetings held concerning shelf mix changes by large retailers.

S corporation (S corp)—a US government defined business classification that avoids the double taxation issue. Profits and losses still pass through to the individual owner's tax returns, but the business itself is not taxed.

Sales channels—a method for bringing products to market to be purchased by consumers.

Sales commitments—the amount of product a producer commits to make or a distributor agrees to sell during a period.

Sales expenses—any costs for materials, salaries, and benefits related to sales.

Sankey—a stainless steel keg that is currently the most universally accepted style and most highly recommended keg in the industry.

Screw-top—a style of closure used with cider or spirits in the larger format bottles.

Seamer—a method for closing a can.

Seasonal pattern—a pattern of demand that are generally consistent in terms of peaks and valleys, and the main forecasting adjustments are in the amount of growth or decline.

Seasonal products—products available during certain seasons or periods of the year.

Seasonals—specialty item products offered during specific seasons (October, Christmas, spring, summer).

Seat yield—the percentage of seats used on average.

Securities regulation—the legalities around properly structuring deals and insuring legal compliance.

Security deposits—a prepaid expense considered a fixed asset.

Security—a negotiable financial instrument for investors represents their investment in a business such as stock, membership units, debt instruments, and right to acquire ownership.

Self-distribution—a brewery or cidery sells directly to a licensed retailer.

Sell by date—date in which product should be sold by to preserve freshness.

Sell sheet—a one-page document with the brand logo, brief story, key selling attributes and differentiating factors.

Serious food—a carefully thought out food program that generates higher revenue and a discerning audience for a pub or restaurant.

Sessionable—beverages with lower alcohol that are more suitable for lengthy drinking sessions.

Set—the choice of products.

Setbacks—the distance the building must be away from the road and property lines.

Setup cost—the fixed cost of purchasing or creating items that is not directly tied to the quantity.

Shared production facilities—a situation where two or more producers share a single production facility.

Sharing economy—a market model where people share access to good and services rather than having individual ownership.

Shelf-talkers—type of promotional display tag.

Shipping allowance—an allowance that lets the producer get an appropriate price on the retail shelf for locations out of their market where shipping costs are reduced to the producer.

Site—the piece of land where a building sits or will be constructed.

Slims—a sixth barrel or roughly 5 gallon keg.

Small business association (SBA)—a program that exists to encourage banks and other lenders to support small firms by guaranteeing part of the loan repayment.

Social media—media content created for websites and apps to help build a brand and story.

Sole proprietorship—the simplest organizational structure. One person owns and runs the business.

Sophisticated investor—an investor that has been determined to have sufficient investment experience and knowledge to weigh the pros and cons of a potential investment.

Space requirements—space required for various activities of a business.

Sparge—rinsing of grain in the lauter tun.

Special requirements—specific qualities that a candidate should possess for a specific position.

Specialty malt—malts that add special flavors and characteristics to beer beyond the base malt.

Spices and flavorings—ingredients such as spices, herbs, fruits, and many other items that add characteristics to craft beverages of all kinds.

Spirit production—the production of spirit product which could be via multiple routes. One direct path used by spirit producers is to buy neutral alcohol or ethanol and redistill it with flavorings to create products like gin or vodka. Similarly, they can buy or produce a wine from grapes, other fruits, agave, or honey and distill those products for various brandies, liqueurs, tequila, and so on. Sugar can be mixed with water and fermented to create rum. The most advanced process is grain-based spirits which involve making a mash like beer and draining off the wort prior to fermenting.

Spirit safe—a device used in traditional whiskey distilleries where the master distiller can observe the spirits running through a device to determine the separation point for heads, hearts and tails.

Spirit tax issues—many countries tax spirits at a very high level, which is why spirits dominate duty free shops around the world. Taxes are the highest for spirits because many countries assert that spirits contribute to alcoholism and the associated societal costs.

Spot market—product that is available at the current price.

Startup team—team of people with certain skills and talents put together to steer the startup of an organization.

Startup—a new company just starting out.

State and municipal development funds—government created loan programs to revitalize certain locations undergoing tough economic times.

Steam heated—a method of heating with steam.

Stock—financial instrument that can be converted into other financial forms.

Storage—space in a facility to hold materials, finished products, kegs, etc.

Strengths—internal elements to the company—advantages, capabilities, and specific resources.

Subscription—a model where consumers pay in advance for the product and receive some product yearly or seasonally in return.

Subscription/admission agreement—covers the assurance by a company to sell at a given price.

Sugar—cane, beet or other base sweetener to supplement other fermentable sugars.

Suggested retail price—the highest selling price to the consumer to which the discount is applied.

Sustainability—the producing of products with minimal negative impact to the environment and society.

Sweat—the process of storing apples for about one week to soften and lose excess water, and increase sugar level.

SWOT analysis—strengths, Weaknesses, Opportunities, and Threats—a useful tool for evaluating how a chosen objective might work in the environment the business is facing.

Table turns—a concept for a restaurant that averages the number of times one table turns (seats a new customer of group of people) in one evening during specific periods of time.

Tables—refers to the configuration and layout of tables in a pub or restaurant.

Tails—spirits extraction from a still with lower than desirable proof and lacking important flavor components.

Tap handles and lines—a unique tap handle with branding and design provided by the producers for every beverage style. Tap handle is connected with a line to the keg.

Tap lines—lines that run from the keg to the tap handle.

Taproom—a facility that sells product by the glass.

Target customer—customers identified as key consumers of a product.

Tasting room—a facility that sells or gives away product by the glass or smaller portions, i.e. tastings.

Taxes—state and federal producer tax.

Team costs—the cost of paying for all managers and employees compensation including burden.

Tenant improvements—improvements paid for by the landlord that meet the needs of a tenant and his/her business.

Term sheet—a simple document outlining the material terms and conditions of business agreement.

Termination—the point where a contract is ended and the proposed outcome of ending the relationship.

Territory—a specific area to market a product.

Third place—refers to a retail space such as a pub or coffee shop which becomes the third place choice of places to be for frequent socialization, behind home and work.

Third-party distribution—distributing through a third party or entity between the producer and retailer.

Threats—external situations that may pose threats to a company.

Three-tier system—a system where wholesalers bridge the gap between the retailer and the producer.

Through the line marketing (TTL)—a hybrid of both ATL and BTL.

Tied house—a structure where breweries own or finance pubs and these pubs must buy beer from the production brewery.

Tote—unit size that holds large amounts like 2,000 pounds of grain.

Trademark—a word, set of words, symbol, or design that is legally registered or established to represent a company, product, or service.

Traditional Brewer—a brewer who has a majority of its total beverage alcohol volume in beers whose flavor derives from traditional or innovative brewing ingredients and their fermentation.

Traditional crowdfund—a business posts a project with a monetary goal and offers rewards.

Transfers—how a member sells, assigns, or disposes of his or her interest in the company.

Turnover—the rate in which employees are retained.

Two-tier system—a method used by producers to sell to the public. In this case, the producer acts as distributor and sells directly to the retailer.

Unpredictable demand—refers to varying demands and times of unexpected increase in or decrease of demand.

Value-added producer grants—a grant to help producers move into value-added agricultural enterprises typically funded by Department of Agriculture.

Variable costs—costs that include labor, utilities, and materials needed to make a unit of each product.

Variety—the number of different styles or items within a category.

Vatting—process where aged spirits are mixed with other barrels from the same production batch.

Velocity—the average number of kegs sold in each account per month.

Vendor and supplier financing—a solution that optimizes cash flow by allowing businesses to borrow money from or lengthen the payment terms to their suppliers.

Vision—the ideal of what a business will become in the long-term.

Visual diagram of process—a visual that supplements the verbal description of the operational plan.

Volume discounts—price discounts for ordering higher volumes of items.

Wash—liquid from mash.

Water and sewer—utilities in a facility for accessing water and disposing of liquid waste.

Water—important ingredient for all craft beverages.

Weaknesses—internal elements to the company that pose disadvantages and may make a company vulnerable.

Weighted average method—a method of averaging previous periods data where periods are weighted according to their perceived importance (i.e., the most recent period may be weighted more than the older periods).

Whiskey barrel—a wood barrel that holds 53 gallons or 200 liters of liquid.

Wholesaler—an entity in the distribution channel that buys in bulk and sells to retailers rather than consumers.

Wine and spirits house—one of three main types of wholesale models which specialize in wine and spirits distribution.

Wine permit—a permit needed for wine or cider makers prior to producing, storing, blending, bottling or wholesaling cider.

Wine—alcoholic beverage made from fermented grape juice.

Work in progress (WIP)—inventory of product that has not been completed such as fermenting beer.

Wort chiller—where the hot wort is pumped to in order to achieve the desired temperature.

Wort—liquid produced from the mash step in brewing.

Yeast—ingredient required by every fermented beverage.

Zones—different spaces within a building with different functions such as an area for single diners and pairs, and area for families with kids, and an area for larger private parties.

Zoning ordinances—rules designed by local governments to separate hazardous industrial areas from farming areas and residential areas.

Zoning permit—a permit for building in a specific zone.

INDEX